THE BANK HOUSE DIRECTORIES

Bradford 1850

THE BANK HOUSE DIRECTORY FOR BRADFORD 1850

Published by BANK HOUSE BOOKS in association with the Local Studies Department of Bradford Central Library

ISBN 9781904408512

Designed and produced in the UK by
BANK HOUSE BOOKS
PO Box 3
NEW ROMNEY TN29 9WJ UK
www.bankhousebooks.com

IBBETSON'S
GENERAL AND CLASSIFIED
DIRECTORY,

STREET LIST AND HISTORY OF BRADFORD

AND THE WOOL TRADE AND WORSTED MANUFACTURES;

COMPRISING ALSO

AN ALPHABETICAL LIST

OF THE

PRINCIPAL MERCHANTS AND MANUFACTURERS,

(WITH THE NAMES OF THE PARTNERS IN EACH FIRM),

THE GENTRY, CLERGY, AND THE VARIOUS TRADESMEN AND SHOPKEEPERS

IN BRADFORD, BOWLING, HORTON AND MANNINGHAM:

COMPLETE LIST OF THE VARIOUS

CONVEYANCES BY RAILWAY, ROAD AND WATER;

POST OFFICE REGULATIONS;

THE PLACES OF DIVINE WORSHIP AND THE PUBLIC BUILDINGS, INSTITUTIONS AND OFFICES; THE CORPORATION OF THE BOROUGH; COURT-HOUSE; THE POOR LAW UNIONS AND REGISTRARS OF BIRTHS, DEATHS, AND MARRIAGES, ETC.

LIST OF YORKSHIRE BANKERS,

WITH THE HOUSES ON WHICH THEY DRAW IN LONDON.

A PLAN OF BRADFORD,

EMBRACING THE LATEST IMPROVEMENTS, ACCOMPANIES THE WORK.

Bradford:

PRINTED AND PUBLISHED BY JAMES IBBETSON.

LONDON:—SIMPKIN, MARSHALL AND CO. LEEDS:—WEBB, MILLINGTON, AND CO. MANCHESTER:—ABEL HEYWOOD.

Price to Subscribers,—in Cloth, 5s. 6d.—in Leather, 6s. 6d. Non-subscribers One Shilling extra.

1850.

PREFACE.

The publisher, in presenting this, the second issue of his Commercial Directory to the notice of the numerous subscribers and the public of Bradford, is sanguine enough to think will adapt itself to all the purposes for which such a work is required; and, taken as a whole, he believes will be found more full and complete than any Directory yet published for this borough.

On the advantages of a Directory which shall exhibit in methodical arrangement the names and residences, as well of the nobility, gentry and clergy, as of the professional gentlemen, the manufacturers, and the various Trades and Industrial occupations, it is unnecessary here to insist.

In the Alphabetical portion is given the names and residences of the principal inhabitants in full; and wherever the private residence of a partner is given, the firm with which he is connected is also named; and being partners are not necessarily ineligible because not housekeepers.

The Classified Directory of Manufacturers, Trades and Professions have been arranged with the discrimination necessary to fit it for its commercial object. Every name or firm will be found under the various heads to which its trade or manufactures extend, and many new heads of trade have been introduced.

A valuable STREET LIST, embracing every new street, place, court, &c. that have arisen since the last publication have been given, with a distinct reference to its locality, and which will be found indispensible in the addressing and despatch of circulars and letters.

The CONVEYANCE LISTS contains separate names of coaches and carriers by railway, road or water,—their times of departure, and the places whence they start.

The HISTORICAL department has been conducted by an eminent literary gentleman, through whose research and industry it is believed the 'Past and Present' of Bradford have been reviewed, and expressed in a manner that has given to history a freshness which few writers impart, and which only an extensive local and topographical knowledge could supply.

A novel feature in Directory compilation,—that of distinguishing, in connection with the trades and professions, the names of such persons as possess the electoral qualification, whether borough or county, and both. In fulfilling our promise in this respect, considerable care and judgment was required, and few errors, it is hoped, have been committed. We have necessarily inserted numbers of persons in the employ of others. Such consideration have not deterred us from our duty.

The changeableness of human affairs is in nothing more conspicuous than the pages of a Directory; even while we write such are taking place. However, at the end of some three years another Directory will be required, the materials for which it is our intention to collect and publish.

A LIST OF BANKERS has been carefully prepared up to the present date.

An accurate Plan of the Town illustrates the work.

Directory Office, 1850.

INTRODUCTORY REMARKS, ETC.

The etymology of the word Bradford has given rise to a variety of curious suggestions, some antiquaries deriving it from *Broad-ford*, others from *brae* a hill, and *ford* the brook at the foot of the hill, and so forth. The most probable derivation seems however the first one here given.

Without tracing back to the very earliest times the history of Bradford, which has been done most carefully by Mr. James in his "History and Topography of Bradford," &c. we may gather much interesting information relative to its existence and ownership from the Domesday Record, and other similar authorities. From that record we learn that Bradford in the time of the survey was the chief vill of the manor, and had six berewicks, or groups of houses dependent upon it. In the inquisition, taken on the oath of Henry, Earl of Derby, 1361, we again find mention of Bradford. The lord of the manor at the time of the conquest was one Gamel, of whom little more is known than that he held the chief manors in this county. The whole of the cultivated lands at this time in the manor of Bradford with its berewicks, was fifteen carucates, or 1500 acres, on which eight ploughs were employed. The value of the manor, prior to the conquest was £4, and the population probably about 750 persons, of whom one third was assigned to Bradford.

The manor soon came into the possession of the family of the Lacies, the lords of Pontefract, and passing from them, into the hands of the Earls of Lancaster, at length became the property of the present owners, the members of the Rawson family, of Nidd Hall, Yorkshire.

In a work like the present it would be foreign to the purpose to dwell at any considerable length upon the ancient history of the town, parish and manor of Bradford. We shall proceed therefore to point out, in the most concise manner possible, some few features connected with the rise and progress of our town and borough, which will be more in harmony with the design of a work entitled a "Directory of the Borough of Bradford."

Ecclesiastical and Sacred Buildings.—The church of St. Peter's, commonly called the Parish Church, was erected in the reign of K. Henry VI, and is a structure of noble proportions, though considerably disfigured by subsequent alterations and additions.—Bierley chapel erected 1766, was consecrated August 30, 1824.—Horton chapel erected 1806, was consecrated 1807.—Christ Church was consecrated Oct. 12, 1815.—St. James' church, built in the year 1836, was consecrated Oct. 12, 1842.—St. John's, Manchester road, was erected 1838-9, and is not consecrated, though there is reason to believe that rite will very shortly be performed.—St. John's church, Bowling, was consecrated in February, 1842.—St. Jude's was consecrated June 20th, 1843.—St. Paul's, Manningham, was consecrated September, 1848.—The church of St. Matthew, Bank foot, will be ready for consecration in a few weeks. The Westgate end of Drewton street has lately been considerably ornamented by the erection of a handsome church for the use of the Scotch Presbyterians of the town. It is in the Doric style, the architects,—Messrs. Mallinson & Healy.

Of the places of public worship which can lay claim to any thing like antiquarian interest, we can only point to the Unitarian Chapel, in what is commonly called Chapel lane, the date of which is about 1710, though there probably had been some place of worship here before, and that its site was in the immediate vicinity of the present one. The Friends' Meeting House was erected about 1680, rebuilt 1811, and enlarged 1825. The Wesleyan Methodists soon struck root in this town, and after displaying much zeal and diligence now stand at the head of all the Christian bodies which are not in direct connection with the Church of England. We desire not, however, to make any invidious comparisons where all have laboured to the best of their several abilities to promote the success of those objects which each have in view.

WOOLLEN AND WORSTED MANUFACTURES.

Wool (*a*) was undoubtedly one of the original articles which constituted a staple of England; prior, however, to 1313, it does not appear to have been manufactured into cloth for exportation. In 960 the manufactories of Flanders were certainly established, and at that time they drew their chief supplies, and for long after, from England. It cannot be doubted, however, that the Britons learned the art of manufacturing it into cloth

(*a*) It has been doubted whether wool be strictly a staple of England; but when the sheep was first introduced into the island, is hidden in the darkness of antiquity. Sheep's wool is generally supposed to be the product of cultivation; we know of no wild animal which resembles the wool-bearing sheep.

from the Romans, although ages elapsed before they were in a condition to supply more than their own wants. In 1172 is the earliest allusion to foreign wool being imported into England. Stowe quotes a charter of Henry I. declaring, that "if any cloth were found to be made of Spanish wool, mixed with English wool, the mayor of London should see it burnt;" "which," says Anderson, "shews the antiquity of English woollen cloths being all made of Spanish wool." The passage, however, admits of another interpretation; for the exportation to the Netherlands was at that time encouraged, and it may be inferred, that the importation of Spanish wool was discouraged, and woollen cloths made only of English wool. At all events, I cannot find under what circumstances Spanish wool was, at this time, at all imported into England.

As early as 1197, broad cloth was certainly made in England. Richard I. cap. 27, declares that "woollen cloth, wherever it be made, shall be all of one breadth; viz. two ells within the lists, and of the same goodness in the middle as in the edges." (*b*)

The pensionary De Witt says, that many of the Flemish and Brabant manufacturers removed, soon after the year 1300, into Holland; and certain it is, that the letters of license which Edward III. granted to weavers and other foreign workmen belonging to the Netherlands, to settle in England, rendered them instrumental in establishing our woollen manufactures. This is not, however, altogether correct; for we see by the regulations of Richard I. for woollens, that broad cloth was made in this country at least as early as 1197, more than a hundred years previous.

The city of Antwerp, in 1312, was the staple port in the Netherlands for English wool; and the English ports for export were Weymouth, Southampton, Boston, Yarmouth, Hull, Lynn, Ipswich, and Newcastle; from which ports alone, by an injunction in 1320, by King Edward II. and from none other, might wool be exported from England. (*c*)

In 1328, the measure and assize of cloth, ray and colour, were regulated by law; "whereby it is directed, the length and breadth of the two sorts of cloth, that the king's aulneger (*d*) shall measure them; and they shall be

(*b*) In 1253 sheep were so scarce in England, in proportion to the demand for wool, that a fleece was estimated at two-thirds of the value of the ewe which produced it, together with the lamb.

(*c*) The Brabant manufacturer Hanks gave his name to the skein of worsted which still retains it; and Thomas Blanket, a weaver in Bristol, has given a bedfellow both to ladies and gentlemen.

(*d*) The office of aulneger was very ancient. Peroult le Tayleur, who held the office in the time of Edward I., having forfeited it, the king, by writ of privy seal, commanded the treasurer to let Pierres de Edmonton have it.—Madox.

forfeited to the king if they be short of the following lengths and breadths, viz.; first, the cloths of ray (not coloured) were to be twenty-eight yards in length, and six quarters broad; secondly, the coloured cloths were to be twenty-six long, and six quarters and a half wide." This is the first time the aulneger is mentioned in the statute-book, and he was so called from an aulne, or ell.

Our kings and parliaments undertook to regulate the dimensions of cloth coming from abroad, no doubt to procure some advantage for the English manufacturers. One John May, the general aulneger, published a treatise, in 1613, called *A Declaration of the State of Clothing now used in this Realm of England*; in which he says, that before the making of cloth—that is, fine cloth—in England, the aulneger was ordained, who exercised that office upon all cloths coming from foreign parts, to measure and try when they were put on land, even as far back as the fifteenth year of King Edward II., in 1322, by letters patent.

One of the most important laws for the establishment of just notions respecting commerce was passed by Edward III., in 1328, abolishing the staples, or, rather, the limitation of the places where the staples were sold; and declaring that all merchant strangers may go and come with merchandise into England, after the tenour of the great charter.

We now approach the era from which the commercial greatness of England may be dated—an event which reflects not more renown on the wisdom of Edward III. than the establishment of the royal navy, and the heroic achievements in France.

Observing that the vast power and riches of the Netherlands proceeded from their woollen manufactures, and that they owed much of their wealth to the wool of England, he became anxious to attract the artificers of that manufacture into this country. In the fourth volume of Rymer's *Fæd.* p. 496, we find the first mention of any effectual measure to accomplish this. It is a letter of protection to John Kemp, (*e*) of Flanders, a woollen cloth weaver, coming over to exercise his trade in England, in the year 1331, and to teach it to such people as shall incline to learn it; the king taking Kemp with all his servants, apprentices, goods and chattels into his royal protection, and promising the same likewise to all others of his occupation, as also to all dyers and fullers, inclined to come and settle in England.

(*e*) John Kemp's descendants are supposed to still survive at Kendal, where he settled; and in the reign of Queen Elizabeth the woollen manufactures of that town were as great as at present. Who has not heard of Kendal Green and Sir John Falstaff?.

Seventy families of Walloons (*f*) were in consequence induced, in that year, to accept of Edward's invitation; and it deserves particular notice, as an instance how much political causes influence the migrations of trade, that this most important event corresponds with the time mentioned by De Witt, in his *History of Holland*, where he says, that "the cloth-makers of Flanders began to be uneasy under their earl, by which they sought other places of settlement elsewhere." In considering, as the mind unconsciously does, the amazing consequences and the wealth which arose from this measure of Edward III., it should still be recollected, that it was not to him altogether that we owe the introduction of woollen manufactures, but only of the fabrics of cloth which the Netherlands were accustomed to make, and which were then the most common in use throughout Europe. Woollen cloth of some kind was, from the time of the Romans, always made in Britain; and when they retired the art was left behind. Nor can it be supposed that our Saxon ancestors had not always manufacturers among them, at least of the coarse cloth used by the common people. It seems historically probable that the higher orders and the nobility for many years imported their clothing from Italy; for it was certainly not before the tenth century that the Netherlands began to acquire any name as woollen manufacturers. Indeed, it admits of no question, that when historians say the woollen manufactures were introduced into England by Edward III., all that is meant can be no more than they were first established by him on a great scale, and encouraged with a view to exportation. Before his time, the common people made, in their own families, such clothing as they required.

From the time of the conquest downwards, the making of some sort of woollen cloth and linen in England is past all doubt; as we have seen, that in the reign of Henry II. there was a guild, or fraternity, of weavers in London. In the charter which Henry III. was obliged to sign in 1225, there is, in the twenty-fifth article, the following stipulation: "That there be one breadth of dyed cloth, russets, and haberjicts; that is to say, two yards within the lists, which perfectly justifies what has been said of the ambiguity of the woollen manufactures of England, without, however, detracting from the great policy of Edward in fostering the same manufac-

(*f*) The woollen manufactures were distributed over the kingdom at the following places:—The manufacturers of fustians, at Norwich; of baize, at Sudbury, in Suffolk; of sayes and serges, at Colchester: of broad cloths, in Kent; of kerseys, in Devonshire: of frieses. in Wales; of cloths, in Kendal; of coarse cloth, in Yorkshire; of cloth, in Hampshire, Berkshire, and Sussex; and of serges, at Taunton, in Somersetshire.

tures as those of the Netherlands, by encouraging their operatives to settle in England.(*g*) But still give the honour due to the heroic and politic Edward; for although from an ancient date there had been a gradual converging of the elements of English commerce, it was not till they received the fiat of his wisdom that they assumed that form and consistency the progress of which constitutes the agreeable object of this undertaking. [For this valuable outline of the history of the woollen manufacture, the writer of these pages is indebted to an article by Mr. Galt on "The Ancient Commerce of England, prior to the reign of Edward III. inclusive."]

Though it may not be generally known, it is nevertheless true, that so late as the middle of the last century, the manufacture of woollen cloths formed the staple trade of Bradford. So early as the thirteenth century we find in the Hundred Rolls of A. D. 1284, the mention of Evans, a weaver of Gomersal, being confined in the prison of Bradford,—a proof that this branch of business was practised in the neighbourhood; and in the fifteenth year of king Edward I. (1287) *Frizinghall*, near Bradford, is spoken of as belonging to Robert de Everingham, which is further confirmation of the same fact. After the civil wars the *woollen* manufactures of Bradford gradually diminished until the period before-mentioned, viz., the middle of the last century, when they were entirely given up. The *worsted* trade beginning to take the place of the *woollen* for the greater convenience of the manufacturers, a large building called the *Piecehall* was erected in the year 1773, the dimensions of which are 144 feet long, by 36 feet broad. Near this building, which stands in Kirkgate, report says, that previous to the erection of the first steam mill in the Holme in 1798, spinning was done by means of a horse-gin, and that this was the common practice of the time.

The earliest attempt at the application of steam power in Bradford was made by a Mr. Buckley, who proposed building a mill in the Manchester road, nearly opposite the Primitive Methodists' chapel, on a plot of ground commonly known as the "Brick Kiln Field." This was in the year 1793, but the opposition which this attempt raised caused him to yield his purpose. In the year 1798, Messrs. Ramsbottom, Swaine and Murgatroyd, midst much public odium and remonstrance, carried a similar design into execution in the "Holme," and erected a steam engine of fifteen horses' power; this done, others soon rose, with what rapidity and to what ex-

(*g*) It is a point probably of easy determination when the woolsacks were introduced into the House of Lords. As Edward was undoubtedly a prince of a poetical taste, it seems not improbable that they were introduced by him about 1376.

tent, the following statement will shew: In the year 1800, 1200 persons were employed in Bradford in trade or manufactures. In 1811, 1595 families were so employed; in 1821, 2452; in 1831, 3867, besides 1605 labourers; in 1835, 6022; whilst in 1841, there were 10,410 persons employed. Again, in 1798, there was but one steam engine, of fifteen horses' power, —in 1819, the power was about 492,—in 1830, 1047,—in 1840, 2000, whilst in 1847 it was computed to be upwards of 3000.

Public Buildings. Little need be said relative to the public buildings, if we except the warehouses of the merchants, many of which are creditable alike to the taste of the architects, and the spirit of the proprietors. We may mention a range of new and substantial warehouses in Bridge street and Hall Ings, the latter built for the occupiers, John Haigh & Co. and Mr. Frederick Schwann, by Mr. Brayshaw,—Mr. John Dixon architect. In all these hoisting machines have been constructed—effecting a considerable saving of labour in transferring goods from the lowest to the middle or higher compartments. Messrs. Thornton, Firth, Ramsden & Co. were the first, we believe, to introduce these into the town. An extremely chaste building—a school, built for the Messrs. Child, in Drewton street, is another addition to those enumerated. It is in the Italian style,—Messrs. Andrews and Delauney architects. It would be unpardonable not to bestow a passing notice upon some few others, which if not to be classed with the highly ornamental, belong to the useful.

The ancient *Toll-booth*, or market-house stood at the junction of Kirkgate, Westgate and Ivegate. The courts Baron and Leet were held in a room above it, the entrance to which about the year 1600 was in Ivegate, and beneath it was the town's dungeon, which yet remains, and is entered from that street. The court-house was called the "Hall of Pleas," in the grant of the manor by King Charles I. The dungeon is so deep that there is now a cellar over it. The *Manor-house* stands probably upon the site of a much more ancient edifice, for we find that in the reign of King Henry VII. the Rawsons "builded a fair place called Bradford-hall." The present house was erected in 1705, and in many respects is deserving of a careful inepection. The foundation of the *Free Grammar School* can be traced back to far distant times. It existed before the dissolution of chantries in the time of King Henry VIII. The trustees of the school were incorporated by letters patent, granted by King Charles II., and dated the 10th of October, 1663. Before the present school-house was erected, there was an ancient one standing on the west side of the church-yard of St.

Peter, (the parish church,) the date of which is unknown. This latter was succeeded by the one existing in North Parade, built in 1820. The *Exchange Buildings* were opened October 1st, 1828, and were erected by Messrs. Stead and Sellers, under the superintendence of the architect. Mr. Francis Goodwin, of London, at a cost of £7000. The *Mechanics' Institute* in 1839, at a cost of £3300. The Infirmary in 1844, at a cost of between £8000. and £9000., Mr. Rawstorne, architect., The Court House in 1834, at an expense of upwards of £7000.

POPULATION.—Scarcely in any town in the United Kingdom has the population increased of late years in the same proportion with that of Bradford. To go no farther back than the beginning of the present century, the period when the great stimulus was given to our native industry by the erection of the factories already spoken of. The increase in the township of Bradford from 1801 to 1841 has been from 6393 to 34560 or 440 per cent. The population of the four townships forming tho parliamentary borough, was in 1801, only 13,264, whilst in 1841, it was 66,718, being an increase of 400 per cent. When these figures are considered along with the fact that the general increase of the population of Great Britain from 1801 to 1841, was but 122 per cent, we are led to see that some powerful cause must have been at work to produce so startling an effect, and that cause is, no doubt, the rapid growth of the home manufactures.

BOROUGH OF BRADFORD.—The borough includes the townships of Bradford, Horton, Bowling and Manningham. The franchise of returning two members to parliament was conferred upon it by the Reform Bill in 1832. The following is a list of the gentlemen elected to serve in the different parliaments since that time.

FIRST ELECTION.—1832.

DAYS OF POLLING 14th and 15th Sep.

Lister	650
Hardy	471
Banks	402

SECOND—JANUARY 10th, 1835.

Hardy	611
Lister	589
Hadfield	392

THIRD—JULY, 1837.

Lister	635
Busfeild	621
Hardy	443
Busfeild, jun.	383

FOURTH—JUNE 30th. 1841.

John Hardy	612
W. C. Lister	540
Wm. Busfeild	536

FIFTH—SEPTEMBER 15th. 1841.

Busfeild	526
Wilberforce	522

SIXTH—JULY 31st. 1847.

Busfeild	937
Col. Thompson	936
Wickham	860
Hardy	812

WEST RIDING OF YORKSHIRE ELECTIONS.

The freeholders in the West Riding far exceed in numbers those of any other county in the kingdom. If proofs were wanting in support of this statement we refer to the memorable and closely contested election of 1807, which made a pretty ample disclosure of their amount, and from which it appears that forty-two years ago upwards of 23,000 freeholders gave their suffrages for county members; and it is very probable that 3000, at least, did not vote.

Since that period there is no reason to suppose the number have been diminished, but on the contrary, through the influence of the various Freeholders' Associations in the leading towns of Yorkshire, it may reasonably be presumed their strength in numbers have *sensibly* multiplied.

WEST RIDING ELECTIONS FROM 1832.

1832. Lord Morpeth - Libl.
Sir G. Strickland, Bt. Libl

1835. Lord Morpeth - Libl.
Sir G. Strickland, Bt. Libl.

1835. May, vice Morpeth, appointed Secretary for Ireland.
Lord Morpeth, Libl. 9066
Hon. J. S. Wortley, C. 6259
18,011 regis.—15,324 voted

1837. Lord Morpeth Libl. 12,576
Sir G. Strickland, L. 11,892
Hon. J.S. Wortley, C. 11,489

1841. Hon. J.S. Wortley, C. 13,165
E. B. Denison, C. 12,780
Lord Milton, Libl. 12,080
Lord Morpeth, Libl. 12,031

1846, Feb. vice Wortley, who succeeded to the peerage as Lord Wharncliffe
Lord Morpeth - Libl.

1846, July, vice Morpeth, Commissioner of Woods and Forests.
Lord Morpeth - Libl.

1847. Lord Morpeth - Libl.
Richd. Cobden - Libl.

1849, vice Morpeth, who succeeded to the Peerage as Earl Carlisle.
E.B. Denison, C. 14,743
Sir C. Eardley, Lib. 11,795

These extracts have been given for information, free from political bias.

Government of the Borough.—Until the recent charter of incorporation, the municpal affairs of the town were managed by a number of the West Riding magistrates, by the watching and lighting commissioners, and by a board of surveyors. On the 9th of June, 1847, the incorporation of the borough was granted, which gave the burgesses the privileges of a mayor, aldermen, common councilmen, &c., the powers possessed by the former being given up and transferred to the Council. The first mayor was Robert Milligan, Esq., who, at the expiration of his term of office, was re-elected to fill the same, which he had done to the entire satisfaction of all parties, whatever might be their political or religious creed. He was succeeded by the present mayor, Titus Salt, Esq., of Crow Nest, who, with 14 Aldermen and 42 Common Council-men, constitute the corporate body.

The Bradford Poor Law Union.—About a year ago this union, which was considered much too large for convenient management, was divided, into two, the one retaining its original name, the other called the North

Bierley Union. Of the former one J. R. Wagstaff, Esq., is superintendent registrar and clerk to the board of guardians. The day of meeting for the despatch of business is Friday.

BRADFORD WATER WORKS.—So long ago as 1790 a company was established and incorporated by parliament for the formation of water works. This not fulfilling its important purpose, a joint stock company was formed under the authority of an act passed in 1842, for the purpose of bringing the water of a famous spring, called Many Wells, into the town.

CANAL AND RAILWAYS.—An act for the construction of a *canal* from Bradford to Shipley, where it should join the Leeds and Liverpool, was obtained in 1771, and in 1774 the canal was opened. Several unsuccessful attempts had been made prior to 1843, to obtain an act authorizing the construction of a *railway* from Bradford to Leeds. In that year, however, on the 9th of May, the bill passed the commons, and on the 11th of June the Lords, and received the Royal Assent a few days afterwards. In the year 1846, an act entitled "*The West Riding Union Railway Act*," received the approval of the houses of Commons and Lords, and the Royal Assent was given August 18th, 1846, for the construction of a series of railways—west and south of Bradford, thus bringing Bradford into connection with the towns of Halifax, Cleckheaton, Hudderfield, Manchester, &c. The first section of this was opened in August of last year, viz.—from Low Moor to Mirfield; a further portion from Low Moor to Bradford will be ready for traffic at the end of the present or the commencement of the next year, and the remainder of the line connecting Bradford with Halifax about the month of July, 1850.

LEEDS AND BRADFORD RAILWAY.

THIS line, which was opened from Leeds to Bradford, July 2nd, 1846, and thence from Bradford to Keighley, Skipton, and Colne, passes a circuitous route of some 14½ miles through a populous district, and has stations at Shipley, Apperley Bridge, Calverley Bridge, Newlay, Kirkstall, &c. The North Western line was opened from Skipton to Ingleton on the 26th July, 1849; and the following " Sketch of the Country," and " Ride from Skipton to Ingleton," with its various associations, will interest the reader:

INGLETON.

This beautiful village is twenty-six miles from Skipton, and nine and three-quarters from Settle. Ingleborough frowns over it, and the river Greta ripples round the base of the heath-clad mountains. The view towards the north from the station is very beautiful, the village and the square-towered church bosomed in the wood, occupying the fore-ground, while the back ground is formed by bold mountain scenery. The railway bridge over the Greta has its piers raised some few feet above the water, but the staging indicates the height of the level of the rails, and gives promise that the aqueduct will not be an unworthy item in the scenery. Lewis, in his Topographical Dictionary, gives the following details about Ingleton.

In the neighbourhood are many romantic objects, amongst which are Raven Roe, a rocky promontory covered with evergreens, and Thornton Force, a curious water-fall; but the most striking of all is Yordas Cave, in the vale of Kingslake, under a mountain called Gray Gareth; the excavation, which is carried through a solid rock of black marble, somewhat resembles the interior of a Throne, and on the left the Chapter House, with petrifactions hanging from the roof, and from the sides issue numerous rills, forming fantastic cascades, which add to its sublimity.

AUSTWICK,

Backed up by the scars, from which the finest blue slate rock has been obtained, but has been little used, owing to the difficulty of transmission to the towns; the facility of transit will now be afforded by the North Western railway. The simple inhabitants of this hamlet have been the object of the jokes of the neighbourhood from time immemorial; by one authority it is stated that the villagers, in an intense desire to study the natural history of the cuckoo, hedged in the bird with the idea of catching it. By another it is possitively affirmed that not one hundred years ago there was but one whittle or knife in the village, which was stuck for the public use in the tree now standing in a broad open space beside the roadway.

GIGGLESWICK.

Is a parish comprising the townships of Giggleswick, Rathmell, Settle, and Stainforth, and is three-quarters of a mile distant from Settle. The living is a discharged vicarage in the archdeaconry and diocese of York, rated in the king's books at £21. 5s. 4d., endowed with £200 private benefaction and £200 royal bounty, and in the patronage of J. Coulthurst and J. Hartley, Esqs. Here is a Free Grammar School founded by Edward VI. in the seventh year of his reign, in which Archdeacon Paley was educated. At the foot of a ledge of rocks in this parish, called the Scar, rises a spring noted for ebbing and flowing, though distant near thirty miles from the sea; the water has been known to rise and fall 19 inches in five minutes. Passing onwards there is a point where the river Ribble winds beside the embankments, then were more rapidly rolled down an incline of 1 in 100 past Mr. Birbeck's house on the left, while we had a glimpse of a very fine view to the right where the village of

RATHMELL

may be seen. The views around this place are said to be rarely equalled; but it contains in itself but one remarkable object, the free public library, in which are contained an excellent assortment of old editions of classical works. A deep cutting presently hid the country from our sight, till we approached Merebeck lying on the right, and Wigglesworth Hall, the property of Earl de Grey, upon the left. At Long Preston, at which point the Clitheroe line was proposed to join the main line, we passed under a handsome skew bridge of three arches, ascended a gradient of 1 in 245, and emerged upon the viaduct over Long Preston Beck. Ascending inclines of 1 in 330 and 1 in 214, we came to Gisburne road bridge, and thence to a good stone skew arch which carries the Skipton turnpike road over the line. Beyond Hellifield, which lies on the right, with the huge Pendle-hill beyond it, we saw on our left a very picturesque group of trees upon a clump which are said to be visible at a great distance; by some the mound is said to bear indications of having been a Roman encampment.

CONISTON COLD.

On a lofty mount near the village is an oval encampment, supposed to be Danish. Tradition relates that at a place called Sweet-Gap, on the north-western side of Coniston moor, the inhabitants endeavoured to arrest the progress of a party of Scotch invaders, and nearly the whole of them was killed.

GARGRAVE.

It is situated four and a half miles from Skipton. The church is dedicated to St. Andrew, and is built in the later English style. The river Aire runs through the village, and the Leeds and Liverpool Canal bounds the outskirts. In the immediate neighbourhood is a Roman encampment, and a fine specimen of tesselated pavement is said also to have been discovered.

The North Western Railway approaches the Liverpool and Leeds Canal a little beyond, and a second time crosses the river Aire. Beyond, far off to the right is Eshton Hall, the residence of Matthew Wilson, Esq., the property in this neighbourhood belongs chiefly to Sir Charles Tempest. On again approaching the Aire, a spot was pointed out where a landslip had taken place, but had been prevented from doing mischief or delaying the works by the vigilance of the contractor.

On the right, at a considerable distance, is Broughton Hall, embosomed in woods; and after passing over the river Aire once more, the observer will perceive Carlton about a mile from the road on the left. At a few hundred yards beyond is the point where the North Western Railway falls into the Leeds and Bradford extension, which gradually approaches it on the right. The joined lines, leaving the canal on the left, take a very sharp curve of 12 chains radius into the station belonging to the Leeds and Bradford Company.

SKIPTON.

A parish comprising the market town of Skipton, the chapelry of Bolton Abbey, and the townships of Barden, Draughton, Embsay with Eastby, East Halton and Bolton, and Stirton with Thorlby, in the eastern division of Staincliff and Ewcross, and the township of Hazlewood and Storiths, and part of that of Beamsley, in the upper division of the wapentake of Claro, West Riding of the county of York. The name, which is variously spelt in Domeday-book, as *Sciptone*, *Sceptone*, *or Sceptetone*, was probably acquired from the vast number of sheep anciently fed in the vicinity. About the close of the reign of William the Conqueror, a castle was built here by Robert de Romille, which in the great civil war was garrisoned for the royal cause, but having been invested by the opposing party, it was surrendered, after a seige of three years, December 20th, 1645, having held out longer than any other fortress in the northern part of the country. In the following year an order was issued from the parliament for its demolition, which in 1649, was partially carried into effect; but it was soon after restored by the Countess of Pembroke who occasionally resided in it. In more modern times it has undergone a thorough repair, and is still a magnificent and commodious residence.

SETTLE.

The name of this town is derived from the Saxon word Setl, a seat: its situation is singular and picturesque, at the base of an almost perpendicular limestone rock which rises to the height of two hundred feet.

The town contains 2000 inhabitants, the parish church being situated at Giggleswick. A new church was erected in 1838, and there are chapels belonging to the Methodists, Independents, and Quakers. The spacious Market-place is now graced by a handsome Town-hall, in the Elizabethan style, built in 1832, at the cost of £5,500 raised in £10 shares, exclusive of the clock, which cost £150. raised by subscription. Beside the court and assembly-rooms, it has apartments for the Savings' Bank, a News room, and the extensive library of the Settle Literary Society, founded in 1760. The inhabitants also participate in the benefits of the richly endowed Grammar School at Giggleswick. At the Spread Eagle, in Settle was born in 1753, that eminent sculptor, Thomas Proctor, and on the walls of the dairy are still preserved some of the efforts of his juvenile years. Below the Market-house is a curious erection called the shambles, which are partly only occupied by butchers. On the top of the round arches, under which are the shambles, are built cottages with rude terraces, while beneath the shambles are cellars, which in the "good (?) old times," were used as dwelling places.

INDEX

TO THE TRADES, PROFESSIONS, PUBLIC BUILDINGS, INSTITUTIONS, ETC.

The various Branches of Trades and Manufactures arranged in strict Alphabetical Order.

ALPHABETICAL DIRECTORY

OF THE

BOROUGH OF BRADFORD,

Including Bradford, Great and Little Horton, Bowling, Manningham, and their Vicinities.

The following ALPHABETICAL DIRECTORY contains the names and addresses of the principal inhabitants of the four townships, comprising the GENTRY, CLERGY, MERCHANTS and MANUFACTURERS, the TRADES and PROFESSIONS, PUBLIC BUILDINGS and OFFICES, &c.

A new feature in Directory compilation has been introduced,—that of distinguishing, in connection with the Trades and Professions, the names of such persons as are qualified as borough and county voters.—The small b. denotes borough voter, c. county voter, and b.c. both. Persons in the employ of others (possessing electoral qualifications) have their names and addresses given.

For facility of reference town and country Manufacturers and Spinners are inserted, with situation of warehouses, works and residences, both in the following Alphabetical and Classified directory.

The FIRMS to which PARTNERS belong are given in parenthesis, with the residence of each partner. Where no occupation is stated the parties are generally in the employ of others.

The Contractions of Names, Streets, &c. are such as will be easily understood.

THE CLASSIFICATION OF TRADES FOLLOWS THE GENERAL ALPHABETICAL LIST.

ABBEY John,[c] provision dealer, Clayton lane, Manchester road

Abbey Ner,[b] 6 Clayton lane, Manchester road

Abbott Robert, school, Brunswick place

Abbs James,[b] linen draper, hosier, and haberdasher, 43 Market st

Abel William,[c] Little Horton lane

Abercrombie David,[b c] merchant (D. Abercrombie & Co.); house Westgrove street

Abercrombie David & Co. stuff merchants, Leeds road

Ackroyd Abraham,[b c] beer retailer, Little Horton lane

Ackroyd Abraham, stone mason, Little Horton lane

Ackroyd Cowling,[b c] worsted spinner and manufacturer, Charles street; works and house Great Horton

Ackroyd Elijah, provision dealer, 44 Bower street, Manchester road

Ackroyd Francis,[b c] butcher, Legrams lane, Great Horton

Ackroyd George,[b] Mount Pleasant, Manningham

Ackroyd John,[c] provison dealer, 189 Manchester road

Ackroyd John,[b c] butcher, 67 Westgate

Ackroyd John,[c] Harris st. Leeds road

Ackroyd Jonathan, butcher, 1 Green lane, Manningham

Ackroyd Joseph, butcher, Bedford street, Wakefield road

Ackroyd Rachel, dress maker, 13 Green lane, Manningham

Ackroyd Robinson,[c] butcher, Manningham

Ackroyd Samuel,[c] farmer, Lady royd, Manningham

Ackroyd Samuel,[b] Lady royd, Manningham

Ackroyd Thomas,[b] spinner (Thos. Ackroyd & Sons); residence Upper House, Birkenshaw

Ackroyd Thos., leather cutter, Bridge st.; house Harris st., Leeds road

Ackroyd Thomas,[c] farmer, Smith's lane, Manningham

Ackroyd Thomas & Sons, worsted spinners and manufacturers, Dale street; works Birkenshaw

Ackroyd William,[c] Wood street, Manningham

Ackroyd William,[b c] grocer and tea dealer, 142 Manchester road

Ackroyd William,[c] provision dealer, 24 Croft street, Leeds road

Ackroyd William, beer retailer, 24 Croft street, Leeds road

Ackroyd William, spinner (Thomas Ackroyd & Co.); house Wheatleys, Birkenshaw

Ackroyd William,[b] spinner (William Ackroyd & Co.); house Otley

Ackroyd William & Co. worsted spinners and manufacturers, 5 Dale street; works Otley

Acworth Rev. James,[b c] M. A., president and theological tutor at the Baptist College, Little Horton

Adams George, provision dealer, Halifax road, Bowling

Adams Joseph, provision dealer, 17 Broomfield terrace, Wakefield road

Adams Rev. William Massey, B. A., (curate of St. Jude's), Hanover sq.

Adamson John,[b] carrier (Pearson & Co.), and agent for the Bradford and Selby Fly Boats' Co. Canal road; house High street

Adamson John & Sons, woolstaplers, Well street

Adcock John,[b] woolstapler (John Adcock & Son); house Broomfield terrace, Wakefield road

Adcock John & Son, woolstaplers, 60 Bridge street

Addison George,[b] spinner (G. W. Addison & Sons); house Chesnut Cottage, Manningham

Addison George Wilson,[b c] spinner (G. W. Addison & Sons); house Hall Field, Bowling

Addison George Wilson & Sons, worsted and woollen yarn spinners, Hall Lane Mill, Bowling

Addison Wiliam Brook,[b] spinner, (G. W. Addison & Sons); house Hall Field, Bowling

Adjusting Office for Weights and Measures, Court House, Hall Ings; Wm. Baxter adjuster

Airedale Independent College, Harrogate road, Undercliffe; Rev. Walter Scott resident theological tutor. —[*See* "Public Buildings and Offices."]

Airey Robt.,[c] Green lane, Manningham

Aked & Robertshaw, woolstaplers, Cheapside

Aked Thomas,[b c] woolstapler, Brook street; house Shipley grange

Aked William,[b c] woolstapler (Aked & Robertshaw); house North parade

Akers Jesse,[c] Great Cross street

Akroyd Edward,[b] manufacturer (Jas. Akroyd & Son); house Bankfield, Halifax & Denton Park, near Otley

Akroyd Edward,[b] Old lane, Bowling

Akroyd Henry,[b] manufacturer (Jas. Akroyd & Son); residence Saville House, Halifax

Akroyd James & Son, stuff manufacturers, merchants and spinners, Booth street; works Copley and Halifax

Akroyd John,[b] Rooley lane, Bowling
Akroyd John,[b c] Victoria st. Nth prde
Akroyd William,[b] cotton-warp dyer, Mawson street, Thornton road; house Belgrave place, Maningham
Aldersley William,[b] butcher, 2 White Abbey
Alderson George,[b c] grocer, tea dealer, coffee roaster, and hop and seed merchant, 1 Bridge street
Alderson John,[b] merchant (Snowden and Alderson); house Bridge street
Alderson Joseph, tailor, Ivegate; house School street, Manningham
ALFRED HOME AND FOREIGN LIFE ASSURANCE COMPANY; agent, Mr. Joseph Thompson, solicitor, Bridge street buildings
Allen Edward,[b] manufacturer (Edward and Robert Allen & Co.); house Vicar lane
Allen Edward and Robert & Co. stuff manufacturers, Charles st.; works PENNYOAK'S MILL, Melbourne street, Leeds road
Allen Matthew,[c] provision dealer, Croft street, Manchester road
Allen Robert,[b] manufacturer (Edward and Robert Allen & Co.); house Leeds road
Allen William,[c] machinist, Westgrove street
ALLIANCE INSURANCE COMPANY; agent Mr. Bentley Greenwood, solicitor, Regent place, Duke street
Allison Sarah, boot and shoe maker, 25 Market street
Ambler Eliza, beer retailer, 116 Bridge street, Wakefield road
Ambler Elizabeth, provision dealer, Manningham
Ambler Henry, worsted spinner and manufacturer, Schuster's buildings, Brook street; works Shaylane and Holmefield Mills, Ovenden; house Ovenden grange
Ambler Illingworth, waste dealer, Albion yard, Ivegate; ho. Clayton
Ambler James,[b] Trees, Manningham
Ambler Jeremiah,[b] curled hair and bagging manufacturer, Skinner lane, Manningham
Ambler Sarah, eating house, Market st
Ambler Thomas,[b] Lillycroft, Manghm
AMERICAN AND AUSTRALIAN PACKET OFFICE, 1 Chapel lane; Edward Collinson agent
Anderson Emma, milliner and bonnet maker, Wakefield road
Anderson George,[b] merchant (Anderson & Yates); house Wilsden hill
Anderson George,[c] worsted manufacturer, Mills's yard, Brook st.; works and house Wilsden
Anderson John, provision dealer, 121 Tumblinghill st. Thornton road
Anderson Joseph, boot and shoe maker, Parkgate, High street
Anderson Joshua,[c] manufacturer (Joshua Anderson & Co.); house Wilsden
Anderson Joshua & Co. worsted spinners and manufacturers, Brook street; works Wilsden
Anderson Michael,[b] Broad street
Anderson Richard, tailor, 1 Quebec terrace, Thornton road
Anderson Ruth, milliner and dress maker, 26 Croft st. Manchester rd
Anderson & Yates, stuff merchants and manufacturers, Leeds road; works Wilsden
Anderton George, spinner (George Anderton & Sons); ho. Cleckheaton
Anderton George & Sons, worsted spinners, Bank street; works at Cleckheaton

Anderton John,[b] Victoria st. Nth prde

Anderton John Ashworth,[b] woolstapler, Hardcastle lane, Well st.; house Victoria st. North parade

Anderton John Braithwaite,[b] Horton

Anderton Jonathan William, agent for silk and cotton warps, &c. 30 Pearson's buildings, Bridge street; house Summerseat place, Horton

Anderton Samuel,[b] spinner (Swithin Anderton & Sons); house Ashfield-place, Great Horton

Anderton Sarah, cloth presser and finisher, Mawson street, Thornton road; house Brunswick place

Anderton Swithin,[b c] spinner (Swithin Anderton & Sons); house Ashfield place, Great Horton

Anderton Swithin & Sons, worsted spinners, Eastbrook Mills, Peel street, Leed road

Anderton William,[b] worsted spinner and manufacturer, Brook street; works and house Bingley

Andrew George,[c] joiner, cabinet maker, and undertaker, mourning and hackney coach and cab proprietor, Silsbridge lane; house Victoria street

Andrew John,[c] Middleton field, Silsbridge lane

Andrews & Delauney, architects and surveyors, and agents for the South Lancashire Building Association, Rennie's buildings, Hall Ings

Andrews John, precept constable, Longcroft place, Silsbridge lane

Andrews William, architect (Andrews and Delauney); ho. Little Horton

Annison Samuel,[c] joiner, cabinet maker and undertaker, Church st

Anti-State Church Association; Mr. James Hanson secretary, Manor row, Cheapside

Appleyard Henry, stuff manufacturer, Booth street; works and house Ibbotroyd, Hebden Bridge

Appleyard James, blacksmith, Quebec terrace, Thornton road

Appleyard Joshua,[b] manufacturer (William Appleyard & Son); house Kingcross street, Halifax

Appleyard William,[b] manufacturer (William Appleyard and Son); house Halifax

Appleyard William & Son, worsted spinners and manufacturers, Schuster's buildings, Brook street; works Wainstalls and Hebble Mills, near Halifax

Archer Edward,[b] cabinet maker and upholsterer, Tyrrel street

Archer Hannah, milliner and dressmaker, 8 Providence street, Silsbridge lane

Armitage George, boot and shoe maker, Back lane, Bowling

Armitage George,[b c] dyer, (George Armitage & Co.); residence Water Lane House

Armitage George,[c] carrier, Thornton road; house Great Horton

Armitage George, boot and shoe maker, Croft st. Wakefield road

Armitage George, boot & shoe maker, 136 Providence st., White Abbey

Armitage George & Co, dyers and finishers, Water Lane Dye Works, Thornton road

Armitage Joseph, boot and shoe maker, North street, North wing

Armitage Samuel,[c] plumber, glazier, and gas fitter, 52 Market st.; house North parade, Manningham lane

Armitage Thomas, joiner, King's court, Northgate; house Back Broad street, Cheapside

Armitage Thomas,[c] Bolton road
Armitage Thomas,[c] Low green, Little Horton
Armstrong Robert,[c] Broad street, Manor row
Arnold John, grocer, tea dealer and coffee roaster, 41 Bridge street
Arnold Solomon, worsted spinner and manufacturer, 13, Bank street; works and house, Eastburn, near Halifax
Arnold Tubal Cain, provision dealer, Longlands street, Westgate
Arnold Rev. William (Catholic), Stott hill, adjoining the chapel
Arton Mr. James,[b c] Hanover square
Arton Mr. Titus, Broad street
Ashley Ascough Leonard, provision dealer, 128 Broom street, Wakefield road
Ashley John,[b] Hanover square
Ashley John,[b c] Summerseat place, Great Horton
Ashley John,[c] Bridge street
Ashley Nathaniel, provision dealer, Bradford moor
Ashley Nathaniel, brazier and tinplate worker, Broadstones
Ashley Thomas,[b c] cattle dealer, Summerseat place, Great Horton
Ashworth Simeon, boot and shoemaker, Old gardens, Cropper lane
Ashworth Thomas,[c] Drewton street
Askwith Joseph, tailor and draper, 91, Westgate
Aspinall Abraham, boot and shoemaker, Bavaria place, Manningham
Aspinall John,[b c] provision dealer, Hope street. Manchester road
Aspinall Joseph,[b c] Victoria street, North parade
Aspinall Samuel,[c] joiner and builder, Regent place, Duke street
Aspinall Mrs. Sarah, Victoria street, North parade
Asquith John,[c] *Furnace Inn*, North Bierley
Asquith Joseph,[b] Holme top, Little Horton
Asquith William, flour and provision dealer, 42 Greenaire place, Silsbridge lane and Westgate
ASSEMBLY AND BILLIARD ROOMS, Exchange buildings, Kirkgate
ASSESSORS OF INCOME AND PROPERTY TAX OFFICE. 14, Exchange street, Kirkgate; James Lambert, solicitor, clerk to the commissioners
Atack Benjamin,[c] Low Moor
Athea John, beer retailer, 4, Longcroft place, Silsbridge lane
Atherton William, leather cutter, Hope street, Manchester road
Atherton William, leather cutter, Hope street, Manchester road
Atkinson Alice, straw bonnet maker, Crown street, Thornton road
Atkinson Caleb,[c] Duke street, Manchester road
Atkinson Edward,[c] Sawrey place, Little Horton lane
Atkinson Edward,[b] spinner (Bottomley, Wilkinson and Co.); house Portland place
Atkinson Francis Whitley,[c] joiner and cabinet maker, Bolton road
Atkinson George,[b c] tailor and draper, 130 Manchester road
Atkinson George, watch and clock maker, 87 George st. Leeds road
Atkinson James, provision dealer, 274 Wakefield road

Atkinson John,[bc] woolstapler, Cheapside ; house 3 Hustler terrace

Atkinson Joseph,[b] plumber and glazier, Vicar lane

Atkinson Joseph, boot and shoe maker, 4, Johnson fold, North wing

Atkinson Joseph,[b] Old lane, Bowling

Atkinson Joseph,[c] John street

Atkinson Joseph,[b] Bridge street

Atkinson Nathan,[b] Bolton road

Atkinson Nathan, grocer and provision dealer, 187 Wakefield road

Atkinson Richard, cooper, 120, Manchester road, and Leeds road; house Vicar lane

Atkinson Robert, plumber, glazier, and gas fitter, Vicar lane

Atkinson Mr. Samuel,[b] Old lane, Bowling

Atkinson Thomas, *Lister's Arms*, Manningham

Atkinson Thomas,[b] beer retailer, 15, Nelson street, Chapel lane

Atkinson Thomas, hackney coach proprietor, Sun yard, Bridge street

Atkinson Thomas, *Spotted House Inn* and Bowling green, Manningham lane

Atkinson William,[bc] Hanover square

Atkinson William Child, schoolmaster, Back lane, Manningham

ATLAS INSURANCE COMPANY; agents Mr. G. A. Busfeild, Market st. Mr. E. A. Barret, Charles street, and Mr. George Humble, Albion court

Audesley John,[c] clothes and stay dealer, 55, Bazaar, Kirkgate, and 1, Primrose terrace, Manningham

Audsley John,[b] Horton road

Audesley William,[b] butcher, 16, Hustlergate; house Great Horton lane

Auty Squire, [bc] draper and provision dealer, 101 Manchester road, and bazaar, Kirkgate

AUXILIARY BIBLE SOCIETY; Depot, Mr. Thos. Wilson's, Bridge street: Rev. Wm. Morgan, B.D. secretary

AUXILIARY TO THE LONDON MISSIONARY SOCIETY; James Garnet, Esq. treasurer, and Rev. J. G. Miall secretary

AUXILIARY TRACT SOCIETY; Depot, 1 Thornton's buildings, Bridge st.; John Rand, Esq. president

Aykroyd Jonathan, [bc] woolstapler (Jonathan Aykroyd and Son); house Haworth.

Aykroyd Jonathan & Son, woolstaplers, Swain street; house, Haworth

BACON Mrs. Mary, Spring House, Manningham

Bailey Mr, John, Leeds road

Bailey Samuel Oldfield, engraver (Masser & Bailey); house Hustler's buildings, Leeds road

Bailey William, clerk, Hill side Villas

Bainbridge James, beer retailer, 110, North wing

Baines John Kirby, beer retailer, Britannia street, Manchester road,

Baines Samuel, worsted spinner and manufacturer, New Piece hall; works and house, Brighouse

Baines Sarah, woolstapler and top maker, Swaine street; res. Thorn House, Manningham lane

Bairstow Abraham,[c] Brownroyd hill top, Bierley

Bairstow Abraham,[c] Hill End, Horton

Bairstow Amos,[b] relieving officer for Bradford West District; house Belgrave place, Manningham

Bairstow Andrew, hair dresser, 12, Queen's Cut, Manchester road

Bairstow Israel,[b c] manufacturer, (Wade & Bairstow);house Halifax
Bairstow James,[c] Bankfoot, Bowling
Bairstow John,[c] grocer, Wilsden
Bairstow Matthew, manufacturer, (Thomas & Matthew Bairstow); house Sutton, near Keighley
Bairstow Paul,[c] butcher, Little Horton lane
Bairstow Sarah Ann, straw bonnet maker, Laister dyke
Bairstow Thomas, manufacturer, (Thomas and Matthew Bairstow); house, Sutton, near Keighley
Bairstow Thomas & Matthew, worsted spinners and manufacturers, Charles street; works, SuttonMill, near Keighley
Baker Matthew, boot and shoe maker, 87, John street, Stott hill
Bakes Isaac Smith,[c] Drewton street,
Bakes Joseph,[b c] Birks, Horton
Bakes William, inspector of nuisances, police office, Swaine street
Bakes William,[b c] *Fleece Tavern*, Great Horton
Baldwin Dan, provision dealer, Sticker lane, Bowling
Baldwin Thomas,[c] Northcroft place, Horton
Balme Abraham,[b]Little Horton green
Balme John, schoolmaster, Great Horton lane
Balmforth Jabez, coal dealer, Victoria street, Silsbridge lane
Balmforth Joseph,[c] smith, Clayton street, Thornton road
Bamford Wm.[c] Carr lane, Bierley
BANK (COMMERCIAL), Market street; Mr. Joseph Hill, manager
BANK (OLD), 24, Kirkgate; Messrs. Henry, Alfred, and William Masterman Harris
Bankart Alfred,[b] merchant, (John Douglas & Co.); house Spring bank, Manningham
Bankart Charles,[b] woolstapler, (Hall & Bankart); house Eldon place
Bankart Mrs. Mary, Eldon place
Banks George,[b] commission buyer, (Banks & Pollard); house Wakefield road
Banks Matthew, provision dealer, Bradford moor
Banks & Pollard, commission agents, makers-up and packers, 28 Leeds road
Bannerman Henry & Sons, stuff merchants, Union street, and Leeds
BAPTIST CHAPELS—[see the Index, "Churches and Chapels"]
BAPTIST COLLEGE, Little Horton lane; president and theological tutor, Rev. James Acworth, A. M.
Barber Rev. John,[b c] A. M., incumbent of North Bierley
Barber Thomas,[b] *Manor House Inn*, Darley street
Barker Benjamin, provision dealer, 52 White Abbey
Barker Greenwood,[b] Hannah gate, Manchester road
Barker James,[b] clerk, Snow Hill
Barker James, woolstapler, 38 Cheapside; house Hanover square
Barker James, beer retailer, 58 Smith street, Manchester road
Barker Jeremiah,[c] Lumby street, Manchester road
Barker Sarah, milliner and straw bonnet maker, 217, Bolton road
Barker Squire,[b] beer retailer, 224, Manchester road
Barker Thomas,[b] furniture broker, 232, Northgate

Barker Thomas Lister,[b] provision dealer, and painter, gilder, &c. George street, Leeds road; paint works Ivegate

Barker William,[c] Wharf street, Bolton road

Barker William,[c] Sterling street, Manchester road

Barlow William Wagstaff, assistant overseer for and registrar of marriages Bradford district; office Court House; res. 175 Bridge street

Barnes John, provision dealer, 37, Black Abbey

Baron George,[b] Esq. Clock House, Manningham, and Drewton

Barraclough Abraham,[c] King street, Manchester road

Barraclough Abraham,[c] Edge End, North Bierley

Barraclough Benjamin,[c] Moorfield, Slack, Bierley

Barraclough Charles,[c] Woodside, North Bierley

Barraclough Mrs. Frances, Upper North Parade

Barraclough Francis,[c] Jer lane, Horton

Barraclough Francis,[c] grocer, Wibsey

Barraclough James, green grocer, Broadstones

Barraclough James,[c] Dudley hill

Barraclough John,[b] joiner and cabinet maker, 68 Westgate

Barraclongh John, wood turner, Spence's Mill, Chapel lane; house Harrogate road

Barraclough John, greengrocer and coal dealer; 125 Bridge street

Barraclough John,[b c] provision dealer, Little Horton

Barraclough John,[c] North parade

Barraclough John,[c] Low moor

Barraclough John,[c] Wibsey bank top

Barraclough John,[c] Low moor side

Barraclough Joseph,[c] Potter street, Birks hall

Barraclough Joshua,[c] North Bierley

Barraclough Mary, provision dealer, Upper West street, Silsbridge lane

Barraclough Mary, *Bishop Blaize Inn*, Westgate

Barraclough Rachael and Margaret, dress makers, 56 John street, Stott hill

Barraclough Samuel,[c] Fiddler-hill farm, Bierley

Barraclough Samuel,[c] Aycliffe lane, Horton

Barraclough Thomas, tailor, Primrose terrace, Manningham

Barraclough William,[c] Moor top, Bierley

Barraclough William, wood turner, Spence's mill, Chapel lane; house John street, Stott hill

Barraclough William,[c] Low moor

Barraclough William, manufacturer, (Dickinson & Barraclough) house Gloucester street, Leeds

Barrans James,[b] Mirey shay

Barrans James,[c] woolstapler, Hustler's buildings, Market street; house, Great Horton

Barrans Jonas, coal dealer, Back Tyrrel street

Barrans Matthew, toll-bar keeper, Bierley lane

Barratt Elizabeth, dress maker, 70 John street, Stott hill

Barratt John, draper, hosier, &c. 38 Leeds road

Barrett Abraham,[b] 43 Bowling hall, Bowling

Barret Edward Alexander, solicitor, and agent for the Atlas Insurance office, Charles street; house, Summerseat place, Great Horton road

Barrett James, watch and clock maker, 1 Wellington st, Stott hill

Barrett Job, tailor, Leach's square, Laister dyke

Barrett Misses, milliners and straw bonnet makers, 302, Leeds road

Barrett William, tailor, 2 Illingworth's court, Westgate

Barrow William, watch and clock maker, jeweller, &c. 2 Bank street

Barthelmes & Buckup, linen and worsted yarn merchants, Dale st., Kirkgate

Barthelmes Emil, merchant, (Barthelmes & Buckup); house Spring gardens

Bartle David, joiner and provision dealer, High street, Great Horton

Bartle George, beer retailer, 16 Croft street, Wakefield road

Bartle John,[b] stuff manufacturer, Hustler's buildings, Market street; works and house Great Horton

Bartle John & Brothers, joiners, Great Horton

Bartle Thomas, dealer in oils, &c. High street, Great Horton

Bartle Timothy,[b] confectioner, and dealer in tea and British wines, 26 and 28 Market street

Barton James, provision dealer, 73, Brick lane

Barton James,[b c] provision dealer, Thornton road

Bastow James, provision dealer, Whetley street, Manningham

Bastow John,[b] Under-the-hill, Horton

Bastow John, surgeon, 48 Wellington street, Stott hill

Bastow John,[b] Aycliffe hill, Horton

Bastow Joseph,[c] Green lane, Manningham

Bastow Jonathan,[b] provision dealer, Great Horton lane

Bastow Moses,[b] Lower beck, Horton

Bastow Paul,[b] Little Horton lane

Bateman Charles,[b] beer retailer, 12, Greenaire place, Silsbridge lane

Bateman Daniel,[bc] Edmund st. Horton

Bateman Mr. James,[c] Park House, Bowling

Bateman John,[c] druggist, Wibsey

Bateman Mrs. straw bonnet maker, 49 High street

Bateman Mr. Samuel,[c] Croft House, Bierley

Bates Henry,[b] 76 Westgrove street

Bates Joshua,[c] woolstapler, 23 Well street; house Hanover square

Bates Mary Ann, milliner and bonnet maker, 53 Manchester road

Bates Miles, wool-comb maker, Silsbridge lane

Bates Sarah, milliner and dress maker, 6 Sharp st. Manchester road

Bates Thomas,[b] Brick lane, Manghm.

Bates William,[c] auctioneer, valuer and furniture broker, 15 Union passage, Kirkgate

Bateson Samuel, butcher, 14 Market st

BATHS (PUBLIC), Woolsorters' Gardens, Manningham lane, and Henry Blackburn's, Great Horton

Batley Ann, dress maker, North wing

Batty Samuel, schoolmaster, Earl street, Manchester road

Baxendale Abraham,[b c] coal owner (David and Abraham Baxendale), Old lane, Bowling

Baxendale David,[bc] coal owner (David and Abraham Baxendale), Old lane, Bowling

Baxendale David & Abraham, coal owners, Bowling lane, Bowling
Baxter Benjamin,[b] pall bearer, &c. 27 North street, Stott hill
Baxter Charles, engraver, copper-plate and lithographic printer, Market st.; house, Manningham
Baxter John, joiner (Baxter and Johnson); house Diamond street
Baxter & Johnson, joiners and builders, Diamond street, Vicar lane
Baxter Joseph,[b c] *Bowling Green Inn*, commercial posting house, and billiard-room, &c. Bridge street
Baxter Moses, provision dealer, 6 Mill street, Canal road
Baxter William,[b c] *White Lion Inn*, 31 Kirkgate
Baxter William, provision dealer, 59 North street, Stott hill
Baxter William, *Old King's Arms*, Westgate
Bayldon William, commission agent, and dealer in cotton warps, Swaine street; house Manor street
BAZAAR FOR GENERAL MERCHANDISE, Market place, Kirkgate
Beach John, surgeon, Rawson place
Bean Joseph, engineer, gas works; house Victoria st. North parade
Beanland Eliza, milliner and dress maker, Keighley old road, Manghm
Beanland Emanuel,[c] Wakefield road
Beanland Frances, stay maker, Cheapside, and 42 Manchester road
Beanland George, school, 30 Pearson's buildings, Bridge street; house James' st., Manchester road
Beauland George Joseph,[c] corn miller; (Geo. Joseph and John Beanland); house Great Horton road
Beanland George Joseph and John, corn millers, Beckside, Horton
Beanland H. smith & farrier, Northgate
Beanland Henry,[c] Bowling old lane
Beanland Jas.[c] Spring row, Manghm.
Beanland John,[c] corn miller (George Joseph and John Beanland); house Great Horton road
Beanland John, builder (John and William Beanland); house Great Horton lane
Beanland John,[b] grocer and provision dealer, 1 Victoria st. North parade
Beanland John & William, joiners and builders, Little Horton lane
Beanland Joseph, provision dealer, Badford moor
Beanland Joseph,[b] woolstapler, 16 Union street, Bridge street; house Broomfield terrace
Beanland Joseph, butcher, Whetley street, Manninghnm
Beanland Joshua,[b c] chemist and druggist, 30 Northgate
Beanland Martin,[c] china, glass and earthenware dealer, 46 Westgate
Beanland Richard,[b] Victoria street, North parade
Beanland Robert,[b] linen draper and hosier, 195 Bridge street
Beanland William, builder (John and William Beanland); house Heber street, Little Horton lane
Beanland William,[b] timber merchant, Northgate
Bearder John,[bc] provision dealer, 89 Sticker lane, Bowling
Beattie Adam,[b] manager for the water-works company; house Northrop's buildings, Westgate
Beattie Jonathan,[b c] Ashfield place, Great Horton
Beaumont George,[c] Back lane
Beaumont Thomas,[bc] surgeon, Laura place, Leeds road

Beaumont William, tea dealer and coffee roaster, 29½ Kirkgate; house Broad street, Manor row
Beaver John,[c] Back lane, Bowling
Beaver William,[b c] woolstapler, 13 Cheapside; house Stone street
Becher Louis, merchant (Gustavus Gumpel and Co.); ho. Drewton st
Beck Benjamin,[c] beer retailer, 14 Southgate
Bedford Mrs. Mary, North parade
Beecroft, Butler & Co. iron and steel manufacturers and merchants, Leeds road; works Kirkstall, near Leeds: John Thornton agent
Beecroft George,[b] joiner (executor of Joseph Beecroft); ho. Tyrrel square
Beecroft George Skirrow,[b] merchant (Beecroft, Butler and Co.); res. Abbey House, Kirkstall
Beecroft John,[b] beer retailer, 1 Duke street, Manchester road
Beecroft John, joiner (executor of Joseph Beecroft); ho. Tyrrel square
Beecroft Joseph (Executors of), joiners and builders, Toad la. Bridge st
Beetham James, hair dresser, 68 White Abbey
Beetham James,[c] Greenhill place, Manningham
Beetham Joseph, clerk of St. John's church, 70 Hope st. Manchester rd
Beetham Thomas,[c] Dudley hill
Beetham William, provision dealer, Swaine green, Bowling
Behrens Edward, merchant (Jacob Behrens); house Hanover square
Behrens Jacob, stuff merchant, Leeds road; ho. Whetley lane, Manghm.
Behrens Solomon Levi & Co. stuff merchants, Swaine street; Mr. J.A. Unna manager
Bell Miss Ann Elizbth. Brunswick pl.
Bell John, *Commercial Inn* and spirit vaults, Tyrrel street
Bell John, draper, (Bell and Prest); house Tyrrel street
Bell Martin, corn and flour dealer, 17 Chapel lane, Bridge street
Bell Mary, straw bonnet maker, 153 Silsbridge lane
Bell and Prest, woollen drapers, Tyrrel street
Bell Thomas,[b] grocer and tea dealer, 104 Manchester road
Bell Thompson, boot and shoe maker, 57 Providence st. White Abbey
Bell William, provision dealer, Greenhill place, Manningham
Bell William, boot and shoe maker, Green hill place, Manningham
Bellwood John,[c] Queen st. Bowlidg
Bennet Charles,[b] Aycliffe hill, Horton
Bennett David, boot and shoe maker, 176 Silsbridge lane
Bennett James Heaton (late Caton), surgeon, Manningham lane
Bennett John, boot and shoe maker, 21 Clayton street, Thornton road
Bennett John, draper, 77 Westgate
Bennet Joseph, boot and shoe maker, 3 King Charles street, Otley road
Bennett William,[c] provision dealer, Great Horton road
Bennett Rev. W.P. curate, Southgate, Great Horton
Benson Joseph, provision dealer, Manningham
Bentham Joseph,[b] agent for French yarns, stuff goods, &c. Market st.; house Whetley lane, Manningham
Bentley Abraham,[b] furniture broker and town beadle, 48 Market street
Bentley Albert, cabinet maker, Hope and Anchor Yard, Bank street; house 16 New st. Leeds road

Bentley Charles,[bc] straw hat and bonnet maker, 58 Kirgate

Bentley Edwin,[b] spinner (Nathan Bentley and Sons); house Primrose hill, Great Horton

Bentley Greenwood, carrier (Joseph Wood and Co.); house Hall Ings

Bentley Greenwood,[b] solicitor (Bentwood and Wood); house Hall Ings

Bentley Greenwood, jun. solicitor, and agent to the Atlas Insurance Co. Regent place, Darley street

Bentley Henry,[b] manufacturer (Nathan Bentley and Sons); house Legram's lane, Horton

Bentley Mr. James,[c] Lower Woodlands, Bierley

Bentley John,[b] Broad st. Manor row

Bentley John,[c] Great Horton

Bentley John,[c] Bowling lane

Bentley Nathan & Sons, worsted spinners and manufacturers, Piece-hall yard; works Legrams, Horton

Bentley Walter,[bc] beer retailer and butcher, Great Horton road

Bentley William,[bc] manufacturer (Nathan Bentley & Sons); house Legrams lane, Great Horton

Bentley & Wood, solicitors, Hall Ings

Berry Benjamin,[bc] machinist (Benjamin Berry and Sons); house Hall lane, Bowling

Berry Benjamin & Sons, machine makers, Prospect Mill, Wakefield rd.

Berry Henry,[bc] mechanist (Benjamin Berry and Sons); house Broomfield terrace, Wakefield road

Berry John (from Wakefield), attorney, and clerk to the deputy-lieutenant for Lower Agbrigg, agent for the County Fire and Provident Life Insurance, the London Indisputable Life Policy, and for the National Benefit Building and Investment Society; office Leeds road—house 20 Victoria st. North parade

Berry Peter,[b] machinist (Benjamin Berry & Sons); house Hall lane, Bowling

Berry Richard, coal, rag, and bone dealer, 20 Keighley st. Silsbridge la.

Berry Thomas, provision dealer, 21 Park street, High street

Berry Thomas,[bc] machinist (Benjamin Berry and Sons); house Mill lane, Bowling

Berry William,[b] machinist (Benjamin Berry and Sons); house Broomfield terrace, Wakefield road

Berwick Brothers & Jamieson, stuff merchants, Swaine street

Berwick James, merchant (Berwick Brothers and Jamieson); house Mount Pleasant, Manningham

Berwick John,[b] butcher, 14 Broadstones, Well street

Berwick John, merchant (Berwick Brothers and Jamieson); house Mount Pleasant, Manningham

Best Dan,[c] Fidler Hill Farm, Bierley

Best Joseph,[bc] Bolton place, Bolton rd.

Best Matthew,[c] Fidler Hill Farm, Bierley

Bibby John,[c] Clayton place, Pit lane

Bible Society (Ladies' Branch); president Mrs. Rand; secretary Miss Taylor

Bickerdike Rev. John,[c] A.M. afternoon lecturer at the parish church; house Broad street, Manor row

Bielby William, provision dealer, 1 Westgrove street

Bierley Iron Works Company (Clayton, Marshalls and Co.); office and wharf Canal road

Billiard Rooms: Exchange buildings, Exchange street, Bowling Green Inn, Bridge street, and E.P. Duggan's, Union street

Billinge Adam, druggist, Halifax road

Billingsley Edward,[bc] manufacturer, (Billingsley, Tankard and Co.); house Bradford moor

Billingsley, Tankard & Co. worsted spinners and manufacturers, Market street; works Bradford Moor

Bilton Mr. James,[bc] Ashfield place, Great Horton

Bilton Mrs. Susannah, Great George st

Bingham George,[b] woolstapler and top maker, 20 Balm st. and 9 Bolton road; ho. 3 Harris st. Leeds rd.

Binns Eleanor, confectioner and tea dealer, 25 Hustlergate

Binns George,[bc] grocer, tea dealer and coffee roaster, 151 George street, Leeds road

Binns George,[bc] merchant (John Wilson and Co.); house Sawrey place, Little Horton lane

Binns Mrs. Hannah, Bridge street

Binns Mr. John,[bc] Leeds road

Binns John, leech dealer, James st.

Binns John,[c] stuff manufacturer, 170 Old Piecehall; works and house Wilsden

Binns Joseph, fishmonger, Bridge street; house Millbank

Binns Joseph, clogger, Great Horton

Binns Mrs. Martha, Victoria street, North parade

Binns Mills, provision dealer, Albert street, Bolton road

Binns Ogden, beer retailer, 53 Victoria street, Thornton road

Binns Richard,[c] confectioner, 47 Silsbridge lane

Binns William,[c] Wood st. Manngham

Binns William,[b] Preston pl. Gt. Horton

Binns William,[b] woolcomb maker, Bolton road

Birchall Edwin, merchant (Edwin Birchall and Sons); house Burley, near Leeds

Birchall Edwin & Sons, stuff and blanket merchants, Leeds road

Birchall William, merchant (Edwin Birchall and Sons); house Thornton road

Bird Isaac Faulkner, portrait painter, Hustler terrace

Bird Samuel, draper, 10 White Abbey

Birkbeck James,[c] Great Horton

Birkbeck John,[b] Drop, Horton

Birkbeck Morris,[c] merchant (Morris Birkbeck and Co.); house Manningham lane

Birkbeck Morris & Co. stuff and yarn merchants, 52 Cheapside

Birkby James, butcher, 174 Silsbridge lane

Birkby William,[c] North Bierley

Birkly John,[c] Row Nook, Bierley

Black Rev. W. F. M.A. senior curate at the parish church; house Hillside Villas

Blackburn Abraham, wool and waste dealer, Liverpool street, Bank st.; house Clayton Heights

Blackburn Bailey,[bc] chemist and druggist, top of Ivegate; house Upper North Parade

Blackburn Henry,[b] hair dresser and perfumer, 29 Hustlergate

Blackburn Henry, public bath establishment, Great Horton lane

Blackburn Henry William, accountant, trustees and receivers' accounts in chancery, or for any of the courts of equity, or bankruptcy made out; office 36 Darley street; house Allerton

Blackburn Isaac,[c] Birkshall Fields, Leeds road

Blackburn John,[b] worsted spinner, Laister Dyke Mill; house New Drop, Leeds road

Blackburn Mrs. Mary, Upper North Parade, Manningham lane

Blackburn Samuel,[b] tobacconist and hatter, and dealer in foreign cigars and fancy snuffs, 38 & 39 Tyrrel st.

Blackburn Thomas, provision dealer, Back lane, Bowling

Blackburn William,[c] Holmetop lane, Little Horton

Blackburn William Howgill,[bc] book and music seller, and printer, stationer, &c. 15 Market street; house Undercliffe

Blades James, clock cleaner, Bowling lane, Dudley Hill

Blakebrough Joshua, boot and shoe maker, High street, Great Horton

Blakeney Richard, boot-tree and last maker, 1 Toad lane, Bridge street

Blakey Mrs. Elizabeth, 47, Darley street

Blakey James, *Barley Mow Inn*, Wakefield road

Blakey Jobson,[b] Manchester road

Blakey Samuel, seedsman and florist, Kelvin Grove public gardens, and 8 Union Passage, Kirkgate

Blamires Benjamin,[b] Manchester road

Blamires Mrs. Elizabeth, High street, Great Horton

Blamires John,[bc] *Pack Horse Inn*, Westgate

Blamires Joseph, clog and patten maker, White Abbey

Blamires Joseph,[c] *Boar's Head Inn*, Market street

Blamires Joseph, provision dealer, Spring row, Manningham

Blamires Luke,[b c] Old road, Horton

Blamires Samuel, agent for the Bradford Flour Mill Society, Great Horton lane

Blamires Samuel,[b c] Cross lane, Great Horton

Blamires Timothy,[c] High street, Great Horton

Bland James, provision dealer, Church hill, Bowling

Bland James, provision dealer, Shear bridge, Great Horton

Bland John,[c] Frederick street, Goodman's End

Bland John, provision dealer, 133, Wakefield road

Bland Jonathan, boot and shoe maker, 73 High street

Bland Luke, provision dealer, 286 Manchester road

Bland Luke, schoolmaster, New Leeds

Boader John, millwright, Horton lane

Boats James, beer retailer, 40 Silsbridge lane

Bocock Jane, provision dealer, 8 Cannon street, Cheapside

Bocock John, painter, Black Bull yard, Westgate

Boddington Rev. John,[bc] Incumbent of Horton; house Great Horton

Boddy Elizabeth, dress maker, 39 Mill lane, Bowling

Bolland David,[c] Lower Woodlands, North Bierley

Bolland John,[c] Dudley hill, Bowling

Bolland William,[b c] plumber, glazier, and gas fitter, Church bank

Bolton Elizabeth, greengrocer, 65 Westgate

Bolton John,[b c] plasterer, 78 Bridge street

Bolton John,[c] Low Moor
Bolton Joseph,[b] provision dealer, Wapping, Northwing
Bolton Lewis,[b] Low green, Horton
Bolton Richard,[b c] provision dealer, Great Horton
Bolton Richard, druggist, Britannia street, Manchester road
Bolton William, plasterer, &c. Southgate, Great Horton
Bonnell Mr. John,[bc] Houghton place, Drewton street
Bonnell Joseph Fearnley,[b] saddler and harness maker, 22 Bridge street
Bonwell John,[c] provision dealer, 3 Kirkgate; house Peel street, Manchester road
Booker Robert Alfred, wool stapler, Swaine street; house Manningham lane
Booth Ann and Sarah, milliners and straw bonnet makers, 38, Manchester road
Booth Benjamin, stone merchant, Bolton road; house Clayton
Booth Elizabeth, school, North parade
Booth George,[b] Manchester road
Booth Mr. James,[c] Thornton Hall
Booth John,[b c] spinner (Smith & Booth); house, 2 Edmund street, Little Horton lane
Booth John,[b] flour dealer, 4 Manchester road; house, Manningham
Booth John,[b] flour dealer, 4 Leeds road; house George street, Leeds road
Booth Jonas,[bc] draper and hosier, High street, Horton
Booth Jonas,[b] Victoria street
Booth Joseph, joiner and cabinet maker, Dudley hill
Booth Joseph,[b] 373 Burnet Field, Bowling
Booth Mr. Nathaniel, North parade
Booth Thomas,[c] boot and shoe maker and provision dealer, Southgate, Great Horton
Booth Mr. William,[c] Thornton Hall
Booth William, grocer and tea dealer, 38 White Abbey
Booth William, vagrant master for Bradford Union; house Toad lane, Bridge street
Borissow Christian Ignatius, professor of the French, German, Italian and Spanish languages, 2 Victoria street, North parade
BOROUGH CONSERVATIVE ASSOCIATION, New Inn, Tyrrel street; William Greenwood, secretary
BOROUGH COUNCIL CHAMBERS, Court House, Hall Ings.—(*See* "Public Offices and Buildings")
BOROUGH COURT HOUSE, Hall Ings; clerk to the West Riding magistrates Mr. G. R. Mossman, solicitor, Hall Ings
BOROUGH MAGISTRATES' CLERK,—Mr. John Rawson, solicitor; office Swaine street
BOROUGH POLICE STATION, Swaine street; Mr. William Leveratt chief constable; superintendent of night police Richard Collinson; John Shuttleworth and Joseph Field detective officers; inspector of nuisances Mr. William Bakes
Bostock John, officer of inland revenue (excise branch), Manchester road
Bostock William, boot and shoe maker, 29 Ivegate
BOTANICAL AND HORTICULTURAL SCIETY; exhibition rooms Ex-

change buildings,—Mr. J. Simpson secretary

Botterill John, dyer, Charles street; works and house Leeds

Bottomley David, butcher, Tyrrel street; house Great Horton

Bottomley David,[b] *Fox and Pheasant Inn*, Little Horton

Bottomley Eli,[b c] provision dealer, 24 Croft street, Wakefield road

Bottomley George,[bc] Horton Grange, Great Horton

Bottomley James,[b] butcher, Great Horton lane

Bottomley John, stuff manufacturer, 8 Cheapside; house Cross School st

Bottomley Jonathan,[b] worsted spinner, Marshall's Mill, Manchester road; house Portland street, Manchester road

Bottomley Joseph, merchant, (Bottomley, Wood & Co.); house Idle

Bottomley Moses & Son, worsted spinners and manufacturers, Brook street; works and house Shelf, near Halifax

Bottomley Moses,[b] butcher, 114 Manchester road

Bottomley Moses,[b] spinner, (Moses Bottomley & Son); house, Shelf

Bottomley Paul, butcher, Back lane, Bowling

Bottomley Samuel,[c] Edmund street, Little Horton lane

Bottomley Samuel,[b] spinner, (Samuel Bottomley & Brothers); house Low Moor

Bottomley Samuel,[b] spinner (Bottomley, Wilkinson & Co.); res. Hallfield House, Bowling

Bottomley Samuel & Brothers, worsted spinners and manufacturers, Swaine street; works and house Low Moor

Bottomley Thomas, merchant (Bottomley, Wood & Co.); house Idle

Bottomley, Wilkinson & Co., worsted spinners and manufacturers, Croft street, and Marshall's Mill, Manchester road

Bottomley William,[b] butcher, Lowclose House, Great Horton

Bottomley William, butcher, 343 Wakefield road

Bottomley, Wood & Co. stone merchants; office canal road

Bottoms James,[b] woolstapler, Back Tyrrel street; house, North parade

Boulton Nathan, boot and shoe maker, Mount street, Bowling

Boulton Samuel, newsvender, stationer, and circulating library, Lumb lane

Boulton Samuel,[b] manufacturer, (Pilling & Boulton); house Lumb lane

Boville Sarah, dress maker, 31, Prospect street, Thornton road

Bower Benjamin, butcher, Back lane, Bowling

Bower Henry, spinner, (William and Henry Bower); house Drighlington, near Leeds

Bower Isaac,[bc] Bunker's Hill

Bower John,[c] wheelwright, Bunker's Hill

Bower Jonas,[b] professor of music, and dealer in piano-fortes, &c. Victoria street, North parade

Bower Samuel,[b c] wheelwright, Thornton road

Bower Samuel,[c] Bunker's Hill, Barkerend

Bower William,[c] Odsal moor-side

Bower William, manufacturer (Wm. & Henry Bower); house Drighlington, near Leeds

Bower William and Henry, worsted spinners and manufacturers, Charles street; works and house Drighlington, near Leeds

Bowes Hannah, provision dealer, 78 Silsbridge lane

Bowes James, watch and clock maker, jeweller, &c. 8 Union passage, and Leeds road

Bowker John, butcher, 191 Bolton road

Bowker John, general dyer, 148 Westgate, and Ship Alley, Well street

Bowker Susannah, provision dealer, 144 White Abbey

Bowles John Holdsworth, plumber, glazier and gas fitter, 2 Black Abbey

Bowling Greens:—Thomas Atkinson (subscription), Spotted House Inn, Manningham lane; John Lumby (public), New Millers' Dam Inn, Thornton road, and Elizabeth Crabtree (public), Coach and Horses Inn, Shipley

Bowling Iron Works (John Sturges & Co.); iron manufacturers, founders, millwrights, and engineers; coal and iron wharf Canal road

Bowman Rev. John, incumbent of Buttershaw

Bowman John, linen draper, hosier, &c. Wakefield road

Bowser John,[c] collector of water rates, Reservoir Cottage, Manningham

Boyce Thomas, tailor, Stott Hill

Boyd James, rag, rope, old metal and waste dealer, Chapel lane and Leeds road

Boyd William, tailor, Bradford Moor

Boyes Mrs. Elizabeth, Black Abbey

Boyes Richard, provision dealer, Laister Dyke

Boyes Robert, head clerk, Midland Railway Company; house Black Abbey

Boykett Charles, gun maker, 73 Chapel lane, Tyrrel street

Boyle Joseph,[b] beer retailer, 83 Westgate

Boyle Joseph,[c] Birks croft, Leeds road

Bracewell John, boot and shoe maker, Wood street, Manningham

Bradford Banking Company, Kirkgate; Mr. Samuel Laycock managing director

Bradford & Calverley Colliery, Bunker's hill (Messrs. Rawson, Clayton & Cousen); agent Mr. Isaac Clayton, 3 Market street

Bradford Charles William,[b] *Brown Cow Inn*, Kirkgate

Bradford Commercial Bank, Market street; Mr. Joseph Hill manager

Bradford Conservative News and Reading Rooms, Albion court, Kirkgate

Bradford and East-Morley Savings' Bank, Kirkgate; Mr. Thos. Haigh actuary

Bradford Exchange, corner of Exchange street, Kirkgate; Mr. Samuel Lord superintendent

Bradford Flour Company, Gordon street, Manchester road; Mr. D. H. Tarbottom manager

Bradford Free Grammar School, Manor row; Rev. John Richards, M. A. head master

Bradford Gas Works (old station), Mill street; New Station Thornton road; Mr. David Swallow superintendent; Mr. Joseph Bean, engineer

BRADFORD INFIRMARY AND DISPENSARY, Westgate; house-surgeon Mr. Knowles; matron Miss Rowley

Bradford Mr. John,[b c] Bradford Moor

Bradford Joseph,[b] hair dresser and perfumer, Chapel court, Kirkgate; house Westgrove street

BRADFORD AND LEEDS RAILWAY STATION, bottom of Kirkgate; Mr. Matthew Crabtree superintendent

BRADFORD LIME WORKS (Joseph Wood); office and kilns Canal road

BRADFORD OLD BANK, 24 Kirkgate; (Messrs. Henry, Alfred, and William Masterman Harris); draw on Barnett, Hoares & Co. London; cashiers Charles Heron and John Pawson

BRADFORD AND SELBY FLY BOATS' Co. (Pearson & Co.), Canal road; John Adamson agent

BRADFORD SUBSCRIPTION LIBRARY, Exchange buildings, Kirkgate; open from 10 till 5; winter closes at 4; Miss Mason librarian

Bradford Mr. Thomas,[b c] Hillside

BRADFORD WATER-WORKS COMPANY, 2 Rennie's buildings, Hall Ings; Mr. Adam Beattie manager

Bradley Catherine, milliner and dress maker, Laister Dyke

Bradley John,[b c] provision dealer, Laister Dyke

Bradley John, smith and farrier, Thornton road; house Westbrook terrace

Bradley Joseph, boot and shoe maker, 13 Priestley street, Bolton road

Bradley Joseph, manufacturer (Wilcocks, Bradley & Co.) ho. Shipley

Braint William, wholesale confectioner, 10 Nelson street, Chapel lane

Braithwaite Samuel, worsted spinner, Marshall's Mill, Manchester road; house Upper North parade

Bramham Henry, butcher, 99 Tumblinghill street, Thornton road

Branson Thomas,[b] grocer and druggist, Wakefield road

Branson William,[b] butcher, 72 Manchester road; house Earl street

Bray George,[c] Croft street, Leeds road

Bray Joseph, pattern-card maker and lithographic printer, Wadkin's fold, Well street

Brayshaw Elizabeth, milliner and dress maker, 298 Leeds road

Brayshaw George,[c] Westpark House, North Bierley

Brayshaw James, chimney sweeper, Mary Farrar yard, Westgate

Brayshaw James, scale-beam maker (John Hill & Co.); house 10 Back School street

Brayshaw William, chimney sweeper, 55 Providence street, White Abbey

Brayshaw William,[b c] builder and stone merchant, Manningham lane; house corner of Lumb lane, Westgate

Brear Grace, *Oak Inn*, Leeds road

Brear John,[c] 316 Leeds road

Brear James, coal dealer, 124 Round hill, Silsbridge lane

Brear Maria, milliner, 134 Silsbridge lane

Brear Thomas,[c] Brickkiln, Manningham

Brear William, piano-forte teacher and tuner, Belgrave place, Manningham

Brearley Daniel,[c] Great Horton

Brearley David,[b c] boot and shoe maker, 47 Westgate
Brewer Abel, tailor, Dudley Hill
Brewer Charles,[c] Foundry street, Vicar lane
Brien Rev. J. T. B. A. curate of national schools, Allerton
Brigg John, manufacturer, (John Brigg & Co.); res. Guard House, Keighley
Brigg John & Co., worsted spinners and manufacturers, Charles street; works Keighley
Brigg Joshua,[b c] commission agent and stuff merchant, Hall Ings; ho. Fountain st. Manningham lane
Brigg William,[c] Market street
Briggs Benjamin,[c] Little Horton lane
Briggs Henry,[b] carver and gilder, and house, sign and decorative painter and paper hanger, 1 North parade; res. Prospect House, Manningham
Briggs James, *Fox and Hounds Inn*, North Wing
Briggs John,[c] tailor, High street, Great Horton
Briggs John, bobbin turner (Robert Briggs & Sons); house Primrose terrace, Manningham
Briggs Jonas, stuff manufacturer, Market street; works and house Birstal
Briggs Jonathan, stuff manufacturer, 183, Old Pieceball; works and house Clayton
Briggs Joseph, looking-glass and picture frame maker, 92, Leeds road
Briggs Joseph, beer retailer, 12 Castle street, Manchester road
Briggs Michael,[b] furniture broker, 149 Bridge street
Briggs Nathaniel,[b c] merchant (Milligan, Forbes & Co.); house Cliff Cottage, near Rawden
Briggs Rawdon, boot and shoe maker, Clayton street, Thornton road
Briggs Robert, jun. bobbin turner (Robert Briggs and Sons); house Primrose terrace, Manningham
Briggs Robert & Sons, bobbin turners and hard wood-dealers, Sugden's Mill, Black Abbey
Briggs Samuel, boot and shoe maker, Lower green, Great Horton
Briggs Thomas, bobbin turner (Robt. Briggs & Sons); house Primrose terrace, Manningham
Briggs Thomas, schoolmaster, Wakefield road, Bowling
Brightman William,[b c] provision dealer and beer retailer, 93 Birk street, Leeds road
Briskham John, *Wheat Sheaf Inn*, Wakefield road
Britton Robert,[c] grocer and tea dealer, British wines, and foreign fruit and hop merchant, 10 Bridge street
Broadbent Henry,[c] Close top, Horton
Broadbent James Sutcliffe, worsted spinner and manufacturer, Hartley's buildings, Brook street; works and house Roundhill, Cleckheaton
Broadbent John,[b c] Mount pleasant, Manchester road
Broadbent John,[b c] Broad street, Manor row
Broadbent John,[b] merchant (John Broadbent & Co.); house Earl st. Manchester road
Broadbent John & Co., stuff merchants, Swaine street
Broadbent Robert,[c] Brick lane, Manningham
Broadbent William,[c] Aycliffe lane, Great Horton

Broadley Henry, hair dresser and toy dealer, top of Ivegate

Broadley & Taylor, boot and shoe makers, 3 North parade

Broadley William, provision dealer, 37 Vicar lane, Leeds road

Bronte Rev. Patrick, B. A. incumbent of Haworth

Brook, Gant and Co., linen and wollen drapers, hosiers, silk mercers, and haberdashers, 10 Westgate

Brook Isaac,[c] Little Horton

Brook and Knowles, stuff merchants, Crossley's buildings, Westgate

Brook John, provision dealer, Sticker lane, Bowling

Brook John,[c] Little Horton

Brook Joseph,[b] blacksmith, Silsbridge lane; house Victoria street, North parade

Brook Luke, tailor, Sticker lane, Bowling

Brook Richard,[b,c] merchant (Brook & Knowles); house Westgate

Brook Richard, draper (Storey and Brook); house Kirkgate

Brook Thomas, furniture broker, 78 White Abbey

Brook William,[c] Victoria terrace, Bolton road

Brooke Richard, provision dealer, 19 Queen street, White Abbey

Brooke William,[b] brush maker, 17 High street

Brooks Edward, wool and top agent, Swaine street

Brooks James, fruit and provision dealer, 87 Birk street, Leeds road

Brooksbank William,[b] watch and clock maker, silversmith and jeweller, 64 Market street

Broscomb Joseph,[b] beer retailer, 49 Black Abbey

Brotherton Thomas,[c] Bradford Moor

Brown Edward, boot and shoe maker, 2, Vicar lane

Brown Frances, milliner and straw bonnet maker, 45 Croft street, Manchester road

Brown Francis, *Golden Lion Inn*, Leeds road

Brown George, tailor, 107 Grace-street, White Abbey

Brown George,[b] spinner (George Brown & Co); ho. Richmond terrace

Brown George & Co., worsted spinners and manufacturers, Charles street; works Fawcetholme Mill, Thornton road

Brown Harriet, milliner and dress maker, Swaine green, Bowling

Brown Henry,[b] Sawrey place, Little Horton lane

Brown Henry, organ builder, Leeds road

Brown Henry,[b c] draper (Brown and Muff); house Melbourne place

Brown Jacob,[b] stationer, circulating library and paper hanger, 8 John street, Northgate

Brown James, engraver, lithographic and copper-plate printer, gold and silver letter manufacturer, 2 Market street; house John street, Northgate

Brown James, coal dealer, Victoria street, Thornton road

Brown James,[b] Victoria street, North Parade

Brown James,[c] Foundry street

Brown John,[b] Broad street, Manor row

Brown Joseph,[b] schoolmaster, Gain lane, Laister dyke

Brown Joseph,[c] woolstapler, top maker and agent, machine broker, &c.

Hustler's buildings, Market street; house Broomfield terrace
Brown Joseph, provision dealer, Leech's Square, Laister dyke
Brown Joseph,[b] High street
Brown Margaret, dress maker, 53 Thornton road
Brown Mary Ann, milliner and bonnet maker, 97 Westgate
Brown Matthew,[b c] woolstapler, Cheapside; house Drewton street
Brown & Muff, linen and woollen drapers, clothers, hosiers, &c. 54 Market street
Brown Sarah, beer retailer, 18 Southgate
Brown Sarah, silk and straw bonnet maker, 32 Britannia street, Manchester road
Brown Thomas,[b] manufacturer (Geo. Brown & Co); ho. Richomnd terrace
Brown Thomas,[b] Houghton place, Drewton street
Brown William King,[b] pawnbroker, 10 Vicar lane
Brown William, tailor, 170 Whetley street, Manningham
Brownbridge Robert,[b] butcher, Wakefield road
Browne James,[b] merchant (James and John Browne); house Spring Lodge, Lower Baildon
Browne James and John, stuff merchants, Court street, Brook street
Brownlee Henry William,[c] Yew House, Thornton
Brumfit Charles,[b] wine and spirit merchant, and wholesale dealer in ale and porter, Bermondsey; house North parade
Brumfit Jacob,[b] Longlands place, Westgate
Brumfit Joseph,[b c] dealer in new and second-hand clothes, silver plate, and musical instruments, jeweller and furniture broker, 80, Market street; house North parade
Brumfit Misses Nancy and Mary, Northgate
Brunt Jacob, beer retailer, 10 Long lands place, Westgate
Brunt Joseph, coal dealer, Thomas street, Brick lane
Brunton William, joiner and builder, Keighley street, Silsbridge lane; house Manchester road
Bryar Joseph, auctioneer and tea agent, Snow hill, Manningham lane
Bryar Mrs. register for servants, Snow hill, Manningham lane
Buck Bolland,[b c] woolstapler, 14 Cheapside; house Fountain street, Manningham lane
Buck & Holmes, woolstaplers, 1 Exchange street, Duke street
Buck & Holmes, worsted spinners, Pennyoaks Mill, Melbourne-street, Leeds road
Buck Thomas,[b c] worsted spinner, (Buck and Holmes); ho. Manor row
Buckanan Andrew, tailor and draper, 3 Paper Hall, Northwing
Buckle Mr. William,[b] High street, Great Horton
Buckley J. H., letter-press printer, 39 Sterling street
Buckley M., hat and bonnet box manufacturer, 39 Sterling street
Buckley Wm. Halstead Greenwood,[b] surgeon, 22 Portland place, Manchester road
Buckup John, merchant, (Barthelmes & Buckup); house Spring gardens, Manningham lane
Building and Investment Society's Rooms, Cheapside; Mr. W. Clough, secretary

Bullock John, clog and patten maker, 26 Brick lane
Bulmer William, butcher, 15 Silsbridge lane
Burgess Susannah, milliner and dress maker, 1 George street, Manchester road
Burghart, Aders, & Co., stuff and yarn merchants, Bermondsey and Manchester
Burke John, provision dealer, 54 Nelson court, Nelson street
Burnett Rev. John, L.L.D. Greenhill House, Leeds road
Burnett Joseph,[c] White Abbey
Burnley James,[c] stone mason, Black Abbey
Burnley John,[b] 121 Oakfold, Bowling
Burnley Joseph,[c] White Abbey
Burnley Samuel,[c] White Abbey
Burnley William, boot & shoe maker, Little Horton lane
Burrows John, tailor, 35 Heber street, Little Horton lane
Burrows John, flour dealer, Great Horton lane
Burrows John,[b] junior, High street, Great Horton
Burrows William, cotton warp dealer, High street, Great Horton
Burton Francis, provision dealer, 620 Wakefield road
Burton Francis, provision dealer, 12 Nelson street, Chapel lane
Burton George, engraver, Leeds road
Burton Misses, school, Chapel street, Leeds road
Burton Robert, provision dealer, 6 Silsbridge lane
Busfeild Johnson Atkinson,[b] solicitor, and treasurer of County Courts, Thornton's buildings, Market st.; house Hall Field, Manningham lane
Bussey Eleanor, provision dealer, Bradford Moor
Butler Ambrose Edmund,[b] merchant (Beecroft, Butler, & Co.); house Kirkstall, near Leeds
Butler George,[b] Victoria street, North Parade
Butler James,[b c] maltster, Dudley hill
Butler John,[c] Longcroft place, Westgate
Butler John,[c] Cheesecake House, North Bierley
Butler John Octavius,[b] merchant (Beecroft, Butler & Co.); house Kirkstall, near Leeds
Butler Joshua, butcher, 85 Bridge st.
Butler Thomas,[b] merchant (Beecroft, Butler & Co.); house Kirkstall, near Leeds
Butterfield Mrs. Ann, North parade
Butterfield Brothers, stuff manufacturers and merchants, 1 Norfolk street, Bridge street; works Prospect Mill, Keighley
Butterfield David,[c] Northstreet, Stott Hill
Butterfield Mr. David,[c] North parade
Butterfield Mrs. Elizabeth, North Parade
Butterfield Francis, solicitor, White Lion yard, Kirkgate; house Bingley
Butterfield Frederick,[b] merchant (Butterfield Brothers); house Cliff Hall, Keighley
Butterfield George, woolstapler, Swaine street; house Springfield place, Manningham lane
Butterfield James,[b c] provision dealer, 122, Longcroft street, Silsbridge lane

Butterfield John,[b] woolstapler (John Butterfield and Son); house Springfield place, Manningham lane

Butterfield John,[b] merchant (Butterfield Brothers); house Cliff Hall, Keighley

Butterfield John and Son, woolstaplers, Swaine street

Butterfield Robert, woolstapler, Swaine street; house Manningham lane

Butterfield Samuel,[c] woolstapler, top maker and agent, Hustler's buildings, Market street; house North Wing

Butterfield William,[b] merchant (Butterfield Brothers); house Cliff Hall, Keighley

Butterfield William, manager (executors of Peter Laycock); house Vicarage

Butterfield William, provision dealer, 46 Sterling street, Manchester road

Butterworth Sidney Aquil a and Co. stuff merchants, printers and dyers, Charles street, Hall Ings

Byles Henry Beuzeville,[b c] bookseller and stationer, 17 Kirkgate; house Hanover square

Byles William,[b c] proprietor and publisher of the *Bradford Observer*, 17 Kirkgate; house Ann Place, Little Horton lane

Byrd Thomas, linen draper, hosier, and haberbasher, 31 Kirkgate

Byrne Patrick William, ironmonger, (Dixon and Byrne); house Summerseat place

Byrom James, painter, gilder and paper hanger, Townhill House, Wakefield road

Byron Robert,[b] veterinary surgeon, Hall Ings

CALEDONIAN INSURANCE COMPANY; agent Mr. Thomas Stephenson, Charles street

Calvert Blakey,[b c] manufacturer, (Lodge Calvert & Son); house Hall lane, Bowling

Calvert Brothers, tailors and drapers, 73 Market street; house Hall lane, Bowling

Calvert George, boot and shoe maker, Castle street, Manchester road

Calvert John, smith and farrier, Well street; house John street

Calvert Lodge,[bc] manufacturer (Lodge Calvert & Son); house 62 Leeds road

Calvert Lodge & Son, worsted spinners and manufacturers, 37 Bank street; works Thornton road

Calvert Mary, linen draper, Wakefield road, Bowling

Calvert Michael,[b c] brazier, and iron and tinplate worker, 13 Ivegate

Calvert Thomas,[b] top of Westgate

Calvert William,[b] greengrocer, 128 Manchester road

Cameron William, provision dealer, 57 Park place, Little Horton

Campbell Richard, locksmith and bell hanger, Reform street, Westgate

Cannan James, hardware dealer, Silbridge lane

Cannan William,[c] druggist and stationer, 149 Bridge street

Cannon John,[c] Bolton road

Cansfield Isaac, provision dealer, 30 Gaunt street, Otley road

Cansfield John,[c] Bolton road

Carey Rev. John (Moravian), Little Horton lane

Carr John, auctioneer, appraiser and valuer, Tyrrel street and Halifax

Carr Joshua,[c] Wakefield road

Carr Mary, draper, Dudley hill

Carr Sarah, boot and shoe dealer, High street, Great Horton

Carr Thomas,[b] provision dealer, 4 Nelson street, Chapel lane

Carritt Ann, dress maker, 97 Brick lane

Carroll Moses, beer retailer, Broomfield, Wakefield road

Carter George, coal dealer, Back fold, North wing

Carter James,[c] butcher, Clayton

Carter John,[b] confectioner, 124 Manchester road

Carter John,[b] Randallwell street, Great Horton road

Carter Jane, dress and straw bonnet maker, top of Park square, Manningham

Carter Joseph, beer retailer, 209 Bolton road

Carter Richard, spindle maker (Holmes & Carter); house Pit lane, Leeds road

Carter Robert, provision dealer, 138 Manchester road

Carter William, tailor, 7 Three street, Silsbridge lane

Carter William, greengrocer, 3 Nelson street, Chapel lane

Carter William,[b] blacksmith, Vicar lane, Leeds road

Carver, Chaplin & Horne, carriers to Bristol, London, &c., Hall Ings; Mr. Samuel Harrison agent

Carver & Co. carriers and agents for the Lancashire and Yorkshire Railway Company, Hall Ings

Carveth George,[b] school, Chapel street, Leeds road ; house Hillside

Cass William,[b] Little Horton lane

Casson Edwin,[b] surgeon, 1 High st.

Casson John, provision dealer, High street, Churchbank

Casson Mary, butcher, 133, Brick lane

Casson William, butcher, Thornton road; house Clayton Heights

Catholic Chapel.—(*See* the index "Church and chapels.")

Caton Richard, m. d. (gone to *Scarboro'*)

Cattle Market—(held on Thursdays), Fair ground, Darley street

Cauthra Jonathan,[c] farmer, Beck side, Horton

Cauthra Joseph,[b] Bracken Hill, Great Horton

Cavalry and Infantry Barracks, Bradford Moor; Mr. Jackson Midgley, barrack-master

Cawthara John, provision dealer, Park square, Manningham

Chadwick John,[b] fruiterer and greengrocer, 47, Westgate

Chadwick John, *Reservoir Inn*, Lady's Walk, Manningham

Challand George, provision dealer, 20 Bowling lane, Manchester road

Chapel Sarah, milliner, 18, School street, Manchester road

Chapman John,[b] tailor and draper, (John Chapman & Co.); house Little Horton lane

Chapman John & Co., hatters, woollen drapers and tailors, 26 Kirkgate

Chapman Joseph,[b c] manufacturer, (Chapman & Lofthouse); house Westgate

Chapman & Lofthouse, stuff manufacturers, 48 Bridge street

Chapman William, silk and woollen dyer, 57 Chapel lane, and 8 Northgate

Charlesworth John,[b] provision dealer, Bowling lane

Charlesworth J. & J. agents for the Haigh Colliery Company; wharf and office Railroad street, Canal road

Charlesworth Thomas, provision dealer, Manningham

Charlesworth Thomas Richard, accountant and general agent, arbitration & bankruptcy business, &c. 49 Darley street; house Sticker lane, Bowling

Charters William Holdsworth,[c] York street, Wakefield road

Chatterton Frederick,[b] confectioner and eating-house keeper, 34 Ivegate

Cheesebrough Alfred,[b] woolstapler, Wakefield road

Cheesebrough Edward,[b] woolstapler, Wakefield road

Cheesebrough James, woolstapler, Westbrook House, Great Horton

Cheesebrough John, worsted inspector 13 Ebenezer street

Cheesebrough Joseph,[bc] woolstapler, Wakefield road

Cheesebrough Leonard,[b] Westgrove street

Cheesebrough William,[bc] woolstapler, Cheapside, Dale street and Exchange street; res. Westbrook House, Great Horton lane

Cheesebrough William, butcher, 30 King street, White Abbey

Chelsea Pensioners' Pay Office, Court House, Hall Ings; Major Orange acting officer

Cherry James,[c] Wellington street, Stott Hill

Cherry John, boot and shoe maker, Stott Hill

Child Daniel,[b] machine maker, Spence's Mill, Chapel lane; house Eccleshill

Child James, provision dealer, 94 Bolton road

Child John, dealer in publications, 137 Brick lane

Child John,[bc] 14 North parade

Childs' Messrs. school, Drewton street; house Upper North parade

Choral Society, Oddfellows' Hall, Thornton road

Chown Rev. J. P. (Baptist), Little Horton lane

Christian Knowledge Society's Depot, 2 Albion Court, Kirkgate; E. J. Mitchell, Esq. president

Church of England Insurance Company; agent, Mr. T. R. Charlesworth, 49 Darley street

Church Missionary Society; Rev. Dr. Burnett president

Church Temperance Society, Christ Church vestry, Darley street

Churchwardens, Mr. Isaac Wright, woolstapler, Bermondsey, and Mr. William Rouse, spinner, Canal road

City of London Life Assurance Company; agent Mr. Marmaduke Foster, solicitor, 70 Market street

Clair John, beer retailer, 88 Adelaide street, Manchester road

Clapham John, manufacturer (Wm. & John Clapham); house Thornton road

Clapham Samuel, spinner (Clapham & Whitaker); house Esholt

Clapham Thomas,[b] beer retailer, 2 Duke street, Manchester road

Clapham & Whittaker, worsted spinners and manufacturers, Schuster's Buildings, Brook street; works Baildon

Clapham William, wheelwright, Manchester road, Bowling

Clapham William,[bc] manufacturer, (William and John Clapham); house Westgrove street

Clapham William,[bc] stuff manufacturer, Swaine street; works and house Wilsden

Clapham William & John, stuff manufacturers, HOLMEFIELD MILLS, Thornton road

Clarance Adolphus, merchant (Adolphus Clarance & Co.); house Stone street, Manor row

Clarance Adolphus & Co., tea, coffee and spice merchants, 34 Kirkgate

Clark Henry,[b] Bankfoot, Bowling

Clark James, wool-comb maker, Southgate

Clark James, provision dealer, 163 George street, Leeds road

Clark John,[c] Lumb lane, Manningham

Clark John,[c] provision dealer, Four lane ends, Manningham

Clark John,[c] New row, Manningham

Clark Joseph, blacksmith, Bradford Moor; house Stanningley

Clark Joshua, provision dealer, Pit lane end, Barkerend

Clark Robert, beer retailer, New road, Great Horton

Clark Robert,[bc] silk mercer (Parkinson & Clark); res. Gilhead House, Little Horton

Clark Thomas,[b] butcher, 76 White Abbey

Clark Thomas, provision dealer, 11 Mill street, Little Horton

Clark Walter,[bc] seedsman, and public tea, fruit, and salad gardens, Manningham lane

Clark William, coal dealer, Tumblinghill street, Thornton road

Clark William Oswald, artist, 12 Wellington street, Stott hill

Clark William, tailor, Wakefield road

Clark William,[c] Mount street, Stott Hill

Clarke Benjamin, tailor, Cherry-tree row, Manningham

Clarke Benjamin,[b] woolstapler, (Clarkes & Ingham); house Croft street, Wakefield road

Clarke Christopher, wheelwright, High street, Great Horton

Clarkes & Ingham, woolstaplers, 8 Broadstones

Clarke John, woolstapler (Clarkes and Ingham); house Croft street

Clarke Jonathan,[b] East street, Leeds road

Clarke William,[b] butcher, Bradford Moor

Clarkson Abraham, boot and shoe maker, 17 Cropper lane, Westgate

Clarkson Richard,[b] provision dealer, 45 Westgate

Clarkson Thomas, corn and flour dealer, Back lane, Bowling

Clarkson Thomas, plumber, (Clarkson & Walton); house Southgate

Clarkson & Walton, plumbers, glaziers and gas fitters, 5 Manchester road

Clayton Charles,[bc] plasterer, High st

Clayton Charles,[bc] shuttle maker, (Charles & John Clayton); house Water lane

Clayton Charles & John, shuttle makers, heald-shafts, temples, and double stocks, &c. Thornton road

Clayton Henry, draper, Arcadia street, Lumb lane, Manningham

Clayton Isaac,[b] coal merchant, (Rawson, Clayton & Cousen); house Apple Hall, Bunker's hill
Clayton Isaac,[bc] Laburnum Cottage, Manningham
Clayton James,[c] Westgate
Clayton James,[c] Laycock's Houses
Clayton James,[b] general commission agent, Charles street; house Broomfield terrace, Wakefield road
Clayton John,[c] Moor top, Bierley
Clayton John, smith and farrier, Market street; house Joseph street, Leeds road
Clayton John, shuttle maker (Chas. and John Clayton); house Thornton road
Clayton John, hair dresser, 40 White Abbey
Clayton John, boot and shoe maker, Cheapside; ho. Wellington street
Clayton John, [bc] merchant (John Clayton, Son & Co.); house Manchester road
Clayton John, Son & Co. stuff merchants and woolstaplers, Exchange street, Kirkgate
Clayton Joseph,[b] merchant (John Clayton, Son & Co.); house Hanover square
Clayton, Marshalls & Co. iron manufacturers, founders, and coal owners; works Bierley,—office and wharf Canal road
Clayton Mary, milliner and dress maker, Wakefield road
Clayton Mary Ann, milliner and straw bonnet maker, Barkerend
Clayton Matthew, provision dealer, Back lane, Bowling
Clayton Richard,[b] Near Birks Hall
Clayton Solomon,[b] professor of music, Victoria street, North Parade
Clayton & Son, tailors, Wakefield road
Clayton Thomas, coal owner, Mirey-shay
Clayton Thomas, [bc] woolstapler, Thornton road; house Sawrey place, Little Horton lane
Clayton Thomas Greenwood,[bc] Esq. ironmaster, (Bierley Iron Works); house Bierley Hall
CLECKHEATON, &c. RAILWAY STATION; passengers' entrances on the Leeds and Wakefield road
Clegg James,[b] Thornton road
Clegg John, provision dealer, 31 Hayworth street, White Abbey
Clegg John, coal dealer, Broomfields, Wakefield road
Clegg John,[b] solicitor (Thompson & Clegg), and steward to the ladies of the manor, Bridge Street Buildings, Bridge street; house Manor row
Clemitshaw John, hackney coach proprietor, Stone street, Manor row; house Lister street, Bermondsey
CLERICAL, MEDICAL, AND GENERAL INSURANCE COMPANY; agent Mr. E. H. Parratt, Broadstones
Cliffe James and Joseph, engineers, iron and brass founders, and railway-wheel manufacturers, Old Foundry, Tyrrel street
Cliffe Joseph,[b] Goodmansend
Cliffe Joseph, engineer (James and Joseph Cliffe); house Tyrrel street
Clifford John,[b] Old lane, Bowling
Clough Ann, provision dealer, 66 Bolton road
Clough Benjamin, brazier, and iron and tinplate worker, 8 White Abbey
Clough Charles,[c] draper, Little Horton lane

Clough Charles,[b] solicitor, (Tolson, Clough, and Taylor), and clerk of county court, and to the Bradford and Wakefield turnpike trust; office Rawson place; house Bolton Grange

Clough George,[b c] carrier, Thornton road; house Park lane, Little Horton

Clough Henry,[c] boot and shoe maker, Little Horton

Clough Henry,[b] carrier and farmer, Park lane, Little Horton

Clough Hudson,[b] spinner, (Smith, Clough & Co.); house Globe Cottage, Manningham

Clough James,[b c] stone merchant, Little Horton lane

Clough James, dealer in London porter, Burton ales, &c. 20 Market street; house Heber street, Little Horton lane

Clough James, woolstapler, Bermondsey; house Birkenshaw

Clough James,[b c] provision dealer, Heber street, Little Horton lane

Clough Jane, provision dealer, 85 Fitzgerald street, Manchester road

Clough John, worsted spinner and manufacturer, Charles st.; works and house Ingrow, near Keighley

Clough John, boot and shoe maker, 176 Wakefield road

Clough John,[b c] provision dealer, High street, Great Horton

Clough John,[b] Back lane, Manningham

Clough John,[b] Spinkwell

Clough Joseph,[b] cabinet maker and upholsterer, 2 Manchester road

Clough Joseph,[b c] provision dealer, Halifax road, Bowling

Clough Maxwell, hair dresser, 578 Bridge street

Clough Robert, worsted spinner and manufacturer, Exchange street; works and house Keighley

Clough Samuel,[c] Woodhouse Hill, North Bierley

Clough Samuel,[c] Little Horton lane

Clough Thomas,[c] schoolmaster, Garden place, Silsbridge

Clough William,[b c] accountant, collector of lighting and watching rates, agent for the West of England Insurance Company, and secretary to the Building & Investment Society; office Swaine street; house Charles street, Leeds road

Clough William,[c] Longcroft place, Westgate

Clough William, green grocer, High street, Great Horton

Clowes Rev. Francis,[b] classical tutor, Baptist College, Little Horton; house Bolton

Cluderay John,[b c] corn and flour dealer, Ivegate; house 6 Westgrove street

Cluderay William,[b] corn, flour, and provision dealer, 134, Westgate; house Simes street, Westgate

Clulow Rev. William Benton,[b] (Independent), Spring gardens

COACH OFFICES, &c.—(See "Conveyance Lists.")

Coates Ann, straw bonnet maker, 284 Leeds road

Coates George,[b] Conservative registrar, Albion court; house Hanover square

Coates Henry, woollen cloth manufacturer, Bradford Moor

Coates James, woollen cloth manufacturer, Bradford Moor

Coates James,[b] Hanover square

Coates Joseph, teacher of vocal music, Thornton road

Coates Joseph, woollen cloth manufacturer, Bradford Moor

Coates Ralph, blacksmith, Hardcastle lane, Well street

Coates Sarah Ann, milliner and dress maker, 8 Northgate

Coates William,[b] master of Post-Office, Union Passage; house Manor row

Coates William,[b c] surgeon, Rawson place, Darley street

Cochrane Mr. James, [b c] Westbrook place, Horton road

Cockcroft John, manufacturer, (John Cockcroft & Son); house Ovenden

Cockcroft John & Son, stuff manufacturers, Brook street; works Ovenden, near Halifax

Cockcroft Joseph, woolstapler, Commercial street; house Heaton

Cockcroft Samuel,[b c] Undercliffe road

Cockcroft Samuel,[b c] beer retailer, Lidget green, Great Horton

Cockcroft Thomas, clogger, Lidget green, Great Horton

Cockcroft Thomas, stuff manufacturer, 24 Old market; works and house Heaton

Cockerham Edward,[b c] High street, Great Horton

Cockin Joseph,[c] Great Horton

Cockin Joseph, carpet dealer (Joseph & James Cockin); house Houghton place, Drewton street

Cockin Joseph and James, carpet dealer and upholsterers, 12 Cheapside

Cocks Thomas, provision dealer, Manningham

Cockshott William, manufacturer, (Wall, Cockshott, & Wall); house Grassington, near Skipton

Cockshott William,[b] chemist and druggist, and dealer in British wines, 32 Westgate

Cockson Samuel,[b] Church street

Cockson William, provision dealer, 1 Mount street, Leeds road

Coe John,[c] North Bierley

Coe Michael,[c] Longcroft pl. Westgate

Colburn John, plumber, glazier, and gas fitter, 7 Croft street, Leeds road

Cole Benjamin,[b] provision dealer, Church hill, Wakefield road

Cole James, engineer, (Cole, Marchent & Co.); house Wakefield road

Cole John,[b c] engineer, (Cole, Marchent & Co.); house Greenhill Cottage, Hall lane, Bowling

Cole, Marchent & Co. engineers, millwrights and iron and brass founders, PROSPECT FOUNDRY, Wakefield road, Bowling

Cole Thomas,[b] Portland street, Manchester road

COLLECTORS' OF TAXES OFFICE, Swaine street, Hall Ings

Colley Maria, straw bonnet maker, 25 Silsbridge lane

Collier John,[b] commission woolcomber, Duckitt's Mill, Nelson st.; house Little Horton lane

Collier William, woolcomber (William Collier & Co.); house Manchester road

Collier William,[b] grocer and provision dealer, 85 Victoria street, North parade

Collier William & Co. commission woolcombers, Duckitt's Mill, Nelson street, Union street

Collinge Halstead,[b] High Bolton road

Collingwood Job, provision dealer, Great Horton

Collins Edward, provision dealer, Bradford Moor
Collins George,[bc] provision and earthenware dealer, 452 Wakefield road
Collins Thomas, veterinary surgeon, Beehive yard, Westgate
Collinson Edward, emigration and general agent, Hustler's buildings, Leeds road; house Green lane, Manningham
Collinson Joseph,[b] Westgrove street
Collinson Richard, superintendent of night police, Swaine street
Collinson William,[c] Bierley lane, Bierley
COMMERCIAL JOINT-STOCK BANK, Market street; Mr. Joseph Hill manager
Connell Sarah, straw bonnet maker, 93 Manchester road
Constantine James, cabinet maker and upholsterer, 76 Bridge street
Cook David, boot and shoe maker, Sticker lane, Bowling
Cook Jabez, dealer in periodicals, 28 White Abbey
Cook James, hair dresser, 127 Bridge street
Cook William, fruiterer and greengrocer, 248 Manchester road
Cook William,[b] woolstapler, 44 Cheapside; house Manor row
Cooke John,[bc] share broker, and agent for the Scottish Union Insurance Company, 38 Bank street; house Edmund street, Little Horton
Cooke William,[b] publication dealer, news-agent and stationer, Ebenezer street, Vicar lane
Cookson John, plumber, glazier and gas fitter, Well street, Kirkgate
Cooper Rev. James,[b c] M.A. incumbent of St. Jude's, Bellevue, Manningham lane
Cooper Jane, wool and waste dealer, Hope and Anchor yard, Bank st.; house Manchester road
Cooper John,[b] provision dealer, 192 Manchester road
Cooper Joseph,[b] Cliffe Wood, Bolton
Cooper Rev. Nathaniel, B. A. assistant curate at parish church, and chaplain of national schools; house Brunswick place
Cooper Thomas,[b] Charles street
Cooper & Wainwright, commission makers-up and packers, Dale street, Kirkgate
Cooper William, maker-up (Cooper & Wainwright); house Stone st. Manor row
Cooper William,[b] brazier, and iron and tin plate worker, 102, Manchester road
Cooper William,[b] Cliffe Wood, Bolton
Copley John,[b] letter-press and lithographic printer, 4 Market street; house Trafalgar street
Copley Thomas, provision dealer, 37 Longlands street, Westgate
Copley William,[b c] Wakefield road
Copley William,[b c] beer retailer, Manningham
Cordingley John, corn dealer, Edward street, Bridge street
Cordingley John,[b c] fell-monger, (John and Samuel Cordingley); house Burnet Field, Bowling
Cordingley John and Samuel, fellmongers and skinners, Manchester road
Cordingley Mrs. Maria, Crescent House, Horton
Cordingley Samuel,[b c] fellmonger, (John and Samuel Cordingley); house Manchester road

Cordingley William,[b c] white leather dresser, Park place, Little Horton

Cordingley William, tailor, 34 Reform street, Westgate

Corless George,[b c] worsted spinner, Upper Croft Mill, Bowling; house Sticker lane, Bowling

Corless Thomas,[b] worsted spinner, Upper Croft Mill, Bowling; house Swaine green, Bowling

Corless William,[b c] worsted spinner, Upper Croft Mill, Bowling; house Swaine green, Bowling

CORONER'S OFFICE, Court House, Hall Ings; Mr. Christopher Jewison coroner

CORPORATION COUNCIL CHAMBERS, Court House, Hall Ings.—[*See* "Public Buildings and Offices"]

Corson Mr. Samuel,[b] Little Horton lane

Cotham Rev. George Tolson, B. A. Wakefield road

Cottam Lawrence,[c] Near Birkshall

Cotton Edward, boot and shoe maker, 7 Westgate; Mr. George Roberts, agent, house Drewton street

Couldwell John, beer retailer, 52 Vicar lane

Coulson John,[b] beer retailer, Wood street, Manningham

Coulters Jonathan,[bc] stuff manufacturer, 14 Hartley's Buildings, Brook street; works Lower West street Mill; house Victoria street, North Parade

COUNTY COURT OF YORKSHIRE for Bradford & surrounding townships, 45 Darley street (held thrice a month); Charles Heneage Elsley, Esq. judge; Mr. Charles Clough, clerk, and Samuel Woodhead high bailiff

COUNTY FIRE AND PROVIDENT LIFE INSURANCE COMPANY; agent Mr. John Berry, attorney, Leeds road, and Mr. A. Sussman, Court st. Leeds road.

COURT HOUSE, Hall Ings; Mr. Charles Ingham superintending constable; Mr. William Baxter inspector of weights and measures, and high constable for East-Morley district.—[For magistrates, sessions &c. see "Public Buildings and Offices."]

Cousen Samuel,[b] coal merchant (Rawson, Clayton & Cousen); house Bunker's Hill

Cousen Samuel, stuff manufacturer, 22 Nag's Head yard, Kirkgate; works Great Horton, house Mireyshay, Bunker's Hill

Cousen Samuel,[b] hair dresser, game dealer and news agent, 13 Kirkgate; house Mount Pleasant, Bunker's Hill

Cousen Samuel Mann,[bc] merchant (Cousen & Thackray); house Milner Field, Bingley

Cousen & Thackray, stone merchants; office and wharf Brunswick place, Northgate

Cousen Thomas,[b] stuff manufacturer, Cross lane, Horton

Cousen William,[b] worsted spinner, Old Piecehall; works and house Great Horton

Cowgill Thomas,[b] grocer and provision dealer, 107 Bridge street

Cowin James,[b] upholsterer (James Cowin & Son); house Northgate

Cowin James & Son, cabinet makers and upholsterers, 59 Northgate

Cowling John,[b] coal and provision dealer, 237 Wakefield road

Cowman William, locksmith and bell hanger, Mawson street, Thornton road; house Wakefield road

Cox Joseph,[b] Wellington place, Little Horton lane

Crabtree Benjamin,[b c] collector of poor rates for Horton township; house and office Manchester road

Crabtree Cornelius,[c] tailor, Southgate, Great Horton

Crabtree Elizabeth, *Coach & Horses Inn*, and bowling green, Shipley

Crabtree George, beer retailer, 15 Peel street, Leeds road

Crabtree James,[b c] George street, Manchester road

Crabtree John,[b] Grammar School st. Manor row

Crabtree John,[b] beer retailer, 95 Bolton road

Crabtree John Anthony, joiner and builder, Salem street, Manor row; house Salem street

Crabtree Joseph,[c] Great Horton lane

Crabtree Mark, potato dealer, Paper Hall, Northwing

Crabtree Matthew,[b c] boot and shoemaker, High street, Great Horton

Crabtree Richard,[c] Greenhill place, Manningham

Crabtree Richard,[b] stone merchant, Lower Globe, Manningham

Crabtree Samuel, tailor, Greenhill Manningham

Crabtree Samuel,[b c] farmer, Lillycroft, Manningham

Crabtree Thomas,[b] butcher, 39 North gate

Crabtree Thomas,[b] provision dealer, 121 Manchester road

Crabtree William, tailor, Southgate, Great Horton

Crabtree William,[c] wool-washer, Mill street, Manchester road; house Manchester road

Crabtree William, watch maker (Harker & Crabtree); house Albion square

Crabtree William, machine maker, Laycock's Mill, Thornton road; house Villier street, Little Horton

Crampton Elizabeth, *Nag's Head Inn*, Kirkgate

Crampton John,[b c] butcher, 13 Hustler gate; house Heber street, Little Horton lane

Crampton William, *Shoulder of Mutton Inn*, Kirkgate

Craven Benjamin, moreen manufacturer, 155 Old Piece hall; works and house Allerton

Craven Benjamin,[c] provision dealer, Daisy hill top, Manningham

Craven Cornelius,[c] Bolton road

Craven Elijah, schoolmaster, Spring street, Manningham

Craven & Harrop, stuff manufacturers, Brook street; works DOLE MILL, Thornton, and WATERLOO MILL, Brook street

Craven Isaac, cabinet maker and upholsterer, 34 Darley street

Craven John,[b] manufacturer (John & Joseph Craven); house Keighley

Craven John, butcher, top of Greenhill, Manningham

Craven John & Joseph, stuff manufacturers, Booth street; works Keighley

Craven Jonas,[b c] manufacturer (Craven & Harrop); house Kipping lane, Thornton

Craven Joseph, manufacturer (John and Joseph Craven); ho. Keighley

Craven Joseph,[b] Whetley lane, Manningham

Craven Joseph,[b] jun. Whetley lane, Manningham

Craven Joshua,[c] stuff manufacturer, 112 Old Piecehall; works and house Allerton

Craven Joshua,[b c] stuff manufacturer, Charles street; works and house Thornton

Craven Thomas,[b c] Peel street, Leeds road

Craven William,[b] Whetley lane, Manningham

Craven William, brick maker, Brick lane; house White Abbey

Crebbin David John, schoolmaster, Chapel street, Leeds road

Cressey William,[b] house agent, 2 Bedford street, Bridge street

Cricket Club Ground, Great Horton road; Mr. Joseph Clayton president

Critchley Henry, provision dealer, 7 Longcroft place, Silsbridge lane

Croft Benjamin, provision dealer, 597 Wakefield road

Croft James,[b c] provision dealer and beer retailer, 111 Back lane, Bowling

Cromack Charles,[b c] butcher, 152 George street, Leeds road

Crompton Charles, agent for double and single cotton yarns, silk warps, oils, &c. Charles street, and Leeds

Crook William,[b c] woolcomb maker, Fawcett's court, Nelson street

Croser William,[b] surgeon, 30 Darley street

Crosland Francis, boot and shoemaker, 5 Croft street, Bridge street

Crosland Robert,[bc] millwright, engineer, and iron founder, wrought and cast-iron railway wheels and axles, tenders, waggons and trucks, Union Foundry, Manchester road; house Horton Crescent

Crosland William, clogger, 636 Wakefield road

Crossley Mrs. Elizabeth, Spring gardens, Manningham lane

Crossley Mrs. Frederick George, Hanover square

Crossley Henry William,[b c] tea dealer and coffee roaster, 31 Ivegate; house Westbrook place, Gt. Horton

Crossley James, tailor, 12 School street, Manchester road

Crossley John,[c] Bowling

Crossley Jonas,[c] Bowling

Crossley Robert,[c] Bowling

Crossley Samuel,[c] Southgate, Horton

Crossley Mr. Thomas,[b] North Parade

Crowther Mrs. Ann, Northbrook place, Bolton road

Crowther Benj.[b] Old lane, Bowling

Crowther Eli, draper, Brick lane, Black Abbey

Crowther George Brown,[bc] assistant overseer and collector of poor-rates for Manningham township, Brick lane, Manningham

Crowther John,[c] Westgrove street

Crowther John,[b] confectioner, 17 Market street

Crowther Rachel, provision dealer, 8 Nelson street, Chapel lane

Crowtrees Colliery, Bradford Moor, Mr. George Pollard proprietor; house Kirkskill Hall, near Otley

Croxall James,[b] agent (Pickford & Co.), 26 William street, Little Horton lane

Cryer Mr. Watson, [b c] Horton road

Cryer Wilson,[b] M.D. Hanover square

Cummins John,[b] linen draper, hosier, haberdasher, &c. 24 Market street

Cunliffe Thomas, fustian manufacturer, 31 Darley street; house Hawksclough, near Hebden Bridge

Cure William,[b c] grocer, tea dealer and coffee merchant, 24 Westgate

DAGLEY John,[b] Hillside

Daker John,[b] beer retailer, Mill street, Canal road

Daker Robert,[c] Mill street, Canal rd.

Dalby James, boot and shoe maker, 9 Park place, Little Horton

Dalby James,[b] stuff manufacturer, Schuster's buildings, Brook street; works Thornton road; house Manor row

Dalby Joseph,[bc] worsted spinner and manufacturer, George Hotel yard; works and house Laister dyke

Dalby Robert, school, 34 Chapel st. Leeds road; house James' street, Manchester road

Dalby Samuel,[b c] worsted spinner and manufacturer, Old Market; works and house Bradford Moor

Dalby Thomas, worsted top maker, 16 Old Piece hall; works and house Clayton

Dale George,[b] hair dresser and perfumer, 37 Market street

Dale John,[b c] bookseller, printer, stationer and bookbinder, Religious Tract Depository, and agent to the National Provident Institution and the Lancashire and Yorkshire Building Society, 1 Thornton's Buildings, Bridge street; house 11 Hanover square

Dalton Margaret, milliner and dress maker, 17 Manchester road

Daly Michael, beer retailer, 71 Westgate

Daniel Mary Ann, straw bonnet maker, 36 Vicar lane

Daniel William,[b] Vicar lane

Darling Benjamin, provision dealer, 101 Northwing

Darling Thomas, butcher, 23 Bower street, Manchester road

Darlington John,[bc] solicitor, and agent in the West Riding for the Guarantee Society, and the Manchester Fire and Pelican Life Insurance Offices, 12 Union passage, Kirkgate; house Shipley Hall

Darnbrough William,[c] Upper green, Horton

Darnbrough William, tailor, Walmsley's buildings, Prospect street, Silsbridge lane

Davidson Joseph, woolstapler, 13 Exchange street, and London

Davison William, tailor, 10 King street, Silsbridge lane

Davy William, officer of inland revenue (excise branch), 34 Westgrove street

Dawson Charles, butcher, 84 Edward street, Wakefield road

Dawson Christopher Holdsworth,[b c] Esq. iron master (Low Moor Iron Works); house Royds Hall

Dawson Daniel,[bc] saddler and harness maker, 1 Bermondsey; house Stone street, Manor row

Dawson George,[bc] furniture broker, 3 Stone street, Manor row

Dawson Hannah, earthenware dealer, 42 Market street

Dawson James, reed and heald maker, 60 Croft street, Manchester road

Dawson John, provision dealer, 164 George street, Leeds road

Dawson John,[bc] *Granby Hotel*, Union street, Bridge street

Dawson Joseph,[b] solicitor, Tyrrel-square, Tyrrel street; house Wadsworth Cottage, Manningham

Dawson Joseph, boot and shoe maker, Chapel lane, Tyrrel street

Dawson Mark, cotton warp agent, Booth street; house Great Horton

Day John,[b] woolcomb maker, 3 Thomas street, Manchester road

Dean Ellen and Christiana, milliners and dress makers, 21 Manchester road

Dean Henry & Son, stuff manufacturers, 15 Old Market; works and house Colne

Dearden William,[c] Wibsey Bankfoot

D'Hauregard Henry, stuff merchant, Leeds road; Mr. Errel manager

Deighton John, hair dresser and fishing tackle dealer, 18 Market street; house Leeds road

Deighton Mary Ann, milliner and dress maker, 86 Leeds road

Delaunay Frederick William, architect (Andrews and Delaunay); house Park place

Demain George, joiner (Demain & Johnson); house Belgrave place, Manningham

Demain & Johnson, joiners and builders, Manor row, Cheapside

Demain William, provision dealer, Upper North Parade, Manningham lane

Denbeigh Benjamin,[b] Brow, Manningham

Denbeigh Elizabeth, provision dealer, 15 Thornton road

Denby John,[bc] moreen manufacturer, 87 Old Piecehall; works and house Spring street, Manningham

Denby John,[bc] woolstapler, Cheapside; res. Manor House, Manningham

Denby Jonas,[bc] Spring st. Manningham

Denby Jonathan,[b] Upper North parade

Denby Jonathan, reed maker, 37 Southgate

Denby Joseph, spinner (Wm. Denby and Sons); house Shipley

Denby Richard, brazier and tin-plate worker, 97 Bridge street

Denby William, spinner (Wm. Denby and Sons); house Shipley

Denby William & Sons, worsted spinners and manufacturers, Court st. Leeds road; works and house Shipley

Denison Benjamin,[c] Belgrave place, Manningham

Denison Dyson,[bc] smith (Dyson and Thomas Denison); house Bridge st.

Denison Dyson & Thomas, smiths and farriers, Bridge street and Tyrrel street

Denison Emanuel, boot and shoe maker, Swaine green, Bowling

Denison Frederick Ramsden,[c] Bridge street

Denisen Joshua,[b] *Malt Shovel Inn*, Kirkgate

Denison Patrick,[bc] provision dealer, 88 Manchester road

Denison Thomas,[bc] smith (Dyson and Thomas Denison); house Shearbridge, Horton

Denton Elizabeth, dress maker, 48 Sterling street, Manchester road

Denton John, wool and waste dealer, Hope and Anchor yard, Bank st.; house Little Horton

Denton John, stone agent, Balm street, Bolton road; house John street, Stott Hill

Denton Joseph, hardware dealer, Bazaar, and Lidget green, Horton

Denton Joshua, greengrocer, Silsbridge lane

Denton Richard,[bc] worsted spinner and manufacturer, 8 and 9 New Piecehall; works and house Great Horton

Denton Samuel,[c] farmer, Legrams lane, Horton

Denton William,[bc] woolstapler and top maker, Swaine street; house Westbrook place, Horton

DEPOSITORY OF THE RELIGIOUS TRACT SOCIETY, 1 Thornton's Buildings, Bridge street

DEPOSITORY OF THE SOCIETY FOR PROMOTING CHRISTIAN KNOWLEDGE, Albion court, Kirkgate

Dewhirst Benjamin, smith and farrier, Vicar lane

Dewhirst John, tailor and draper, 57 High street, Churchbank

Dewhirst John,[bc] Water side, Manningham

Dewhirst Sarah, milliner and dress maker, Belgrave place, Manningham

Dewhirst Simon, tailor, Great Horton lane

Dewhirst Thomas, provision dealer, Providence street, Silsbridge lane

Dewhirst Thomas,[c] worsted spinner, Piecehall yard, Kirkgate; works Laister dyke, house Bradford Moor

Dewhirst Thomas,[bc] sharebroker, and agent for the Yorkshire Insurance Company, 10 Union passage, Kirkgate; house Upper North parade

Dewhirst Thomas,[b] Back la. Bowling

Dewhirst William,[c] Westgrove street

Dewhirst William,[b] merchant (Wm. Dewhirst & Co.); house Richmond place, Great Horton

Dewhirst William,[c] Brunswick place

Dewhirst William, plumber and glazier, Beckside, Great Horton

Dewhirst William & Co. stuff merchants, Leeds road

Dibb & Co. woolstaplers, Commercial street, Canal road

Dibb John,[bc] woolstapler (John Dibb and Co.); house Stone street, Manor row

Dick Archibald,[b] schoolmaster, High street, Barkerend

Dickinson & Barraclough, stuff manufacturers, Charles street; works Hope Mill, Hunslet, near Leeds

Dickinson George,[b] beer retailer, Well street

Dickinson Jonathan, manufacturer (Dickinson and Barraclough); ho. Blenheim square, Leeds

Dickinson William Leddicote,[b] *Wharf Hotel*, Bolton road

Diggles James,[b] grocer and provision dealer, 158 and 160 Westgate

Diggles John,[bc] pork butcher, 23 Ivegate; house Westgate

Dilger Engelbert, clock maker (Dilger, Winterhalder and Co.); house Hustlergate

Dilger Theodore, hardware, china and toy dealer, 15 Hustlergate

Dilger, Winterhalder & Co. clock makers, 18 Hustlergate

Dilley Phillip, baker, Back lane, Bowling

DIOCESAN CHURCH BUILDING SOCIETY; Rev. Dr. Burnett president

DIOCESAN EDUCATION SOCIETY;—George Pollard, Esq. treasurer

DIRECTORY (BOROUGH) OFFICE, and map and plan publishing establishment, 20 Bridge street

Dixon & Byrne, general furnishing ironmongers, stove-grate manufacturers, and agents for the Experience Life Insurance Company, 77 Market street

Dixon James,[bc] tailor (Dixon and Masser); house Westbrook place, Great Horton

Dixon Jeremiah,[b] provision dealer, 4 Duke street, Manchester road

Dixon John, tailor, 54 Earl street, Manchester road

Dixon John,[bc] builder, plasterer, &c. Swaine street; house Drewton st.

Dixon John, officer of inland revenue (excise branch), Dudley Hill

Dixon Joseph, clog and patten maker, 58 White Abbey

Dixon & Masser, tailors and drapers, 8 Bridge street

Dixon Robert, clogger, 102 Queen's Cut, Manchester road

Dixon Thomas,[b] ironmonger (Dixon and Byrne); house Whetley lane, Manningham

Dixon Thomas,[b] land agent and surveyor, and agent for the Yorkshire Fire and Life Insurance Company, Bridge street buildings, Bridge st.; house Spring gardens

Dixon Thomas,[b] bar, pig and sheet iron and steel merchant, railway tire bars, &c. Thornton road; res. Whetley House, Manningham

Dixon William, butcher, Belgrave place, Manningham

Dobson Christopher, provision dealer, Swaine green, Bowling

Dobson Edward,[bc] basket and skip maker, 33 Westgate

Dobson Henry,[bc] Birks, Horton

Dobson John, horn and tortoise-shell comb manufacturer, John street, Leeds road; house 87 Thornton rd.

Dobson Mary, new and second-hand clothes dealer, 2 Ivegate

Dobson Stephen,[c] Swaine green, Bowling

Dobson Thomas,[b] coal and provision dealer, 300 Manchester road

Dobson William,[bc] George st. Leeds rd.

Dodgson Mary, straw hat and bonnet maker, 24 Hustlergate

Dodsworth William,[c] machine maker, Thornton road; house Prospect row, Thornton road

Donisthorpe & Co. worsted top manufacturers (and top machine patentees), Tyrrel street

Donisthorpe George Edmund, manufacturer (Donisthorpe & Co.); house Hunslet, near Leeds

Donisthorpe Joseph,[b] worsted top agent, Tyrrel street; house Hall lane, Bowling

Dooley Henry,[b] *Albion Inn*, Leeds road

Dove Jacob,[b] currier (William and Jacob Dove); house Hanover sq.

Dove Thomas Pashley,[bc] furnishing ironmonger, brazier and tinman, 17 Ivegate

Dove William & Jacob, curriers, leather cutters and gutta-percha dealers, 16 Darley street, and Call lane, Leeds

Dovener William, provision dealer, Milton street, Wakefield road

Douglas James,[bc] merchant (Douglas, M'Candlish & Co.); house Edmund street, Little Horton lane

Douglas James,[bc] surgeon, Drewton street, Manningham lane

Douglas John,[bc] merchant (John Douglas & Co.); house Rose Mount

Douglas John & Co. stuff merchanst, Hall Ings

Douglas, M'Candlish & Co. stuff merchants, &c. Butterworth's buildings, Ivegate

Douglas Robert,[b] travelling draper and tea dealer, 114 Westgate

Douglas William,[bc] merchant (Russell, Douglas & Co.); house Manningham lane

Dover Rev. J. H. M. A. incumbent of Wilsden

Dowley Henry, [c] Back lane, Birkshall Fields

Dowling Cornelius,[c] Milton street, Wakefield road

Dowling John,[c] Milton street, Wakefield road

Dowling Michael,[bc] provision dealer, and bacon, cheese and butter factor, 51 Market street; house Leeds road

Downes Absolom,[c] Beck hill, Bowling

Downes John,[c] Bunker's Hill

Downes Joseph,[c] Fidler Hill Farm, North Bierley

Downing Caroline, day and boarding school, Spring gardens

Dowson Rev. Henry,[b c] (Baptist), Brick lane, Thornton road

Dowson John, nail maker, Wakefield road

Dracup Abraham, clog and patten maker, 18 Broadstones and 76 Silsbridge lane

Dracup Daniel,[b] Solitary, Horton

Dracup Edmund,[b] Pickles lane, Great Horton

Dracup Edward,[b] shuttle maker, Great Horton

Dracup George,[c] Pickles Hill lane, Great Horton

Dracup James,[c] High street, Horton

Dracup Nathaniel,[b] shuttle maker, High street, Great Horton

Dracup Richard, provision dealer, High street, Great Horton

Dracup Samuel,[bc] shuttle and jacquard machine maker, Cliffe lane, Great Horton; house Upper green

Dracup Squire, boot and shoe maker, High street, Great Horton

Drake Andrew,[b] provision dealer and beer retailer, Brick lane and Clayton street, Thornton road

Drake & Fawcett, bookbinders and pattern-card makers, 21 Market st.

Drake John, bookbinder (Drake & Fawcett); house Victoria street, North Parade

Drake Joseph, provision dealer, 54 Clayton street, Thornton road

Drake Joseph,[c] Cropper lane

Drake Moses,[b] Paradise Green, Manningham

Drake William, veterinary surgeon, 90 Northgate

Drake William Thurman,[c] Paradise Green, Manningham

Driver John, wheelwright, Cutler Height lane, Dudley Hill

Driver Peter,[b c] auctioneer and valuer, Procter's Buildings, Leeds road; house Park street

Drummond James,[b c] manufacturer, (Hill & Drummond); house Lillycroft, Manningham

Drury Rupert Alexander,[b] surgeon-dentist, North parade, Manningham lane

Duce James,[b] Wakefield road

Duckett John Broughton,[b] chemist and druggist, 3 Tyrrel street; house Great Horton lane

Duckett Thomas,[b] Little Horton lane

Duckitt Charles,[c] Hillside Villas
Duckitt Miss Jane, North Parade
Duckitt Mrs. Sarah, James street
Duckitt William,[b] manager (Yorkshire Banking Company); house Belle-vue, Manningham lane
Duckworth James,[b] Smith street, Manchester road
Duckworth John,[c] Saville street, Leeds road
Duckworth Joseph, cabinet maker (Duckworth & Watson); house Tyrrel court
Duckworth Joseph,[c] John street, Stott Hill
Duckworth & Watson, cabinet makers and upholsterers, Tyrrel court
Duckworth William,[c] Park street
Dugdale Robert, beer retailer, Ivegate
Duggan Edwin Patrick,[b] horse-breaker and beer retailer, 42, Union street
Duncan Thomas,[b] spinner (William Ackroyd & Co.); house Otley
Dunlop George,[b] Melbourne place, Little Horton
Dunn John, provision dealer, Wake-field road
Dunn Mary, *Bermondsey Hotel*, Lis-ter street, Bermondsey
Dunn Matthew, joiner (Dunn and Stoddart); house Vicar lane
Dunn & Stoddart, joiners and cabinet makers, Vicar lane; works Market street
Dunwell Jonathan,[b] boot and shoe maker, 46 Manchester road
Durham James,[b] Manchester road
Dyson Henry Leah,[b c] Cropper lane

EARLE Rev. J. B. A. incumbent of Clayton
Earnshaw David, hair dresser, 167 Wakefield road
Eastburn William, boot and shoe maker, 10 Sterling street, Man-chester road
EASTERN COUNTIES RAILWAY EN-QUIRY AND PARCEL OFFICE, Mid-land Station, bottom of Kirkgate
Eastwood George, provision dealer, 10 Silsbridge lane; house Provid-ence street
Eastwood John,[c] Queen street, Bow-ling
Eastwood John,[c] Low Moor
Eastwood Jonathan, machine maker, Portland street, Manchester road; house Earl street, Manchester road
Eckroyd Edmund, manufacturer, (Thomas Eckroyd & Sons); house Westgrove street
Eckroyd Thomas,[b] manufacturer (Thomas Eckroyd & Sons); house Horton
Eckroyd Thomas & Sons, stuff manu-facturers, Charles street; works Perseverance Mill, Thornton road
Ecroyd Benjamin,[b c] conveyancer, and secretary to the Friends' Provident Institution, 67 Market street; house Ashfield terrace, Horton road
Ecroyd William, spinner (William Ecroyd & Son); house Lomeshaye, near Burnley
Ecroyd William & Son, worsted spin-ners and manufacturers, Brook st.; works Lomeshaye, near Burnley
Edgar Robert,[b] linen draper, haber-dasher and hosier, 27 Market st.
EDINBURGH LIFE ASSURANCE COM-PANY; agent Mr. Fowler, solicitor, 32 Darley street
Edmeston Robert,[b] Crowther street, Manchester road

Edmonds Rev. J. H. B. A. curate, High street, Great Horton

Edmondson Abraham, butcher, High street, Great Horton

Edmondson Christopher,[b] butcher, 27 Manchester road; house Wibsey

Edmondson Christopher, confectioner, 23 Westgate

Edmondson Jacob, mattress and cushion maker, Bowergate, Chapel lane

Edmondson Robert,[c] Holroyde Hill, North Bierley

Edmondson Thomas, noils and waste dealer, Albion yard, Ivegate; house Allerton

Edwards John,[c] painter (Haley and Edwards); ho. Preston place, Great Horton

Edwards Mrs. dress maker, 10 Wellington street, Northwing

Egan William,[b c] gun maker, and dealer in powder and shot, &c. 21 Hustlergate

Eggleston Rev. J. B. A. incumbent of Denholme

Elgey George Allison,[b] woolstapler, Swaine street; house Bridge street

Elgey Joseph Bowron,[b] woolstapler, Swaine street; house Bridge street

Ellinthorpe Robert,[b c] butcher, 462 Wakefield road

Elliott William, provision dealer, 23 Nelson street

Ellis Ellen, dress maker, Arcadia st. Lumb lane, Manningham

Ellis George,[b] Jer lane, Horton

Ellis Henry, brazier and tinplate worker, 16 Triangle street, Manchester road

Ellis & Holmes, stuff mannfacturers, Charles street; works Dub Mill, Bingley

Ellis James,[b] overseer, registrar of births and deaths, and government tax collector for Bowling township; office and house Hall lane, Bowling

Ellis James,[bc] miller, (Ellis and Priestman); house *Ireland*

Ellis John,[b] machine broker, Roebuck yard, Bridge st.; house Manchester road

Ellis John,[b] worsted spinner and manufacturer, Charles street; works and house Dudley Hill

Ellis John,[b] painter, paper hanger and provision dealer, Dudley Hill

Ellis John,[b] beer retailer and provision dealer, 35 George street, Manchester road

Ellis Joseph,[b c] manufacturer (Ellis and Holmes); house Bingley

Ellis Joseph,[b] beer retailer and provision dealer, Leeds road

Ellis Luke,[c] North Bierley

Ellis Mannasseh, provision dealer, Dudley Hill

Ellis & Priestman, corn millers, 1 Manchester road, and Queen's Mill, Millbank

Ellis Rebecca, dress maker, Wakefield road

Ellis Sharp, patten maker, Black Bull yard, Westgate

Ellis Thomas,[b] provision dealer and druggist, Thornton lane, Little Horton

Ellis Watson, boot and shoe maker, 12 Manchester road; house Fitzgerald street

Ellison John, flour dealer, 65 High st

Ellison Samuel,[b] *Coach and Horses Inn*, Bradford Moor

Ellison Thomas,[b] corn and flour dealer, Brick lane, Well street, and Chapel lane; house Union street

Ellissen Phillip David, stuff merchant, Booth street; manager Mr. Weil

Elsley Charles Heneage, judge of the County Court; house York

Elsworth Ann, straw bonnet maker, 555 Wakefield road

Elsworth Jeseph,[b] provision dealer, 555 Wakefield road

Eltoft Ann, boot, shoe and stay dealer, (and register for servants), 24 Darley street

Eltoft George,[b] Elizabeth street, Little Horton

Ely Benjamin, gardener, Northgate

Emanuel & Son, stuff and yarn merchants, Exchange street, Kirkgate; manager Mr. J.F. Rieckmann

Emmett Emanuel,[b] woolstapler, Bermondsey; house Birkenshaw

Emmett James,[c] Low Moor Side, North Bierley

Emmott James, hackney coach proprietor, Nelson square

Emmott Samuel,[b] cabinet maker, 61 John street, Westgate

Emsley George, stuff manufacturer, 30 New Piece Hall; works and house Queen's Head, Clayton

Emsley James & John, grocers and provision dealers, 38 Bolton road and 204 Manchester road

Emsley Jonathan, [b c] Hollingwood lane, Great Horton

Emsley Robert,[b] Mill lane, Bowling

Engelmann Anton,[b] manager (Hermann Samson & Leppoc); house Hanover square

England John,[b] Park Field, Manningham

England Joseph, coach builder, 54 Threadneedle street; house Tumblinghill street, Thornton road

England Samuel, wheelwright and jobbing smith, Thornton road

England William, tailor and draper, 14 School street, Cheapside

English Mrs. milliner and dress maker, 44 Wellington street, Stott Hill

Equity and Law Life Assurance Society; agent Mr. Charles Lees, solicitor, Albion court

Errel William, manager (H. D'Hauregard); house Sawrey place, Little Horton lane

Eshelby George, butcher, Dudley Hill

Evans James, blacksmith, Back Green lane, Manningham

Everdell Maria, milliner and straw bonnet maker, 12 John street, Westgate

Exchange Buildings, corner of Exchange street, Kirkgate, comprising News-room, Library, and Lecture rooms; Mr. Samuel Lord superintendent

Exchange Subscription Library, Exchange street; opens at 10 and closes at four winter, summer five o'clock; Miss Mason librarian

Excise Officers—(Inland Revenue); supervisor John Roberts, 24 Victoria street, North parade, *officers*—John Bostock, Manchester road; John Dixon, Dudley Hill; Thomas Wright, Undercliffe; William Davy, 34 Westgrove st.; John Penket, 12 Canal terrace, Bolton road, and Richard Wynn, Shipley

Exley John, English and foreign wool dealer, Cheapside; house Victoria street, North Parade

Exley Joseph, boot and shoe maker, Sticker lane, Bowling

EXPERIENCE LIFE ASSURANCE COMPANY; agents Messrs. Dixon and Byrne, ironmongers, Market street

FACER John, beer retailer, 177 Wakefield road

Facer Thomas,[b] Bridge street

Fairbank Alice, currier and leather cutter, Westgate

Fairbank John Tertius, architect, 36 Darley street; house Hanover sq.

Fairbank Joseph,[b] jeweller (Wilson and Fairbank); house Spring gardens, Manningham lane

Fairbank Thomas, currier and leather cutter, 75 Northgate

Fairbank William, boot and shoe maker, 132 Queen street, Manchester road

Fairbank William, Crossley Hall Colliery, Allerton

Falkingham Jeffrey, coal dealer, Brick row, Thornton road

Falkingham Jeffrey,[b] provision dealer, 59, Westgate

Falls Thomas, draper, Preston place, Great Horton

Fanshaw Robert,[b] chemist and druggist, High street, Great Horton

Farish James,[b c] spinner (Richard Tetley & Co.); house Crowther street, Manchester road

FARMERS' AND GRAZIERS' ASSURANCE ASSOCIATION; agents Mr. G. T. Lister, Drewton st., and Mr. George Thornton, solicitor, 10 Duke street, Darley street

Farnell Henry James,[b] Westgrove st.

Farnell James, corn dealer, 150 Westgate

Farnell John, draper, 138 Westgate

Farrand Henry, fruit, egg, and herring dealer, 70 Manchester road; house Portland street

Farrand Jonathan,[c] cabinet maker and undertaker, 71 Frederick street, Wakefield road

Farrar David, cotton doubler, Thompson's Mill, Thornton road; house Tumblinghill street, Thornton road

Farrar & Gillham, hatters, hosiers, and glovers, tailors, drapers, and outfitters, 20 Kirkgate

Farrar Henry,[b c] tailor, &c. (Farrar and Gillham); house Crossbanks, Shipley

Farrar James, Halifax and Huddersfield daily carrier, Back Tyrrel st.

Farrar Jonathan, butcher, Dudley Hill

Farrar Joseph,[b c] hatter, and agent for the Halifax, Bradford, and Keighley Insurance Company, 1 Market street; house Drewton st.

Farrar Joseph, rope and twine manufacturer, Chapel lane, Tyrrel street

Farrar Joseph,[b] Bolton road

Farrar Richard, pork butcher, 109 Bridge street

Farrar Robert,[c] Silsbridge lane

Farrar Samuel,[c] Sunny Bank, Manningham

Farrar Sarah Ann, straw bonnet maker, Frederick street, Wakefield road

Farrar Squire,[b] provision dealer and district post, High street

Farrar Squire, clerk, Hustler Park, Leeds road

Farrar William,[b] M. D. surgeon, 10 Darley street, and Richmond House, Great Horton road

Farrar William,[c] Southgate

Fawbert James & John, boot and shoe makers, 40 Barkerend

Fawcett James, stuff manufacturer, Charles street; works and house Greenfield, near Halifax

Fawcett John,[b] boot and shoe maker, North Parade and Tyrrel street; house Northgate

Fawcett John,[c] Silsbridge lane

Fawcett Rev. Joshua,[c] M.A. (incumbent of Low Moor); ho. Parsonage, Low Moor

Fawcett Mary Ann, milliner and dress maker, 39 Croft street, Manchester road

Fawcett Ralph,[c] bookbinder (Drake and Fawcett); house 11 Silsbridge lane

Fawcett Richard,[bc] woolstapler, Cheapside; house Manningham ln.

Fawcett William, tax collector and deputy registrar for Bowling district, Hall lane, Bowling

Fawthorp Joseph, worsted spinner and manufacturer, New Pieceball; works Brow Mill, Clayton; house Queen's Head, Clayton

Fawthorp Thomas, tailor, 10 Croft street, Bridge street

Fearnley Edmund,[b] Westgrove street

Fearnley George, provision dealer, Otley road

Fearnley George, beer retailer, Otley road

Fearnley James, beer retailer, Broom street, Wakefield road

Fearnley John, beer retailer, Thornton road

Fearnley John, wheelwright, Thornton road

Fearnley Richard,[c] Truncliffe, Bierley

Fearnley Robert,[bc] beer retailer, Stott Hill

Fearnley Mrs. Sarah, Manor row

Fearnley Thomas,[c] North Bierley

Fearnley Thomas, engineer (Thomas Thwaites & Co.); house Westbrook street, Great Horton road

Fearnley Thomas,[c] Captain street, Stott Hill

Fearnley Samuel,[b] Well street

Fearnley Mr. William, Trafalgar st.

Fearnside Mr. John,[bc] top of Westgate

Feather Edward,[b] Lister hills, Horton

Feather Joseph, boot and shoe maker, Manchester road

Featherstonehaugh Martha & Jane, milliners and dress makers, Upper North Parade

Fell Christopher, chemist and druggist, 36 White Abbey

Fell James, whitesmith and bellhanger, 17 Nelson street; house Bower street, Manchester road

Fell Mary, beer retailer and provision dealer, Providence street, White Abbey

Fenton John, butcher, 160 Manchester road; house Wibsey

Fenton James, boot and shoe maker, Uppercroft row, Bowling

Fenton Sarah, locksmith, 15 Market street

Ferrand William,[bc] Victoria street, North parade

Fether William,[c] Back Regent street, Manningham

Field John,[c] Bowling lane

Field John, fishmonger, Bridge street; house Tyrrel street

Field Joseph, police detective officer, Swaine street

Field Samuel,[c] worsted spinner, and manufacturer, Brook street; works Millbank; house Hanover square

Fielden John,[b] William street, Horton

Fielden Mary Ann, milliner and dress maker, William street, Little Horton lane
Field William, surgeon, Dudley Hill, and Tong
FieldhouseBenjamin, provision dealer, Southgate, Great Horton
Fieldhouse Moses,[c] Pickles hill lane, Great Horton
Fieldhouse Reuben,[b] Bradford Moor
Fieldhouse Thomas, beer retailer, Bradford Moor
Fieldhouse William,[c] provision dealer, Bradford Moor
Fieldhouse William,[b] Rooley, Bowling
Fieldsend William, provision dealer, 17 Brick row, Thornton road
FIRE-ENGINE STATIONS:—Borough, adjoining the police office, Swaine street,—Richard Collinson superintendent; Leeds and Yorkshire Insurance Co.'s,—Exchange street; Mr. Edwin Olivant, superintendent, 36 Heber st. Little Horton lane
Firth Betty, provision dealer, Leach's square, Laister Dyke
Firth Charles,[b] beer retailer, Uppercroft row, Bowling
Firth Constantine, boot and shoe maker, 25 Oak street, Leeds road
Firth Daniel,[bc] woolstapler, Bermondsey; house Sterling street, Manchester road
Firth Edward,[b] Eastsquire lane, Manningham
Firth Elizabeth, provision dealer, 30 Mill lane, Manchester road
Firth George Enoch,[b] Eastsquire lane, Manningham
Firth Henry,[b] junr. beer retailer, 44 Westgate
Firth Isaac, spinner (Isaac Firth & Son); house Lilly lane, Halifax
Firth Isaac & Son, worsted spinners and manufacturers, 22 Bank street; works Lilly lane, Halifax
Firth James,[b] yarn merchant, 6 Commercial street; house Bowling
Firth James, auctioneer, 15 Broadstones, Well street
Firth John,[bc] *White Hart Inn*, Dudley Hill
Firth Joseph,[c] Raw Nook, Bierley
Firth Joseph, boot and shoe maker, 45 Bridge street
Firth Nathan, soda-water and ginger beer manufacturer, Manningham
Firth Samuel,[b] Eastsquire lane, Manningham
Firth Samuel,[b] grocer and tea dealer, 80 Westgate
Firth Samuel, spinner (Samuel and John Firth); house Lilly lane, Halifax
Firth Samuel and John, worsted spinners and manufacturers, 14 New Piecehall; works and house Lilly lane, Halifax
Firth Thomas,[c] Bierley lane, Bierley
Firth Thomas, plasterer, Manningham
Firth Thomas, tailor, Dudley Hill
Firth Thomas,[b] spinner (Thomas Firth & Co.); house Earl street, Manchester road
Firth Thomas & Co. worsted spinners, Caledonia Mills, Manchester road
Firth William, carrier, Thornton road
Firth William,[c] Great Horton
Firth William,[b] shuttle maker, New row, Manningham
Firth William, provision dealer, 169 Bolton road
Firth William, merchant (Thornton, Firth, Ramsden & Co.); house Kirkstall, near Leeds

Firth William,[b] North Parade

Fisher George,[b] dealer in London and Dublin porter, Scotch and Burton ales, &c. Schuster's buildings, Brook street; house 55 East street, Leeds road

Fison Cornell, manufacturer (Harris and Fison); house Primrose Hill, Great Horton

Fison Thomas Sparham,[b] merchant, (Forster & Fison); house Rawden

Fison William,[b] worsted spinner and manufacturer, Charles street; works Foundry Mill, Manchester road; house Manor row

Flather Emanuel, coal dealer, Smith street, Manchester road

Flatman John & Samuel, woolstaplers, Wood's Court, Cheapside, and Westgate, Wakefield

Fletcher Abraham, boot and shoe maker, Albion court, Kirkgate

Fletcher Rev. Adam (Wesleyan), Hunt yard, Great Horton road

Fletcher James,[c] Little Horton lane

Fletcher James,[c] North Bierley

Fletcher James, boot and shoe maker, 79 Portland street, Manchester rd.

Fletcher John,[c] Manchester road

Fletcher John,[c] Great Horton lane

Fletcher Mark,[c] Brownroyd Hill, Bierley

Fletcher Richard,[b c] Westgrove st.

Fletcher Richard,[c] John street, Stott Hill

Flinn Edward, hardware dealer and umbrella maker, Bazaar, and 14 Providence street, Westgate

Floral and Horticultural Society;—Exhibition rooms, Exchange Buildings; Mr. J. Simpson, secretary

Forbes Henry,[b c] merchant (Milligan, Forbes & Co.); res. Summerhill House, near Rawden

Ford Thomas,[c] Hill top, Low Moor

Forrest Francis Hanson, beer retailer, Westgate

Forrest James,[b] *Royal Oak Inn*, Kirkgate

Forrest James, butcher, 25 Nelson street; house 12 Hope street, Manchester road

Forrest Samuel,[c] boot and shoe maker, 27 Otley road

Forster & Fison, wool merchants, and commission wool and top agents, Hustler's Buildings, Leeds road

Forster William Edward,[b] merchant (Forster & Fison); house Lane End, Rawden

Foster Abraham,[c] beer retailer, 100 Westgate

Foster Henry,[c] spinner (William & Henry Foster); house Denholme

Foster John, stuff manufacturer, New Piecehall; works and house Lower Heywood, Midgley

Foster John,[b] manufacturer (John Foster and Sons); res. Prospect House, Clayton

Foster John,[b c] Sterling street, Manchester road

Foster John & Sons, worsted spinners and manufacturers, Piecehall yard; works Black Dyke Mills, Clayton

Foster Jonas, jacquard machine maker, card cutter, &c. 50 Victoria street, Manchester road

Foster Jonathan, hair dresser, 3 Nelson street, Chapel lane

Foster Jonathan, coal dealer, Manchester road

Foster Joseph,[b c] woolstapler (Shepherd & Foster); house St. James' square, Manchester road

Foster Joseph,[b c] schoolmaster, John street, Westgate

Foster Joseph,[c] provision dealer, 28 Longlands street, Westgate

Foster Joseph,[b] *Bee Hive Inn*, Westgate

Foster Marmaduke,[bc] solicitor, and agent to the City of London Assurance Company, 70 Market street; house Brunswick place

Foster William,[b] provision dealer, 26 Silsbridge lane

Foster William,[b c] New Market and Canal side

Foster William,[c] spinner (William & Henry Foster); house Denholme

Foster William & Henry, worsted spinners and manufacturers, New Piecehall; works Denholme Mill

Foulds John,[b] clog and patten maker, 186 Manchester road

Foulds Joseph, boot and shoe maker, 20 Providence street, White Abbey

Foulds Thomas, boot and shoe maker, 69 Manchester road

Foulds William, clog and patten maker, 74 Silsbridge lane; house Longcroft place

FOUNTAIN BREWERY, Manchester road; Joseph Pullan proprietor

Fowler Edward,[b] solicitor, and agent for the Edinburgh Life Assurance Company, 32 Darley street; house Ann place, Little Horton lane

Fowler Elizabeth, dress maker, Belgrave place, Manningham

Fox Amos, boot and shoe maker, Great Horton lane

Fox Charles, boot and shoe maker, Lidget Green, Great Horton

Fox Edmund Keighley,[b c] woolstapler (Edmund & William Fox); house Horton road

Fox Edmund & William, woolstaplers, Roe Buck yard, Ivegate

Fox Gregory,[c] Hollinwood lane, Great Horton

Fox Henry,[c] boot and shoe maker, High street, Great Horton

Fox Jabez, stuff manufacturer, Industry Mill, Dudley hill; house Tong

Fox Kelitah, joiner, Greenhill place, Manningham

Fox Peter,[b] provision dealer, High street, Great Horton

Fox Richard Gott,[b c] *White Swan Inn*, 31 Market street

Fox Sarah, beer retailer, Southgate, Great Horton

Fox Theodosia, milliner and straw bonnet maker, 153 Manchester road

Fox Thomas,[b] provision dealer, 56 Westgrove street

Fox William,[b c] butcher, High street, Great Horton

Fox William, provision dealer, 18 Providence stret, White Abbey

Franee Samuel,[b] grocer and tea dealer 24 Broadstones, 141 Bridge street, and 7 Tyrrel street; house Wellington place, Little Horton lane

Francis Joseph, beer retailer, 80 Manchester road

Francis Thomas, brass founder, Lumby street, Manchester road

Frank John Philip,[b] merchant (John Philip Frank & Co.); house North Parade, Manningham lane

Frank John Philip & Co. merchants and foreign agents for the Bowling Iron Works, corner of Exchange street, Duke street

Frankland John Bailey,[c] Victoria st. North parade

Frankland William Henry,[c] Victoria street, North parade

Franks Isaac, optician, mathematical instrument maker, and lecturer on the eye, 71 Market street, and Leeds

Franks Robert, boot and shoe maker, and provision dealer, 300 Leeds road

Fraser Rev. Daniel, M. A. (Independent), and classical tutor, Airedale College, Undercliffe

Frear Bryan, coal dealer, Wakefield road

FREEHOLDERS' LAND AND BUILDING ASSOCIATION, 4 Bridge street; Mr. William German secretary

Freeman Ambrose, watch maker, 98 Manchester road

Freeman Joseph, tanner, Thornton road

Freeman William,[b c] comb manufacturer, (Simonett & Freeman); house Chapel street, Leeds road

FREE MASONS' HALL, Duke street, Darley street

French Adam,[b] John street, North gate

French John,[b] machinist (Wright, Wood & French); house Tetley row

French Thomas Russell,[b] Skinner lane

FRIENDS' MEETING HOUSE—[*See* "Churches and Chapels."]

FRIENDS' PROVIDENT INSTITUTION; agent Mr. Benjamin Ecroyd, Hustler's buildings, Market street

FRIENDS' RAGGED SCHOOL, Millbank

Frost Rev. Joseph Loxdale,[c] A. M. incumbent of Bowling; house Wakefield road

FRUIT, EGG, BUTTER AND VEGETABLE MARKET, Rawson place, and Fair Ground, Darley street

Fryer John,[b] woolstapler, Commercial street; house Manchester road

Fryer John,[b] beer retailer, 100 Manchester road

Fugill Joseph,[b] stuff merchant, Chapel lane, Tyrrel street; house Spring gardens

Fuller Thomas, woolcomber (Wm. Collier & Co.); house Manchester

Furby Martha, schoolmistress, Broom street, Wakefield road

Furnell George, provision dealer, 35 Lumb lane, Manningham

Furness Joseph, provision dealer, Back lane, Bowling

Furst Bernard & Co. stuff merchants, Hall Ings; manager Mr. Louis Goldstein

GALE Septimus, boot-tree and last maker, 11 Toad lane; house Fitzgerald street

Gallen John Jardine, M. D. surgeon and dentist, Drewton street;—Thursdays only, from ten till six

Gallimore James,[b] Heber street, Little Horton lane

Galloway James,[c] boot and shoe maker, Halifax road, Bowling

Galloway John, provision dealer, 44 Sterling street, Manchester road

Galloway John, boot and shoe maker, Halifax road, Bowling

Galloway John, provision dealer, Bowling lane

Galloway Squire,[c] Fiddler Hill Farm, North Bierley

Galloway William,[b c] *Fleece Inn*, 208 Manchester road

Gamble George,[c] Leeds road, Bradford Moor

Gamble Mrs. John, Brunswick place

Gamble Mrs. school, Stott Hill

Gamble Richard, provision dealer, Swaine green, Bowling

Gamble Robert, manor bailiff, Stott Hill

Gamble Sarah, grocer and tea dealer, 90 Westgate

Gamble Samuel,[c] Newland House, Calverley Moor

Gant James Greaves Tetley,[b], solicitor, and agent for the Life Association of Scotland, 3 Market st.; res. Rose Cottage, Bolton

Gant William, draper (Brook, Gant & Co.); house Westgate

GARDENERS' (ANCIENT FREE); Relieving lodge (England's Freedom), Shoulder of Mutton Inn, Kirkgate

Garner Edward,[c] Chapel green, Great Horton

Garner Joseph,[c] merchant (Joseph Garner & Co.) house Manchester road

Garner Joseph & Co. stuff merchants, 30 Pearson's Buildings, Bridge street

Garnett James and William, worsted spinners, Barkerend, High street, and Union street mills

Garnett James,[b c] worsted spinner, (James & William Garnett); res. Mill House

Garnett Mrs. Richard, Butler House, Barkerend

Garnett William,[b c] worsted spinner (James and William Garnett); house Hill Side

Garside Benjamin,[c] Carr lane, North Bierley

Garside Joseph,[c] Low Moor side

Garside William,[c] Low Moor side

Garthwaite John, blacksmith, High street, Great Horton

GAS WORKS (new station) Thornton road; old station, Mill street, Canal road; Mr. David Swallow, superintendent; Mr. Joseph Bean, engineer

Gaukroger Samuel, provision dealer, 21 Silsbridge lane

Gaunt Fanny, milliner and dress maker, Belgrave place, Manningham

Gawthorp Joseph,[c] Manningham

Gelderd Robert,[b] provision dealer, 88 Thornton road

Geoghegan James, beer retailer, Hope street, Manchester road

George James,[b] Manningham

George William,[b c] solicitor (Rawson and George); and agent for the Protestant Dissenters' and General Assurance Company, Swaine st.; house Grosvenor place

German William,[b c] basket and skep maker, 4 Bridge street; house Elizabeth street, Little Horton

Gibbon Thomas,[c] Manchester road

Gibson George, grocer and tea dealer, 180 Manchester road

Gibson Jabez.[b] beer retailer, Dudley Hill

Gibson John,[c] East street, Leeds road

Gibson Jonathan, contractor, 8 Chapel street, Leeds road

Gibson Joseph, butcher, Well street, Leeds road

Gibson Mrs. milliner and dress maker, 8 Chapel street, Leeds road

Gilderdale John, dealer in tea, coffee tobacco, cigars and fancy snuffs, 28 Bowling Green, Bridge street, and Wakefield

Gill Benjamin Farrar,[b c] apothecary, High street

Gill Hugh, bailiff for Pontefract Court, Goodman's End

Gill John, highway surveyor, Vicar lane

Gill Joshua, boot and shoe maker, 126 Broom street, Wakefield road

Gill Michael,[b] Hillside Villas

Gill Stephen,[c] milk dealer, 118 Longlands street, Westgate

Gill Tamar, dress maker, Spring st, Manningham

Gill William, tailor, 257 Manchester road

Gillett Henry, provision dealer, 85 Victoria street, North Parade

Gillham Thomas, tailor (Farrar and Gillham); house Houghton place, Drewton street

Gilliard John,[b] beer retailer, 112 Manchester road

Gledhill Henry,[b] *Prince of Wales Hotel*, Leeds road

Gledhill James,[b] Stott Hill

Gledhill James,[c] Leeds road

Gledhill Thomas, cab, hackney, and mourning coach and hearse proprietor, Prince of Wales yard, Leeds road

Gledhill William, stone mason and builder, 72 Leeds road

GLOBE FIRE AND LIFE INSURANCE COMPANY; agents Mr. Alfred Sussmann, Court street, Leeds road, and Mr. William Clough, Swaine street, Hall Ings

Glover Henry, paper dealer and stationer, 5 Bermondsey; house St. James' square, Manchester road

Glover John,[b c] spinner (Richard Tetley & Co.); house Broomfield terrace, Wakefield road

E

Glover Mr. Mark Spink,[b c] Sawrey place, Little Horton lane

Glover Mr. William,[b c] North Parade

Glyde Rev. Jonathan,[b c] (Independent), Melbourne place, Little Horton lane

Glyde William Evans,[b c] Melbourne place, Little Horton lane

Goddard Richard William, manufacturer (Whitehead, Goddard & Co.); house Spring gardens

Godwin Rev. Benjamin,[b] D. D. (Baptist), Westmount, Horton road

Godwin John Vennimore,[b c] merchant (Milligan, Forbes & Co.); house Ashfield place, Horton road

Goggs Henry, provision dealer, 29 Wellington street, Stott Hill

Goldsbrough William,[c] Middleton Field, Silsbridge lane

Goldstein Louis, manager (Furst Bernard & Co.); house Little Horton lane

Goldstein Martin, stuff merchant, Swaine street, Hall Ings

GOMERSALL COLLIERY; wharf and office School street, Railroad street

Gomersall Joshua,[b c] card maker, Dudley Hill; house Tong

Gomersall Jonathan,[b c] card maker, Dudley Hill; house Tong

Goodair Joseph, provision dealer, 183 Whetley Fold, Manningham

GOODCHILD'S COMMERCIAL AND TEMPERANCE HOTEL, Market place, Kirkgate

Goodchild James,[b c] boot and shoe dealer, Market place, Kirkgate

Goodchild Robert, house, sign and ornamental painter and gilder, 223 Manchester road

Goodhall John,[c] Clayton place, Pit lane

Goodwin James, china and earthenware dealer, 133 Manchester road

Goodyear Richard, beer retailer, Canal road

Gordon John,[b] surgeon, 27 Bridge street

Gornall Thomas, tailor, Church hill, Wakefield road

Gosling Lee, hair dresser, 252 Manchester road

Gosling Matilda, hair dresser, 266 Manchester road

Gott John,[b c] soft soap manufacturer, Wharf street; house Drewton st.

Gott William,[b] Stone street, Manor row

Gough John, boot and shoe maker, 1 North street, Northwing

Gould Thomas, hair dresser, 73 Bridge street

Gouldsbrough Hannah, dress maker, 10 James' street, Northgate

Gouldsbrough William,[b c] beer retailer, 93 Bridge street

Gourlay Andrew,[bc] tea dealer and draper, Southfield place, Manningham

Gourlay James,[b c] draper and tea dealer, Victoria street, North parade

Gourlay Thomas, [b c] draper and tea dealer, Fountain street, Manningham lane

Graham George,[b c] draper and tea dealer, 16 Victoria street, North Parade

Graham Joseph, beer retailer, Back lane, Bowling

Graham Mark, woollen flock dealer, Albion yard, Ivegate

Graham Thomas, brazier and tinplate worker, 29 Hope street, Manchester road

Grainge James,[b] auctioneer and valuer, 7 Union Passage, Kirk-gate; house Apple Hall, Barkerend

Grainge John, beer retailer, 20 Brick lane, Black Abbey

GRAMMAR SCHOOL (FREE), Manor row; Rev. John Richards, M. A. head master; Mr. George Voigt, B. A. and Mr. Hubert Lewis, B. A. assistant masters

Grandage William,[b] manager, (Bowling Old Dyehouse), Hall lane, Bowling

Grassington Job, brazier and tinplate worker, 205 Bolton road

Gray John,[b] blacksmith, 68 Manchester road

Gray Thomas,[c] blacksmith, Thornton

Greasley Isaac Monson,[b] traveller, Charles street, Leeds road

GREAT BRITAIN MUTUAL LIFE INSURANCE COMPANY; agents Mr. Charles Woodcock, 4 Bridge street, and Mr. H. Neumann, Charles st.

Greaves John, wine and spirit merchant, Tyrrel street; house Westbrook place, Horton road

Greaves Joseph,[b c] Little Horton lane

Greaves William,[b c] *Horse and Trumpet Inn*, 208 Manchester road

Greaves William Hansley, merchant (William Dewhirst & Co.); house Manningham lane

Green Benjamin, wheelwright, 49 Leeds road

Green Mrs. Hannah, Duckworth lane, Manningham

Green James,[c] Lower Woodland, North Bierley

Green James,[b c] joiner and cabinet maker, Colliergate, Swaine street; house Manor row

Green John,[b c] Bolton road

Green John, wheelwright, top of Westgate
Green John, joiner and builder, Mill lane, Little Horton
Green Joseph,[c] Bierley lane, Bierley
Green Robert Fletcher, manufacturer (Robert Fletcher Green & Son); house Headingley, near Leeds
Green Robert Fletcher & Son, worsted spinners and manufacturers, Hartley's Buildings, Brook street; works Burley, near Leeds
Green Samuel,[c] Hillside, Undercliffe
Green Thomas,[b] provision dealer, Undercliffe
Greenhough Benjamin,[b] provision dealer, 47 Victoria street, North Parade
Greenhough John,[b] painter, paper hanger, gilder, &c. Garden place, Westgate
Greenhough John,[b c] machine broker, Roebuck yard, Ivegate; house Westgate
Greenhough Thomas,[c] Tyrrel court
Greenhough Thomas Lister, confectioner, 157, Wakefield road
Greenhough William,[c] Bowling
Greenlay Thomas, boot and shoe maker, 22 Darley street
Greenwood Alfred, butcher, 79 High street
Greenwood Benjamin, spinner, (Joseph & Benjamin Greenwood); house Thornton road
Greenwood Benjamin,[b c] surgeon, 51 Portland place, Manchester road
Greenwood David, clog and patten maker, 24 Leeds road
Greenwood Edmund,[b c] Barkerend
Greenwood Frederick Smith,[b c] ale and porter dealer, Duke street, Cheapside
Greenwood George Oates,[b c] stuff merchant, Hall Ings; house Ann's place, Little Horton lane
Greenwood John,[b c] Bolton place, Bridge street
Greenwood John,[b] brush manufacturer, and dealer in matting, &c. 58 Market street
Greenwood John,[b] Brownroyd, Horton
Greenwood John Wilson,[b] provision dealer, High street, Great Horton
Greenwood Joseph,[b c] provision dealer, Great Horton lane
Greenwood Joseph,[b] Four Lane Ends, Manningham
Greenwood Joseph,[c] Woodhall Hills, Calverley
Greenwood Joseph & Benjamin, worsted spinners and manufacturers, 38 Liverpool street, Bank street; works Thornton road
Greenwood Joseph,[c] spinner (Joseph and Benjamin Greenwood); house Thornton road
Greenwood Luke, stone mason, Great Horton
Greenwood Sharp, draper, hosier, &c. 48, White Abbey
Greenwood Thomas, agent for stuff goods, yarn, &c. Charles street
Greenwood Thomas,[c] clog and patten maker, 105 Bridge street
Greenwood Mr. William,[b c] Croft st.
Greenwood William,[c] White Abbey
Greenwood William,[b] junior, stuff manufacturer, Brook street; works and house Oxenhope, near Keighley
Greenwood William Watson,[b c] corn miller, Bankfoot Mill, Halifax road, Bowling
Greetham Joseph, butcher, 35 Bank street; house Spring street, Manningham

Gregory Thomas, manufacturer (T. Gregory & Brothers); house Shelf

Gregory Thomas & Brothers, worsted spinners and manufacturers, 23 Old Market; works Shelf, near Halifax

Grimshaw John, beer retailer, 32 Providence street, White Abbey

Grunwell John,[c] 1 Birks street, Leeds road

GUARANTEE SOCIETY; agent for the West Riding Mr. John Darlington, solicitor, 12 Union passage, Kirkgate

GUARDIAN FIRE AND LIFE INSURANCE COMPANY; agent Mr. Benjamin Ecroyd, Thornton's Buildings, Market street

Gummersall Joseph,[b] *Waterloo Hotel*, Lister Hills, Little Horton

Gumpel Gustavus & Co. stuff merchants, 5 Chapel lane; manager, Mr. Louis Becher

Guthrie William,[b] plumber, glazier and gas fitter, 4 Chapel lane; house 8 King street, Manchester road

HAGGAS William, worsted spinner and manufacturer, Hustler's Buildings, Market street; works and house Oakworth hall, nr. Keighley

HAIGH COAL COMPANY (Lofthouse and Rothwell), office Railroad st.; J. & J. Charlesworth agents

Haigh Edward,[b] manufacturer (Lythall and Haigh); house Hanover square

Haigh George,[c] manufacturer, (Geo. Haigh & Co.); house Stone street, Manor row

Haigh George & Co. stuff manufacrers, Brook street; works Holme Mill, Canal road

Haigh Mr. Henry,[b] Manor row

Haigh James, beer retailer, 201 Bridge street

Haigh John,[b c] Smiddles, Bowling

Haigh John & Co. stuff merchants, Hall Ings

Haigh Matthew,[b] Westgrove street

Haigh Richard,[b] boot and shoe maker, Westgrove street

Haigh Samuel,[b c] butcher, 256 Manchester road

Haigh Thomas,[b] accountant and share broker, Savings' Bank, Kirkgate

Haigh Thomas, dyer and stover, Charles street; works and house Newlay, near Leeds

Haigh Thomas,[c] Edmund street, Little Horton lane

Haigh William,[b] boot and shoe maker, Dudley Hill, Bowling

Haigh William, boot and shoe maker, Mitchell's Buildings, Manchester road

Haigh William Chapman,[b] general agent, woolstapler, and silk and cotton warp dealer, Swaine street and Exchange street; house Horton Villa

Hailstone Edward,[b c] solicitor (Saml. and Edward Hailstone); house Horton Hall

Hailstone Samuel,[b c] solicitor (Saml. and Edward Hailstone); house Horton Hall

Hailstone Samuel & Edward, solicitors, offices 37 Manchester road

Haining Jane and Hannah, day and boarding school, Hanover square

Haining Mr. Thomas,[b] Hanover square

Hainsworth John,[b] Beck side, Horton

Hainsworth John, new and old bookseller, and circulating library, 32

Manchester road; house Bower street

Hainsworth John & Son, woolstaplers, 47 Union street

Hainsworth Reuben, woolstapler, (John Hainsworth & Son); house Farsley

Hainsworth William,[b] sizing dealer, Hustler's Buildings, Market street; house Pudsey

Halcro Augustus John, auctioneer, appraiser and general agent, 22 Piecehall yard, Kirkgate; house Queen street, Bowling

Haley Abraham, beer retailer, Diamond street, Vicar lane

Haley Charles,[c] 12 Ebenezer street

Haley Christopher,[b] iron founder, Foundry street, Vicar lane; house Ebenezer street

Haley Dan, provision dealer, High street, Great Horton

Haley Dan, butcher, High street, Great Horton

Haley Edward, painter (Haley and Edwards); house Hunsworth

Haley & Edwards, house, sign and furniture painters, gilders, &c. Roebuck Yard, Market street

Haley Ellen, milliner and dress maker, 25 Thornton road

Haley Enoch,[b] iron founder, Thornton road; house Westgrove street

Haley Jonas,[b c] blacksmith, Dudley Hill, Bowling

Haley Joseph,[b] iron founder, Mill st. Manchester road; house Lower Thomas street, Manchester road

Haley Joshua,[bc] woolstapler, 6 Broadstones; house Sawrey place, Little Horton lane

Haley Richard,[b c] provision dealer and druggist, High street, Great Horton

Haley Thomas,[c] Bierley lane, Bierley

Haley Samuel, school master, 13 Duke street, Manchester road

Haley William,[c] Great Horton

Haley William, provision dealer, 1 Fawcett court, Nelson street

Halifax, Bradford and Keighley Insurance Company; agent Mr. Joseph Farrar, 1 Market street

Hall & Bankart, wool agents, Bermondsey

Hall Edmund,[b] wool agent (Hall & Bankart); house North Parade

Hall Francis Stuart,[b] woollen draper, 33 Kirkgate

Hall John,[b] Oaks lane, Bowling

Hall John,[b] working cutler and surgical instrument maker, 40 Market street

Hall John,[b], hosiery manufacturer, 61 Northgate

Hall Joseph, green grocer, Northgate

Hall Joshua,[b] woolstapler, Cheapside; house Hanover square

Hall Robert,[b] George street, Leeds road

Hall Thomas, grocer and tea dealer, 42 Leeds road

Hellewell James,[b] Little Horton Green

Hellewell Mary Ann, milliner and dress maker, Broomfield terrace, Wakefield road

Halliday George,[c] attorney's clerk, 4 Green lane, Manningham

Halliday John, commission agent for warp and yarns, stuff goods, paper, &c. Hartley's Buidings, Leeds road

Halliday Joseph, tailor, 46 George street, Manchester road

Halliday Richard,[c] provision dealer, Ebenezer street

Halliday William, [b] Manchester road

HALLIWELL ASH PUBLIC GARDENS, Manningham lane; James Walker proprietor

Hallpike William, painter, gilder, &c. Great Horton road

Halstead Benjamin,[c] Hope street, Manchester road

Halstead Isaac,[b] iron founder, Thornton road; house 10 Nelson square

Halstead John, woolstapler, Bermondsey; house Quebec street, Wakefield

Hamilton Mary, provision dealer, Church Steps

Hammond Benjamin,[bc] cattle dealer, Manningham lane

Hammond Mrs. Isabella, Great Horton road

Hammond James,[b] *Market Tavern*, Rawson Place, Darley street

Hammond James, accountant, Wood's Yard, Cheapside

Hammond James, milk dealer, 50 White Abbey

Hammond James,[bc] spinner (Wm. Rouse & Co.); ho. Brunswick Place

Hammond John,[c] *Turf Tavern*, Heaton

Hammond John,[b] butcher and provision dealer, 4 Melbourne street, Leeds road

Hammond Joseph, woolcomb maker, Ship Alley, Well street; house Leeds road

Hammond Joseph,[b] provision dealer, Four Lane Ends, Manningham

Hammond Richard,[c] Wood street, Manningham

Hammond, Turner, & Sons, stuff merchants, &c. Charles street and Manchester

Hancock William, tailor and draper, 23 Thornton's Buildings, Bridge street; house Broad street

Handby Cornelius, tailor, 3 Ivegate; house Stotthill Place

Handforth Edward,[c] Low Moor

Hannay Johnston, [b] John street, Northgate

Hannay Mary Ann, milliner and dress maker, 10 John street, Westgate

Hanrahan John, tailor, 21 Longcroft Place, Westgate

Hansom Richard,[b] law stationer, 12 Parkgate, Peckover Walks

Hanson Daniel, provision dealer, 43 Northgate

Hanson Henry,[b] Rooley, Bowling

Hanson James,[c] boarding and day school, Manor Row

Hanson John, [b] beer retailer, 81 Wapping road

Hanson John, hair dresser and toy dealer, 29 Westgate; house 3 James street

Hanson John,[b] farmer, Cliffe lane, Horton

Hanson Joseph,[b] tailor, 178 Wakefield road

Hanson Joseph, provision dealer, 178 Wakefield road

Hanson Joseph,[c] Hill Top, North Bierley

Hanson Thomas, leather dresser, Westbrook terrace; house Thornton road

Hanson Thomas Anderson, stuff merchant and manufacturer, Leeds road

Hanson William,[c] High street, Stott Hill

Hanson William Sturdy, merchant (Scarf & Hanson); house Summerseat place, Horton road

Hardaker Benjamin, tailor and draper, 20 Hustlergate; house Frederick street, Bridge street

Hardaker Henry,[b c] clog and patten maker, 12 White Abbey

Hardaker James, provision dealer, 18 Longlands street, Westgate

Hardaker James, watch and clock maker, 12 Providence street, Silsbridge lane

Hardaker James,[c] Manorile lane, North Bierley

Hardaker Thomas, boot and shoe maker, 32 White Abbey

Hardcastle George,[b] auctioneer, valuer and surveyor, 53 Westgate

Hardcastle Joseph,[b] woolstapler, (Joseph Hardcastle & Co.); house Undercliffe

Hardcastle Joseph & Co. woolstaplers, 256 Bolton road

Hardcastle Sarah Ann, confectioner, 53 Westgate

Hardwick Thomas, coal dealer, 29 Thompson's Alley, Silsbridge lane

Hardy Abraham,[c] Heaton Hill, North Bierley

Hardy Charles,[b c] Esq. iron master, (Low Moor Iron Works); house Odsal Hall

Hardy Henry, grocer, tea dealer and butter factor, Market street, corner of Bridge street

Hardy John, Esq.[c] iron master (Low Moor Iron Works); house 3 Portland place, London

Hardy John,[b] Quaker lane, Horton

Hardy Jonathan,[c] Ditch Side, North Bierley

Hardy Joseph, coal dealer, High st. Black Abbey

Hardy Squire, long and short wool dealer, Hustler's Buildings, Market street; house Dudley Hill

Hardy Stephen,[c] Hill Top, North Bierley

Harewood Richard,[b] Melbourne place, Little Horton lane

Hargrave Richard,[b] merchant (Jennings & Hargrave); house York place, Leeds

Hargreaves Benjamin, woolstapler, Charles street; house Westgate Hill, Tong

Hargreaves Charles,[b c] smith, (Chas. and Michael Hargreaves); house Longcroft place, Westgate

Hargreaves Charles and Michael, general smiths, gas fitters, palisading and screw-bolt manufacturers, Cropper lane, Westgate

Hargreaves David, boot and shoe maker, 212 Manchester road

Hargreaves James,[b c] Edward street, Wakefield road

Hargreaves John,[b c] commission wool agent, Union street; house Hanover square

Hargreaves John,[b c] Croft street, Leeds road

Hargreaves John,[c] Victoria street, North Parade

Hargreaves Joseph,[bc] worsted spinner and manufacturer, Booth street; works and house Shipley

Hargreaves & Kennedy, engineers, millwrights, and iron founders, Wellington Foundry, Queen's Cut, Manchester road

Hargreaves Michael,[b] smith (Charles & Michael Hargreaves); house Butterfield row, Manningham

Hargreaves Peter, whitesmith, Ship Alley, Well street; house Broad street, Manor row

Hargreaves Richard, house, sign and furniture painter, Tyrrel court, Tyrrel street

Hargreaves Sarah, confectioner, and dealer in ale, porter, and British wines, &c. 30 Kirkgate

Hargreaves Thomas Henry,[b] Houghton Place, Drewton street

Hargreaves Mr. William,[b c] North Parade

Hargreaves William,[b] Victoria street, North Parade

Hargreaves William,[b c] engineer, (Hargreaves & Kennedy); house Arundel street

Harker & Crabtree, watchmakers and jewellers, 162 Manchester road

Harker George,[b c] Paperhall street, Otley road

Harker James,[c] Hill Top, Bierley

Harker John,[c] Parkfield, Manningham

Harker John,[b] tallow chandler, Wakefield road

Harker John,[b] provision dealer, Railroad street, School street

Harker John,[c] Garnett street, Leeds road

Harker Mary, dress maker, Railroad street, School street

Harker Richard, watch maker (Harker & Crabtree); house Albion square

Harker Simon, coach builder and hackney coach proprietor, Vicar lane

Harker Thomas, wholesale confectioner, Wakefield road

Harker William, worsted spinner and manufacturer, Brook street; works VICTORIA MILL, Bowling; house Wakefield road

Harland Brothers, house, sign, and decorative painters, gilders, and paper hangers, 14 Hustlergate

Harland Edward,[b] painter (Harland Brothers); house Westgrove street

Harland Elizabeth, schoolmistress, 43 Chandos street, Wakefield road

Harland John, chemist and druggist, Brick lane

Harland John, painter (Harland Brothers); house Westgrove street

Harland Richard, painter (Harland Brothers); house Westbrook street

Harpin Benjamin,[c] Low Moor

Harpley John, boot and shoe maker, draper, &c. Laister Dyke

Harris Alfred,[b c] Esq. Spring Lodge, Manningham lane

Harris & Fison, stuff manufacturers, Charles street; works VICTORIA MILL, Manchester road

Harris James,[b] provision dealer, Dudley Hill

Harris Richard Peckover,[b] manufacturer (Harris & Fison); house Great Horton road

Harris William Masterman,[b c] Esq. Edmund street, Little Horton lane

Harrison Alfred, beer retailer, Bradford Moor

Harrison Mr. Benjamin,[b c] Hustler terrace

Harrison Eden, linen-draper and milliner, 104 Westgate

Harrison Elizabeth, dress maker, 40 Northgate

Harrison George,[c] Bowling lane

Harrison James,[bc] woolstapler, Bermondsey; house Stone street

Harrison John,[c] Bowling Old lane

Harrison John,[b] saddler, Halifax road, Bowling

Harrison John,[b] provision dealer, 49 Silsbridge lane

Harrison John, stuff manufacturer, 13 Old Pieceball; works and house Shelf, near Halifax

Harrison John,[b] Bridge street

Harrison John, woolstapler, Liverpool street, Bank street; house Spring street

Harrison John Seppings,[b] solicitor, Bridge Street Buildings, Bridge street; house Shipley

Harrison Joseph,[c] Stone street

Harrison Joseph,[b c] grocer, tea dealer, and oil and tallow chandler, 55 Westgate; house Southfield place, Manningham

Harrison Joseph, beer retailer, 68 Bedford street, Wakefield road

Harrison Joseph,[c] Bowling old lane

Harrison & Laycock, woolstaplers, Cheapside

Harrison Miles,[b] provision dealer, 10 Fawcett court, Nelson street

Harrison Richard, merchant (Harrison & Singleton); house Woodlesford, near Leeds

Harrison Robert,[b] beer retailer, 39 Westgate

Harrison Samuel, beer retailer, 41 Lumb lane

Harrison Samuel,[b c] agent (Carver, Chaplin & Co.); house Sterling st. Manchester road

Harrison Samuel,[b c] woolstapler, (Harrison & Laycock); house Regent place, Duke street

Harrison & Singleton, timber merchants; wharf and office Canal road and Leeds

Harrison Stephen, boot and shoe maker, 96 Bedford street, Wakefield road

Harrison Rev. Thomas,[b] (Catholic) Stott Hill, adjoining the chapel

Harrison Thomas,[b] stuff manufacturer, Wakefield road, Bowling

Harrison Thomas,[b] china and earthenware dealer, 118 Manchester road

Harrison Thomas,[b] Edmund street, Little Horton

Harrison William,[b] provision dealer, and beer retailer, Back lane, Bowling

Harrison William,[b] school, Prospect street, Silsbridge lane; house 10 Southfield place, Manningham

Harrop Henry,[b c] manufacturer (Craven & Harrop); house Ball street, Thornton

Harrop William,[b] stuff manufacturer, Charles street; works and house Cullingworth

Harrowby John,[b] reed and heald maker, Little Horton lane

Harrowby Robert,[b] Hanover square

Harrowby Sarah, straw bonnet maker, John street, Westgate

Hartley Ann, register for servants, 19 James street, Northgate

Hartley Benjamin, schoolmaster, Southgate, Great Horton

Hartley Brothers, timber merchants, rolling-board and packing case makers, Bridge street

Hartley Elizabeth, straw and silk bonnet maker, Thornton road

Hartley Henry, stuff manufacturer, Brook street; works and house Tawden, near Colne

Hartley Isaac,[b] Little Horton Green

Hartley James,[b] John street, Stott Hill

Hartley James, auctioneer and furniture broker, Well street

Hartley James, Temperance hotel, Well street

Hartley James, manufacturer, (Jas. Hartley & Son); house Skipton

Hartley James,[c] jun. Trafalgar street, Manor row

Hartley James & Son, stuff manufacturers, Hope and Anchor yard, Bank street; works Skipton

Hartley Jane and Margaret, milliners and straw bonnet makers, 78 John street, Stott Hill

Hartley Jarvis, wool top maker, Hustler's Buildings, Market street; house York street, Wakefield road

Hartley John, provision dealer, Cross lane, Great Horton

Hartley John, merchant (Hartley Brothers); house Musgrave Fold, Leeds

Hartley John,[c] beer retailer, 460 Wakefield road

Hartley John, provision dealer, Great Horton

Hartley John,[b] John street, Northgate

Hartley John,[c] Manor street, Manor row

Hartley Joseph, clog and patten maker, 25 Northwing

Hartley Joseph, wool dealer, (Whittaker & Hartley); house Allerton

Hartley Peter,[b] provision dealer, Little Horton

Hartley Richard, provision dealer, 69 High street

Hartley Samuel, cabinet maker and upholsterer, Leeds road; house Bowling

Hartley Stephen,[c] Little Horton lane

Hartley Thomas, merchant, (Hartley Brothers); house Cavalier Hill, Leeds

Hartley Thomas,[b c] William street, Little Horton lane

Hartley William, provision dealer, Crown street, Thornton road

Hartley William, coal dealer, Brick lane, Black Abbey

Hartley William, worsted spinner, Thompson's Mill, Thornton road; house Great Horton lane

Hartley William, soda water, lemonade, &c. manufacturer, Thornton street, Thornton road

Haslam John,[b] Leeds road

Haste Joshua,[b] Northgate, Horton

Haste Josiah,[bc] William street, Horton

Hattersley Frederick,[b] machinist, (Samuel Hattersley & Son); house Crossbanks, Shipley

Hattersley George, worsted spinner and manufacturer, flyer, roller and power-loom maker, Charles street; works and house Keighley

Hattersley Samuel, [b] machinist (Samuel Hattersley & Son); house 46 Darley street

Hattersley Samuel & Son, engineers general tool makers, and spindle and flyer makers, WESTBROOK WORKS, Thornton road

Hattersley William,[c] Hall lane, Bowling

Hatton William,[b c] Great Horton road

Hawkins Thomas, tailor, 83 Wakefield road

Hawksworth Esther, straw bonnet maker, 18 Cropper lane

Hawley John, boot and shoe maker, 27 Westgate; house Cross street

Hay Abraham, provision dealer, Butterfield's row, Manningham

Hayes Michael, beer retailer, Pool's Alley, Silsbridge lane

Haywood James,[b] beer retailer, Church bank, Well street

Heads Thomas, schoolmaster, Great Horton road

Healey Thomas,[b] architect (Mallinson & Healey); house Sawrey place, Little Horton lane

Heap Mrs. Hannah, Manor street

Heap Joseph, joiner and cabinet maker, Brick lane; house Horton Bank Top

Heaton Christopher,[c] Joseph street, Leeds road

Heaton George,[c] Manningham

Heaton John Driver,[c] Joseph street, Leeds road

Heaton Peter, tailor, 48 King street, Manchester road

Heaton Robert,[c] Little Horton Green

Heaton Robert, woolstapler, Cheapside; house Sutton, near Keighley

Heaton Thomas Driver,[bc] highway tax collector, Garnet street, Leeds road

Heaton William,[b] clog and patten maker, Manningham

Hebden John, fishmonger, Bull's Head yard, Westgate; house Reform street, Westgate

Hebden William, fishermonger, 25 Rawson Place, Northgate

Heckley James, boot and shoe maker, 23 Fitzgereld street, Manchester road

Helliwell Benjamin, woolstapler, Commercial street; house Baildon

Helliwell Henry, woolstapler, Commercial street; house Baildon

Helliwell Joseph,[b] provision dealer, 300 Wakefield road

Helliwell Joseph,[c] farmer, Stock's Green, Manningham

Henderson Rev. Peter, A. B. curate of New Leeds National School; house Hanover Square

Henry A. & S. & Co. stuff merchants, Bermondsey, and Manchester

Henry Elizabeth, dress and bonnet maker, 32 Earl street, Manchester road

Hepper Christopher,[b] auctioneer, valuer, and furniture broker, Old Post Office Buildings, Bridge street

Hepper James,[c] general commission agent, lime merchant, wharfinger, and agent to the Leeds and Liverpool Canal Carrying Company, Thornton road, and canal wharf, Shipley

Heppinstall Henry, school and postmaster, Lillycroft, Manningham

Hepworth James,[bc] *Hit or Miss Hotel*, Sticker lane, Bowling

Hepworth William,[c] Dudley Hill

Heron Charles, cashier (Bradford Old Bank); house Kirkgate

Heron James,[b] Hanover Square

Heron Peter,[bc] linen draper, hosier, and haberdasher, 69 Westgate; house Leeds road

Heron Thomas,[b] Victoria street, North Parade

Heron William, boot and shoe maker, Brown street, Wakefield road

Hertz Heinrich D. stuff merchant, Brook street, and Bond street, Leeds

Hertz Martin, merchant (Martin Hertz & Co.); house North Parade

Hertz Martin & Co. yarn and stuff merchants, Tyrrel street

Heselton John Allison,[b] agent fo

silk warps, &c. Union street; house 52 Westgrove street

Heselton George Thomas,[b] Primrose Hill, Great Horton

Hesling John, grocer and provision dealer, North street, Stott Hill

Hewitt Benjamin, clothes dealer, 33 John street, Northgate

Hewitt Edward Smith, tailor and draper, 10 Manchester road; house Bedford street

Hewitt James, tailor, 82 Bedford street, Wakefield road

Hewitt & Knowles, timber merchants, school street, Manor row

Hewitt Samuel, merchant, (Hewitt & Knowles); house Northholme street

Hewitt Wiliam, provision dealer, 10 Prospect street, Thornton road

Hey Josepb, dealer in Orleans, stuff fents, &c. Primrose terrace, Manningham

Hey Joseph, hackney coach proprietor, King street, Leeds road

Heymann & Alexander (late A. J. Saalfeld & Co.) stuff and yarn merchants, Charles street

Heyworth Samuel, coal and provision dealer, Bradford Moor

Hibbert Thomas,[b] William street, Little Horton

Hick Joseph,[b c] chemist and druggist, Broadstones; ho. Hanover square

Hick Joseph, professor of music, Drewton street

Highmes John, boot and shoe maker, Sunnyside, Lumb lane, Manningham

Hill Abraham,[b] dealer in merinos and stuffs, York street, Bridge street

Hill Charles,[b c] Hall lane, Bowling

Hill & Drummond, worsted spinners and manufacturers, Booth street; works Manningham

Hill Edmund, provision dealer, Little Horton

Hill Edward, boot and shoe maker, 5 Arundel street, Manchester road

Hill Edward, boot and shoe maker, 27 Nelson street, Chapel lane

Hill Elizabeth, maltster, 20 Manchester road

Hill, Hardaker Hill & Co. flag merchants, Balme street, Bolton road

Hill James,[c] provision dealer, Little Horton

Hill John, maltster, 57 Westgate

Hill John,[b] grocer and tea dealer, 254 Manchester road

Hill John, beer retailer, 32 Melbourne street, Leeds road

Hill John, watch and clock maker, Whetley street, Manningham

Hill John,[bc] manufacturer, (Hill and Drummond); house Manningham lane

Hill John,[b] weighing machine maker (John Hill and Co.); house Springfield place, Manningham

Hill John & Co. scale-beam and weighing machine makers, 8 Cheapside

Hill Jonas,[b c] joiner and builder (J. and T. Hill); house Westgate

Hill Jonas & Thomas, joiners and builders, Churchbank, Well street

Hill Joseph,[b] manager (Commercial Bank); house Manor row

Hill Joseph,[b] grocer and tea dealer, 41 Market street; house Springfield place, Manningham

Hill Joshua,[c] provision dealer, 49 Lumb lane

Hill J. & W. & Sons, slaters and slate dealers, Vicar lane

Hill Luke Crosby,[b] woolstapler, Broadstones; house Manor row

Hill Nott, boot and shoe maker, 15 Burrow street, Manchester road

Hill Oliva & Eliza, milliners, 30 Westgate

Hill, Smithies & Nelson, slaters, and slate and stone merchants, Well street

Hill & Sutcliffe, slaters, Canal side, Bolton road

Hill Thomas,[b] joiner and builder, (Jonas & Thomas Hill); house Westgate

Hill Thomas Hardaker,[b c] (Hill, Smithies & Nelson); house 50 Westgrove street

Hill Thomas, provision dealer, Dudley Hill, Bowling

Hill Thomas, professor of music, Cropper lane

Hill William,[c] slater (Hill & Sutcliffe); house Cheapside

Hill William,[c] Whetley street, Manningham

Hillam David,[c] Low Moorside

Hillam Joseph,[c] Thornton lane, Little Horton

Hillas Abraham,[c] blacksmith, 213 Manchester road; house Great Horton road

Hillas Samuel, tailor, Wakefield road

Hiller Harry, commission merchant, 16 Dale street, and Manchester

Hinchliffe George,[c] Little Horton lane

Hinchliffe James,[c] Hill top, North Bierley

Hinchliffe Mary, beer retailer, 1 Melbourne street, Leeds road

Hinchliffe Thomas, provision dealer, 29 Brook street, Leeds road

Hinchliffe Thomas,[b] machine maker, Little Horton

Hindle Edmund, damask and fancy stuff manufacturer, Victoria Buildings, Cheapside

Hindle Thomas,[b c] tailor and draper, 23 Darley street

Hinds and Walmsley, tailors and drapers, 36 Market street

Hird Alexander,[b] umbrella maker, 28 Hustlergate; house Ebor street, Little Horton lane

Hird, Dawson & Hardy, coal, iron, and steel merchants, and iron and brass founders,—works Low Moor; office and wharf Canal road

Hird Isaac, worsted spinner, 97 Old Piecehall; works and house Keighley

Hird James,[b] clerk, Old Brewery, Great Horton road

Hird James, draper, hosier, &c. 35 Westgate

Hird James, Hall lane, Bowling

Hird John, provision dealer, 18 Providence street, Westgate

Hird Joseph, hat maker, 82 Queen street, White Abbey

Hird William,[b c] house, sign and ornamental painter and gilder, 92 Northgate

Hirst Edward, hair dresser, 42 Silsbridge lane

Hirst Joseph,[b] wool and waste dealer, Roebuck Yard, Ivegate

Hirst Joseph,[b] Lister Hills, Horton

Hirst Joseph,[b] farmer, Snap, Horton

Hirst Joseph and William Henry, woolstaplers, Leeds road

Hirst Thomas,[b c] Bridge street

Hirst William Henry,[b] woolstapler (J. & W. H. Hirst); house Halifax

Hoadley Ann, beer retailer, Northgate

Hoadley & Pridie, damask manufacturers, 20 Nag's Head yard; works ARCHER STREET MILLS, Halifax

Hoadley Thomas, manufacturer, (Hoadley & Pridie); house Halifax

Hoadley Thomas, fruit dealer, Northgate

Hobson Marmaduke, pork dealer, 16 Manchester road

Hodgson Benjamin, provision dealer, 1 Nelson court, Nelson street

Hodgson Elizabeth, dress and bonnet maker, North Parade, Christ Church

Hodgson James, boot and shoe maker, 27 Nelson street, Chapel lane

Hodgson John, stuff manufacturer, Brook street; works and house Sunderland, near Halifax

Hodgson John,[c] Bank Top, North Bierley

Hodgson John,[b] [c] provision dealer and butter factor, 60 Garnett street, Leeds road

Hodgson Joseph,[b] solicitor, and commissioner for taking affidavits for the county palatine of Lancaster, 12 Hustlergate; house Nelson square, Great Horton

Hodgson Michael,[b] grocer and tea dealer, 73 Westgate

Hodgson Thomas,[b] Eastbrook lane

Hodgson Thomas,[b] *Prospect Inn*, Bolton road

Hodgson William, tailor, Mary Farrar yard, Westgate

Hodgson William, tailor, 106 Silsbridge lane

Hodgson William,[b] Harris street, Leeds road

Holden Mr. Peter Kenyon,[b] [c] Hanover square

Holden William, beer retailer, 42 Northwing

Holdsworth Edward,[c] green grocer, High street, Great Horton

Holdsworth Mrs. Elizabeth, Snow Hill

Holdsworth Elizabeth, milliner and dress maker, 79 Westgrove street

Holdsworth Ellen, milliner and dress maker, 2 Portland street, Manchester road

Holdsworth George, merchant (John Holdsworth & Co.); house Stoneyroyd, near Halifax

Holdsworth Isaac,[b] Peel street

Holdsworth James, woolstapler and top agent, Cheapside; house Sterling street, Manchester road

Holdsworth James,[b] provision dealer, Barkerend

Holdsworth John,[c] Wakefield road

Holdsworth John, merchant (John Holdsworth & Co.); house Shaw Lodge, near Halifax

Holdsworth John, tailor, 36 Wellington street, Stott Hill

Holdsworth John & Co. stuff and blanket merchants, and stuff manufacturers and spinners, Norfolk street, Bridge street; works SHAW LODGE MILLS, Halifax

Holdsworth Jonas,[c] Hollingwood lane, Great Horton

Holdsworth Jonathan,[c] Russel street, Great Horton

Holdsworth Joseph, dyer, Old Market, Market street; works and house Wakefield

Holdsworth Joseph, school master, Back lane, Bowling

Holdsworth Joseph, provision dealer, Great Horton

Holdsworth Joseph,[c] Paradise Green, Horton

Holdsworth Miss, school, Fountain street, Manningham lane

Holdsworth & Raistrick, boiler, gasometer, railway carriage, and wrought-iron tank makers, and general smiths, &c. Croft street, Manchester road

Holdsworth Samuel,[b] farmer, Rooley, Bowling

Holdsworth Samuel,[c] Quaker lane, Horton

Holdsworth Thomas, provision dealer, 191 Wakefield road

Holdsworth Thomas,[b c] boiler maker (Holdsworth & Raistrick); house Westgrove street

Holdsworth & White, stuff manufacturers, Prospect Mill, Bowling

Holdsworth William,[b] manufacturer (Holdsworth & White); house Hall lane, Bowling

Holdsworth William,[b] provision dealer, 72 Bolton road

Holdsworth William, merchant (John Holdsworth & Co.); house Shaw Lodge, near Halifax

Holgate John, draper, (Proctor and Holgate); house Kirkgate

Holgate John,[c] Park square, Manningham

Holgate Mary, straw bonnet maker, 5 Cannon street, Cheapside

Holgate Robert, hair dresser, 19 Bank street

Holgate William, tailor, 16 Union Passage; house George street, Leeds road

Holgate William,[bc] hair dresser and perfumer, 10 Market street; house Stone street

Holland Joseph,[b] manufacturer (Saml. Holland & Co.); res. Slade House, near Halifax

Holland Samuel & Co. worsted spinners and manufacturers, Charles street; works Slade Syke, near Halifax

Holliday John,[c] Fitzgerald street, Manchester road

Holliday Read & Co. manufacturing chemists, and patentees of the self-generating gas lamps, Well street, and Huddersfield; Thomas Cobb, agent

Holliday Richard, boat builder, Bradford dock, Canal side

Holliday Mr. Thomas,[b c] Mount Pleasant, Manningham

Hollings Abraham,[bc] provision dealer, Legrams lane, Horton

Hollings Isaac Butler,[c] Manningham

Hollings John,[b] fruiterer, game dealer, and fishmonger, Bowling green, Bridge street; house Tyrrel court

Hollings Mr. Joseph,[c] West House, Manningham

Hollings Joseph,[b] Horton road

Hollings Mark,[c] Legrams lane, Horton

Hollings Thomas,[c] West House, Manningham

Hollingworth William, boot and shoe maker, Wadkin's Fold, Well street

Holloway William Henry,[b] wine and spirit merchant, ale, porter and cider vaults, beneath the Exchange, Kirkgate; house Eldon place

Holmes Benjamin,[b] Undercliffe

Holmes Benjamin,[c] Low Fold, Bolton

Holmes & Carter, spindle and flyer makers, Victoria Mill, Bowling

Holmes Charles,[c] farmer, Sticker lane, Bowling

Holmes Edward Stephen,[b] hat manufacturer, 36 Bridge street; house Fountain street, Manningham lane

Holmes Ellen, provision dealer, Wakefield road

Holmes Hartley,[b c] wool dealer (John and Hartley Holmes); house Manningham

Holmes James, boot and shoe maker, Dudley Hill, Bowling

Holmes James, spindle manufacturer (Holmes and Carter); ho. Bowling

Holmes John,[b] wool dealer (John & Hartley Holmes); house Hanover square

Holmes John,[b] farmer, Hollingwood lane, Great Horton

Holmes John,[b] Providence street, White Abbey

Holmes John & Hartley, dealers in noils and short wool, Back Tyrrel street

Holmes Joseph,[b] spinner and woolstapler (Buck & Holmes); house 3 Park place

Holmes Joseph,[b] beer retailer and provision dealer, 28 Joseph street, Leeds road

Holmes Joseph,[b] paper hanger, gilder and picture frame maker, 53 Darley street

Holmes Richard, commission agent and manufacturer, 19 Talbot Yard; house Heaton

Holmes Richard, provision dealer, Wakefield road

Holmes Samuel,[b] surgeon, 40 Darley street

Holmes Thomas, manufacturer (Ellis and Holmes); house Baildon

Holmes Thomas,[bc] share broker, and agent to the Manchester Fire Assurance and Pelican Life Assurance Companies, 10 Exchange street; house Darley street

Holmes Thomas & Son, drapers, silk mercers and undertakers, 36 Darley street, and Kirkgate

Holmes William, clerk of parish church, 45 Stott Hill

Holmes William Wainman,[b] Victoria street

Holroyd & Barstow, dyers and bleachers, New road, Great Horton

Holroyd Esther, beer retailer, 18 Silsbridge lane

Holroyd John, tailor and draper, 41 High street

Holroyd John,[c] High street, Great Horton

Holroyd Joseph,[c] New road, Great Horton

Holroyd Matthew, boot and shoe maker, Sticker lane, Bowling

Holroyd Robert,[c] Back lane, Horton

Holroyd Samuel,[c] Great Horton

Holt Benjamin,[b] appraiser and machinery broker, general commission agent and dealer in washing leather, &c. Bank street, and Mawson street, Thornton road; house Westgrove street

Holt Bryan, coach proprietor (Holt and Scaife); house George street, Leeds road

Holt John, organ builder (John and William Holt); house Preston place, Great Horton

Holt John & William, organ builders, Preston place, Great Horton

Holt & Scaife, cab and omnibus proprietors, West street, Vicar lane

Holt William,[b] organ builder (John and William Holt); house Preston place, Great Horton

Homily & Prayer Book Society; depot 5 Westgate; treasurer Chas. Walker, Esq.

Hope John,[b] Victoria street, North Parade

Hopkins Elizabeth, dress maker, 8 Parkgate, High street

Hopkins Joseph, brass founder, Thornton road; house 8 Parkgate, High street

Hopkinson William,[b c] beer retailer, 7 Wapping

Hopkinson William, provision dealer, 5 Well street

Hopper John, boot and shoe maker, 2 King street, Manchester road

Hopper John,[b] Hope street, Horton

Hornby Henry, provision dealer, Back lane, Bowling

Hornby Mary, milliner and straw bonnet maker, Garnett Yard, Union st.

Horne Charlotte, dress maker, 125 Bolton road

Horne James,[c] Folly Hall, North Bierley

Horne John,[c] Heaton Hill, North Bierley

Horne John,[c] Fiddlerhill Farm, North Bierley

Hornell James,[b] M. D. surgeon, Rawson place, Darley street

Horrocks James, tailor, 3 Hayworth street, White Abbey

Horsfall George, joiner, Cure's court, Westgate; house North Parade

Horsfall John,[c] merchant (William Horsfall & Brothers); house Bolton royd, Manningham

Horsfall John Garnett & Co. worsted spinners and manufacturers, Charles street; works Northwing

Horsfall Joshua, wool and waste dealer, Hope and Anchor Yard, Bank street; house Little Horton

Horsfall Joshua,[c] Bower street, Manchester road

Horsfall Thomas,[b] merchant (Wm. Horsfall & Brothers); house Burley Hall

Horsfall Timothy,[b] merchant (Wm. Horsfall and Brothers); house Hawksworth Hall

Horsfall William, merchant (Wm. Horsfall & Brothers); res. Calverley House

Horsfall William & Brothers, foreign wool merchants, and English wool commission agents, Broadstones

HORTON MECHANICS' INSTITUTE, Church school, Great Horton

HORTON POST OFFICE, Great Horton road; John Wood postmaster

Hotchin Jonathan, agent for the Gommersall Coal Company, Thornton road

Hotchin Sarah, milliner and dress maker, 121 Bridge street

Hotchin William, coal dealer, Broomfield, Wakefield road

Hough Mrs. Sarah, Manor row

Housoncroft Thomas, *Prince of Wales Tap*, Leeds road

Howard Elizabeth, butcher, 191 Wakefield road

Howard Joseph, provision dealer, 36 Manchester road

Howarth John,[b c] farmer, Crowtrees, Manningham

Howitt George, cloth worker and packer, 1 Church bank, Well st.; house Lister Hills, Little Horton

Howroyd Charles,[b c] plasterer (Howroyd & Duckworth); house Smith street

Howroyd and Duckworth, plasterers, Smith street, Manchester road

Howson Eccles, coal dealer, 214 Manchester road

Hoyle David,[c] North Bierley

Hubbard James & Son, wool merchants, Hall Ings and Leeds

Hubbard John Rothery, merchant, (James Hubbard & Son); house 14 Park place, Leeds

HUDSON BRICK WORKS, Leeds road

Hudson George,[c] Beldon Hill, Horton

Hudson James, woollen cloth manufacturer, Bradford Moor

Hudson James,[b] beer retailer, Wakefield road

Hudson Jane, milliner and dress maker, 120 Park square, Manningham

Hudson John, brick maker, (Hudson Brick Works); house Leeds road

Hudson John, boot and shoe maker, 87 Wakefield road

Hudson John, jun. brick maker (Hudson Brick Works), house Wapping

Hudson John,[c] worsted top maker, 98 Old Piece Hall; works and house Ilkley

Hudson John,[c] St. James' street

Hudson Jonathan,[c] North Bierley

Hudson Joseph,[c] Ivegate

Hudson Joseph,[b] pawnbroker, 9 Portland street, Manchester road

Hudson Joseph, medical botanist, Thornton road

Hudson Martha, straw bonnet maker Church hill, Wakefield road

Hudson Nathan,[b] Clarence street, Manchester road

Hudson Pharoah, brick maker (Hudson Brick Works), house Wapping

Hudson Thomas,[c] Beacon Hill, Great Horton

Hudson Thomas,[c] Chapel Green, Great Horton

Hudson William, brick maker, (Hudson Brick Works); ho. Wapping

Hudson William, hackney coach proprietor, Victoria street, Silsbridge lane

Huggan Thomas,[b c] boot and shoe maker, 46, Kirkgate

Humble George, solicitor (Lees & Humble); house Brunswick place

Humble John, carrier (daily) to Leeds, Illingworth's Court, Westgate

Humphries Samuel, hair dresser, 81 High street

Hunter John,[b c] tailor and draper, 2 Market street; house Manningham lane

Hunter Thomas,[b] tailor and draper, 4 Westgate; house Drewton street

Hunter Thomas, merchant (Milligan, Hunter & Co.); house Hanover square

Hunter William, plumber, glazier and gas fitter, 1 Kirkgate

Hunton William,[b] haberdasher, Berlin wool, hosiery and lace dealer, and baby-linen warehouse, 8 Darley street; house Brunswick place

Hurtley Thomas, boot and shoe maker, 11 Green lane, Manningham

Hustler George,[b c] comb manufacturer (Isaac Hustler & Son); house Manchester road

Hustler Isaac & Son, horn & tortoise shell comb manufacturers, 84 Manchester road

Hustler James,[c] North street, Stott Hill

Hustler John Milner, architect (Tuke & Hustler); house York

Hustler Joseph,[c] Dudley Hill

Hustler Joseph Oddy, tailor, and clerk of St. James's church, 3 Castle st. Manchester road

Hustler William,[c] Wakefield road

Hutchinson Eliza, dress maker, 3 Illingworth's Court, Westgate
Hutchinson John,[c] boot and shoe maker, 53 Chapel lane, Tyrrel street
Hutchinson John, gardener and seedsman, Well street
Hutchinson Samuel,[b] general commission agent, Charles street; house Summerseat place, Great Horton
Hutchinson William, hair dresser, 119 Park Square, Manningham
Hutley William,[b] White Abbey
Hutton Bartholomew, coal dealer, 12 Fawcett Court, Nelson street
Hutton John,[bc] Barkerend
Hutton Jonathan,[b] Manchester road
Hutton Thomas,[c] Bedford street, Bridge street
Hutton William, confectioner, 166 Stott Hill

IBBETSON James, printer, publisher and stationer, and London and provincial news agent, 20 Bridge street
Ibbetson John, hackney coach proprietor, Thompson's Buildings, Silsbridge lane
Ickringill Abraham, butcher, 63 Black Abbey
Iles Henry,[c] Mount street, New Leeds
Illingworth Alfred,[b] Hanover square
Illingworth Mrs. Ann, Manningham lane
Illingworth Armitage, moreen manufacturer, 178 Old Piecehall; works and house Allerton
Illingworth Booth,[b] joiner (Booth & Thomas Illingworth); house Fountain street, Manningham lane
Illingworth Booth & Thomas, joiners and builders, Southgate
Illingworth Charles, tailor, Four-Lane Ends, Manningham
Illingworth Daniel,[bc] worsted spinner and manufacturer, Providence Mill, Thornton road; house Great Horton road
Illingworth Henry,[b] surgeon, 26 James' street, Westgate
Illingworth Herr,[c] tailor, Brick lane, Manningham
Illingworth Isaac,[c] Manningham
Illingworth Jeremiah, coal dealer, Park Square, Manningham
Illingworth John,[bc] draper, hosier, and haberdasher, 80 and 66 Westgate
Illingworth Jonas,[c] joiner and builder, Southgate
Illingworth Jonas,[c] joiner and builder Mawson street, Thornton road; house Westbrook street
Illingworth Jonathan Ackroyd,[bc] surgeon, 14 Westgate
Illingworth Joseph,[b] woolstapler (Illingworth & Kenion); house Spring gardens
Illingworth & Kenion, commission agents and woolstaplers, Charles street, Hall Ings
Illingworth Martha, bonnet maker and milliner, Broadstones
Illingworth Mazeppa, dress maker, 23 Queen street, White Abbey
Illingworth Rachael, milliner and dress maker, 1 Keighley Old road
Illingworth Samuel, moreen manufacturer, 59 Old Piecehall; works and house Allerton
Illingworth Samuel,[b] farmer, Southgate, Great Horton
Illingworth Thomas,[c] draper, 2 Black Abbey

Illingworth Thomas,[b] joiner (Booth and Thomas Illingworth); house 2 Southgate

Illingworth Titus,[c] tailor, Spring row, Manningham

Illingworth William, worsted spinner and manufacturer, Schuster's Buildings, Brook street; works and house Halifax

Illingworth William,[c] Wellington st. Stott Hill

Imeson Matthew, boot and shoe maker, 5 Melbourne street, Leeds road

Imperial Fire Assurance Company; agent Mr. J. R. Wagstaff, solicitor, Charles street

Independent Chapels.—[*See* index "Churches and Chapels."]

Independent College (Airedale) Otley road; Rev. Walter Scott resident theological tutor; Rev. Danl. Fraser classical tutor.

Independent Order of Odd Fellows' District Head Offices (Manchester Unity), Oddfellows' Hall, Thornton road

Infirmary and Dispensary, Lumb lane; house-surgeon Mr. Knowles, matron Miss Rowley.—[See "Public Buildings and Offices."]

Ingham Benjamin, cabinet maker, 172 Back lane, Bowling

Ingham Charles,[c] chief constable to the West Riding Magistrates, Court House, Hall Ings

Ingham James, [b c] woolstapler (Ingham & Taylors); house Springfield place, Manningham lane

Ingham John,[c] woolstapler (Clarkes & Ingham); house Hall lane, Bowling

Ingham Joseph, agent for silk and cotton warps, stuff goods, &c. Hope and Anchor yard, Bank st.; house Leeds road

Ingham Martha, straw bonnet maker, 99 Brick lane

Ingham Nancy, beer retailer, Back lane, Bowling

Ingham & Taylors, woolstaplers, Booth street, Hall Ings

Ingham Timothy,[b c] auctioneer, furniture broker, and sheriff's officer, 34 Market street

Ingham William,[c] beer retailer, Back lane, Bowling

Ingham William, joiner, Back lane, Bowling

Ingle Elizabeth, *Rawson's Arms*, Market street

Ingle & Smith, land agents and surveyors, and agents for the Architects', Engineers' and Builders' Insurance Company, 1 Albion court, Kirkgate

Ingle Thomas, surveyor (Ingle and Smith); house Rawson's Arms, Market street

Ingle William, *Woodman Inn*, 157 George street, Leeds road

Inland Revenue Officers (Excise Branch); *supervisor* Mr. John Roberts, 24 Victoria street, North Parade; *officers*, John Bostock, Manchester road; William Davy, 34 Westgrove street; John Penket, 12 Canal terrace, Bolton road; Thomas Wright, Undercliffe; Jno. Dixon, Dudley Hill, and Richard Wynn, Shipley

Irving Christopher, [b c] grocer and tea dealer, 42 Westgate

Irving Harriet, milliner and dress maker, King street, White Abbey

Irving John, boot and shoe maker, 210 Manchester road

Irving William, chemist and druggist and dealer in tea and coffee, &c. 20 Northrop's Buildings, Westgate

Isitt George,[c] grocer and tea dealer, 61 Kirkgate; house Darley street

Isherwood William,[c] Fitzgerald st. Manchester road, Horton

Isles John, worsted spinner and manufacturer, 1 and 7 Old Piecehall; works and house Illingworth, near Halifax

JACKSON Abraham, provision dealer, 274 Manchester road

Jackson John, provision dealer, Legrams lane, Horton

Jackson John,[c] furniture broker, 61 Westgate, and Silsbridge lane

Jackson Jonathan,[b c] agent, Manchester road

Jackson Joseph,[c] Wibsey, North Bierley

Jackson Samuel,[b] provision dealer, 52 George street, Leeds road

Jackson Thomas, provision dealer, 26 Clarence street, Manchester road

Jackson Mr. William,[b c] Brunswick terrace

Jackson William,[b] linen draper and hosier, Manchester road

Jagger Abraham,[b] corn and flour dealer, 44 Manchester road

Jagger John, merchant (Thomas and John Jagger); house Northowram

Jagger Jonas, stuff manufacturer, Hope and Anchor Yard, Bank street; works and house Clayton Heights

Jagger Samuel,[c] Northwing

Jagger Thomas, stone merchant, (Thomas and John Jagger); house Northowram

Jagger Thomas & John, flag merchant, Bolton road

James John, managing clerk (Tolson, Clough & Taylor); house Tyrrel street

Jamieson Thomas, merchant (Berwick Brothers & Jamieson); house North Parade, Manningham lane

Jaram Edward N.[b] draper & hosier, 302 Manchester road

Jardeen Richard, tailor, 122 Bridge street

Jardine Ann & Son, linen drapers, hosiers, &c. Ivegate

Jardine James,[b] Mill lane, Bowling

Jarratt William, provision dealer, top of Green lane, Manningham

Jarvis George, tailor, 41 George street, Leeds road

Jenkins James, tailor and hatter, 123 Manchester road

Jenkinson Rachel, beer retailer, Silsbridge lane

Jenkinson Robert, tailor, 62 Joseph street, Leeds road

Jennings & Hargrave, stuff merchants, Leeds road

Jennings Henry, merchant (Jennings and Hargrave); house 8, Park place, Leeds

Jennings Mr. John, Southgate, Great Horton

Jennings John,[b] farmer, Cutler lane, Tong

Jennings John,[bc] butcher, Mill street, Canal road

Jennings John,[b] farmer, Lowclose house, Great Horton

Jennings Jonas,[b c] relieving officer for Bowling and Horton townships; house Great Horton road

Jennings Jonathan,[c] stuff manufacturer, Bank street; works and house Hewnden, Wilsden

Jennings Mr. William,[b c] Houghton place, Drewton street

Jennings William & Son, worsted spinners and manufacturers, 4 Hartley's Buildings, Brook street; works and house Windhill, Shipley

Jessop Joseph,[b] gunsmith, Albion Court; house 3 Fountain street, Manningham lane

Jessop Samuel,[c] Little Horton

Jewison Christopher, borough coroner, office Court House; residence Rothwell, near Leeds

Johnson George,[b c] Crowther street, Manchester road

Johnson George, joiner (Demain and Johnson); house Manor street

Johnson John, beer retailer, 62 Duke street, Wakefield road

Johnson John,[c] Bradford Moor

Johnson Mary, straw bonnet maker, 135 Vicar lane

Johnson Mary, milliner and dress maker, Burrow street, Manchester road

Johnson Richard,[b c] provision dealer, Swaine green, Bowling

Johnson Samuel,[c] Mill lane, Eccleshill

Johnson Thomas, joiner (Baxter & Johnson); house Brook street

Johnson Thomas,[b c] butcher, 12 Old Market place; house Westgate

Johnson William provision dealer, 57 Regent street, Duke street

Johnson William,[b] butcher, 7 Well street

Johnson William & Co. hatters, 30 Ivegate

Jolly Henry,[c] Back Mount street, Stott Hill

Jolly Isaac,[c] Providence street, White Abbey

Jolly John,[c] Thornton road

Jolly Joshua, tobacco-pipe maker, 21 Albion street, Silsbridge lane

Jones Alice, milliner and dress maker, 4 John street, Westgate

Jones Elizabeth, beer retailer and provision dealer, Wakefield road

Jones Morris, boot and shoe maker, 4 Castle street, Manchester road

Jones Samuel, beer retailer, 23 Bower street, Manchester road

Jordan William, beer retailer, Broom street, Wakefield road

Josling William, boot and shoe maker, 24 West street, Vicar lane

Jowett Ann, provision dealer, Great Horton lane

Jowett Ann, nursery gardens, seeds, plants, &c. Manningham lane

Jowett Daniel,[b] farmer, Southgate, Great Horton

Jowett Edmund,[b] woolstapler, worsted spinner and manufacturer, Union Passage and Upper North Parade, Manningham lane

Jowett Ellen, beer retailer, Cross st. Westgate

Jowett James,[c] Low Green, Horton

Jowett James, constable to the West Riding magistrates, Court House, Hall Ings

Jowett James,[b c] Longcroft place, Westgate

Jowett Jane Elizabeth, milliner and bonnet maker, Great Horton lane

Jowett John,[c] Bank-bottom, Horton

Jowett Jonas,[c] *Horse and Jockey Inn*, Low Moor

Jowett Jonas, printers' joiner, Southgate; house Great Horton road

Jowett Jonathan, stuff manufacturer, Hope and Anchor Yard, Bank st.; works and house Clayton

Jowett Joseph,[bc] Upper North Parade, Manningham lane

Jowett Joseph,[c] Albion street, Silsbridge lane

Jowett Nathan, provision dealer, 21 Ebor street, Little Horton lane

Jowett Samuel,[c] Bowling Old lane

Jowett Thomas & Co. stuff manufacturers, Old Market; works and house Bingley

Jowett William, beer retailer, Lumby street, Manchester road

Jowett William,[b] provision dealer, 88 Silsbridge lane

Joyce John, tailor, Longlands street, Westgate

KAYE Ellis Cunliffe Lister,[b c] Esq. Manningham Hall

Kaye John,[c] Whetley street, Manningham

Kaye John,[b] grocer and provision dealer, Leeds road

Kaye John, beer retailer, 1 Silsbridge lane

Kaye John Cunliffe,[c] Addingham

Kaye Miles, tailor, 50 Tumblinghill street, Thornton road

Kaye Thomas,[c] coal master, Bierley lane

KEIGHLEY AND BRADFORD, &c. RAILWAY STATION, bottom of Kirkgate; Mr. Matthew Crabtree superintendent

Keighley Daniel,[c] Daisy lane, Manningham

Keighley Gilbert William, spinner (G. W. & S. Keighley & Co.); house Keighley

Keighley G. W. & S. & Co. worsted spinners & manufacturers, Charles street; works Keighley

Keighley James, dyer and finisher (George Armitage & Co.); house Belle Vue

Keighley James,[b] plumber, glazier, and gas fitter, Chapel court, Kirkgate; house Belle Vue

Keighley James, beer retailer and provision dealer, 38 Silsbridge lane

Keighley Jeremiah,[c] John street, Northgate

Keighley John, tailor and draper, Frederick street, Wakefield road

Keighley Sugden, spinner (G. W. & S. Keighley & Co.); house Keighley

Keighley William,[b c] boot and shoe maker, Great Horton road

Kell Matthew, beer retailer, 18 Longcroft place, Westgate

Kellett Charles,[c] Heaton Hill, North Bierley

Kellett Daniel, Heaton Hill, North Bierley

Kellet James,[c] Low Moor

Kellett James,[b] beer retailer, 178 Manchester road

Kellett John, provision dealer, High street, Great Horton

Kellett Jonas,[c] Gracechurch street, White Abbey

Kellett Joseph,[c] North Bierley

Kellett Maria, straw bonnet maker, 5 Church bank

Kellett Thomas, boot and shoe maker, 106 Wapping road

Kellett William,[c] Bank-bottom, Horton

Kelley John, provision dealer, 132 Bridge street

Kelley William, provision dealer, Shear Bridge, Great Horton

Kelly James, provision dealer, Great Horton road

Kelly Rev. William, M. A. incumbent of Shipley

Kelsall John,[b] clogger, 197 Bridge street

Kenion Edward,[b c] woolstapler, (Illingworth & Kenion); house North Parade

Kennedy John,[c] engineer (Hargreaves & Kennedy); house Queen's Cut, Manchester road

Kennedy Richard,[b c] provision dealer, 132 Victoria street, Manchester road

Kenyon Mr. Edward,[b c] North Parade, Manningham lane

Kershaw Abel,[c] Wadsworth Mill, Haworth

Kershaw George,[b] farmer, Oaks Fold, Bowling

Kershaw Henry, spinner (Samuel & Henry Kershaw); house Allerton

Kershaw James,[c] New-road-side, Denholme

Kershaw Miss Mary, Victoria street, North Parade

Kershaw Samuel, joiner and cabinet maker, Bowling lane

Kershaw Samuel, spinner (Samuel & Henry Kershaw; house Allerton

Kershaw Samuel & Henry, worsted spinners & manufacturers, Charles street; works Allerton

Kershaw Sarah, dress and bonnet maker, 31 Green lane, Manningham

Kershaw Titus,[c] Bull Hill, Haworth

Kershaw William,[c] Wadsworth Mill, Haworth

Kerstein G. manager (Reuss, Kling & Co.); house Drewton street

Kessler & Co. stuff merchants, Bermondsey; Mr. George R. Wiechus manager

Kirby Amelia and Sister, day and boarding school, Skinner lane, Manningham

Kirby Mr. Charles Douglas, North Parade, Manningham lane

Kirk George,[b] chemist and druggist, 94 Manchester road; house Elizabeth street, Little Horton lane

KIRKSTALL, LEEDS, &c. RAILWAY STATION, bottom of Kirkgate; Mr. Matthew Crabtree superintendent

Kitchenman J. Charles,[c] blacksmith, Bierley lane, North Bierley

Kitchenman Samuel, beer retailer, and dealer in London porter and Burton ales, Leeds road

Kitchin John, moreen manufacturer, 94 Old Piecehall; works and house Clayton

Kitchin John,[c] Whetley Fold, Manningham

Kitson Jane, milliner and bonnet maker, 72 Hope street, Manchester road

Knapton Abraham, flour dealer, Ber-

Kitson John,[c] Thorp-Idle, Calverlye

mondsey; house Manningham

Knapton James, agent for stuff goods, yarn, warps, &c. 20 Market street; house Manningham

Knapton Jonas,[bc] Westgrove street

Knight Beanland,[c] Chapel street

Knight Edward,[c] Chapel street, Leeds road

Knight George,[b] *Craven Heifer Inn*, Four Lane Ends, Manningham

Knight Jonas,[c] High street, Horton

Knight Joseph,[b c] coal owner, Little Horton lane

Knowles David, watch and clock maker, 19 Manchester road

Knowles Ezra, boot and shoe maker, 32 York street, Bridge street

Knowles George, timber dealer (Hewitt & Knowles); house School st.

Knowles George, boot and shoe maker, Dudley Hill, Bowling

Knowles Mrs. Hannah, Fountain st. Manningham lane

Knowles Isaac,[c] Birksland, Leeds road

Knowles John,[c] Woodhouse Hill, North Bierley

Knowles Jonas,[bc] steward to the Ladies of the Manor, Rawson Place

Knowles Jonas, merchant (Brook and Knowles); house Rawson place

Knowles Jonathan, ale and porter brewer, Denholme Gate, Thornton; business attendance on Thursdays, New Inn, Tyrrel street

Knowles Joseph,[c] boot and shoe maker Halifax road, Bowling

Knowles Sarah, temperance hotel, 14 King street, Manchester road

Knowles Squire, beer retailer, Greenaire place, Silsbridge lane

Knowles William, provision dealer, Bavaria place, Manningham

Kyme Thomas, tailor, 22 Croft street, Bridge street

LACY John Womersley, beer retailer, 3 Churchbank, Well street

Ladies' Auxiliary Society; James Garnett, Esq. treasurer; Rev. J. G. Miall secretary

Ladies of the Manor, Misses Mary and Elizabeth Rawson, Nidd Hall, near Knaresborough

Lamb John,[b] school, Manchester road; house Chapel street

Lambert David, coal dealer, Summer street, White Abbey

Lambert Edward,[b] farmer, Oak House, Manningham

Lambert George,[b c] *White Horse Inn*, 23 Kirkgate

Lambert James,[b] solicitor, and clerk to the commissioners of taxes, 14 Exchange street, Kirkgate; house Shipley

Lambert James, stuff manufacturer, 14 Old Market; works and house Haworth

Lambert Thomas,[b] farmer, Wakefield road

Lancashire and Yorkshire Building Society; agent Mr. John Dale, 1 Thornton's Buildings, Bridge st.

Lancashire and Yorkshire Railway Station, Passengers' entrance on the Leeds and Wakefield roads; Goods' warehouse Vicar lane

Lancaster Judith, cotton warp dealer, 32 Hustlergate

Lancaster Robert, clogger, 1 Paperhall, Northwing

Land Richard, boot and shoe maker, Uppercroft Row, Bowling

Lapage George,[c] Croft street, Leeds road

Lapage John, provision dealer, Back lane, Bowling

Lapage Joseph,[c] Clarence street, Manchester road

Lapage William,[b] Chapel street, Leeds road

Lassen Edward Samuel,[b] merchant (Heymann & Alexander); house 3 Eldon place

Lauckland Joseph,[b] tailor, 48 Chapel lane, Tyrrel street

Law Ann, card maker, Dudley Hill

Law James,[b c] Melbourne place

Law James, boot and shoe maker, 87 Bridge street

Law Richard,[b] [c] butcher, Brunswick place and shambles

Lawson James,[b] cork manufacturer, Chapel lane, Tyrrel street

Lawson William Watson,[b] linen draper, hosier, laceman and haberdasher, 22 Ivegate

Laycock Abraham,[b] earthenware and provision dealer, Wakefield road

Laycock David,[c] Little Horton lane

Laycock George, collector of taxes, Great Horton

Laycock Henry,[b] [c] linen draper, silk mercer and haberdasher, 17 Westgate

Laycock James,[c] plasterer, 2 Longcroft place, Silsbridge lane

Laycock James,[b] [c] woolstapler (Harrison & Laycock); house Spring Gardens.

Laycock John, hay and straw dealer, 28 Well street; house Duke street, Darley street

Laycock John, schoolmaster, West Parade, Brick lane, Manningham

Laycock John, boot and shoe maker Victoria street, Manningham

Laycock John,[b] Westgate

Laycock Joshua, provision dealer and beer retailer, 16 King Charles st.

Laycock Peter (executors of), wine and spirit merchant, and ale, porter and black beer brewer, top of Ivegate; John Middlebrook manager

Laycock Robert,[c] Union street, Bridge street

Laycock Samuel,[c] Low Moor-side

Laycock Thomas, fishmonger, Church Hill, Bolton road

Laycock Thomas, boot and shoe maker, 20 Butterfield terrace, Manchester road

Laycock Thomas,[c] Fiddlerhill Farm, North Bierley

Lea Henry,[b] worsted spinner, Victoria Mill, Wakefield road; house Back lane, Bowling

Lea Henry,[b] jun. worsted spinner, Back lane, Bowling

Lea Henry,[c] Field House, Manningham

Lea John,[c] Bridge street

Leach Elizabeth, linen draper and hosier, 81 Westgate

Leach George Henry,[b] worsted spinner, Charles street; works Phœnix Mill, Thornton road; house Northbrook place, Bolton road

Leach John,[c] Townend, Westgate

Leach John & Son, gardeners and seedsmen, and public tea, fruit and salad gardens and bath, Manningham lane

Leach Joseph,[c] Undercliffe

Leach Joseph,[c] Lower Kipping, Thornton

Leach William,[b] [c] plumber, glazier, and gas-fitter, Leeds road

Leachman Robert Gilchrist, tailor, 25 Prospect street, Silsbridge lane

League Building Association; agent Benjamin Walker, 8 Market street

Learoyd Abraham,[c] grocer and tea dealer, 50 Manchester road

Leather George Henry,[b] worsted spinner and silk agent, Charles street; works Mill street, house Edmund street, Little Horton lane

Leavens Robert, wood and ivory turner, 212 Bolton road

Ledgard John,[b c] *Old Globe Inn*, Manningham

Ledgard John, beer retailer, Manningham

Ledgard Thomas,[c] High Spring street, Manningham

Lee Frederick,[c] Manningham

Lee George,[b] & Son, tailors, 43 John street, Westgate

Lee Hannah, wine and spirit dealer, Westgate; house Northgate

Lee Joseph,[b] Banktop, Great Horton

Lee Joshua, tailor and draper, 26 High street

Lee J. M. solicitor, Pearson's Buildings, Bridge street

Lee William,[b c] farmer, Bradford Moor

Lee William,[b] provision dealer, Commercial street, Canal road

Leeds and Bradford, &c. Railway Station, bottom of Kirkgate; Mr. M. Crabtree superintendent

Leeds and Liverpool Canal Company; Robert Nicholson principal agent, Salem street, Manor row; carrying agent James Hepper, Thornton road, and Canal wharf, Shipley

Leeds and Yorkshire Insurance Company; agents Mr. Hy. Thornton 10 Duke street, and Terry & Watson, 9 Market street

Lees Charles,[b c] solicitor (Lees and Humble); house Laura place, Leeds road

Lees & Humble, solicitors; Charles Lees commissioner for taking recognizances of insolvent debtors, and affidavits in the Irish courts, and agent for the Equity and Law Life Assurance; George Humble commissioner for taking acknowledgments of married women, and agent for the Atlas Insurance Company, offices 5 Albion Court, Kirkgate

Leeming Isaac,[b] Earl street, Manchester road

Leeming James,[b c] machinist (John Leeming & Son); house Manor st.

Leeming John,[b c] machinist (John Leeming & Son); house Manor st.

Leeming John & Son, machine makers and iron founders, Northholme Mill, Railroad street, School st.

Leeming Mr. Samuel,[b c] Brick lane, Manningham

Leeming William, cart and waggon cover, &c. manufacturer, 7 Old Market, Market street

Leng William, beer retailer, Paperhall, Northwing

Lenham Thomas, wood turner and carver, 9 Reform street, Westgate

Levee Maria, milliner and dress maker, 52 Vicar lane

Lever John, provision dealer, Broom street, Wakefield road

Leveratt William, chief constable, Police office, Swaine street

Lewis Benjamin, tailor and draper, Well street

Lewis Hubert, B. A. assistant master, Grammar School, Manor row

Lewty Clara, dress maker, 59 Fitzgerald street, Manchester road

Lewty John, hackney coach proprietor, North Parade, Manningham lane

Leyland Francis, beer retailer, Beckside, Great Horton

Libraries:—*Subscription*, Exchange Buildings, Exchange street; Conserative, Albion Court; Oddfellows'

Darley street, and Mechanics' Institute, Leeds road: *Circulating*:—James Ibbetson, 20 Bridge street; Joseph Lund, 82 Westgate; Jacob Brown, John street, Westgate; Thomas Waterhouse, Darley st.; Samuel Boulton, 4 Lumb lane; Jno. Hainsworth, 32 Manchester road; Thomas Umpleby, 2 Lumby street, Manchester road, and Wm. Cooke, 1 Ebenezer street, Vicar lane

Liebert Bernhard, commission agent and stuff merchant, Hall Ings and Manchester

LIFE ASSOCIATION OF SCOTLAND; agent Mr. J. G. T. Gant, solicitor, 3 Market street

Light John,[b] woolstapler, 39 Darley street; house Ann's place, Little Horton lane

LIGHTING AND WATCHING OFFICE, Swaine street; William Clough collector

Lightowler Charles,[b c] *Church Steps Inn*, Bolton road

Lightowler James, *Golden Lion Inn*, Leeds road

Lightowler Jonas, tailor, Southgate, Great Horton

Lightowler Joseph,[c] Buttershaw, North Bierley

Lincey John, boot and shoe maker 90 Bedford street, Wakefield road

Lincey Sarah, milliner and dress maker, 90 Bedford street, Wakefield road

Lindley Sarah, milliner and dress maker, 182 Manchester road

Lister Benjamin, provision dealer, High street, Great Horton

Lister Benjamin, fruiterer, 91 Manchester road

Lister George Thompson,[b c] land and general agent, valuer & auctioneer, Drewton street; house Holling House, Bolton

Lister James, beer retailer and provision dealer, Park place, Little Horton

Lister John, woolstapler, Swaine st.; house Birkenshaw

Lister John,[b] grocer and druggist, Wood street, Manningham

Lister Joseph,[b] Thornton road

Lister Joseph,[c] George street, Leeds road

Lister Joshua Brook,[b c] wool merchant and cotton warp manufacturer, Booth street; house Little Horton lane

Lister Reuben,[c] Back lane, Horton

Lister Robert,[b] earthenware and provision dealer, Wakefield road

Lister Samuel Cunliffe,[bc] woolcomber and top maker, (and combing machine patentee), Mill street, Canal road; house Manningham Hall

Lister Samuel Cuncliffe, machine top maker (Donisthorpe & Co.); house Manningham Hall

Lister Thomas, Esq. Manningham Hall

Lister Thomas, worsted spinner and manufacturer, 79 Old Piecehall; works and house Idle

Lister Thomas,[c] Cockpit Hill, Horton

Lister William Hemingway, *Angel Inn*, Westgate

Liversedge Jabez,[b c] beer retailer and butcher, Great Horton road

Liversedge John,[b c] provision dealer, Great Horton road

Liversedge Joseph,[c] Low Green, Horton

Liversedge Thomas,[b c] boot and shoe maker, and registrar of births and deaths for the west district, 16 Ivegate

Liversedge William, boot and shoe maker, 63 Hope street, Manchester road

Liversedge William,[c] Middleton Field, Westend street

Lockwood Charles, agent (Schunck, Souchay & Co.); house Mount Pleasant

Lockwood Edward, boot and shoe maker, 48 Bedford street, Manchester road

Lockwood James, Little Horton

Lockwood William, beer retailer, 64 Bolton road

Lodge John, cow medicines, Longlands street, Westgate

Lofthouse Richard,[c] manufacturer, (Chapman & Lofthouse); house North Parade

Lofthouse & Rothwell (Haigh Coal Company); office Railroad street; J. & J. Charlesworth agents

Lofthouse William, hair dresser, Great Horton road

Lofthouse William,[b] fruiterer and game dealer, 1 Market place, Darley street; house Brick lane

London Union Assurance Company; agent Mr. R. Ridehalgh, solicitor, Tyrrel square

Long Charles, butcher, 35 George street, Leeds road

Long James, beer retailer, Hardcastle lane, Well street

Long Joseph,[c] tailor, Temperance terrace, Spring street, Wharf street

Long Thomas, beer retailer, 97 Gracechurch street, White Abbey

Longbottom Thomas, green grocer, 44 Market street

Longbottom Thomas, wool and waste dealer, Hope and Anchor Yard, Bank street; house Market street

Longbottom Thomas, provision dealer, 579 Wakefield road

Longbottom William, [b] provision dealer, Milton street, Wakefield road

Longfield Joshua, [b c] Bolton place, Bridge street

Longfield William,[b] draper (William Longfield & Co.); house Kirkgate

Longfield William & Charles, linen drapers, hosiers, and silk mercers, 30 Kirkgate

Longfield William & Co. woollen drapers, 30A, Kirkgate

Longstaff John Dixon, hair dresser, 13 High street

Longthorn Thomas, saddler and harness maker, 111 Bridge street

Lonsdale Daniel, provision dealer, 3 James' street, Manchester road

Lonsdale Robert, beer retailer, Mount street, Bowling

Lord John,[b] draper (William & John Lord); house Kirkgate

Lord Samuel, superintendent of the Exchange, Kirkgate; house Broad street, Manor row

Lord William,[b] draper (William and John Lord); house Kirkgate

Lord William & John, linen drapers, hosiers, silk mercers, &c. 52 Kirkgate

Lothersdale Lime Company (Wm. Spencer & Sons); office Railroad street, School street; John Hargreaves agent

Loveday William, saddler, Dudley Hill, Bowling

Lowe Mary Ann, milliner and dress maker, 5 Stone street, Manor row

Lowe Thomas,[b] hat manufacturer,

22A Kirkgate; house 11 Broad street, Manor row

Lowenthal Siegmund,[b] merchant, (John Douglas & Co.); house Eldon place

Low Moor Iron Works (Messrs. Hird, Dawson & Hardy); office and wharf Canal road

Lownden Joseph, stuff finisher (Lownden & Robertons); house Leeds

Lownden & Robertons, woollen and stuff finishers, Westbrook terrace, Thornton road

Lowndes James, beer retailer, 57 Croft street, Manchester road

Lowndes William,[b] Queen street, Manchester road

Lucas Robert, boot and shoe maker, 4 James' street, Manchester road

Luccock John Darnton, merchant (Luccock, Lupton & Co.); house Sheepscar, Leeds

Luccock, Lupton & Co. stuff merchants, Bridge street

Ludlam Benjamin, smith and farrier, Spink's Buildings, Black Abbey

Lumb Abraham,[b c] pawnbroker, Old Market; house Upper North Parade, Manningham lane

Lumb Elizabeth, *Old Crown Inn*, 11 Ivegate

Lumb George, schoolmaster, Hall lane, Bowling

Lumb John Binns,[c] Northbrook place

Lumb Luke, tailor, Little Horton lane

Lumb Misses, milliners and straw hat and bonnet makers, 1 Westgate

Lumb Samuel draper, 89 Brick lane

Lumb Samuel, draper and hosier, 140 Manchester road

Lumby George,[b] farmer, Sticker lane, Bowling

Lumby John, *New Millers' Dam Inn*, (and bowling green), Thornton road

Lumby Richard,[b] farmer, Scholemoor, Horton

Lumby Mr. Samuel,[b c] Scholemoor, Horton

Lumley Joseph, bookbinder, stationer, and pattern-card maker, Hustler's Buildings, Leeds road; house Leeds road

Lund Joseph,[b] bookseller, binder and stationer, news agent and music seller, and circulating library, 82 Westgate

Lund Luke,[b] butcher, 6 White Abbey

Lund William, stuff manufacturer, Hope and Anchor Yard, Bank street; works and house Keighley

Lupton Ann, milliner and dress maker, 156 Bridge street

Lupton Charles, merchant (Luccock, Lupton & Co.); house Newton Green, Leeds

Lupton Henry,[b] Bolton place

Lupton John,[b] worsted spinner and manufacturer, Charles street; works Laister Dyke, house Eccleshill

Lupton John,[b c] currier and leather cutter, 38 Chapel lane; house Laura place, Leeds road

Lupton Joseph, merchant (Luccock, Lupton & Co.); house Blenheim Square, Leeds

Lupton Joshua,[b c] woolstapler (Richard Lupton & Son); ho. Manor row

Lupton Richard & Son, woolstaplers, 24 Cheapside

Lupton Richard,[b] woolstapler (Richard Lupton & Son); house Manor row

Lynn James, eating-house, 7 Kirgate

Lythall & Haigh, stuff manufacturers,

Swain street; works Caledonia Mill, Manchester road

Lythall William,[c] manufacturer (Lythall & Haigh); house Little Horton lane

M'CANDLISH John Thompson, merchant (Douglas, M'Candlish & Co.); house Victoria street, North Parade

M'Clennan William Johnstone,[b] travelling tea dealer and draper, 51 Westgrove street

M'Crea Henry Charles, manufacturer (M'Crea & Shephard); house Elm Cottage, Halifax

M'Crea & Shephard, worsted spinners and manufacturers of damasks, &c. Charles street; works Crosshills Mill, Halifax

M'Croben John,[b] linen draper, silk mercer, hosier and haberdasher, 25 Kirkgate

M'Intyre Michael, cutler, Poole's Alley, Silsbridge lane

M'Kay James, new and second-hand clothes dealer, Well street

M'Kean Andrew,[bc] merchant (M'Kean, Tetley & Co.); house Brunswick place

M'Kean, Tetley & Co. stuff merchants, Leeds road

M'Kell William, provision dealer, Lillycroft, Manningham

M'Laurin Andrew Scott,[b] merchant (A. S. M'Laurin & Co.); house 26 Spring Gardens

M'Laurin A. S. & Co. stuff merchants, Tyrrel street

M'Lean Thomas, provision dealer, Croft street, Manchester road

M'Math James,[b] travelling tea dealer and draper, Victoria street, North Parade

M'Meeking Gilbert, travelling tea dealer and draper, 50 Westgrove street

M'Michan James, travelling draper and tea dealer, Victoria street, North Parade

M'Michan John Little,[b] surgeon, 23 Thornton's Buildings, Bridge street

M'Nulty Edward, clothes dealer and cleaner, John street, Northgate

M'Nulty Michael,[b] Great Cross street

M'Taggart William,[b] grocer and tea dealer, 3 Silsbridge lane

M'Turk William,[b] M.D. Manor row

M'William James, travelling tea dealer, 16 Green lane, Manningham

Maden Samuel,[c] coal dealer, 74 White Abbey

MAGISTRATES' CLERKS' OFFICES; Borough—Mr. Rawson, solicitor, Swan street; West Riding—Mr. Mossman, solicitor, Hall Ings

Mahony Michael Joseph,[b] wool merchant, Brook street, Hall Ings; house Manor row

Malim George, grocer and tea dealer, 140 Westgate

Malim Margaret, school, 35 Victoria street, North Parade

Mallinson & Healy, architects, surveyors and valuers, Tyrrel street

Mallinson James, architect (Mallinson & Healy); house Halifax

Mallinson Joseph, coal dealer, Bolton road

MANCHESTER FIRE AND LIFE INSURANCE COMPANY; agents Mr. Thomas Holmes, 10 Exchange street, and Mr. John Darlington 10 Union Passage, Kirkgate

Manning Robert Frederick, tailor

and draper, 79 Market street

MANNINGHAM POST OFFICE, Lillycroft; Henry Heppinstall postmaster

Mann James,[b] provision dealer, 68 Hope street, Manchester road

Mann Jonas,[c] North Parade

Mann Joseph, green grocer, 199 Wakefield road

Mann Joshua,[b] merchant (Thomas and John Mann & Co.); house Manville, Great Horton

Mann Thomas & John & Co. stuff merchants, White Lion Yard, Kirkgate

Mann William,[c] provision dealer, Manchester road

Mann William, boot and shoe maker, Belgrave place, Lumb lane

MANOR OFFICE, Messrs. Clegg & Thompson, solicitors, Bridge Street Buildings, Bridge street

Marchbank John, hair dresser, 136 Westgate

Marchent James, engineer (Cole, Marchent & Co.); house Prospect Foundry, Bowling

Margerison Mr. Ellis,[b c] Bolton Royd

Margerison John Lister,[b] wool agent (Margerison & Sutcliffe); house 5 Park place

Margerison Mr. Richard,[b c] Bolton Royd

Margerison Mr. Samuel,[b c] Manor row, Cheapside

Margerison & Sutcliffe, commission wool agents, Bermondsey

Margeson Isaiah, boot and shoe maker, 29 Prospect street, Silsbridge lane

Markham Joseph,[b] provision dealer, 129 Manchester road

Marriott & Brearley, milliners and dress makers, 62 Earl street, Manchester road

Marsden Ann, grocer and tea dealer, 1 Union street, Bridge street

Marsden Benjamin,[b] butcher and provision dealer, Sticker lane, Bowling

Marsden James,[b c] grocer and tea dealer, 8 Ivegate; house North Parade, Manningham lane

Marsden James, beer retailer, Bradford Moor

Marsden John,[bc] farmer, Sticker lane, Bowling

Marsden Squire,[b] *Moulders' Arms Inn,* Sticker lane, Bowling

Marsden Thomas,[b c] Cross street, School street

Marsden William, professor of music, School street

Marshall James,[b] woolstapler, Bermondsey; house Spring gardens

Marshall John,[c] Calverley

Marshall John, butcher, 12 Barkerend, High street

Marshall Joseph,[b] joiner and furniture broker, Bolton road

Marshall Samuel, tea dealer and coffee roaster, 185 Bridge street

Marshall Thomas, boot and shoe maker, 2 Gracechurch street, White Abbey

Marshall William,[b] ironmonger, brazier and tinplate worker, 4 Kirkgate; house Eccleshill

Marten William,[b c] wool merchant, 28 Cheapside; res. Undercliffe House, Bolton

Martin Joseph, provision dealer, 128 Wakefield road

Martin Samuel,[b c] Hustler terrace

Martin Samuel Dickinson, surveyor, land agent and valuer, 51 Darley street, and Albion place, Leeds

Martin Thomas,[b] Victoria street

Marvell John, boot and shoe maker, Silsbridge lane .

Maskell George, provision dealer, 43 Edward street, Bridge street

Mason Christopher,[b] draper and grocer, 537 Wakefield road

Mason George,[b] manufacturer (Henry and George Mason); house Cross lane, Great Horton

Mason Henry,[b] manufacturer (Henry and George Mason); house Clayton Heights

Mason Henry & George, worsted spinners and manufacturers, Market street; works Cliff Mill, Great Horton

Mason Thomas, iron master (John Sturges & Co.); house Copthernwick

Mason William,[b] accountant and share broker, Bridge Street Buildings, Bridge street; house James' street

Mason William,[b] provision dealer, corn factor and maltster, 2 Cropper lane, Westgate

Massa John, provision dealer, Ellis street, Bermondsey

Masser & Bailey, engravers, lithographers and draughtsmen, Hustler's Buildings, Leeds road

Masser Joseph Fallowfield, engraver (Masser & Bailey); house Fallowfield terrace, Leeds

Masser Thomas,[b] tailor (Dixon and Masser); house Sawrey place, Little Horton lane

Mather James Stuart,[b] Victoria st. North Parade

Mathers Mary Ann, straw bonnet maker, 173 Back lane, Bowling

Matthews Alfred M. surgeon-dentist, 6 North Parade, Christ Church

Maud George,[c] Clayton place, Pit lane

Maud James,[c] Belgrave place, Manningham

Maud Samuel,[b c] Green lane, Manningham

Maud Timothy,[b c] draper, hosier, silk mercer and haberdasher, 42 Kirkgate and 65 Westgate

Maud & Wilson, chemists and druggists, 10 Bridge street; Mr. Thomas Wilson agent for the British and Foreign Bible Society

Maude Joe, painter, (Joe & John Maude); house Leeds road

Maude Joe & John, painters, gilders, and paper hangers, Hustler's Buildings, Bridge street

Maude John, painter, (Joe & John Maude); house Hillside Villas

Mawson David,[b] architect, 29 West-end Buildings, Lister Hills, Little Horton

Mawson Henry Ogle, bookseller, printer, stationer, and agent for the Minerva Life Assurance Company, 43 Kirkgate; house Stone street

Mawson Joseph, provision dealer, 149 Silsbridge lane

Mawson Mary Elizabeth, milliner and bonnet maker, Primrose terrace, Manningham

Mawson Sarah, eating-house, 21 Kirkgate

Meade Richard Henry,[b] F.R.S. surgeon, Manor row

MECHANICS' INSTITUTE, Leeds road; Mr. John Dale honorary secretary, Edward Starkey librarian

MECHANICS' INSTITUTE, Church school room, Great Horton

MEDICAL LIBRARY AND SOCIETY, Infirmary, Lumb lane, Westgate

Medley David,[b c] hair dresser, 98 Manchester road

Medley Elizabeth, dress maker, 73 Manchester road

Mellor Mary, coal dealer, 28 Portland street, Manchester road

MERCANTILE LIFE ASSURANCE COMPANY; agent Mr. H. B. Byles, 17 Kirkgate

Mercer James,[c] Daisy Hill, Manningham

Mercer Jonas,[b] Leeds road

Mercer Miss Mary, High street

Mercer Thomas,[c] Hazlehirst Brow, Manningham

Merrall Brothers, worsted spinners and manufacturers, 3 Hartley's Buildings, Brook street; works Haworth, near Keighley

Merrall Edwin, manufacturer (Merrall Brothers); house Haworth

Merrall Hartley, spinner (Merrall Brothers); house Haworth

Merrall Michael,[b] machinist (Naylor and Merrall); house Manchester road

Merrall Michael, manufacturer(Merrall Brothers); house Haworth

Merrall Stephen, manufacturer (Merrall Brothers); house Haworth

Metcalf Benjamin, toll-bar keeper, Laister Dyke

Metcalf Elizabeth, milliner and bonnet maker, Thornton road

Metcalf James, organist, and pianoforte teacher and tuner, Spring gardens, Manningham lane

Metcalf John,[b] Bedford street, Bridge street

Metcalf John, wool and waste dealer, Brumfit's Yard, Kirkgate

Metcalf John,[b] hair dresser, 14 Manchester road; house Earl street

Metcalf Thomas, toll-bar keeper, Wakefield road

Metcalf Thomas,[c] Ilkley street, Green lane, Manningham

Metcalf William,[b c] architect and surveyor, Bridge Street Buildings, Bridge street; house Sawrey place, Little Horton lane

METHODIST CHAPELS.—[*See* index "Churches and Chapels."]

Meyer George Solomon,[b] stuff merchant, 7 Lister street, Bermondsey; house Eldon place

Meynel Robert,[b c] *Seven Stars Inn*, Wakefield road

Miall Rev. James Goodeve,[b] (Independent), Brunswick place

Micklethwaite James, stuff manufacturer, Hustler's Buildings, Market street; works aud house Wakefield

Middlebrook John,[b] (executor Peter Laycock), 35 Ivegate; house Bingley

Middleton Christopher,[b] provision dealer, Hannahgate, Manchester road

Middleton David,[b] butcher, 52 Manchester road

Middleton Joseph,[b] provision dealer, Bradford Moor

Middleton Thomas,[bc] travelling tea dealer and draper, Brunswick place

Midgley Ann, *Wool Packs Inn*, Well street

Midgley John,[b] beer retailer, Broomfield, Wakefield road

Midgley John, boot and shoe maker, 32 Prospect street, Thornton road

Midgley Richard,[c] Gracechurch street, White Abbey

Midgley Thomas, locksmith, 1 Cure's Court, Westgate

Midgley Thomas,[b] butter dealer, 7 Providence street, White Abbey

Midgley William,[b c] provision dealer, Bridge street, Wakefield road

MIDLAND RAILWAY COMPANY, general carriers; goods' warehouse and office, Railroad street, Canal road; Robert Boyes head clerk

MIDLAND RAILWAY STATION; passengers' entrance and parcel office bottom of Kirkgate

Miller George, butcher, 108 Wakefield road

Millett James, beer retailer, 2 Mason street, Thornton road

Milligan, Forbes & Co. stuff merchants, Exchange street, Kirkgate

Milligan Harrison,[b c] merchant (Milligan John, Son & Co.); house 2 Ashfield place, Horton road

Milligan, Hunter & Co. stuff merchants, Exchange street, Kirkgate

Milligan Mr. James,[b] Houghton place, Drewton street

Milligan John, Son & Co. stuff merchants, Leeds road

Milligan Robert,[b] manufacturer (Robt. and William Milligan); house Houghton place, Drewton street

Milligan Robert,[b c] merchant (Milligan, Forbes & Co.); res. Acacia House, near Rawden

Milligan Robert,[b] merchant (Milligan, Hunter & Co.); house Hanover square

Milligan Robert & William, stuff manufacturers, Charles street; works Thornton road

Milligan Walter,[b c] manufacturer (Walter Milligan & Son); house Harden, near Bingley

Milligan Walter & Son, stuff manufacturers, Brook street; works Harden, near Bingley

Milligan William, manufacturer (Robert & William Milligan); house Regent place, Duke street

Millington John,[c] Park square, Manningham

Mills Edward, furniture broker, 2 Bower street, Manchester road

Mills Henry, provision dealer, 122 Manchester road

Mills James William, stuff merchant, and agent for silk and cotton yarns, Hustler's Buildings, Market st.; house North Parade

Mills Robert, provision dealer, 141 Manchester road

Mills Thomas,[b c] cabinet maker, and carver, gilder and upholsterer, 45 Market street; house Hanover square

Milner Daniel,[b] Victoria street, North Parade

Milner John,[b] commission agent, Sawrey place, Little Horton lane

Milner John,[b c] manufacturer (John Milner & Co.); house Manor row

Milner John & Co. worsted spinners and manufacturers, 11 Exchange street; works Clayton

Milner Jonas, hair dresser, Laister Dyke

Milner Joshua,[b] tailor and draper, 3 Bridge street

Milner Thomas,[b] grocer and tea dealer, 8 Well street, and 26 Ivegate; house Salem street

Milnes Enoch,[c] cabinet maker and upholsterer, 28 Manchester road

Milnes Henry,[b c] *Odd Fellows' Arms*, Manchester road

Milnes Isaac,[b c] spinner (John Taylor & Co.); house Horton road

Milnes John,[b] provision dealer, Back lane, Bowling
Milnes John, schoolmaster, 28 Manchester road
Milnes Robert,[c] Clarence street, Manchester road
Milnes Samuel,[c] Millholme Yard
Milnes William,[bc] Hustler's Gardens, Undercliffe
Milthorp Mr. Thomas,[c] Hanover square
Milthorp William,[b] paper manufacturer, Swaine street: works Poole, near Otley; house Manor row
MINERVA LIFE ASSURANCE COMPANY; agent Mr. H. O. Mawson, 43 Kirkgate
Minns Elizabeth, midwife, 74 Birks street, Leeds road
Minton Edward Smith,[b] commission agent, Shipley
Mirfield John,[b c] woollen cloth manufacturer, Bradford Moor
Mirfield John, provision dealer, Bradford Moor
Mirfield William,[c] Back Coach row, Bradford Moor
Misdale Frederick, piano-forte rooms, 1 Grammar School street, Manor row
MISSIONARY SOCIETY (branch of the London); Depositories 1 Thornton's Buildings, Bridge street, and 17 Kirkgate
Mitchell Edmund Johnson,[b c] stuff merchant, Manor row; house Spring gardens
Mitchell Francis & John, worsted spinners and manufacturers, Hustlergate; works Stowell's Mill, Manchester road
Mitchell Henry, stuff manufacturer, 16 Hartley's Buildings, Brook st.; works and house Hebden Bridge
Mitchell Henry, coal dealer, 32 Queen street, White Abbey
Mitchell Henry,[b] Fountain street
Mitchell James, worsted spinner and manufacturer, New Piece Hall; works and house Lane Ends, near Keighley
Mitchell John,[c] York street, Wakefield road
Mitchell John, grocer, corn and provision dealer, and district post office, Dudley Hill, Bowling
Mitchell John,[b c] corn miller, Bowling Old Mill; house William st. Little Horton lane
Mitchell John, joiner and cabinet maker, 125 Westgate
Mitchell John,[b] manufacturer (Francis & Jno. Mitchell); house Bowling
Mitchell John, merchant (A. & S. Henry & Co.); house Eldon place
Mitchell John,[c] Low Moor
Mitchell Joseph, spinner (Shaw and Mitchell); house Bolton road
Mitchell Joseph, temperance coffee house, 46 Union street
Mitchell Joshua, tallow chandler, 30 Ivegate
Mitchell Joshua,[b c] Manchester road
Mitchell Reuben,[c] stuff manufacturer, Millgate, Horton
Mitchell Thomas, *Old Red Gin*, Bowling lane
Mitchell Thomas, farrier, Bradford Moor
Mitchell Thomas,[c] manufacturer (Turner & Mitchell); house Burnet field, Bowling
Mitchell Thomas,[b c] Legrams lane, Horton
Mitchell William,[c] Swaine green, Bowling

Mitchell William, provision dealer, 2 Lumb lane

Mitton Henry,[b] agent (Henry Mitton & Co.); house Hillside Villas

Mitton Henry & Co. oil, paint and colour merchants and commission agents, 20 Nag's Head Yard, Kirkgate

Mitton Rev. Welbury,[b] incumbent of St. Paul's, Manningham

Monies James,[b] draper (James Monies & Co.); house 2 Exchange street

Monies James & Co. linen and woollen drapers, hosiers, haberdashers, carpet dealers, silk mercers and undertakers, 30 Kirkgate and 2 Exchange street

Moody Nathaniel,[b c] provision dealer, 216 Manchester road

Moore James, manufacturer, (Thomas and James Moore); house Shibden Head, near Halifax

Moore John, manufacturer (John Moore & Son); house Morton, near Bingley

Moore John & Son, stuff manufacturers, Brook street; works Morton, near Bingley

Moore John, cabinet maker, Wakefield road

Moore Thomas, manufacturer (Thos. and James Moore); house Shibden Head, near Halifax

Moore Thomas & James, stuff manufacturers, New Piecehall; works Shibden Head, near Halifax

Moore William, letter-press printer and stationer, Little Horton green

Moorhouse Robert, hair dresser, Chapel lane, Bridge street

Moorhouse Smith, provision dealer, 27 Silsbridge lane

Moorhouse William, wool and waste dealer, Great Horton

Moorhouse William,[b c] *White Horse Inn*, Great Horton

Moran Michael, beer retailer, 84 Thornton road

Morgan Rev. William,[b c] B. D. incumbent of Christ Church; house Snow Hill, North Parade

Morrell John,[b] grocer, tea dealer and coffee roaster, provision merchant and bacon, cheese and butter factor, Tyrrel street; house opposite

Morrell Robert,[b] corn dealer (Robert Morrell & Co.); house Westgate

Morrell Robert & Co. corn and provision dealers, 17 and 92 Westgate

Morren John, woolstapler, Cheapside; house 17 Spring gardens

Morris Benjamin Gough, bookbinder and pattern-card maker, Swan Yard, Market st.; house Mount, Bunkers' Hill

Morris Mr. Christopher,[b] Great Horton

Morris Joseph,[b c] solicitor, and clerk to the North Bierley poor-law Union, 36 Darley street; house Greenside, Allerton

Morritt William,[c] Edward st. Croft street

Mortimer Ann, dress maker, 185 Wakefield road

Mortimer David, butcher, Tyrrell st.; house Great Horton

Mortimer David,[b c] farmer, Paradise, Horton

Mortimer Eli,[c] Throstle Nest, Manningham

Mortimer George,[b c] *Rose and Crown*, New road, Great Horton

Mortimer John,[b c] farmer, Daisyhill, Manningham

Mortimer Richard,[b c] woolstapler, 63 Commercial street, Canal road; house Laister Dyke

Mortimer William,[b c] Bradford Moor

Mortimer William, agent for cotton and silk warps, stuff goods, &c. 21 Market street; house Westbrook terrace, Horton

Mortimer William Dawson,[b] tea dealer and coffee roaster, 68 Market street; house 8 William street, Little Horton lane

Morton George,[b] paper stainer (Geo. Morton & Son); house Summerseat place, Great Horton

Morton George & Son, paper stainers, 39 Market street

Morton Lupton, plasterer and colourer, 70 Northgate

Morton Matthew,[b] grocer and tea dealer, 84 Westgate

Moses & Son, tailors, hatters and outfitters, 19 Bridge street

Moss Dennis Topham, linen draper, hosier, &c. 5 Manchester road; house Leeds

Moss William, provision dealer and shoe maker, 8 Leeds road

Mossman George Robert,[b c] solicitor, and clerk to the West Riding magistrates acting at Bradford, commissioner for taking bail in the Insolvent Debtors' court, and for taking acknowledgments of married women; office Hall Ings; house 5 Eldon place

Moulson Hiram,[b] *Black Bull Inn*, Little Horton lane

Moulson John,[b c] farmer, Old lane, Bowling

Moulson Miles,[b] stone mason, Great Horton road

Moulson William,[c] Holme top, Little Horton

Mountain Eliza, straw bonnet maker, 6 Lister street, Bermondsey

Mountain William,[b] cooper and sieve maker, 111 Westgate

Moxon Emma, milliner and dress maker, Manchester road

Moxon John,[c] Thornton street, Thornton road

Mudd Edward, butcher, 2 Wellington street, Northwing]

Muff Bentley,[b] butcher, Halifax road, Bowling

Muff Charles, beer retailer and butcher, Back lane, Bowling

Muff John, smith and farrier, Cutlerheight lane, Dudley Hill

Muff Richard,[c] Clayton place, Pit lane

Muff Thomas Parkinson,[b] draper, (Brown & Muff); house Hanover square

Muldoon James, fruit dealer, Northgate

Muller George, commission agent, Charles street, Hall Ings

Munday James, butcher, Dudley Hill, Bowling

Murgatroyd Benjamin, dyeing manager (Bowling Old Dyehouse), Hall lane, Bowling

Murgatroyd Benjamin,[b] stone merchant, Whetley street, Manningham

Murgatroyd Charles,[b] general dyer, 56 Manchester road

Murgatroyd James,[c] Crown street, Thornton road

Murgatroyd John, butcher, Little Horton lane

Murgatroyd John, stuff manufacturer, Swain street; works and house Midgley, near Halifax

Murgatroyd John,[c] Park square, Manningham

Murgatroyd Joseph, linen draper, silk mercer, hosier and haberdasher, 6 Tyrrel street

Murgatroyd Joshua, beer retailer, Thornton road

Murgatroyd Joshua,[c] Silsbridge lane

Murgatroyd Thomas,[b c] George st. Manchester road

Murgatroyd William,[b c] wool merchant, and agent for silk warps, &c. Charles street; house Bank Field, Cottingley

Murgatroyd William,[b c] Banktop, Horton

Murgatroyd William,[c] Beldon Hill, Horton

Murphy Martin, beer retailer, 10 Providence street, Silsbridge lane

Muscham Thornton, flour dealer, Great Horton road

Muscham William, coal dealer, Cropper lane, Westgate

Musgrave Samuel,[b] woolstapler (S. & S. Musgrave); house Pudsey Townend, near Leeds

Musgrave Samuel & Simeon, woolstaplers, Swaine street

Musgrave Simeon,[b] woolstapler (S. & S. Musgrave); house Pudsey Townend, near Leeds

Mutual Provident Society; Mr. John Cooke, agent, 38 Bank street

Myers David,[b c] joiner and provision dealer, 113 Queen street, Manchester road

Myers Isaac,[bc] *Star Inn*, Westgate

Myers John,[c] Beckside, Horton

Myers John,[c] Holme lane top, Horton

Myers Susannah, provision dealer, Uppergreen, Horton

Myers Thomas,[b c] overseer of Horton township; house and office Cross lane, Great Horton

NALTON Thomas, tailor and draper, 12 Cheapside; house Otley road

Nathan N. P. & H. stuff merchants, Bermondsey; manager Mr. J. Philips

National Provident Insurance Company; agent Mr. John Dale, 1 Thornton's Buildings, Bridge st.

National Schools—[*See* "Academies and Public Schools"]

Natural History Society and Museum, Mechanics' Institute, Leeds road

Naylor Abraham,[b] wheelwright, Bowling lane, Bowling

Naylor & Co. earthenware, old metal and rag dealers, 152 Bridge street

Naylor George,[bc] George street, Manchester road

Naylor Isaac,[c] New row, Manningham

Naylor Joseph, druggist and grocer, Bradford Moor

Naylor Joseph,[c] Belgrave place, Manningham

Naylor & Merrall, machine makers, Providence Mill, Manchester road

Naylor William, provision dealer, New row, Manningham

Naylor William,[b] machinist (Naylor and Merrall); house Manchester road

Neal Charles, joiner (Shaw & Neal); house Arundel street, Manchester road

Neesom James,[b c] grocer, tea dealer, coffee roaster, and hop merchant, 43 Market street; house Hanover square

Nelson Michael,[b] slater (Hill, Smithies & Nelson); house James' street, Westgate

Nelson Richard,[b] boot and shoe maker, White Abbey

Nesbit George, school, and teacher of commercial writing, 17 Stone street, Manor row

Nesbit Susannah, seminary, 17 Stone street, Manor row

Neumann H. merchant (Heymann and Alexander); house Manor row

Newbould Michael,[b] butcher, 12 Kirkgate; house High street

Newbould Thomas,[b] boot and shoe maker, 41 John street, Stott Hill

Newby Richard,[b] [c] chemist and druggist, and dealer in tea, coffee, and tobacco, 10 Kirkgate, 1 Church Steps, and Manchester road; house Spring Gardens

Newby William,[b] fruiterer, game dealer and register for servants, Tyrrel street; house Tyrrel court

Newcastle - on - Tyne Insurance Company; agent Mr. William Mason, Bridge Street Buildings, Bridge street

Newell Henry Frederick,[b] linen draper, hosier and haberdasher, 34 Kirkgate

Newell John, joiner and cabinet maker, Broadstones; house Hardcastle lane

Newington Samuel Tompsett,[b] china, glass and Staffordshire warehouse, 1 Tyrrel street

Newsholme Thomas, noils and waste dealer, Albion Yard, Ivegate; house Hannahgate, Manchester road

Newsome William,[c] Peel street, Leeds road

Newspaper—"The Observer," 17 Kirkgate; published on Thursday mornings, and a second edition, with report of the day's markets, early in the afternoon; Mr. Wm. Byles proprietor

Newton and Duckett, linen drapers, hosiers, &c. 55 Manchester road

Newton Reuben, tailor, 304 Mitchell's Buildings, Manchester road

Nichols James,[c] Black Abbey

Nichols John,[c] Thornton road

Nichols Sarah Elizabeth, silk and straw bonnet maker, 1 Fitzgerald street, Manchester road

Nichols Rev. William, curate, Haworth

Nicholson Hirst, tripe dealer, 35 Westgate

Nicholson John, pattern card and pocket book maker & bookbinder, 1 Bermondsey; house 3 Prospect terrace, Manor Row

Nicholson John,[b] organ builder, 6 Melbourne street, Leeds road

Nicholson John, boot and shoe maker, 42 Bower street, Manchester road

Nicholson John Ellis,[c] Southgate, Horton

Nicholson Richard,[b] provision dealer, 10 Cross Wellington street, Stott Hill

Nicholson Robert,[b] manager for the Leeds and Liverpool Canal Company; house and office Salem st. Manor row

Noble Elizabeth, bonnet maker, 117 Park square, Manningham

Normington Isaac, worsted spinner and manufacturer, George Hotel Yard; works Junction Mill, Laister Dyke; house Netherwood green

Norris John Michael,[b] Primrose Hill, Horton

North Bierley Union Board Room

36 Darley street; Joseph Morris, solicitor, clerk

Northbrook Vitriol Works—Wharf street, Canal road; George Henry Leather proprietor

North Isaac,[b] farmer, Car bottom, Bowling

North John, butcher, Halifax road, Bowling

North William, saddler, Halifax road, Bowling

North William, seedsman, and public tea, fruit & salad gardens, Low Moor

Northrop Mrs. Martha, James street

Northrop William, provision dealer, 13 Tumblinghill street, Thornton road

Northwood George, solicitor, Darley street; house Apperley Bridge

Nowell John,[b] provision dealer, High street

Nowell John, *Blue Lion Inn*, Manchester road

Nowell Proctor,[b c] Canal terrace, Bolton road

Nuisance (Borough) Office, Swain street; William Bakes inspector

Nursey Mrs. school, Hanover square

Nursey Mr. William, Hanover square

Nutter Joseph,[bc] cabinet maker, paper hanger and upholsterer, North Parade

Nutton Lawrence, clog and patten maker, 7 Clayton lane, Manchester road

OATES Samuel,[b] Wakefield road

"Observer" Office, 17 Kirkgate, published on Thursday mornings, and a second edition, with report of the day's market, early in the afternoon; Mr. Wm. Byles proprietor

Odd-fellows' Hall, and district head offices (m.u.) Thornton road

Odd-fellow' Literary Institution and News Rooms, Darley street; Ralph Fawcett secretary

Oddy George, rope and twine manufacturer, 19 Kirkgate

Oddy James,[b] merchant (James Oddy & Sons); house Westgate Hill, Tong

Oddy James & Sons, wool merchants, Brook street, Hall Ings

Oddy John, medical botanist, King street, Manchester road

Oddy Joseph,[b] merchant (James Oddy and Sons); house Westgate Hill, Tong

Oddy Joseph, butcher, 176 Manchester road; house Wibsey

Oddy Mark, rope and twine manufacturer, bags, sacking, &c. 68 Market street; house Hall lane, Bowling

Oddy Mary Ann, milliner and bonnet maker, Wakefield road, Bowling

Oddy Micah, stuff manufacturer, Hope and Anchor Yard, Bank st.; works and house Northowram

Oddy Sam,[b] house, sign and decorative painter and gilder, paper hanger, &c. 19 Market street

Oddy Mrs. Sarah, Hall lane, Bowling

Oddy Thomas,[b] merchant (James Oddy & Sons); house Westgate Hill, Tong

Oddy William, agent for sizing and leather skeps, pickers, picking straps, laces, &c. 65 Market st.; house Hall lane, Bowling

Oddy William, provision dealer, Bradford Moor

Ogden Elizabeth, milliner and straw bonnet maker, 54 Northgate

Ogden James,[c] Wood street, Manningham

Ogden Jonas,[c] farmer, Wilsden

Ogden Michael & Co. woollen drapers, hatters, hosiers, &c. 29 Kirkgate

Ogden Thomas,[b c] joiner (Pickard & Ogden); house Bradford Moor

O'Hara Paul,[b] new and second-hand clothes dealer, 102 Westgate

Old Brewery, Great Horton road; William Whittaker & Co. proprietors

Oldfield Elizabeth, dress maker, 22 School street, Manor row

Oldfield Richard,[b] Bolton road

Oldfield William,[c] Victoria street, North Parade

O'Leary Randall,[b] silk dealer, &c. Great Cross street, George street

Olivant Edwin,[b c] superintendent of the Leeds and Yorkshire fire engines, 36 Ebor street, Little Horton lane

Onion Edward,[b c] machinist (Onion and Wheelhouse); house Great Cross street, Leeds road

Onion Joseph,[b] Burras Engine, Bowling

Onion & Wheelhouse, machine makers, and iron and brass founders, Frederick street, Bridge street

Operative Conservative Association, New Inn, Tyrrel street; W. Greenwood secretary

Operative Conservative News Room and Library, Albion Court, Kirkgate

Osborn William,[b] boot and shoe maker, 104 Bridge street

Outhwaite John,[c] M. D. Eldon place

Outhwaite Thomas,[bc] *Junction Hotel*, Leeds road

Outhwaite William Thomas,[b] chemist and druggist, 45 Kirkgate

Overend James, provision dealer, Sticker lane, Bowling

Overend Richard, stuff manufacturer, New Piecehall; works and house Cross Hills, near Keighley

Overseers' Offices : — *Bradford District*, Court House, Hall Ings; *Horton*—Cross lane; *Bowling*—Hall lane; *Manningham*—Lumb lane

Oxtoby Thomas, [b c] cabinet turner, 6 Cross street, Westgate; house Earl street, Manchester road

PADGETT William,[b] worsted spinner, Waterloo Mill, Victoria street, Manchester road; house 47 King street

Paley John Green,[b] Esq. ironmaster, (Bowling Iron Works); house Harrogate

Paley Thomas, Esq. ironmaster, house London

Pape Thomas,[b] gardener, Undercliffe

Parker George, hay and straw dealer, Thornton road; house Southgate

Parker Elizabeth, milliner and dress maker, 4 Southgate

Parker Hannah & Mary, Friends' bonnet makers, 3 Tyrrel street

Parker Henry, rag and waste dealer, Wharf street, Bolton road

Park Henry,[c] provision dealer, High street, Great Horton

Parker James, beer retailer, Hall lane, Bowling

Parker James, brass founder, Hall lane, Bowling

Parker James,[c] Saltpie, Great Horton

Parker Jeremiah,[c] *Lower Globe Inn*, Manningham

Parker John,[b] [c] farmer, Old road, Horton

Parker Lydia, provision dealer, Great Horton road

Parker Mrs. Catholic bookseller, Stott Hill

Parker Mrs. dress and shroud maker, 74 John street, Stott Hill

Parker Mrs. milliner and straw bonnet maker, Chapel street, Leeds road

Parker Samuel,[b] smith and farrier, Brook street; house Hillside Villas

Parker Samuel,[c] Cross lane, Horton

Parker William, grocer, tea dealer and coffee roaster, 3 Tyrrel street

Parker William,[b] provision dealer, 131 Brick lane

Parkin Caroline, milliner and dress maker, 63 Bower street, Manchester road

Parkin John, nail maker, top of Westgate; house Longlands street, Silsbridge lane

Parkinson Benjamin,[b] [c] farmer, Westsquire lane, Manningham

Parkinson and Clark, linen and woollen drapers, silk mercers, hosiers, and haberdashers, 27 Kirkgate

Parkinson Edward,[b] [c] grocer (Edwd. and William Parkinson); house Hanover square

Parkinson Edward & William, grocers and tea dealers, 21 Kirkgate

Parkinson George, tailor, Wood st. Manningham

Parkinson George,[b] [c] draper (Parkinson & Clarke); house Kirkgate

Parkinson John,[b] Mount Carmel, Little Horton

Parkinson John, boot and shoe maker, 163 Whetley street, Manningham

Parkinson John, boot and shoe maker, 39 York street, Bridge street

Parkinson John,[b] printer, stationer, and news agent, 2 Union street; house 4 Bedford street

Parkinson Joseph,[b] [c] tea dealer, tobacco manufacturer, and hop merchant, 2 Old Market, Market st.

Parkinson Joshua,[c] Providence street, White Abbey

Parkinson, Mitchell & Co. worsted spinners & manufacturers, Swaine st

Parkinson Samuel, woolstapler (Saml. and Thomas Parkinson); house Market street

Parkinson Samuel & Thomas, woolstaplers, Exchange street

Parkinson Thomas, woolstapler (Sam. and Thomas Parkinson); house Market street

Parkinson William, grocer (Edward and William Parkinson); house Hanover square

Parkinson William,[b] surgeon, Well street, corner of Hardcastle lane

Parkinson William,[b] worsted spinner, Waterlane Mill, Thornton road; house 64 Westgrove street

Parratt Charles, boot and shoe maker, Green lane, Manningham

Parratt Edward Hawksworth,[b] [c] ironmonger, and agent to the Clerical, Medical and General Insurance Company, 1 Broadstones; house Drewton street

Parratt Jonathan,[c] Melbourne street, Leeds road

Parratt Joseph,[b] Westgrove street

Parratt Richard,[b] [c] provision dealer, Bradford Moor

Parratt Robert, boot and shoe maker, 28 Croft street, Bridge street

Parratt Samuel, boot and shoemaker, Bradford Moor

Parratt Samuel, boot and shoe maker, 8 Lister street, Bermondsey

Parratt Thomas,[b] [c] High street

Parratt Thomas Williamson, engraver, Bridge street Buildings, Bridge street; house Legrams, Great Horton road

Parratt William,[c] Parratt's row, Bradford Moor

Parry Robert, bookbinder and pattern card maker, 15 Market street; house Primrose terrace, Wood street

Parsons J. H. surgeon-dentist (successor to Mr. Graves); Thursdays only, at Mrs. Pattinson's, Manningham lane

Passavant Philip Jacob,[b] merchant (P. J. Passavant & Co.); house Greenhill Hall, Bingley

Passavant Philip Jacob & Co. yarn merchants, Cheapside

Passavant Philip John, merchant, (P. J. Passavant & Co.) house Greenhill Hall, Bingley

Pastoral (Church) Aid Society; Rev. James Cooper secretary

Patchett James,[b] [c] hatter, 48 Kirkgate, corner of Market street; house Leeds road

Patchett John, Leeds road

Patchett Joshua, tailor, Otley road

Patchett Joshua,[c] Duckworth lane, Manningham

Patchett Timothy,[c] Manningham

Patchett William, fent dealer, 34 Manchester road; house Clarence street

Patterson Robert,[b] merchant (Robert Patterson & Co.); house Ashfield place, Great Horton road

Patterson Robert & Co. stuff merchants, 38 Bridge street

Pattinson Mrs. Ann, Manningham lane

Pattison John,[b] boot and shoe maker, 13 John street, Westgate

Pattison William, tailor, Uppercroft row, Bowling

Pattison William, tailor, Swaine green, Bowling

Pawson Benjamin,[b] [c] boot and shoe maker, 18 Victoria street, White Abbey

Pawson John,[b] cashier, (Bradford Old Bank); house Chapel street, Leeds road

Peacock Eliza & Sarah, milliners and dress makers, 244 Leeds road

Peacock Harker, butcher, 179 Brick lane

Peacock James,[b] grocer & tea dealer, 246 Leeds road

Peacock John,[b] beer retailer, 41 Vicar lane

Peacock John,[b] grocer and tea dealer, 63 Northgate; house Leeds road

Peacock William, boot and shoe maker, 2 North street Court, Wellington street

Pearce Thomas Massey,[b] clerk (Walkers' & Co. Bridge street), and agent to the Scottish Provident Institution; house Ivy Cottage, Thornton road

Pearsen Abraham,[c] provision dealer, Primrose terrace, Manningham

Pearson & Company, Bradford and Selby Canal carriers, Canal road; John Adamson agent

Pearson Miss Eliza, Manor row

Pearson Gent,[c] stuff manufacturer, 187 Old Piecehall; works and house North Bierley

Pearson Hannah, beer retailer, 23 High street

Pearson Henry,[b c] ironmonger and hatter, 30 and 32 Bridge street; house Great Horton road

Pearson James,[b c] farmer, Sams Mill, Horton

Pearson John, locksmith and bell hanger, Albion Yard, Ivegate; house Eccleshill

Pearson Joseph, joiner and cabinet maker, High street

Pearson William, provision dealer, Halifax road, Bowling

Pease Henry & Co. manufacturers of Orleans, Paramattas, &c. Hall Ings; works and house Darlington

Pease Richard, brass founder, lacquerer and finisher, 79 Chapel lane

PECKETT'S COMMERCIAL EATING HOUSE, Market place, Kirkgate

Peckett John,[b] Manor Hall, Kirkgate

Peckover Daniel,[b] wool merchant (Peckover & Ferrand); house Wood Hall

Peckover & Ferrand, woolstaplers, Dale street and Duke street

Peel Alfred,[c] provision dealer, Great Horton

Peel Edward,[b] provision dealer, Southgate, Great Horton

Peel John,[b] house, sign and decorative painter and gilder, paper hanger, &c. 64 Bridge street

Peel Samuel,[c] boot and shoe maker, Great Horton road

Peel Thomas, stuff manufacturer, Market street; works and house Cononley, near Skipton

Peel Thomas,[c] Southgate, Horton

Peel Thomas,[c] Mill lane, Horton

Peel William, provision dealer, 51 Lumb lane

Peel William,[b c] merchant (William Peel & Co.); res. Springfield House, Manningham

Peel William & Co. stuff manufacturers and merchants, 40 Bridge street

PELICAN LIFE INSURANCE COMPANY; agents Mr. Thomas Holmes, 10 Exchange street, and Mr. John Darlington, Union Passage

Pellett Emanuel Lines, tailor, 49 Queen street, Manchester road

Pemberton Catherine, dress maker, 18 Queen street, White Abbey

Penket John,[b] officer of inland revenue (excise branch), 42 Canal terrace, Bolton road

Pennington John,[b] woolstapler, Cheapside; house Victoria street, North Parade

Penny Mr. Edward,[b c] Leeds road

Perfect Henry Goodwin,[b] woolstapler, Hall Ings; house Bolton

Petty Charles James,[b] North Parade, Manningham lane

Petty George, pottery moulder, Cross street, Wakefield road

Petty Henry, provision dealer, 598 Wakefield road

Petty James,[b] Wakefield road

Petty Robert,[b c] Edward street, Leeds road

Phelps Jane, straw bonnet maker, 139 Gracechurch street, White Abbey

Philipp Joseph,[b] general agent, 60 Market street; house 10 Victoria street, North Parade

Phillips George, butcher, 202 Manchester road

Philips J. manager (N. P. & H. Nathan); house Park place, Manningham lane

Phillips Mary, saddler and harness maker, 8 Piecehall Yard; house Old Market

Phillips Thomas,[c] Manchester road

Pickard Edward,[b] Hillside Villas

Pickard Henry,[c] iron and tin-plate worker, 282 Leeds road

Pickard James,[b] [c] house and sign painter and gilder, 2 Melbourne street, Leeds road

Pickard John, boot and shoe maker, 10 King street, Manchester road

Pickard Joseph,[c] provision dealer, 2 Anngate, High street

Pickard & Ogden, joiners and builders, Silsbridge lane

Pickard William, joiner and builder, Bradford Moor

Pickard William, provision dealer, 189 Bridge street

Pickard William,[b] joiner (Pickard & Ogden); house Longcroft place, Westgate

Pickford & Company, general carriers; office and warehouse Brook street, James Croxall agent

Pickles Eli,[c] Westsquire lane, Manningham

Pickles George,[b] Goodmansend

Pickles Hannah, *Wellington Inn*, High street

Pickles Henry, hair dresser and umbrella maker, 27 Northgate

Pickles John, beer retailer, Swaine Green, Bowling

Pickles John, hair dresser, 52 Westgate

Pickles John,[c] provision dealer, Manningham

Pickles John,[c] Longlands place, Westgate

Pickles Jonathan,[c] Longlands street, Westgate

Pickles Joseph,[b] linen draper and hosier, 43 Westgate

Pickles Thomas, hair dresser, Brick lane, Manningham

Pickles William,[c] Holme Top, Little Horton

Pickles William,[b] plasterer and colourer, 69 York street, Bridge street

Pickup Mark,[b] solicitor, 14 Union Passage; house Prospect Square, Bowling

Piercy John, provision dealer, 222 Manchester road

Pilkington William, greengrocer and gardener, Victoria street, Manningham

Pilling & Boulton, worsted spinners, Westholme Mill, Thornton road

Pilling John, beer retailer, 39 King street, Manchester road

Pilling Mr. Joseph,[b] Little Horton lane

Pilling Joseph,[b] jun. miller (Wm. & Joseph Pilling); house Little Horton lane

Pilling Moses,[b] spinner (Pilling & Boulton); house Crow Nest, Legrams lane

Pilling Robinson, boot and shoe maker, High street, Great Horton

Pilling William,[b] miller (William & Joseph Pilling), house Little Horton lane

Pilling William & Joseph, corn millers, Manchester road

Pittam Samuel,[b] tailor, 30 Chapel lane, Tyrrel street

Pitts Joseph, tailor, Dudley Hill, Bowling

Pitts Mark, tailor, Dudley Hill, Bowling

Pitts Samuel,[b] beer retailer, Back lane, Bowling

Platts Charles,[b] farmer, Wakefield road

Police Station (Borough), Swain street;—William Leveratt chief constable; superintendent of night police Richard Collinson; John Shuttleworth and Joseph Field detective officers; William Bakes inspector of nuisances

Pollard George, coal owner, Crow Trees Colliery, Bradford Moor; house Kirkskill Hall, near Otley

Pollard James, boot and shoe maker, 2 Threadneedle street, Vicar lane

Pollard John,[b] boot and shoe maker, 14 John street, Westgate

Pollard John, boot and shoe maker, Back lane, Bowling

Pollard Joshua,[bc] ironmaster and coal owner, (John Sturges & Co.); house Scarr Hall, Bradford Moor

Pollard Joshua,[b] commission maker-up, (Banks & Pollard); house Wakefield road

Pollard Joseph, boot and shoe maker, 6 Hope street, Manchester road

Pollard Maria, provision dealer, 20 Chapel lane, Tyrrel street

Pollard Richard,[b] woolstapler, Bermondsey; house 101 Earl street, Manchester road

Pollard Samuel, boot and shoe maker, Wakefield road

Pollard Samuel, provision dealer, Millbank

Poole Benjamin, commercial and temperance eating house, Tyrrel st.

Poole David, joiner and cabinet maker, Bowling lane, Bowling

Poole George, agent and appraiser, 85 Silsbridge lane

Poole Jacob, provision dealer, 53 Northwing

Poole Joseph,[c] cabinet maker and broker, 22 Silsbridge lane

Poole Thomas, boot and shoe maker, Crown street, Thornton road

Poole William,[b] beer retailer, 81 Thornton road

Poole William,[c] horn comb maker, 100 Silsbridge lane

Poor Law Guardians' Board Room, Charles street; John Reid Wagstaff clerk

Poors' Rate Office, Court House, Hall Ings; Mr. W. W. Barlow assistant overseer

Poppleton Joe, surgeon, Hall Ings

Popplewell Benjamin,[b] worsted spinner, Greenwood's Mill, Portland street; house Sterling street, Manchester road

Popplewell Benjamin Briggs,[bc] wine and spirit merchant, 43 Market street; house Eldon place

Porritt Jonathan, worsted spinner and manufacturer, 10 Old Piecehall; works and house Birkenshaw

Porter George,[b] Westgrove street

Porter Mary Ann, dress maker, Arcadia street, Lumb lane

Porter Sarah, beer retailer, 46 Longlands street, Westgate

Porter William, furniture broker, 76 High street

Postlethwaite William,[bc] school master, Bradford Moor

Post Office (General), Union Passage, Kirkgate; Mr. William Coates postmaster

Poulter William, tailor, Belgrave place, Lumb lane

Powell Rev. Benjamin,[b c] incumbent of Wigan, Lancashire; house Horton Old Hall

Powell Mr. Francis Sharp, Horton Old Hall

Pratt Christopher,[c] upholsterer (Pratt and Prince); house North Parade

Pratt James, hosier, Bradford Moor

Pratt John,[b c] chemist and druggist, Ivegate; house Hanover square

Pratt John, wheelwright, Sedgwick street, White Abbey

Pratt Mary Ann, school mistress, Bradford Moor

Pratt & Prince, cabinet makers and upholsterers, North Parade

Pratt William,[c] Mount street, Leeds road

PRAYER BOOK AND HOMILY SOCIETY, depot 5 Westgate; Charles Walker, Esq. treasurer

Pregel George, merchant (George Pregel & Co.); house North Parade

Pregel George & Co. stuff merchants, Swaine street

Preller Emilius, merchant (P. J. Passavant & Co.); house Melbourne place, Little Horton lane

Prest John,[b c] draper (Bell & Prest); house Halifax

Prest William,[b] boot and shoe, and watch and clock maker, jeweller, &c. 22 Well street

Preston Benjamin, fent dealer, 8 Manchester road; house Manningham

Preston James, stuff manufacturer, 20 Bank street; works and house Trawden

Preston John, agent for stuff goods, cotton and worsted yarn, &c, 20 Bank street; house Primrose terrace, Manningham

Preston John, chemist and druggist, 45 Silsbridge lane; house Westgate

Preston Nanny, provision dealer, 152 Westgate

Preston William,[b] provision dealer, 54 Manchester road

Pridie Benjamin, manufacturer (Hoadley & Pridie); house Halifax

Priestley Abraham,[b] *Hope and Anchor Inn*, Bank street, Market street

Priestley James,[b] provision dealer, Dudley Hill, Bowling

Priestley Job, moreen manufacturer, 103 Old Piecehall; works and house Allerton

Priestley John, stuff manufacturer, Bank street; works and house Wibsey

Priestley John, provision dealer, High street, Great Horton

Priestley John,[c] Jer lane, Horton

Priestley Joseph, provision dealer, 2 Castle street, Manchester road

Priestley Samuel, professor of music, Green lane, Manningham

Priestley Simeon, damask manufacturer, 22 Nag's Head yard, Kirkgate; works and house Illingworth Moor, near Halifax

Priestman John,[b c] miller (Ellis & Priestman); res. Whetley House, Manningham

Priestman John, manufacturer (John Priestman & Co.); res. Whetley House, Manningham

Priestman John & Co. stuff manufacturers, Brook street; works Ashfield Mill, Thornton road

Prince Edward,[b] butcher, 6 Well street; house Brook street

Prince Joseph,[b] *Airedale Hotel*, Otley road

Prince Thomas, upholsterer (Pratt & Prince); house Fitzgerald street

Procter & Holgate, linen drapers, hosiers, and haberdashers, 67 Kirkgate

Procter James,[b c] stuff manufacturer, 10 Hartley's Buildings, Brook street; works and house Leeds road

Procter John, coal dealer, Silsbridge lane

Procter Samuel,[b c] coach and harness maker, Leeds road; house 40 Church street, Peckover Walk

Procter William, draper (Procter & Holgate); house Kirkgate

PROTESTANT DISSENTERS' AND GENERAL INSURANCE COMPANY; agent Mr. William George, solicitor, Swaine street

Proud William, tailor, 32 Park street

Pullan Joseph,[b c] ale and porter brewer (Fountain Brewery), Manchester road; house Great Horton road

Pullan William,[b] schoolmaster, Great Horton

Pulman Samuel,[c] cloth-presser and finisher, flock dealer, &c. 18 James' street, Northgate

Punt William, coal dealer and shoe maker, 202 Bolton road

Pye Reuben, hair dresser, Leeds road

Pyrah Joseph, cabinet maker, Great Horton road

Pyrah Maria, dress maker, 37 Providence street, White Abbey

Pyrah William,[c] Bolton road

QUINSEY Mary, new and second hand clothes dealer, 36 Ivegate

Quitzow Augustus, merchant (Quitzow, Schlesinger & Co.); house Melbourne place, Little Horton lane

Quitzow, Schlesinger & Co. yarn merchants, Bermondsey

RABY Benjamin, toll bar keeper, Little Horton lane

RAILWAY COMPANIES, PASSENGERS' STATIONS AND WAREHOUSES—[For directors, engineers, &c. see "Public Buildings and Offices"]

Lancashire and Yorkshire—Passengers' New Station on the Leeds and Wakefield roads; Goods' warehouse Vicar lane

Midland Counties—Bradford & Leeds, &c.—Passengers' Station bottom of Kirkgate; Goods' warehouse, Railroad street, Canal road

Raine Thomas, worsted spinner, Spence's Mill, Chapel lane; house 28 Jonasgate, Manchester road

Raistrick James, tailor, 232 Manchester road

Ramsbottom Henry Robert,[b c] manufacturer (John Rand & Sons); house Legrams lane

Ramsden David,[b c] merchant (Thornton, Firth, Ramsden & Co.); house Sawrey place, Little Horton lane

Ramsden Henry,[b] dentist, 29 Darley street

Ramsden Jabez,[b] farmer, High street, Great Horton

Ramsden John,[b c] reed and heald manufacturer, WATERLOO MILL, Brook street; house North Parade

Ramsden J. & Co. stuff manufacturers, Waterloo Mill, Charles street, Brook street

Ramsden Joseph, coal dealer, Wood street, Manningham

Ramsden Joseph,[b c] joiner and timber merchant, High street, Great Horton

Ramsden Mrs. Mary, Westgrove st.

Ramsden Mary Ann, milliner and straw bonnet maker, 2 Nelson court, Nelson street

Ramsden Thomas,[b c] wheelwright, High street, Great Horton

Ramsay James,[c] Portland street

Rand John,[b c] manufacturer (John Rand & Sons); house Whetley Hill, Manningham

Rand John & Sons, worsted spinners and manufacturers, 22 Nag's Head Yard, Kirkgate; works Horton lane

Rand William,[b c] spinner (John Rand and Sons) house Horton lane

Randall Rev. F. A. M. incumbent of Eccleshill

Randall Thomas,[b] farmer, Undercliffe

Raper Joseph,[b] druggist and grocer, 175 Bridge street

Rastrick James,[c] provision dealer, 80 Bolton road

Rastrick Martha, provision dealer, 29 Croft street, Leeds road

Ratcliffe James, manufacturer (James Ratcliffe & Son); house Ovenden, near Halifax

Ratcliffe James & Son, stuff manufacturers, Charles street; works Ovenden, near Halifax

Ratcliffe John, provision dealer, Badger's square, Bowling

Ratcliffe John,[b] butcher, 7 Bridge st.

Ratcliffe Thomas, engraver (Thomas Ratcliffe & Co.); house Ebor st.

Ratcliffe Thomas & Co. engravers, lithographers, and pattern-card makers, Butterworth's Buildings, Ivegate

Rathmell Miss Mary, Melbourne place

Raw John, road surveyor, Spinkwell terrace, Bolton road

Raw John,[c] Richmond street

Raw Thomas, clog and patten maker, 164 Manchester road; house Bowling lane

Rawling William, maker of the Whitworth red bottle, 79 Providence street, White Abbey

Rawnsley Frederick, chemist and druggist, 16 White Abbey

Rawnsley John,[b c] currier, gutta percha dealer, and leather cutter, 35 Market street; house Salem street

Rawnsley Mrs. dress maker, 17 Peel street, Northwing

Rawson, Clayton & Cousen (Bradford and Calverley Colliery), Bunker's Hill; office 3 Market street, Mr. Isaac Clayton agent

Rawson & George, solicitors; John Rawson town clerk, and clerk to the borough magistrates; agents for the South Lancashire Building Association; William George agent for the Protestant Dissenters' and General Assurance Company; offices Swaine street, Hall Ings

Rawson Henry,[b] Westgrove street

Rawson John, cotton spinner (Sutcliffe & Rawson); house Westgrove street

Rawson John,[b c] solicitor (Rawson and George); house Ashfield place, Great Horton road

Rawson Mark,[c] John street, Stott Hill

Rawson Mr. T. W. Duckworth lane, Manningham

Rawson William Henry, coal merchant (Rawson, Clayton & Cousen); house Sowerby Bridge

Rawsthorne Mr. Walker,[b] Westbrook place, Horton

Rawsthorne William, architect and land surveyor, North Parade; house Westbrook place, Horton

Ray Sarah, milliner and dress maker, 40 Adelaide street, Manchester rd.

Rayner Edward, provision dealer, 35 Portland street, Manchester road

Rayner Edward,[c] Well Close, Great Horton

Rayner Joseph, blacksmith, 17 Mill street, Canal road

Rayner Moses,[c] Bowling

Rayner Richard,[c] Dunkhill, Idle

Raynes William, boot and shoe maker, 10 Market street; house Stone street, Manor row

Read Henry,[b c] ironmonger, brazier, and tin and iron-plate worker, 29 Market street; house Sawrey place, Little Horton lane

Read John,[c] North street, Stott Hill

Read Joseph,[b c] joiner, Fitzgereld st. Manchester road; house Sawrey place, Little Horton lane

Reaney James,[b] ale and porter dealer, and registrar of births and deaths for Horton and Manningham districts, 6 James' street, Westgate; house Great Horton road

Reaney Margaret, *George Hotel* and posting house, Market street

Reese Charles,[b] Chapel court, Kirkgate

REFORM CLUB NEWS AND READING ROOMS, 4 Bridge street; William German secretary

REGISTRARS OF BIRTHS AND DEATHS &c. under the New Act—*See* "Public Buildings and Offices"

RELIEVING OFFICERS: *Bradford East District*—Jonas Booth; office Charles street—*Bradford West and Manningham* —Amos Bairstow; office Lumb lane—*Horton and Bowling*—Jonas Jennings; office Hall lane, Bowling

Rendle Thomas, machine and furniture broker Ivegate, and beer retailer, 260 Manchester road

Rennard Ambrose,[b] tailor and draper, 27 Victoria street, North Parade

Rennards Thomas,[b] stuff merchant, Union street, Bridge street; house Spring gardens

Rennie, Tetley & Co. stuff merchants, Leeds road

Renton James, watch and clock maker, jeweller, &c. 16 Well street; house 28 Victoria street, North Parade

Renton Thomas,[b c] woolstapler, 9 Well street; house 4 Bellevue, Manningham lane

Renwick William, fruit dealer, 37 Darley street; house 26 Providence street, Westgate

Reuss, Kling & Co. stuff merchants, Colliergate, Hall Ings; manager Mr. G. Kerstein

Revell Elizabeth, milliner and dress maker, 324 Bowling lane, Manchester road

Revell Emanuel, boot and shoe maker, 51 Chandos street, Wakefield road

Reynard Marmaduke,[c] Great Horton

Reynolds Ann, *Unicorn Inn*, Ivegate

Reynolds Benjamin, rope and twine manufacturer, Bradford Moor

Reynolds Patrick, tailor, Regent st. Manningham

Reynolds William,[b c] Stott Hill

Rhodes Ann, milliner and bonnet maker, 120 Westgate

Rhodes Ann & Mary, milliners and

dress makers, 66 Greenaire place, Silsbridge lane

Rhodes Benjamin,[c] stuff manufacturer, 108 Old Piecehall; works and house Heaton

Rhodes Charles,[c] wireworker (Henry and Charles Rhodes); house Greenhill place, Manningham

Rhodes Charles,[b] earthenware, china, glass and toy warehouse, and painter, gilder and paper hanger, 2 Cheapside; house 112 Westgate

Rhodes Charles,[c] Lidget green, Horton

Rhodes Francis,[c] North Bierley

Rhodes Henry, general wireworker (Henry & Charles Rhodes); house Hope street, Manchester road

Rhodes Henry & Charles, general wireworkers, Toad lane, Bridge st.

Rhodes Isaac,[b,c] butcher, Skinner lane, Manningham

Rhodes James[b,c] timber merchant, packing case, and making-up board manufacturer, Wharf street, Bolton road; house adjoining

Rhodes James,[b,c] saddler and harness maker, Well street

Rhodes James,[b] decorative painter, carver, gilder and paper hanger, Chapel court, Kirkgate; house 78 Victoria street, North Parade

Rhodes John,[b] stone mason, Legrams lane, Horton

Rhodes John, agent for grey goods, canvas, paper, &c. 22 Nag's Head Yard, Kirkgate; house 26 Westgrove street

Rhodes John, coach builder, Bray's Yard, Leeds road

Rhodes John,[b,c] furnishing ironmonger, 18 Kirkgate; house Victoria street, North Parade

Rhodes John, woolstapler, Ship Alley, Well street

Rhodes John, quarry owner, Legrams lane

Rhodes John,[b] jun. woolstapler (John and Joseph Rhodes); res. Broad Lane House, Pudsey

Rhodes John & Joseph, juniors, woolstaplers, Brook street

Rhodes Joseph, jun. woolstapler (Jno. and Joseph Rhodes); house Well street

Rhodes Joseph & Son, curriers, leather cutters, and gutta percha dealers, 18 Well street

Rhodes Joseph,[b,c] currier (Joseph Rhodes & Son); house Well street

Rhodes Joseph,[c] Little Horton

Rhodes Manoah,[b,c] working jeweller, gold and silversmith, cutler, optician, and watch and clock maker, 6 Westgate

Rhodes Moses,[c] Providence street, White Abbey

Rhodes Mrs. Mercy, Black Abbey

Rhodes Paul, *Nelson Inn*, Northgate

Rhodes Thomas,[b] provision dealer, 2 Providence street, White Abbey

Rhodes Timothy,[b,c] *Ship Inn*, 12 Well street

Rhodes Mr. William,[b] Darley street

Rhodes William,[b] currier (Joseph Rhodes & Son); house High street

Rhodes William, general wire worker, 11 Northgate

Rhodes William,[c] whitesmith, bellhanger, scale-beam maker, &c. Thornton road and 99 Westgate

Rhodes William,[b] tailor, 153 Bridge street

Rhodes William,[c] Four Lane Ends, Manningham

Rhodes William, butcher, 43 High street

Rhodes William, cab and hackney coach proprietor, Quebec Terrace, Thornton road

Rich Miss Ann, Fountain street, Manningham lane

Richards Rev. John,[c] M.A. head master of Grammar School, Manor row

Richardson Benjamin, boot and shoe maker, 68 Bolton road

Richardson Francis (late Wells), wine and spirit merchant, 120 Westgate

Richardson Henry, whitesmith, scale-beam maker, &c. 5 Bedford street, Wakefield road

Richardson Joseph, portrait painter and teacher of drawing, Canal Terrace, Bolton road

Ridehalgh Richard,[bc] solicitor (Wells & Ridehalgh); house Belvedere, Manningham lane

Ridehough John, beer retailer, 4 Toad lane, Bridge street

Ridings Edwin, worsted spinner, Charles street; works CannonMill, Great Horton; house Lower Springhead, Clayton

Ridley George,[b] plumber, glazier and gas fitter, 19 Westgate

Ridsdale George Wilson, engraver,&c. Belgrave place, Manningham

Rieckmann J. F. manager (Emanuel and Son); house Manningham la.

Rigg James, [b] stuff manufacturer, New Piecehall; works Marsh Hill Mill, Manchester road; house St. James' square

Rigg Martha, dress and bonnet maker, Sterling street, Manchester road

Rigg Samuel,[b] stuff manufacturer, Sterling street, Manchester road

Riley Alexander, boot and shoe maker, Little Horton

Riley Francis,[b] provision dealer, Uppercroft row, Bowling

Riley James,[b] provision dealer, Back lane, Bowling

Riley James, baker and flour dealer, Sterling street, Manchester road

Riley John,[b] provision dealer, 39 Melbourne street, Leeds road

Riley John, clog and patten maker, 109 Brick lane

Riley John,[c] High Spring street, Manningham

Riley Matthew, auctioneer, 2 Keighley Old road, Manningham

Riley Thomas, Preston place, Horton

Rimmington Felix Marsh,[b] dispensing chemist and druggist, 6 Ivegate; house Eastbrook terrace

Ripley Edward,[b] dyer (Edward Ripley & Son); house Bowling Lodge

Ripley Edward & Son, dyers, Bowling Old Dyehouse, Bowling

Ripley Henry William,[b] dyer (Edward Ripley & Son); house Lightcliffe, Halifax

Ripley James,[b] cab and coach proprietor, 178 Bridge street

Ripley Mary, worm medicines, 178 Bridge street

Ripley William,[b] grocer and provision dealer, 8 North street, Northwing

Rishworth Henry, worsted spinner and manufacturer, 13 Hartley's Buildings, Brook street; works Castle Mill, Keighley; residence Croft House, Keighley

ROADS' NUISANCE OFFICE, Police Station, Swaine street; William Bakes inspector

Roberton Alexander, stuff finisher, (Lowden & Robertons); house Tumblinghill street, Thornton road

Roberton George, stuff finisher (Lowden & Robertons); ho. Walmsley's Buildings, Tetley Row

Roberts Abednego,[c] Laister Dyke

Roberts Benjamin, cutler and surgical instrument maker, 5 Darley street; house Darley street

Roberts Benjamin,[b] grocer and provision dealer, 308 Leeds road

Roberts Benjamin,[b] surgeon-dentist, 42 Darley street

Roberts Elizabeth, schoolmistress, Great Horton road

Roberts George, agent to Edward Cotton, Westgate; ho. Drewton st.

Roberts Henry,[b] worsted spinner and manufacturer; Bank street; works and house Bailiff Bridge

Roberts James,[b c] spinner and manufacturer, Charles street; works Uppercroft Mill, Bowling; house Laister Dyke

Roberts James,[c] Cropper lane

Roberts John, supervisor of inland revenue (excise branch), 24 Victoria street, North Parade

Roberts John, grocer and tea dealer, 25 Westgate

Roberts John,[b] accountant and agent, 11 Harris street, Leeds road

Roberts John Walker,[b] surgeon, 9 Rawson place, Darley street

Roberts Jonathan,[c] provision dealer, 106 Victoria street, Thornton road

Roberts Joseph,[b c] *Farm Yard Inn*, Back lane

Roberts Joseph,[b c] grocer, tea dealer and hop merchant, 50 Westgate

Roberts Joshua, stuff finisher, Keighley street, Silsbridge lane; house Regent place, Duke street

Roberts Joshua, London and Dublin porter merchant, and dealer in Scotch and Burton ales, 5 Manor row; house Regent place

Roberts Richard,[c] Low fold, Back lane

Roberts Thomas, clog and patten maker, 26 Well street; house High street

Roberts William, beer retailer, Bradford Moor

Roberts William, beer retailer, Broomfield, Wakefield road

Roberts William, woollen cloth manufacturer, Bradford Moor

Roberts William,[c] Pit lane, Barkerend

Robertshaw Ann, straw bonnet maker, Mortimer row, Bradford Moor

Robertshaw Isaac, moreen manufacturer, 142 Old Piecehall; works and house Allerton

Robertshaw James, stuff manufacturer, George Hotel Yard, Brook street; works and house Allerton

Robertshaw Jeremiah,[b] woolstapler (Aked & Robertshaw); house Stone street, Manor row

Robertshaw Job,[b] butcher, Southgate, Great Horton

Robertshaw John,[b] Back lane, Bowling

Robertshaw John, provision dealer, Belgrave place, Manningham

Robertshaw John, provision dealer, Southgate, Great Horton

Robertshaw Joseph,[b] Stone street, Manor row

Robertshaw Joseph, provision dealer, Belgrave place, Manningham

Robertshaw Joshua, land valuer and provision dealer, 77 Silsbridge lane

Robertshaw Jonathan,[c] Crag lane, Horton

Robertshaw Thomas,[b c] Peel street

Robertshaw William,[b c] Cross street, School street

Robinson Charles, beer retailer, 67 York street, Bridge street

Robinson Charles, stuff manufacturer, 22 Nag's Head Yard, Kirkgate; works Spence's Mill, Chapel lane; house York street, Wakefield road

Robinson Dan,[b] carver and gilder, printseller, artists' oil and colourman, barometers, &c. 20 Well street

Robinson Esther, provision dealer, Sticker lane, Bowling

Robinson Francis, smith and farrier, 240 Wakefield road; house Paper Hall, Northwing

Robinson Israel,[c] York street, Bridge street

Robinson James, spinner, (James (Robinson & Co.); house Thornton road

Robinson James & Co. worsted spinners, Phœnix Mill, Thornton road

Robinson John, beer retailer, Spink place, Black Abbey

Robinson John, provision dealer, Little Horton

Robinson John Thomas, dealer in noils and short wool, 4 Commercial street, Canal road; house Hanover square

Robinson Jonas, professor of music, Greenaire place, Westgate

Robinson Joseph, clogger, Wakefield road

Robinson Joseph,[c] stuff manufacturer and agent for silk and cotton yarn and stuff goods, Old Market place; house Clayton

Robinson Joseph,[c] stuff manufacturer, 22 Nag's Head Yard, Kirkgate; works Spence's Mill, Chapel lane; house York street, Wakefield road

Robinson Josiah, provision dealer, Greenhill place, Manningham

Robinson Lund, chemist and druggist, 83 High street

Robinson Michael, cabinet maker, Smith street, Manchester road

Robinson Ralph, tailor, 60 Manchester road

Robinson Thomas, tailor, 13 Albion court, Kirkgate

Robinson William,[b] worsted spinner and manufacturer, 31 Bank street; works and house Keighley

Robinson William,[b c] travelling tea dealer, Regent place, Duke street

Robinson William, chemist and druggist, 2 Silsbridge lane

Robson John,[b] provision dealer, 74 George street, Leeds road

Robson John,[b c] provision dealer, 7 Wakefield road

Robson John Lawty, school, Lumb lane, Manningham

Robson William, beer retailer, 33 Wellington street, Stott Hill

Rochfort Valentine,[b c] wool broker, hosier, and wholesale stay manufacturer, &c. 17 Union Passage, Kirkgate; house adjoining

Rodley John,[b] beer retailer, 13 George street, Leeds road

Roe Benjamin,[c] Prospect street, Silsbridge lane

Roe Martha, straw bonnet maker, Arcadia street, Manningham

Roe Simeon, provision dealer, 103 Westgate

Rogers George,[b c] worsted spinner, and manufacturer of stuffs, coburgs,

&c. also agent for the Scottish (Widows' Fund) Assurance Society, Charles street; works BEEHIVE MILL, Thornton road; house Manor row

Rogerson John, merchant (Rogerson & Thackray); house London

Rogerson Michael,[b] chemist and druggist, 2 Darley street, and 31 & 33 North Parade; house Park place

Rogerson & Thackray, stone merchants; wharf and office Canal road

Rooks George,[b] grocer and provision dealer, 9 and 11 Broadstones

Roper Charles,[c] Daisy lane, Manningham

Roper John,[b c] Sawrey place, Little Horton lane

Rose Rev. Henry (Baptist), 25 Westgrove street

Rosse, the Right Hon. the Earl of, Heaton Hall

Rothwell Benjamin, plasterer, colourer, &c. Wakefield road

Rouse Mr. David,[b c] Manor place, Manor row

Rouse Francis,[b c] Esq. Belvedere, Mannningham lane

Rouse Mrs. Mary, Manor row

Rouse William,[b c] manufacturer (Wm. Rouse & Co.); house West Lodge, Horton

Rouse William & Co. worsted spinners and manufacturers, Market street; works BRADFORD MILLS, Canal road

Routh Mrs. straw bonnet maker, 29 Gaunt street, Otley road

Rowbotham Henry,[c] brazier, John street

Rowbotham John, brazier and tinplate worker, 113 Bridge street

Rowntree Isaac,[b] grocer, and corn, flour & provision dealer, 146 Manchester road

Rowntree Thomas, tailor, 1 Burnley Fold, Black Abbey

Rowntree Thomas, jun. tailor, 3 Saltpie street, Black Abbey

Rowntree William, tailor, York street, Bridge street

Rowsby John,[b c] Mount street, Leeds road

ROYAL EXCHANGE ASSURANCE COMPANY; agents Mr. Alfred Sussman, Court street, Leeds road, and Mr. C. Woodcock, 4 Bridge street

Rudd Jeremiah, *Four Ashes Inn*, High street, Great Horton

Rudd Jeremiah, wool and waste dealer, High street, Great Horton

Rudd John, *King's Arms Inn*, High street, Great Horton

Rudd John, butcher, High street, Great Horton

Rudd Robert,[b c] general and furnishing ironmonger, 35 Kirkgate

Ruddock Edward Harris, marble mason and sculptor, Leeds road; house 85 Otley road

Ruddock Joseph, cattle dealer and butcher, Belgrave place, Manningham

Rusby Richard, provision dealer, Little Horton

Rushton George, provision dealer, Belgrave place, Manningham

Rushworth John,[b] Garnet street, Leeds road

Rushworth Jonas, provision dealer, Park square, Manningham

Rushworth Joseph Taylor, woolstapler, 1 Well street; house Victoria street, North Parade

Rushworth Mary, milliner and dress maker, 40 Garnett street, Leeds road

Rushworth John,[c] Garnett street, Leeds road

Rushworth William, provision dealer, 3 Queen street, White Abbey

Russell, Douglas & Co. stuff merchants, Leeds road

Russell John,[b c] merchant (Russell, Douglas & Co.); house Horton Grange

Russell Joseph, draper and stuff merchant, 8 Bank street; house Oak place, Edgbaston, Birmingham

Russell Joshua, provision dealer, 80 Northwing, High street

Russell Mary, beer retailer, 82 Northwing, High street

Russell Peter,[b] linen draper, hosiery and shawl warehouse, 56 Kirkgate

Rycroft John,[c] Tumblinghill street, Thornton road

Rycroft Mary, dress and bonnet maker, Little Horton lane

Ryland Rev. John Howard (Unitarian), Hanover square

SAALFELD A. S. & Co. (present firm Heymann & Alexander), stuff and yarn merchants, Charles street, Hall Ings

SABBATH OBSERVANCE SOCIETY; Rev. William Morgan secretary

Sadler James, pork butcher, 5 Kirkgate

Sadler James,[b] *Ram's Head Inn*, Silsbridge lane

Sagar Henry,[b c] grocer and tea dealer, 5 Broadstones

Sagar John, hair dresser, 86 Manchester road

Sagar John, butcher, Melville street, Great Horton

Sagar John, fent dealer, 1 Croft st. Bridge street

Sagar Joseph,[b] Galloway Farm, Bowling

Sagar Robert,[b] Spring row, Manningham

Sagar Samuel,[b] provision dealer, White Abbey

Sagar Stephen,[b] butcher, Belgrave place, Manningham

Sagar Tubal, engineer, and agent for Messrs. W. & C. Mathers (of Manchester) patent metallic pistons, 56 Longcroft place, Westgate

Sagar William, potato dealer, 49 Duke street, Manchester road

Salt Titus,[bc] spinner (mohair and alpaca), and stuff manufacturer, Brook street; works Union street, and Silsbridge lane; house Crow Nest, Lightcliffe

Samson & Leppoc, stuff merchants, Hall Ings; manager Mr. Anton Engelmann

Sanderson George,[b] provision dealer and beer retailer, Lidget green

Sargeant John, schoolmaster, Preston place, Great Horton

Saunders Edward, printers' joiner, and wood type cutter, Prospect st. Silsbridge lane

Saunders Moses,[c] Bridge House, Haworth

Savage William,[b] chemist and druggist, and district post, 113 Westgate

Saville John,[b c] Clayton place, Pitlane

Saville Jonas,[c] provision dealer 135 Crown street, Brick lane

SAVINGS' BANK (East Morley and Bradford), Kirkgate; Mr. Thomas Haigh actuary

Saxton Lot,[b] St. James' square

Scaife John, hackney coach proprietor, Quebec terrace, Thornton road

Scaife William, coach proprietor (Holt and Scaife); house West street, Vicar lane

Scaife George,[b] Abraham gate, Manchester road

Scarf & Hanson, stuff and blanket merchants, Hall Ings

Scarf Thomas Wilkinson, merchant (Scarf & Hanson); house Summerseat place, Horton road

Scarlett Samuel Wharton,[b] letterpress printer, King's court, Northgate

Schafer John Henry & Co. importers of foreign wool, Hustler's Buildings, Market street; house Brunswick place

Schlesinger Andrew, merchant (Quitzow, Schlesinger & Co.); house Springfield place, Manningham lane

Schlesinger Julius, merchant (Steinthal & Co.); house Stone street, Manor row

Schlesinger Martin, manufacturer (A. Tremel & Co.); res. Whetley House, Manningham

Schofield John, joiner, Great Horton

Scholefield Ann Martha, milliner and bonnet maker, 52 Fitzgerald street, Manchester road

Scholefield James, schoolmaster, Regent street, White Abbey

Scholefield John, *Royal Engineer Inn*, Dudley Hill

Scholefield John, joiner, Low green, Great Horton

Scholefield Joseph, merchant (Thorpe, Scholefield & Co.); house Mill lane, Bowling

Scholefield Michael, boot and shoe maker, Back lane, Bowling

Scholefield Richard Mortimer,[b c] share broker, Market street; house Hanover square

Scholefield William Freer, woolstapler, 8 Duke street and 2 Mill Hill, Leeds

Scholefield William,[b c] *Black Swan Inn*, Thornton road

Scholey Mary Ann, milliner and dress maker, 83 Westgrove street

Scholey Stephen, linen draper, Thornton road

Schonfeld Michael, stuff merchant, Hall Ings; house Park place

School of Industry, Northgate, Miss Elizabeth Piper, superintendent

Schunk, Souchay & Co. stuff and yarn merchants, Brook street; Mr C. Lockwood manager

Schuster Leo,[c] merchant (Leo Schuster Brothers & Co.); house Penge place, Sydenham, Kent

Schuster Leo Brothers & Co. stuff merchants, Charles street, Hall Ings and Manchester

Schwann Frederick, stuff merchant, Booth street, Hall Ings

Scott John,[b] Hardcastle field, Horton

Scott Patience, provision dealer, Southgate, Great Horton

Scott Rev. Walter,[c] theological tutor, Airedale Independent College, Otley road

Scott Walter,[c] jun. Airedale College, Otley road

Scott William, smith and farrier, Church bank, Well street

Scott William, clogger, 314 Mount Leeds road

Scottish Equitable Assurance Company; agent Mr. C. Heron, Old Bank, Kirkgate

SCOTTISH PROVIDENT INSTITUTION; agent Mr. T. M. Pearce, Messrs. Walkers', Bridge street

SCOTTISH UNION FIRE AND LIFE INSURANCE COMPANY; agent Mr. J. Cooke, 38 Bank street

SCOTTISH (WIDOWS' FUND) LIFE ASSURANCE COMPANY; agent Mr. C. Rogers, Charles street

Scully Ambrose,[b] furnishing ironmonger and cutler, 7 Ivegate; house Nelson square, Great Horton

Sedgwick Ellen, beer retailer, 42 Westend street, Silsbridge lane

Sedgwick John, cabinet maker and wood turner, Nelson street; house King street, Manchester road

Sedgwick Robert, cabinet maker and wood turner, King street

Sedgwick William, colourer, School court, Northwing

Seed Anne, milliner and straw bonnet maker, 94 Westgate

Seed Edward,[b] currier and leather cutter, Well street; house Vicar la.

Selby Samuel,[b] commission agent and share broker, Cheapside; house Hanover square

Selix Ulas, steward of Union Club, Manor row

Sellers Ann, straw bonnet maker, 162 George street, Leeds road

Sellers George, butcher, Dudley Hill

Sellers Eli, boot and shoe maker, 19 Tumblinghill street, Thornton road

Sellers John, cabinet maker, paper hanger and undertaker, 162 George street, Leeds road

Sellers John,[c] Bridge street

Semon Charles, stuff merchant (Semon, Siltzer & Co.); house Springfield place, Manningham lane

Semon Mrs. Mary Ann, Sawrey place, Little Horton lane

Semon, Siltzer & Co. stuff merchants, 76 Tyrrel street

Senier George & Co. chemists and druggists, 15 Westgate

Senior John,[b c] pawnbroker, 14 Darley street; house Belle Vue, Manningham lane

Senior John,[b] Wakefield road

Senior Mary, straw bonnet maker, Church hill, Wakefield road

Settle Abraham, boot and shoe maker, Four-lane Ends, Manningham

Settle Samuel Ellick,[b] provision dealer, West Parade, Manningham

Sewell Christopher,[b c] watch and clock maker, 37 Westgate

Sewell William, beer retailer, 6 Bedford street, Manchester road

Seymour William, provision dealer, Bradford Moor

Shackleton Ann and Mary, milliners and straw bonnet makers, 2 Tyrrel street

Shackleton Benjamin, hair dresser, eating house keeper, and beer retailer, Bowergate, Chapel lane

Shackleton Benjamin,[c] Great Horton road

Shackleton Benjamin,[c] High street, Great Horton

Shackleton Betty, milliner and dress maker, 183 Manchester road

Shackleton Ellis, hair dresser, 15 Providence street, Westgate

Shackleton Hannah, straw bonnet maker, 34 Westgate

Shackleton Isaac,[b] Millbank

Shackleton James,[b] woolstapler, School street, Manor row; house Victoria street, North Parade

Shackleton James,[c] Prospect row, Silsbridge lane
Shackleton James,[c] Manchester road
Shackleton John, linen draper, Southgate, Great Horton
Shackleton Joseph, furniture broker, Longcroft place, Westgate
Shackleton Robert,[b c] *Fleece Inn*, Bank street and Hustlergate
Shackleton Samuel,[c] Pickles Hill, Horton
Shackleton Thomas,[b] boot and shoe maker, Holmetop, Little Horton
Shackleton Thomas, provision dealer, Great Horton road
Shackleton William,[b] ironmonger, brazier and tinman, 23 Broadstones
Shackleton William,[b] Piecehall keeper, Piecehall Yard, Kirkgate
Shann Mr. James,[b] Hanover square
Sharman Jonathan,[c] Shipley
Sharman William,[c] Bolton road
Sharp Abraham, joiner and furniture broker, 20 Sedgwick street, White Abbey
Sharp Daniel,[b] farmer, Brownroyd, Horton
Sharp David Wilkinson,[b] worsted spinner and manufacturer, 24 Exchange street, Kirkgate; works and house Bingley
Sharp Frederick, beer retailer, 24 White Abbey
Sharp Henry, furniture broker, Wakefield road
Sharp James,[b] farmer, Sticker lane
Sharp James, worm medicines, Croft street, Manchester road
Sharp James, provision dealer, 10 Chain street, Silsbridge lane
Sharp James, coal agent, Darley st
Sharp John,[b c] chemist and druggist, 75 Westgate and White Abbey
Sharp John, jacquard machine and shuttle maker, Victoria Mill, Bowling; house 174 Wakefield road
Sharp John,[b c] Birks Hall
Sharp John,[b] farmer, Rooley, Bowling
Sharp Jonas, worsted spinner and manufacturer, Brook street; works and house Bingley
Sharp Joshua,[bc] grocer and tea dealer, Wakefield road
Sharp Mary, dress and bonnet maker, Primrose terrace, Manningham
Sharp Misses, milliners and straw bonnet makers, 6 Darley street
Sharp Mungo, boot and shoe maker, 43 George street, Manchester road
Sharp Samuel, tailor, 10 Longlands street, Westgate
Sharp Simon, draper and grocer, Green lane, Manningham
Sharp Simon, Manchester road
Sharpe Squire,[b c] butcher, 29 and 31 Milk street, Manchester road
Sharp Squire,[b] provision dealer, 291 Manchester road
Sharp Thomas, provision dealer, 254 Manchester road
Sharp William,[b] farmer, Brownroyd, Horton
Sharp William, provision dealer, Silsbridge lane
Sharp William, provision and flour dealer, Broadstones
Sharp William,[b] provision dealer, School street, Cheapside
Sharp William, hair dresser, Wakefield road
Shaw Abraham, joiner (Shaw and Neal); house William street, Little Horton lane
Shaw Benjamin, spinner (Shaw and Mitchell); house York street.

Shaw Edward, provision dealer, 9 Wellesley street, North street

Shaw Isaac,[c] Arundel street, Manchester road

Shaw John, linen draper, hosier, &c. 97 Manchester road

Shaw Martha, dress maker, Bradford Moor

Shaw & Mitchell, worsted spinners, Northholme Mill, Leeming street, Canal road

Shaw and Neal, joiners and builders, Arundel street, Manchester road

Shaw William, draper, hosier, &c. 44 Vicar lane

Shaw William,[b] grocer and tea dealer, Southfield place, Lumb lane

Shaw William, butcher, 129 Bridge street

Shaw William, grocer and provision dealer, Wakefield road

Shaw William, *Lister's Arms Inn*, Manchester road

Shaw William, tailor, Little Horton

Shaw William,[b,c] farmer, Thornton lane, Horton

Shaw William,[b] provision dealer, Bazaar, and Smiddles lane, Bowling

Sheard John, tailor, Spring street, Wharf street

SHEFFIELD ASSURANCE COMPANY; E. H. Parratt agent, 1 Broadstones

Shephard Abraham, spinner (Smith & Shephard); house Tumbling-hill street, Thornton road

Shepard George Hollins, milk dealer, 29 Bedford street, Wakefield road

Shephard John, manufacturer (Mc Crea & Shephard); house Hailfax

Shepherd & Foster, woolstaplers, Swaine street, Hall Ings

Shepherd John, provision dealer, Back lane, Bowling

Shepherd Robert,[b,c] provision dealer, Southgate, Great Horton

Shepherd Samuel, [c] Pickles Hill, Horton

Shepherd William,[c] Manchester road

Shepherd William,[b,c] woolstapler, (Shepherd & Foster); house Undercliffe lane, Northwing

Sherwood Rev. William,[b,c] M.A. incumbent of St. James's, Manchester road; house St. James's square

Shields George, coal dealer, Crowther street, Manchester road

Shields Richard, coal dealer, Lumby street, Manchester road

Shires Mary, provision dealer, 13 Duke street, Darley street

Shires Mary Ann, provision dealer, 7 Nelson street, Chapel lane

Shoesmith Joseph, provision dealer, Dudley Hill

Shreeve Mary Ann, milliner and dress maker, North Parade

Shutt Hermann, stuff merchant (Emanuel & Son); house Spring gardens

Shuttleworth John, police detective officer, Swaine street

Shuttleworth William, boot and shoe maker, 13 Longcroft place, Westgate

Shuttleworth William, boot and shoe maker, 82 Silsbridge lane

Shuttleworth William, spinner (Wm. Shuttleworth & Co.); house North Bierley

Shuttleworth William & Co. worsted spinners and manufacturers, Charles street; works North Bierley

Sichel Augustus Sylvester,[c] stuff merchant, Leeds road

Sichel Silvester Emil, [c] merchant (A. S. Sichel); house Closetop, Horton

Siddall Mary Ann, straw bonnet maker, 6 George street, Leeds road

Sidney Mary, straw bonnet maker, 103 Manchester road

Silson John, provision dealer (Joseph and John Silson), Victoria street, White Abbey

Silson Jonas, earthenware dealer, 24 Silsbridge lane

Silson Joseph, earthenware dealer (Joseph & John Silson); house Baildon

Silson Joseph & John, earthenware and rag dealers, Reform street, Westgate

Silson William, provision dealer, Green lane, Manningham

Siltzer John L. merchant (Semon, Siltzer & Co.); house Cliff Cottage, Manningham

Silverwood Richard, provision dealer, 109 Providence street, White Abbey

Simonett & Freeman, ivory and box comb manufacturers, Spence's Mill, Chapel lane

Simonett John,[b] comb manufacturer (Simonett & Freeman); house Chapel street, Leeds road

Simpson Christopher, boot and shoe maker, Spring street, Bolton road

Simpson Elizabeth, linen draper, hosier, haberdasher and glover, 6 and 41 Market street; house Commercial street

Simpson George, boot and shoe maker, 2 Providence street, White Abbey

Simpson James,[b] boot and shoe maker, 76 Leeds road

Simpson John,[c] Trafalgar street, Manningham lane

Simpson John,[b] green grocer, 30 Well street; house Commercial st.

Simpson John,[c] Bower street, Manchester road

Simpson Joseph, professor and teacher of piano-forte & organ, High street

Simpson Joseph, waste dealer, Oak street, Leeds road; house Garnett street, Leeds road

Simpson Thomas,[b c] Chapel street, Leeds road

Simpson William, coal dealer, top of Park square, Manningham

Simpson William, provision dealer, Green lane, Manningham

Simpson William, coal dealer, Bradford Moor

Simpson William,[c] plasterer, Chapel-street, Leeds road

Simpson William,[c] Manchester road

Singleton William, merchant (Harrison & Singleton); house Park place, Leeds

Singleton William & Co. ale and porter brewers; office and stores Chapel lane, and Brunswick Brewery, Leeds

Skaife George,[c] Abraham gate, Bower street

Skelton Jane, milliner and dress maker, 9 Ebor street, Little Horton

Skelton John,[c] Melbourne street, Leeds road

Skirrow John,[b c] currier and leather cutter, 4 Well street, and John street, Northgate; house Westgate

Skirrow Thomas, butcher, Wakefield road

Slater Paul, boot and shoe maker, 9 Old Market; house Hope street, Manchester road

Slater Richard, Gay lane, Laister Dyke

Slatery John, tailor, Park square, Manningham

Smallpage & Son, tailors and drapers, 10 Darley street, and 3 Albion st. Leeds

Smedley Ann, milliner and dress maker, 9 Westgrove street

Smith Abraham,[b] butcher, Sticker lane, Bowling

Smith Abraham,[c] Wood street, White Abbey

Smith Abraham,[b] cooper, Darley st. and corner of Richard street, Leeds road

Smith Alfred, confectioner, 93 Westgate

Smith Benjamin, worsted spinner and manufacturer, Market street; works and house Farnhill, Kildwick

Smith & Booth, worsted spinners, Leeming Mill, bottom of Southgate

Smith Briscoe, stuff manufacturer, Market street; works and house Crosshills, near Keighley

Smith Charles, provision dealer, 170 Manchester road

Smith Christopher,[b c] pork butcher, 9 Ivegate

Smith, Clough & Co. worsted spinners and manufacturers, Brook st; works Globe Mill, Thornton road

Smith David Harris,[b c] grocer (Smith and Tuke); house Melbourne place, Little Horton lane

Smith Edward,[b c] provision dealer, George street, Leeds road

Smith Eli,[b] boot and shoe maker, 12 Nutter's Buildings, Northgate

Smith Elizabeth, shawl fringer and embroiderer, 53 Chapel lane

Smith George, stay maker, 81 Bedford street, Manchester road

Smith George,[b c] joiner, builder, and timber merchant, Thornton road; house Sawrey place, Little Horton lane

Smith George,[b] grocer, tea dealer, and coffee roaster, 2 Tyrrell street; house Great Horton road

Smith George Priestley, surgeon, Wakefield road

Smith Hannah, milliner and dress maker, 2 Sedgwick street, White Abbey

Smith Henry, boot and shoe maker, 145 George street, Leeds road

Smith Mr. Hodgson,[b c] Harris street

Smith Isaac,[c] butcher, Silsbridge la. and 64 Westgate

Smith James, worsted spinner, Pennyoaks Mill, Melbourne street, Leeds road; house Leeds road

Smith James, boot and shoe maker, Thornton street, Thornton road

Smith John,[c] Providence street, Silsbridge lane

Smith John,[b c] butcher, Four Lane Ends, Manningham

Smith John, beer retailer, 4 Silsbridge lane

Smith John,[b] beer retailer, High street

Smith John,[b] spinner (Smith and Booth); house Thornton road

Smith John,[b] beer retailer, 95 Bridge street

Smith John, coal dealer, King street, Manchester road

Smith John,[b] millwright & engineer, Albion Works, Thornton road; res. Townend house, Westgate

Smith John, provision dealer, 21 Gracechurch street, White Abbey

Smith John, boot and shoe maker, 18 Nelson court, Nelson street

Smith John,[b] locksmith, Portland st.; house Bedford street

Smith John,[b] [c] farmer, Closetop, Horton

Smith John, millwright (Thwaites & Co.); house Westgate

Smith Jonas, worsted spinner, Uppercroft Mill, Swaine green, Bowling; house Bowling

Smith Jonas,[b] [c] brazier and furnishing ironmonger, 40 Westgate

Smith Joseph,[b] spinner (Smith and Shephard); house Cropper lane

Smith Joseph, coal dealer, Foundry street, Vicar lane

Smith Joseph,[b] stay maker, 13 Darley street

Smith Joseph, manufacturer (Joseph Smith & Co.); house Dudley Hill

Smith Joseph, surveyor (Ingle and Smith); house Upper North Parade

Smith Joseph,[b] *Odd Fellows' Hall Inn*, Thornton road

Smith Joseph,[b] [c] land surveyor and agent, Thornton's Buildings, Market street; house Little Horton lane

Smith Joseph & Co. stuff manufacturers, George Hotel Yard, Brook street; works Dudley Hill

Smith Mr. Joseph,[b] [c] Tyrrel square

Smith Mr. Joshua,[b] [c] Little Horton lane

Smith Lawrence,[b] [c] farmer, Legrams lane

Smith Margaret and Isabel, dress makers, 37 Green lane, Manningham

Smith Martha, straw bonnet maker, 157 Manchester road

Smith Mary, milliner, 40 Wakefield road

Smith Mary, confectioner, 88 Westgate

Smith Michael, tailor, Great Horton road

Smith Michael, manufacturer (Michael and Samuel Smith); house Dudley Hill

Smith Michael & Samuel, stuff manufacturers, Brook street; works Dudley Hill

Smith Noah, butter factor and stuff manufacturer, 18 Old Market; house Pickles Hill, near Keighley

Smith Pollard,[b] Green lane, Manningham

Smith Prince,[c] butcher 11 Silsbridge lane

Smith Richard,[b] William street, Little Horton lane

Smith Richard,[c] Sterling street, Manchester road

Smith Robert Dixon,[b] [c] Drewton st.

Smith Ruth, beer retailer, 71 Westgate

Smith Samuel, basket and skep maker, 2 Market place, Darley street

Smith Samuel,[c] Holme top, Horton

Smith Samuel,[b] manufacturer (Michael & Samuel Smith); house Elizabeth street, Little Horton

Smith Samuel,[b] [c] dyer (Samuel Smith & Brothers); res. Field House, Horton

Smith Samuel & Brothers, general dyers, Charles street; works Great Horton

Smith & Shephard, worsted spinners, Alland's Mill, Thornton road

Smith & Speed, woolcomb makers, Westbrook terrace, Thornton road

Smith Thomas,[b] [c] dyer (Samuel Smith & Brothers); res. Croft House, Thornton road

Smith Thomas,[c] Sterling street, Manchester road

Smith Thomas, stuff manufacturer, Old Market place; works and house Crosshills, near Keighley

Smith Thomas, beer retailer, Hardcastle lane, Broadstones

Smith Thomas, whitesmith and bellhanger, Bowergate, Chapel lane

Smith Thomas, provision dealer, Thornton street, Thornton road

Smith & Tuke, grocers, tea dealers, and tallow chandlers, 37 Bridge street

Smith Mr. William,[b c] Brunswick place

Smith William,[b c] grocer and tea dealer, 40 Manchester road and 48 Westgate

Smith William, grocer, Wood street, Manningham

Smith William,[b] spinner (Smith and Clough); house Westend Buildings, Horton

Smith William, toll bar keeper, 157 Manchester road

Smith William, stuff manufacturer, Brook street; works and house Shelf, near Halifax

Smith William, butcher 35 Silsbridge lane

Smithies Abraham,[b] slater (Hill, Smithies & Nelson); house Great Horton

Smithies Benjamin,[c] Bradford Moor

Smithies Hannah, milliner and bonnet maker, Hall lane, Bowling

Smithies John,[b c] Hall lane, Bowling

Smithson John, broker, and dealer in new and old books, 218 Manchester road

Smithson Miles,[b] tobacco manufacturer (Smithson, Sugden & Co.); house 5 Regent place, Duke street

Smithson, Sugden & Co. tobacco manufacturers, 53 Westgate, and High street

Snow Nicholas Mason,[b] watch and clock maker, jeweller, &c. 24 Piece-hall Yard; house Salem street

Snow Mrs. Sarah, Snow Hill

Snow William,[b c] carver and gilder, Brunswick place

Snowden & Alderson, wool merchants, Swaine street

Snowden George,[b] merchant (William Dewhirst & Co.); house Hanover square

Snowden James,[b] Wakefield road

Snowden John,[b c] merchant (Snowden & Alderson); house Ann place, Little Horton lane

Snowden Robert,[b c] Bedford street, Bridge street

Society for Promoting Christianity among the Jews; J. Hollings, Esq. secretary

Society for the Propagation of the Gospel; Rev. John Burnett, L. L. D. president

South Lancashire Building Association; agents Messrs. Andrews & Delaunay, Hall Ings, and Rawson & George, Swaine street

Southwell Emanuel, butcher, Providence street, Silsbridge lane

Southwell John, butcher, John street, Westgate

Sowden Benjamin, butcher, 71 Bolton road

Sowden Joseph, boot and shoe maker, 25 Wharf street, Bolton road

Sowden Joseph,[b c] brazier, and iron & tinplate worker, 63 Market street; house Bolton

Sowden Joseph, provision dealer, Four Lane Ends, Manningham

Sowden Richard,[b c] Undercliffe

Sowden William,[b] provision dealer, 193 Bridge street

Sowden William,[b] Sterling street, Manchester road

Speak Jonas,[b] beer retailer, 3 Burrow street, Manchester road

Speak Paul, worsted spinner and manufacturer, 18 Hartley's Buildings, Brook street; works and house Clayton

Speed William, woolcomb maker, (Smith & Speed); house Manchester road

Speight Benjamin, provision dealer, Preston place, Great Horton

Speight John,[b] woolstapler, Bermondsey; house Eccleshill

Speight John,[c] boot and shoe maker, 34 Fitzgerald street, Manchester road

Speight Jonas,[b] file maker and beer retailer, 13 North street, Northwing

Speight William,[b c] boot and shoe maker, Vicar lane

Speight William,[bc] dyer, Preston place, Great Horton

Spence George,[b] provision dealer, Broadstones

Spence Samuel,[b] hay, straw and flour dealer, 5 Nelson street; house Chapel lane

Spencer Grace, provision dealer, 1 Spring street, Northwing

Spencer John, horse clipper, Hall Ings

Spencer John, stuff manufacturer, 50 Old Market; works and house Hainsworth, near Keighley

Spencer John,[b] Bradford Moor

Spencer John Sharp, clog and patten maker, Church steps

Spencer Mrs. dress maker, Well st.

Spencer Mrs. milliner and dress maker, 7 High street

Spencer Richard,[b] registrar of births and deaths for the East District of Bradford, Church street, High st.

Spencer Richard & Thomas, bookbinders and stationers, Broadstones

Spencer Thomas,[c] Carr House, Shelf

Spencer Thomas, butcher, 7 York st. Bridge street

Spencer William, provision dealer, Bradford Moor

Speyer Charles G. & Co. stuff merchants, Swaine street; house Westgrove street

Spiro Ferdinand, stuff manufacturer, Booth street, Hall Ings; works Westholme Mill, Thornton road; house Manningham lane

SPRINGHEAD BREWERY, Regent st. White Abbey; Clement Taylor proprietor

Spurr David,[b] Wakefield road

Spurr Emanuel,[b] Wakefield road

Spurr Nancy, silk and straw bonnet maker, Church hill, Wakefield road

STAFF OFFICERS' AND PENSIONERS' PAY OFFICE, Court House, Hall Ings; Major J. E. Orange acting officer

STAMP OFFICE, 5 Westgate; Mr. C. Stanfield sub-distributor

Standeavens Sarah, dress and bonnet maker, 1 Lumb lane, Westgate

Stanfield Charles, bookseller, printer and stationer, and agent for the Sun Fire and Life Office, 5 Westgate

Stansfield Mrs. Elizabeth, Belle Vue, Manningham lane

Stansfield Hepworth,[c] Idle Green, Idle

Stansfield John Slater,[b] miller; house Mount pleasant, Manningham

Stanley Samuel Haigh,[b] chemist and druggist, 58 Kirkgate

Stapleton Harriet, dress maker, Belgrave place, Lumb lane

Stapleton Thomas,[c] Mount street, Stott Hill

Stapleton William, tailor and draper, 230 Leeds road

STAR INSURANCE OFFICE; agents Mr. A. Sussmann, Court street, and Mr. Selby, Cheapside

Starkey Edmund, provision dealer, 22 George street, Leeds road

Starkey Edward, librarian, Mechanics' Institute; house George street

Stead & Brook, plasterers and colourers, Back Tyrrel street

Stead Charles,[b] Elizabeth street, Little Horton lane

Stead Charles,[c] Hall lane, Bowling

Stead James,[b] farmer, Bank top, Horton

Stead James, provision dealer, Keighley Old road, Manningham

Stead Mr. John,[b c] North Parade

Stead John, provision dealer, 29 Three street, Silsbridge lane

Stead John,[b] Wakefield road

Stead Jonathan,[c] stone mason, Broad street, Manor row

Stead Joseph, beer retailer, 7 Prince street, Manchester road

Stead Joseph, tailor, Bradford Moor

Stead Joseph,[b] *Brunswick Hotel*, Thornton road

Stead Joseph Hitchin,[b] boot and shoe maker, 76 Manchester road

Stead Thomas,[b c] Elizabeth street, Little Horton lane

Stead William,[b c] grocer (William Stead & Co.); house Hall lane, Bowling

Stead William & Co. grocers, tea dealers and coffee roasters, 20 Ivegate, and 56 Market street

STEAM PACKET OFFICE, Hustler's Buildings, Leeds road; agent Edward Collinson

Steel Daniel, boot and shoe maker, 31 Queen street, White Abbey

Steel Edward, boot and shoe maker, 9 Bridge street; E. C. Cooke agent

Steel George, beer retailer, 11 Wellington street, Northwing

Steel Henry, grocer and tea dealer, 99 Brick lane

Steel John,[b c] surgeon, 86 Westgate

Steel Mary Ann, straw bonnet maker, Wakefield road

Steel Sarah, *Craven Heifer Inn*, Bowling lane

Steinthal & Co. commission merchants, Booth street, Hall Ings

Steinthal Henry Michael, merchant (Steinthal & Co.); house Eldon place

Stell Ann, beer retailer, Bridge st.

Stelling Robert, tailor, 13 Bedford street, Wakefield road

Stelling Thomas,[b] furnishing ironmonger, 62 Kirkgate

Stenton William, confectioner, Wakefield road

Stephenson Benjamin, joiner (John Stephenson & Sons); house Great Horton road

Stephenson David,[b c] joiner, & land agent, Little Horton Green

Stephenson Frederick, saddler and harness maker, 14 Market street; house 33 Hanover square

Stephenson James, butcher, 2 North street, Northwing

Stephenson James, joiner (John Stephenson & Sons); house Great Horton road

Stephenson John,[b c] joiner (John Stephenson & Sons); house Horton road

Stephenson John, *Ivy Hotel*, Barkerend, High street
Stephenson John,[c] Earl street, Manchester road
Stephenson John & Sons, joiners, Great Horton road
Stephenson John, beer retailer, 21 Barkerend
Stephenson John, *Junction Inn*, Laister Dyke
Stephenson Moses,[c] joiner, Clayton lane, Manchester road
Stephenson Thomas,[b] dealer in hard and soft soaps, candles, oils, glue, &c. Charles street; house Manningham
Stephenson William,[b c] *Durham Ox Inn*, Queen street, White Abbey
Stephenson William, butcher, Queen street, White Abbey
Stephenson William, provision dealer, Little Horton
Stillings Thomas, chemist, Green row, Thornton road
Stirk George,[c] provision dealer, 48 Lumb lane
Stirk Martha, provision dealer, 1 Bower street, Manchester road
Stocks Brothers, grocers, tea dealers, and coffee roasters, 27 Ivegate
Stocks Henry,[b] grocer, tea dealer, and coffee roaster, 58 Kirkgate
Stocks James, stuff manufacturer, 12 Hartley's Buildings, Brook street; works and house Queen's Head, near Halifax
Stocks Joseph,[b] provision dealer, Southgate, Great Horton
Stoddart John, joiner (Dunn & Stoddart); house William street, Little Horton lane
Stoner Christopher, furniture broker, 154 Westgate; house Cropper la.
Stoner David,[b] joiner and builder, Church bank, Vicar lane; house Peckover Walks
Storey & Brook, woollen drapers, 37 Kirkgate
Storey James,[c] Mount street, Stott Hill
Storey John, draper (Storey and Brook); house Briggate, Leeds
Storey Thomas,[c] Longcroft place, Westgate
Stott Eli,[b] agent, iron works, Wakefield road
Stott Jeremiah, shoe maker, 33 Black Abbey
Stott Joseph, provision dealer, 37 Smith street, Manchester road
Stott Joseph Whitley,[c] Bower street, Manchester road
Stow Brothers & Co. stuff merchants, Hall Ings
Stow Matthew, merchant (Stow Brothers & Co.) house Hanover sqr. Leeds
Stow William Fenwick, merchant (Stow Brothers & Co.); house Redhall, Roundhay, near Leeds
Stowell John,[b c] farmer, Holme top, Little Horton
Stowell Squire,[b c] manufacturer, (Stowell, Sugden & Co.); house Little Horton
Stowell, Sugden & Co. stuff manufacturers, Bank street; works Holme Top Mill, Little Horton
Stoyles Jonathan, boot and shoe maker, 6 Margerison street, Cheapside
Sturges George William, ironmaster (John Sturges & Co.); house 64 Bridge street
Sturges John & Co. coal owners and iron founders, engineers, mill-

wrights, &c. (Bowling Iron Works); office and wharf Canal road, and coal staith, Manchester road

Subscription Library, Exchange Buildings, Exchange street; opens at ten and closes at four in winter, summer at five o'clock; Miss Mason librarian

Sucksmith Mr. William,[b c] Manchester road

Suddards Edward,[b] wool and waste dealer, Hope and Anchor Yard, Bank street; house Little Horton

Suddards Eli,[c] Low Green, Horton

Suddards Robert,[c] Wood street, Manningham

Suddards Samuel,[b] butcher, High street, Great Horton

Sugden Mrs. Ann, Park place

Sugden Benjamin,[b] tobacco manufacturer (Smithson, Sugden & Co.); house 2 Westgate

Sugden David,[c] Providence street, Silsbridge lane

Sugden Emma Jane, dress maker, 25 Manchester road

Sugden George, boot and shoe maker, 141 Leeds road

Sugden George,[b] (manufacturer (Stowell, Sugden & Co.); house Little Horton

Sugden George, coal and provision dealer, 3 Providence street, Silsbridge lane

Sugden James,[c] Goodmansend

Sugden James,[b c] butcher, 77 Kirkgate

Sugden James, manufacturer (Jonas Sugden & Brothers); house Dockroyd, near Keighley

Sugden John,[b c] stone mason, Upper Globe, Manningham

Sugden John, rag, bone and old iron dealer, Back Tyrrel street

Sugden John, spinner (Jonas Sugden & Brothers); house Dockroyd, near Keighley

Sugden John, spinner (William and John Sugden); res. Eastwood House, near Keighley

Sugden John,[b] woolstapler (Sugden and Webster); house Wakefield road

Sugden John, stuff manufacturer, and agent for stuff goods and worsted yarn, Brook street; works and house Dudley Hill

Sugden John,[b c] butcher, Tyrrel st. house 22 Spring Gardens

Sugden John,[b c] Goodmansend

Sugden John,[c] Garnett's Gardens, High street

Sugden John,[b] *Horse Shoes Inn*, Tyrrel street

Sugden Jonas, spinner (Jonas Sugden & Brothers); res. Oakworth House, near Keighley

Sugden Jonas & Brothers, spinners (genappe and heald yarn) and stuff manufacturers, Piecehall Yard; works Dockroyd

Sugden Joseph, woolstapler, Cheapside; house Brighouse, near Halifax

Sugden Joseph,[b c] *Bull's Head Inn*, Westgate

Sugden Mrs. Mary, North Parade

Sugden Moses,[b] *Ring O' Bells Inn*, Bolton road

Sugden Robert, manufacturer (Jonas Sugden & Brothers); res. Vale Mill, near Keighley

Sugden Samuel, joiner and builder, Dudley Hill, Bowling

Sugden Samuel, boot and shoe manufacturer, 43 Vicar lane

Sugden Thomas, stuff manufacturer, 17 Old Market; works and house Lane End, near Keighley

Sugden & Webster, woolstaplers and top makers, Hustler's Buildings, Market street

Sugden William,[c] Spring gardens, Manningham lane

Sugden William,[b] draper, hosier and haberdasher, 4 Broadstones

Sugden William, spinner (William and John Sugden); house Heaton Hall

Sugden William, *Barrack Tavern*, Bradford Moor

Sugden William,[c] Bowling lane

Sugden William and John, worsted spinners, 44 Old Market place; works Keighley

Sugden Zaccheus, provision dealer, Peel street, Leeds road

SUN FIRE AND LIFE ASSURANCE COMPANY; agent Mr. Charles Stanfield, 5 Westgate

Sunderland Simeon, provision dealer, 45 Bedford street, Wakefield road

Sunderland Thomas,[b] provision dealer, Great Horton

SUPERVISOR OF INLAND REVENUE, (Excise Branch), Mr. John Roberts, 24 Victoria street, North Parade

SURVEYORS OF THE HIGHWAYS' OFFICE, 2 Swaine street; Thomas Driver Heaton collector

Sussmann Alfred, agent for paper and packing materials, &c. Court street, Leeds road; house Park place, Manningham

Sutcliffe Aaron, provision dealer, 104 Silsbridge lane

Sutcliffe Abraham, stuff manufacturer, 106 Old Piecehall; works and house Great Horton

Sutcliffe David Lord,[c] Low Moor

Sutcliffe James, chemist and druggist, 26 Westgate

Sutcliffe John,[c] worsted spinner and manufacturer, Bank street; works and house Low Moor

Sutcliffe John, furniture broker, Leeds road; house Vicar lane

Sutcliffe John,[c] Back lane

Sutcliffe John, flour dealer, 109 Northwing

Sutcliffe John, slater (Hill & Sutcliffe); house Tumblinghill street, Thornton road

Sutcliffe John, landscape and portrait painter, over 25 Ivegate

Sutcliffe Jonas,[b] farmer, Pickles lane, Horton

Sutcliffe Jonas,[b] commission agent, Hope and Anchor Yard, Bank st.; house Cottingley

Sutcliffe Joseph,[b c] cotton spinner (Joseph & Robert Sutcliffe); house Spring gardens

Sutcliffe Joseph & Robert, cotton warp spinners and agents, Brook street; works Idle

Sutcliffe Joseph,[b] commission agent Hope and Anchor Yard, Bank st.; house Shipley

Sutcliffe Joseph,[b] farmer, Southgate, Horton

Sutcliffe Joseph,[c] North Bierley

Sutcliffe Martha, provision dealer, Little Horton lane

Sutcliffe Mary, dress maker, 7 Peel street, Northwing

Sutcliffe, Rawson & Co. cotton warp spinners, Laycock's Mill, Thornton road

Sutcliffe Robert, cotton spinner (Jos. and Robert Sutcliffe); house Idle

Sutcliffe Robert, boot and shoe maker, High street

Sutcliffe Robert, salt and whiteing dealer, 157 Leeds road

Sutcliffe Thomas,[b] Thornton lane, Little Horton

Sutcliffe Samuel, cabinet maker and upholsterer, 138 and 140 George street, Leeds road

Sutcliffe Samuel,[b] cotton spinner (Sutcliffe & Rawson); house Brunswick place

Sutcliffe Saville, provision dealer, 143 Manchester road

Sutcliffe William,[b] worsted spinner and manufacturer, Bank street; works Dudley Hill; ho. L. Horton

Sutcliffe William,[b] agent (Margerison & Sutcliffe); house Drewton street

Sutcliffe William,[b c] general dyer, Bowling New Dyehouse; house Little Horton

Sutcliffe Wilson,[b] manager (Bowling Old Dyehouse), Hall lane, Bowling

Swaine Abraham,[c] Wibsey, North Bierley

Swaine Isaac,[b] 4 Sterling street, Manchester road

Swaine Jane, milliner and dress maker, 29 Wakefield road

Swaine John,[c] Aycliffe hill, Horton

Swaine John,[b c] grocer, draper, and provision dealer, 176 North Brook street, Bolton road

Swaine John,[b] chemist and druggist, Manchester road

Swaine John Tempest,[c] Aycliffe lane, Horton

Swaine Jonathan,[b] agent (Swaine & Wilcock); house Earl street, Manchester road

Swaine Joseph,[c] Aycliffe lane, Horton

Swaine Leah, *George and Dragon*, High street, Great Horton

Swaine Richard,[c] New Road, Horton

Swaine Thomas,[b] *Black Bull Inn*, Wood street, Westgate

Swaine and Wilcock, commission agents, 40 Old Market place, Market street

Swaine William, beer retailer, Thornton road

Swaine William,[b] provision dealer, Great Horton

Swaine William,[c] Aycliffe lane, Horton

Swallow David,[b c] manager of gas works, Manor street, Manor row

Swift George, boot and shoe maker, 46 Bower street, Manchester road

Swire Samuel,[b] provision dealer, Dudley Hill, Bowling

Swithenbank John, boot and shoe maker, 31 Bedford street, Wakefield road

Swithenbank John,[b c] cork leg maker, 100 Bridge street; house Hill side Villas, Otley road

Swithenbank Mr. John,[b c] Stot Hill

Swithenbank John,[c] Shearbridge, Horton

Swithenbank Joseph, boot and shoe maker, 28 Brook street, Leeds rd.

Swithenbank Joshua, provision dealer, 17 Prospect street, Thornton road

Swithenbank Samuel, tobacconist, 3 Chapel lane; house Edward street, Wakefield road

Swithenbank Samuel, boot and shoe maker, 23 Chain street, Silsbridge lane

Swithenbank Sarah, provision dealer, 13 Broadstones

Sykes Abraham,[b] dealer in Orleans, stuffs, &c. Wakefield road

Sykes Ellen, milliner and dress maker, 253 Manchester road

Sykes George, boot and shoe maker, 524 Wakefield road

Sykes James,[b] provision dealer, Wakefield road

Sykes Joseph,[c] Northgate, Horton

Sykes Samuel, pork butcher, 87 Manchester road

Sykes Sarah, linen draper, hosier, &c. 96 Manchester road

Sykes Sarah, milliner and straw bonnet maker, 5 Vicar lane

Sykes Sarah, coal and provision dealer, 1 Chandos street, Wakefield road

Sykes Walter, watch and clock maker, Wakefield road

TAINNINGCLIFFE Benjamin, butcher, Back lane, Bowling

Talbot James, hair dresser, 58 Manchester road

Tankard Mr. Benjamin,[c] Sawrey place, Little Horton lane

Tankard Benjamin, clog and patten maker, 178 Silsbridge lane

Tankard Elizabeth, milliner and dress maker, 7 Ebor street, Little Horton lane

Tankard Mr. John,[b] [c] Manchester road

Tankard John,[b] manufacturer (Billingsley, Tankard & Co.); house Bradford Moor

Tankard Matthew, worsted spinner, Uppercroft Mill, Swaine green, Bowling; house Bowling

Tankard Joseph,[c] Holme top, Little Horton

Tankard Noah,[b] [c] Ebor street, Little Horton lane

Tate Dinah & Mary, milliners and dress makers, 14 King street, White Abbey

Tate Richard, house, sign and decorative painter and gilder, top of Darley street, ; house George st. Wakefield road

Tate Richard,[b] *Britannia Inn*, George street, Wakefield road

Tate Robert, provision dealer, Manchester road

Tatham Benjamin,[c] Thornton road

Tattersall John, plasterer and marble mason, Leeds road; house George street, Leeds road

Taylor Charles, plumber, glazier and gas fitter, Church bank, High street

Taylor Christian Henry,[b] surgeon, 12 Darley street

Taylor Clement,[b] [c] *Victoria Inn*, and Springhead Brewery, Spring row, Manningham

Taylor George,[c] Little Horton lane

Taylor Gideon,[b] provision dealer, 1 Black Abbey

Taylor James, worsted spinner, Greenwood's Mill, Portland street; house Croft street, Manchester road

Taylor James, basket maker, 38 Market street

Taylor James Somerville,[b] [c] woolstapler, and agent for cotton warps, Charles street; house Little Horton lane

Taylor John,[b] [c] manufacturer (John Taylor & Co.); house Nelson square, Horton

Taylor John, solicitor (Tolson, Clough & Taylor); house Eldon place, Manningham lane

Taylor John,[c] Green lane, Manningham

Taylor John,[c] provision dealer, Birkshall, Bowling

Taylor John & Co. stuff manufacturers and spinners, Old Market; works Fawcetholme Mill, Thornton road

Taylor Joseph,[c] provision dealer, Church street, High street

Taylor Joseph (late Fisher), ale and porter dealer, Brook street

Taylor Mr. Joshua,[b c] Bellevue, Manningham lane

Taylor Martha, hair dresser and perfumer, tobacconist and toy dealer, 11 and 13 Bridge street

Taylor Mrs. Mary, boarding and day school, Bellevue, Manningham la.

Taylor Mrs. Mary, Spring gardens

Taylor Peter, flour dealer, 226 Leeds road

Taylor Phillip, corn and flour dealer, 61 Manchester road

Taylor Richard, cooper, 23 Hustlergate

Taylor Richard Goodchild, provision dealer, Cannon street, Cheapside

Taylor Rev. Thomas,[b] (Independent) Little Horton lane

Taylor Thomas, provision dealer, 81 Otley road

Taylor Thomas, joiner and builder, Salem street, Manor row; house Salem street

Taylor Thomas, provision dealer, 38 Thornton street, Thornton road

Taylor Thomas, hair dresser, 86 Silsbridge lane

Taylor Thomas,[b] tea and fruit gardens, nursery and seedsman, Manningham lane

Taylor Thomas & Sons, worsted spinners and manufacturers, Old Pieceball; works and house Hey Mill, near Halifax

Taylor William,[b] M.D. Eldon place

Teal John, hair dresser, Back lane, Bowling

Teal Mrs. Martha, Leeds road

Teasdale John, boot and shoe maker, 42 Thornton road

Tee Samuel Laycock,[b] Westbrook House, Horton road

TEMPERANCE HALL (for public meetings, soirees, festivals, &c.), Chapel street, Leeds road

TEMPERANCE (TEETOTAL) HALL, Southgate; George Wilson hallkeeper

Tempest John Plumbe,[bc] Esq. Tong Hall, Tong

Tempest Thomas R. Plumbe,[bc] Esq. Tong Hall, Tong

Tennant Elizabeth, dress maker, 15 Westgrove street

Tennant Jonathan, provision dealer, 15 Westgrove street

Terry Benjamin,[b c] solicitor (Terry, Watson and Fowler); house Bolton Cottage

Terry John,[b] manufacturer (William and John Terry); house Dudley Hill

Terry Joseph,[b] stuff manufacturer, Wakefield road

Terry Sarah Ann, straw bonnet maker, Laister Dyke

Terry, Watson & Fowler, solicitors, and agents to the Leeds and Yorkshire Insurance Company, 9 Market street

Terry William,[b] spinner (William and John Terry); house Dudley Hill

Terry William & John, worsted spinners and manufacturers, Hope and Anchor Yard, Bank street; works Dudley Hill

Tetley Ann, milliner and dress maker, Uppercroft row, Bowling

Tetley Benjamin,[b] auctioneer and appraiser, Leeds road

Tetley Charles, worsted spinner and manufacturer, Cannon Mill, Great Horton road; house adjoining

Tetley Edward Theophilus,[b c] Edmund street, Little Horton lane

Tetley Mrs. Elizabeth, Westgate

Tetley George Greenwood,[b c] merchant (Rennie, Tetley & Co.); house Manningham Lodge

Tetley Joseph,[b] farmer, Brow, Manningham

Tetley Mark, provision dealer, Cutlerheight lane, Dudley Hill

Tetley Mark,[c] Fieldhouse Cottage, Manningham

Tetley Richard,[b c] spinner (Richard Tetley & Co.); house Crowther st. Manchester road

Tetley Richard & Co. worsted spinners, CALEDONIA MILL, Duke st. Manchester road

Tetley Robert,[b] woolstapler, 66 Bridge steeet; house Tong

Tetley Samuel,[b] provision dealer, Wakefield road

Tetley Samuel,[b] merchant (M'Kean Tetley & Co.); house Edmund street, Little Horton lane

Tetley Samuel,[c] Pape's Gardens, Undercliffe

Tetley William,[b] Crowther street, Manchester road

Tetley William,[c] Daisy Hill, Manningham

Thackray Mr. Henry,[b c] Bowling Ing

Thackeray Henry William, pawnbroker (Henry William & J. R. Thackeray); house Hillside Villas

Thackeray Henry William & James Robert, pawn brokers, clothiers, and jewellers, 47 and 48 Vicar lane

Thackeray James Robert, pawnbroker (H. W. & J. R. Thackeray); house Hillside Villas

Thackray Joseph,[b] merchant (Rogerson & Thackray); house Shelf

Thackray Thomas,[b] merchant (Cousen & Thackray), house Brunswick place

Thackwray Martha, straw hat and bonnet maker, 20 Darley street

THEATRE ROYAL, Duke street, Darley street; Mr. John Moseley proprietor

Thistlethwaite John,[b c] woolstapler (John Thistlethwaite & Co.); house 3 Westbrook place, Horton

Thistlethwaite John & Co. woolstaplers, 42 Cheapside

Thomas Abraham,[b c] surgeon, Cross lane, Great Horton

Thomas Rev. George, B. A. incumbent of Thornton

Thomas Henry, provision dealer and draper, Southgate, Great Horton

Thomas Samuel, beer retailer, 10 Brick row, Thornton road

Thomas Squire,[b] farmer, Pickles hill, Horton

Thomas William Jacob,[b] chemist and Druggist, 110 Manchester road

Thompson Ann & Mary, confectioners, North Parade, Christ Church

Thompson Benjamin,[b] brewer (Wm.

Whittaker & Co.); house Parkgate, near Otley

Thompson Benjamin, maltster, Bradford Old Brewery, Horton road

Thompson & Clegg, solicitors; Joseph Thompson clerk to the Bradford Waterworks Company, and John Clegg to the ladies of the manor, Bridge street Buildings, Bridge st.

Thompson & Co. new and old clothes dealers, 125 Westgate

Thompson George, blacksmith, North gate

Thompson George, hatter, 9 John street, Stott Hill

Thompson James,[b] travelling draper and tea dealer, Victoria street, North Parade

Thompson John,[c] Stone street, Manor row

Thompson John, portrait painter, Lumb lane

Thompson John, chimney sweep, 1 Back Fold, Northwing

Thompson John, boot and shoe maker, 95 Tumblinghill street, Thornton road

Thompson Rev. Joseph (Wesleyan), Leeds road

Thompson Joseph,[c] slater and slate dealer, Canal side, Bolton road; house Longcroft place, Westgate

Thompson Joseph,[c] solicitor (Thompson & Clegg); house Mount Pleasant, Shipley

Thompson Robert,[b c] boot and shoe maker, 141 Longcroft place, Westgate

Thompson Robert, brush maker, 87 Westgate

Thompson Thomas, moreen manufacturer, 62 Old Piecehall; works and house Allerton

Thompson Thomas,[c] boot and shoe maker, 156 Westgate

Thompson Thomas,[c] joiner, furniture broker and undertaker, 95 Bedford street, Wakefield road

Thompson Thomas, wheelwright, High street, Great Horton

Thorburn Thomas,[c] Darley street

Thorn Charles, chemist and druggist, 24 Britannia street, Manchester road

Thornton Benjamin, stuff manufacturer, Charles street; works and house Gomersall, near Leeds

Thornton Benjamin, wheelwright, High street

Thornton David,[b] Leeds road

Thornton, Firth, Ramsden & Co. commission stuff merchants, Thornton road

Thornton George, solicitor, and agent to the Farmers' and Graziers' Assurance Association, 10 Duke street, Cheapside; res. Cottingley House, Bingley

Thornton George, plumber and glazier, 94 Northgate

Thornton Henry,[b] architect, and agent to the Leeds and Yorkshire Insurance Company, 10 Duke st.; house Cottingley

Thornton Isaac,[b] Undercliffe

Thornton James,[b c] *Cock and Bottle Inn*, 93 High street

Thornton Jerre,[b] farmer, Manchester road

Thornton John,[b] Undercliffe

Thornton John,[b] cabinet maker and upholsterer, 21 Westgate

Thornton John, beer retailer, Vicar lane

Thornton John, coal dealer, Victoria street, Manningham

Thornton John,[b] merchant (Thornton Firth, Ramsden & Co.); house Carlton place, Horton

Thornton Mr. Johnson, Bierley House

Thornton Joseph, *King's Head Inn*, Buttershaw, North Bierley

Thornton Mr. Joshua, Bierley lane

Thornton William,[c] Barkerend, High street

Thornton William,[b] Southgate, Horton

Thorpe James, provision dealer, Wakefield road

Thorpe John,[b] merchant (Thorpe, Scholefield & Co.); house John st. Leeds road

Thorpe, Scholefield & Co. timber merchants, rolling board and packing case makers, John street, Leeds road, and Wakefield road, Bowling

Thresh Abraham,[c] wool and waste dealer, 36 Bank street; house Green lane, Manningham

Thresh James, hair dresser, 13 Manchester road

Thwaites Robinson, [b c] machinist (Thwaites & Co); house Horton rd.

Thwaites Thomas,[b c] plumber, glazier, gas fitter and lead merchant, 12 Tyrrel st.; ho. Westbrook place

Thwaites Thomas & Co. engineers, iron founders and millwrights, ALBION WORKS, Thornton road

Tillotson Joseph,[b c] machine maker, smiths' work, &c. PENNYOAKS MILL, Melbourne street, Leeds road; house Lyndhurst street

Tillotson Miles,[b] merchant (Wright & Tillotson); house Grosvenor place

Tillotson Thomas,[c] Bolton road

Tillotson William, wholesale salt dealer, Fawcett court, Nelson st.

Tiplady Samuel,[b] saddler and harness maker, 73 Chapel lane, Tyrrel street

Titherington Eli, worsted spinner and manufacturer, New Piecehall; works and house Midgley, near Halifax

Tobler, Amschel & Co. stuff merchants, Tyrrel street; manager Mr. Samuel Webster

Todd David, commission wool comber, Albion Works, Thornton road

Todd John, [b] woolcomber (John Todd & Son); house Great Horton road

Todd John, tailor and draper, 19 Manchester road

Todd John & Son, commission wool combers, Duckitt's Mill, Nelson st.

Todd Jonathan, woolcomber (John Todd & Son); house Great Horton road

Tolson, Clough & Taylor, solicitors; Charles Clough clerk of the County Court and to the Bradford and Wakefield turnpike road, Rawson place, Darley street

Tomlinson Christopher, provision dealer, Roundhill place, Silsbridge lane

Tommis Mary, provision dealer, Bowling lane

Tommis William, coal owner and provision dealer, Wakefield road

Toothhill Jonathan,[c] Daisy Hill Top, Manningham

Topham Aaron,[c] Lidget Green, Horton

Topham Edward, stuff manufacturer, Victoria Mill, Wakefield road; ho. Bowling

Topham John, beer retailer, 39 Black Abbey

Topham John,[b] gardener, Great Horton lane

Topham Maria Dorothy, engraver, lithographer, and gold and silver letter manufacturer, 24 Hustlergate; house 26 Ebor street

Topham Nathaniel,[c] Lidget Green, Horton

Topham Richard Busfeild,[b] chemist and druggist, 36 Westgate

Tordoff Daniel,[b] farmer, Beldon hill, Horton

Tordoff John, (John Tordoff & Son); house Bellevue, Manningham lane

Tordoff John & Son, tea dealers and coffee roasters, and chicory, cocoa, chocolate, blue and starch manufacturers, 46 Kirkgate

Tordoff Mary, *Hare and Hounds Inn*, Banktop, Great Horton

Tordoff Samuel,[c] Mill street, Manchester road

Tordoff Squire,[c] boot and shoe maker, 16 Sterling street, Manchester rd.

Tordoff Thomas Denbeigh,[b] tea dealer (John Tordoff & Son); house Drewton street, Manningham lane

Tordoff William,[b c] Bolton road

Towers Thomas, provision dealer, Clayton lane, Little Horton

Towle Thomas, John and Benjamin, cotton spinners, 12 Union Passage, Kirkgate; works and house Borrowash Mill, near Derby

Town Clerk (and clerk to the borough magistrates) Mr. John Rawson, solicitor, Swaine street

Town Edward Henry,[c] ale and porter dealer, 21½ Ivegate

Town Francis,[b c] boot and shoe maker, 21 Ivegate and 15 Market st.; house Belgrave place, Manningham

Townend Ann, milliner and dress maker, 2 Portland street, Manchester road

Townend George,[c] James street

Townend George, spinner (George Townend & Brothers); house Cullingworth, Bingley

Townend George & Brothers, worsted, heald and genappe yarn spinners and stuff manufacturers, Schuster's Buildings, Brook street; works Cullingworth, near Bingley

Townend John,[b c] woolstapler, Bank street; house School street, Cheapside

Townend Martha, confectioner, Wakefield road

Townend Simeon,[b c] worsted and heald yarn spinner and stuff manufacturer, Charles street; works and house Thornton

Townend William, confectioner, 82 Manchester road

Town's Offices—for watching, lighting, highways, police, &c. Swaine street, Hall Ings

Townson Richard, provision dealer, 36 Bolton road

Tradesmens' Protection Society, (Bradford branch); Mr. Henry Farrar secretary, 20 Kirkgate

Trees Thomas & Co. general dyers, 8 Bower street, Manchester road

Trees William,[b] dyer (Thomas Trees & Co.), Bower street, Manchester road

Tremel Adolphus,[b c] manufacturer (Adolphus Tremel & Co.); res. Field House, Manningham

Tremel Adolphus & Co. worsted spinners and manufacturers, Hall

Ings; works FIELDHEAD MILLS, Thornton road

Trigg Edwin, grocer and tea dealer, Broadstones

Trout John Ridgill,[c] Green lane, Manningham

Tuke Daniel,[b] grocer (Smith & Tuke); house Horton road

Tuke & Hustler, land agents, valuers and surveyors, Darley street, and Blake street, York

Tuke William,[b] surveyor (Tuke & Hustler); house Hillside Villas

Turley Mrs. straw bonnet maker, and register for servants, 18 High street

Turner Charles, provision dealer, 84 Croft street, Wakefield road

Turner Charles Timothy,[b c] woolstapler and cotton warp and top agent, Charles street; house Spring Gardens

Turner Edward,[b] Wakefield road

Turner George,[b c] manufacturer (Turner & Mitchell) house Ashfield place, Great Horton road

Turner John, stuff manufacturer, 25 New Piecehall; works Conolly, house Crosshills, Keighley

Turner John,[b] manufacturer (John and Robert Turner); house Legrams lane

Turner John and Robert, stuff manufacturers, Booth street; works Holmetop Mill, Little Horton

Turner Jonas,[c] stone mason, Park gate, High street

Turner Jonas, auctioneer, appraiser, and eating-house keeper, 49 Kirkgate

Turner & Mitchell, worsted spinners and manufacturers, Unicorn Yard, Hustler gate; works Manchester road

Turner Robert,[b c] manufacturer (John and Robert Turner); house Legrams lane

Turner Robert,[b] pork butcher, 65 John street, Northgate

Turner Samuel,[b c] School street

Turner Thomas, smith and farrier, Cross street, Westgate; house Albion street, Silsbridge lane

Twycross George,[b] woolstapler (Jas. Twycross & Son); house Horton road

Twycross James & Son, woolstaplers, Commercial street; house Lister terrace, Horton road

Tyas John,[b] cabinet maker and upholsterer, 115 Westgate

UMPLEBY Thomas, publication dealer and news agent, 2 Lumby street, Manchester road

UNION CLUB HOUSE, Manor row; Mr. Ulas Selix steward

UNITED INDEPENDENT ORDER OF ODD FELLOWS; head office (Bradford district) Odd Fellows' Hall, Thornton road

Unna Jacob Arnold,[b] manager (S. L. Behrens & Co.); res. Grove House, Manor row

Unwin David, beer retailer, Lillycroft, Manningham

Unwin Joshua,[b] stuff manufacturer, Queen's Mill, Thornton road; house North street, Northwing

Unwin Samuel, hat manufacturer, Tyrrel street; house Quebec terrace, Thornton road

Uttley William, beer retailer, 24 Sedgwick street, White Abbey

Uttley William, tailor, 46 Union st. Bridge street

VAGRANT OFFICE for Bradford Union, Toad lane, Bridge street; William Booth master

Varey Matthew,[c] clerk, Spring row, Manningham

Varley Caroline, straw bonnet maker, 5 Keighley Old road, Manningham

Varley John,[b] worsted spinner and manufacturer, Piecehall Yard; works and house Stanningley

Varley Martha, milliner and dress maker, 167 Wetley street, Manningham

Verity Mary, milliner & dress maker, 79 Bolton road

Verity William,[b] Hall lane, Bowling

Vickerman John,[b c] Victoria street, North Parade

Vint George, stone merchant (George Vint & Brothers); house Idle

Vint George & Brothers, stone merchant; wharf and office Canal side, Bolton road

Virr Alfred, hair dresser, 42 Northgate

Virr Harriet, milliner and dress maker, 58 Bedford street, Manchester road

Virr William, hair dresser, 15 Well street

Voigt George, B. A. assistant master, Grammar School, Manor row

WADDILOVE Richard,[b] beer retailer, 41 Victoria street, Manchester rd.

Waddilove Thomas,[b] beer retailer, 4 Nelson court, Nelson street

Waddilove William,[c] Cross street, Manningham

Waddington George,[b] grocer and provision dealer, 45 Silsbridge lane

Waddington Henry, wool and waste dealer, Hope and Anchor Yard, Bank street; house Keighley

Waddington Isaac, governor of workhouse, High street

Waddington John,[b] Edmund street, Little Horton

Waddington Jonathan, provision dealer, 41 Hope street, Manchester road

Waddington Joseph,[b] grocer, tea dealer and tallow chandler, 76 Westgate

Waddington Richard,[b c] engineer, and iron founder, railway carriage wheel and axle manufacturer, &c. Railway Foundry, Manchester road and Thornton road; house Horton road

Waddington Samuel, coal dealer, Victoria street, Silsbridge lane

Waddington Thomas,[b c] hatter (Thos. and William Waddington), Ivegate

Waddington Thomas & William, hat manufacturers, 23 Ivegate

Waddington William,[c] hatter (Thos. and William Waddington), Ivegate

Waddington William, woolcomb maker, Albion street, Silsbridge la.; house Keighley street

Waddington William, beer retailer, Broomfields, Wakefield road

Wade & Bairstow, stuff manufacturers, Market street; works Laneclose Mill, Great Horton

Wade Charles Duckitt, manufacturer, (Joseph Wade & Sons); house Well street

Wade Elizabeth, *New Inn* and spirit vaults, Tyrrel street

Wade Mr. James,[b c] Horton road

Wade John,[c] Hill End, Horton

Wade John, provision dealer, 463 Wakefield road

Wade John,[b] spinner (Joseph Wade and Sons); house Well street

Wade John,[c] druggist and tea dealer, 43 King street, Manchester road

Wade John,[b c] manufacturer (Wade and Bairstow); house High street, Great Horton

Wade Mr. Joseph,[bc] Horton road

Wade Joseph,[b c] junr. manufacturer (Josh. Wade & Sons); house Well street

Wade Joseph,[b c] manufacturer (Josh. Wade & Sons); house Well street

Wade Joseph & Sons, worsted spinners and manufacturers, Old Market place; works VICTORIA MILL, Canal road

Wade Thomas, hair dresser, 16 Westgate

Wadsworth Eli,[b] grocer and tea dealer, 108 Manchester road

Wadsworth Richard,[b] provision dealer, Leeds road

Wadsworth Thomas, provision dealer, Leeds road

Wager William,[c] Belgrave place, Manningham

Wagstaff John Reid,[b c] solicitor, and superintendent registrar of Bradford and North Bierley districts, clerk to the board of the Bradford Poor-law Union, and agent for the Imperial Insurance Co. Charles street; house Belle Vue, Manningham lane

Wagstaff Mr. William,[b c] 175 Bridge street

Wainwright Grace, provision dealer, Swaine Green, Bowling

Wainwright James,[c] Captain street, Stott Hill

Wainwright John,[c] Bridge street

Wainwright John Wilson,[b c] maker-up (Cooper & Wainwright); house Bridge street

Wainwright John Wilson, beer retailer, Bridge street

Waite John,[c] Silsbridge lane

Waite John,[c] Great Horton road

Walbank Nathaniel, stuff manufacturer, Old Piecehall; works Keighley; house Spring Gardens

Walker Abraham,[c] White Abbey

Walker Benjamin,[b] glue manufacturer, Shipley; business attendance at the Wellington Inn, High street, on Thursdays

Walker Benjamin,[b] bookseller, printer and stationer, and engraver in wood, 8 Market street; house Garnett street

Walker Charles,[b c] manufacturer (Walkers' & Co.); res. Hallfield House, Manningham lane

Walkers' & Co. worsted spinners and manufacturers, Bridge street

Walker George, provision dealer, Clarence street, Manchester road

Walker James, grocer and provision dealer, 24 Otley road

Walker James, brass founder and lacquerer, Northgate

Walker James, Temperance hotel, Northgate

Walker James, basket maker, Brumfit's Yard, Kirkgate; house Regent place, Duke street

Walker James G. basket maker, 25 James street, Northgate

Walker John,[c] Crowther street, Manchester road

Walker John, provision dealer, Hill Top, Manningham

Walker John, draper and hosier, Wakefield road

Walker John,[b] chemist and druggist, 106 Manchester road
Walker Mr. Joseph, Elizabeth street, Little Horton lane
Walker Mr. Joseph,[b] Smith lane, Manningham
Walker Mrs. Mary, Manchester road
Walker Mary Ann, school, Sawrey place, Little Horton lane
Walker Mary & Harriet, milliners and dress makers, 43 Arundel street, Manchester road
Walker Matthew,[c] Darley Gap, near Bingley
Walker Rachel, confectioner, 69 Market street; house Leeds road
Walker Richard,[b] saddler, trunk and harness maker, 17 and 19 Darley street; house Victoria street
Walker Robert,[c] provision dealer, 56 Frederick street, Wakefield road
Walker Robert,[c] Bierley lane
Walker Sarah, coal dealer, Wildboar street, Bolton road
Walker Thomas,[b] Wakefield road
Walker William,[c] Clayton street, Cropper lane
Walker William, beer retailer, Hill Top, Manningham
Walker William,[b c] new and second-hand clothes dealer, jeweller, &c. 3 Westgate
Walker William,[b c] manufacturer, (Walkers' & Co.); house Bowling Hall
Walker William,[b] woolstapler, Bermondsey; house Mill lane, Bowling
Walker William, schoolmaster, Back lane, Bowling
Walker William, tailor, 60 Chapel lane, Tyrrel street
Wall, Cockshott & Wall, worsted spinners and manufacturers, Old Piece-hall; works Linton Mills, Grassington, near Skipton
Wall Francis, spinner (Wall, Cockshott and Wall); house Linton, Skipton
Wall John, manufacturer (Wall, Cockshott & Wall); house Linton, Skipton
Wallace Rev. Alexander (Presbyterian), Hanover square
Wallace Matthew, boot and shoe maker, 12 Wellington street, Stott Hill
Waller Charles, grocer and tea dealer 14 Kirkgate; house Fountain st.
Wallis Brothers, linen drapers, hosiers and silk mercers, 22 Westgate, and Briggate, Leeds
Wallis Joseph, boot and shoe maker, 199 Bolton road
Walls William, provision dealer, 38 Wellington street, Stott Hill
Walmsley Isaac,[b c] *Albion Hotel*, Ivegate
Walmsley James,[b] boot and shoe maker, 66 Market street
Walmsley James, tailor (Hinds & Walmsley); house Edward street
Walmsley John,[c] grocer and tea dealer, 66 Kirkgate
Walmsley John,[c] Clarence street, Manchester road
Walmsley Sarah Ann, milliner and dress maker, 45 Arundel street, Manchester road
Walmsley Thomas, Clarence street, Manchester road
Walsh Alice, milliner and dress maker, 14 Keighley Old road, Manningham
Walsh Jeremiah, general dyer, 45 George street, Leeds road

Walsh John, provision dealer, Victoria street, Manningham

Walton George,[b] house, sign and decorative painter, gilder and paper hanger, North Parade, Christ Church

Walton James George,[b] Garnet street, Leeds road

Walton John, house and sign painter, 11 Lumby street, Manchester road

Walton John,[c] Bower street, Manchester road

Walton Joseph,[b] cloth presser and finisher, Westbrook terrace, Thornton road ; house Adelaide street

Walton Joseph, blacksmith, Queen street, Manchester road

Walton Miriam, dress maker, 58 Greenhill place, Manningham

Walton Robert, linen draper and hosier, 196 Manchester road

Walton Thomas, plumber (Clarkson and Walton); house Richard street, Leeds road

Walton Thomas,[b] beer retailer, 103 George street, Leeds road

Walton Thomas,[b,c] *Queen's Arms Inn*, 135 Manchester road

Walton Thomas,[b] waste dealer (Walton & Wittam); house George st. Leeds road

Walton William, provision dealer, Lidget green, Horton

Walton & Wittam, waste dealers, Albion Yard, Ivegate

Warburton Hannah, milliner and dress maker, 55 Silsbridge lane

Warburton William, house, sign and decorative painter, Brunswick place ; house Drewton street

Ward Edwin, carver and gilder, 12 Wellington street, Stott Hill

Ward Elizabeth, provision dealer, King street, Manchester road

Ward Henrietta Clayton, milliner and dress maker, 53 Victoria street, North Parade

Ward John,[bc] collector of income tax, &c. Chapel street, Leeds road

Ward Samuel,[c] Westsquire lane, Manningham

Ward Mrs. Sarah, Spring gardens

Ward Thomas,[c] Bedford street, Bridge street

Ward William cabinet maker, paper hanger, &c. Westgate; house Westgrove street

Wardle Thomas, brazier and iron and tinplate worker, 43 Silsbridge lane

Wardle William,[b] brazier and tinplate worker, High street, Great Horton

Wardle William, joiner and cabinet maker, 19 Bedford street, Wakefield road

Wardman Benjamin, butcher, Bolton road

Wardman Elizabeth, milliner and dress maker, 19 Chapel lane, Tyrrel street

Wardman Henry,[b c] printer and stationer, 18 Chapel lane, Tyrrel st.

Wardman Joseph,[c] Wharf street, Bolton road

Wardman Martha, grocer and tea dealer, 2 Nelson street, Chapel la.

Wardman Samuel,[c] Chapel Yard, Kirkgate

WASHING ESTABLISHMENT FOR DOMESTIC LINEN, &c. Railroad street, School street; Edmund Johnson Mitchell proprietor

WATCHING AND LIGHTING OFFICE

Swaine street; Mr. Wm. Clough collector

Waterhouse John,[b] farmer, West-squire lane, Manningham

Waterhouse Joseph,[b c] farmer, Bank-top, Horton

Waterhouse Joseph, hair dresser, 119 Manchester road

Waterhouse Richard,[b c] new and second hand clothes dealer, 67 New Market place, Kirkgate

Waterhouse Robert,[b c] commercial coffee rooms and eating house, 4 Bank street, Market street

Waterhouse Thomas, new and old English and foreign bookseller, 25 Darley street

Waterhouse Thomas, stuff manufacturer, 163 Old Piecehall; works and house Keighley

Waters John, provision dealer, 48 Nelson court, Nelson street

WATERWORKS COMPANY'S OFFICE, 2 Rennie's Buildings, Hall Ings; Mr. Adam Beattie, manager, res. Northrop's houses, Westgate

WATERWORKS COMPANY'S STATION AND DEPOT FOR PIPING, &c. Thornton road; Mr. James Garfoot superintendent

Watkins Thomas,[b c] butcher, 133 Bridge street

Watkins William,[b c] plane and tool maker, Cure's court, Westgate; house Ebor street, Little Horton lane

Watkins William, china and earthenware dealer, 133 Bridge street

Watkinson Benjamin,[c] Peel street, Leeds road

Watkinson Henry,[b] worsted top and yarn merchant, Commercial street, Canal road; house Trafalgar st. Manor row

Watkinson Miss, school, Little Horton lane

Watmuff Charles,[c] 147 George street, Leeds road

Watmuff Emma, milliner and dress maker, 147 George street, Leeds road

Watmuff Joe, boot and shoe maker, 26 Northgate

Watmuff Stephen,[c] George street, Leeds road

Watson James, provision dealer, 13 Brick row, Thornton road

Watson Jeremiah, provision dealer, 20 Prospect street, Thornton road

Watson John,[b] travelling tea dealer and draper, Hanover square

Watson John,[b] solicitor (Terry, Watson & Fowler); house Melbourne place

Watson John, cabinet maker (Duckworth & Watson); house Otley rd.

Watson Levi, boot and shoe maker, 268 Manchester road

Watson Mr. Peter,[b c] Snow Hill

Watson Richard,[b] clerk, Preston place, Great Horton

Watson Stephen,[b c] draper (William & Stephen Watson); house School street

Watson William,[b] Skinner-lane End, Manningham

Watson William,[b] farmer, New road, Horton

Watson William,[b] draper (William and Stephen Watson); house Kirkgate

Watson William & Stephen, linen drapers, hosiers and haberdashers, 6 Kirkgate, and Bermondsey

Waud Brothers & Co. stuff manufacturers, Brook street; works BRITANNIA MILLS, Portland street, Manchester road

Waud Christopher & Co. mohair, alpacca and worsted spinners, Brook street; works BRITANNIA MILLS, Portland street, Manchester road

Waud Christopher,[b c] spinner (Christopher Waud & Co.) house Spring place, Manningham lane

Waud & Co. wholesale provision dealers, and bacon, butter and cheese factors, 5 Market street

Waud Edward,[b c] manufacturer (C. Waud & Co.); house Portland st. Manchester road

Waud Robert, provision dealer (Waud and Co.); house Snow Hill

Waud William,[b] brush manufacturer and provision merchant, 1 and 10 Darley street; house Manor row

Waugh John,[c] Park square, Manningham

Waugh William,[b c] joiner and builder, Four Lane Ends, Manningham

Weatherhill Joseph,[c] joiner and builder, Eastbrook lane, Leeds road

Webster Ann, milliner and straw bonnet maker, 19 Barkerend

Webster Frances and Elizabeth, dress and straw bonnet makers, Leeds road

Webster George,[b] butcher, Dudley Hill, Bowling

Webster George, woolstapler (Sugden & Webster); house Victoria street, North Parade

Webster George,[b] stone mason, Sticker lane, Bowling

Webster George,[b] boot and shoe maker, Dudley hill, Bowling

Webster Isaac,[b] worsted spinner, Greenwood's Mill, Portland street; house Sterling street, Manchester road

Webster Isaac,[b] engineer (Cole, Marchent & Co.); house Laister Dyke

Webster James, hair dresser, Silsbridge lane; house Albion street

Webster John,[b] Back lane, Bowling

Webster Richard,[c] market collector and constable, Stone street

Webster Joseph,[b] Elizabeth street, Little Horton

Webster Robert,[b c] pawnbroker, 29 Chapel lane, Tyrrel street

Webster Samuel, manager (Tobler, Amschel & Co.); house Westgrove street

Webster William,[b] engineer, Back lane, Bowling

Webster William,[b c] butcher, Bradford Moor

WEIGHTS' AND MEASURES' ADJUSTING OFFICE, Court House; Mr. William Baxter adjuster

Weil Leopold, manager (P. D. Ellissen); house Hanover square

Wells John,[b] Wakefield road

Wells Joseph, machine maker, Back lane, Bowling

Wells Joshua, boot and shoe maker, 174 Manchester road

Wells & Ridehalgh, solicitors to the Bradford Banking Company; Richard Ridehalgh clerk to the gas works, and agent for the London Assurance Company; office Tyrrel court, Tyrrel street

Wells Thomas Hollingworth, boot and shoe maker, Wakefield road

Wells William,[b c] solicitor (Wells & Ridehalgh); house Eldon place

Wells William, worsted spinner, Laycock's Mill, Thornton road

WESLEYAN CHAPELS—(*See* index "Churches and Chapels"

WESLEYAN MISSIONARY SOCIETY, Eastbrook—Lodge Calvert, Esq. treasurer; Mr. William Whittaker, secretary

West James,[b] Undercliffe

West John,[c] boot and shoe maker, Longcroft place, Westgate

West Joseph, joiner and cabinet maker, Sticker lane, Bowling

West Joshua, boot and shoe maker, Tyrrel court, Tyrrel street

West Samuel,[c] Bunker's Hill, High street

West Thomas,[b] provision dealer, Otley road

WEST OF ENGLAND INSURANCE COMPANY; agent Mr. William Clough, Swaine street

WESTERN INSURANCE COMPANY; agent Mr. Charles Lees, solicitor, Albion Court, Kirkgate

WEST RIDING (branch) GUARANTEE SOCIETY; agent Mr. John Darlington, solicitor, Union Passage, Kirkgate

WEST RIDING CONSTABLES' OFFICE, Court House, Hall Ings; Mr. Charles Ingham and Mr. James Jowett constables

WEST RIDING MAGISTRATES' CLERK, Mr. Robert Mossman, solicitor; office Hall Ings

WEST RIDING UNION RAILWAY COMPANY; Passengers' station—entrances from the Leeds and Wake-roads; goods' warehouse Vicar ln.

Westwood Henry, butcher, 54 Westgt.

M

Whalley John Henry, stuff manufacturer, Brook street; works and house Trawden, Colne

Wharf Richard,[b] butcher, 89 Manchester road

Wharton George, boot and shoe maker, 33 Bank street; house Pratt's Buildings, New Leeds

Wharton Thomas,[c] Silver street, Leeds road

Wheater Henry, joiner and cabinet maker, 62 King street, Manchester road

Wheater Joshua,[c] beer retailer, 38 Queen street, Manchester road

Wheater Richard,[c] Bowling

Wheater Thomas, provision dealer, 125 Silsbridge lane

Wheatley Maria, *White Lion Inn*, Kirkgate

Wheelhouse William,[b c] machinist (Onion & Wheelhouse); house Great Cross street, Leeds road

Whewall James, hosiery, ready-made linen, &c. warehouse, 44 Kirkgate, and Halifax

Whipp Robert, grocer and tea dealer, 42 Vicar lane

White Abraham,[c] manufacturer (Holdsworth & White); house Mill lane, Bowling

White Charles, boot and shoe maker, 34 Chain street, Silsbridge lane

White Charles, gilder and picture frame maker, Bolton street, Barkerend

White Isaac,[b c] woolstapler, William street, Little Horton

White John,[b] currier and leather cutter, Albion Court, Mondays and Thursdays only; house Bingley

White John,[c] Wood street, Manningham

White Samuel, stuff manufacturer, George Hotel Yard; works and house Allerton

White Stephen, woolstapler, Commercial street, Canal road; house Allerton

White Thomas,[c] tailor, Low Green, Great Horton

White Thomas, moreen manufacturer, 178 Old Piecehall; works and house Allerton

White Walter,[b] letter press printer, 22 Piecehall Yard, Kirkgate; house Spring gardens

Whitehead Eliza, milliner and straw bonnet maker, 16 Kirkgate

Whitehead, Goddard & Co. worsted spinners and manufacturers, Charles street; works Canal road

Whitehead James, beer retailer, 60 Westgate

Whitehead John, provision dealer, 29 Sterling street, Manchester rd.

Whitehead John,[b c] cabinet maker and upholsterer, 14 Well street

Whitehead Joseph, coach builder, Chapel lane, Tyrrel street; house Chapel lane

Whitehead Joseph,[b c] manufacturer Whitehead, Goddard & Co.); house Victoria street, North Parade

Whitehead Richard, cabinet maker and furniture broker, 24 Bridge street

Whitehead Samuel, joiner, Albion Yard, Ivegate; house Little Horton

Whitehead William,[b c] spinner (Whitehead, Goddard & Co.); house Victoria street, North Parade

Whitham Thomas, butter factor and provision dealer, 53 King street, Manchester road

Whiteley Thomas, joiner and cabinet maker, Bolton street, Barkerend

WHITEWOOD COAL COMPANY; office and wharf, Railroad street,—John Hargreaves agent

Whitley Isaac,[b] worsted spinner and manufacturer, 19 Hartley's Buildings, Brook street; works Thornton road; house William street, Little Horton

Whitley Joseph,[b c] noils and short wool dealer, Hustler's Buildings, Market street; house Victoria st. North Parade

Whitley Nathan,[b] worsted spinner and manufacturer, George Hotel Yard, Brook street; works and house Dudley Hill

Whitley Richard, woolstapler, Hustler's Buildings, Market street; house Preston place, Great Horton

Whitley Sarah Ann, milliner and dress maker, Simes street, Westgate

Whitley Squire, boot and shoe maker, 98 Westgate

Whitley William,[b c] English and foreign wool dealer, Cheapside; house George street, Leeds road

Whittaker Clough, beer retailer, 15 Barkerend

Whittaker Edmund, warp sizer, Thornton road; house Sandholme, Todmorden

Whittaker Harriet, straw bonnet maker, Bavaria place, Manningham

Whittaker & Hartley, wool and waste dealers, Roebuck Yard, Market st.

Whittaker James, clogger, High st. Great Horton

Whittaker James,[c] Spring street, Wapping

Whittaker John Harper, manufacturer (Clapham & Whittaker); house Baildon

Whittaker Jonas, provision dealer, 86 Bridge street

Whittaker Michael,[c] Belle Isle, Haworth

Whittaker Timothy, wool dealer (Whittaker & Hartley); house Wilsden

Whittaker William, coal dealer, Bolton road

Whittaker William,[c] *White Hart Inn*, Thornton road

Whittaker William,[b] wheelwright, Dudley Hill, Bowling

Whittaker William,[c] Little Horton lane

Whittaker William & Co. ale and porter brewers, OLD BREWERY, Horton road

Whittam Robert,[c] Spring street, Manningham

Whittam Thomas,[b] King street, Manchester road

Whittam William,[b] fellmonger, Brumfit's Yard, Kirkgate; house Victoria street, North Parade

Whitworth Hannah, provision dealer, 188 Bridge street

Whitworth John, manufacturer (R. Whitworth & Co.); house Ovenden Hall

Whitworth Robert, spinner (Robert Whitworth & Co.); house St. James's road, Halifax

Whitworth Robert & Co. worsted spinners and manufacturers, New Piecehall; works Lee Mill, Halifax

Whitworth William, manufacturer (Robert Whitworth & Co.); house St. James's road, Halifax

Wickett Benjamin,[c] Bridge street

Wickham Henry Wickham,[b] [c] Esq. ironmaster (Low Moor Ironworks); house Kirklees Hall

Wickham Lamplugh Wickham,[b] Esq. ironmaster, (Low Moor Iron works); house Lightcliffe

Widdop William, tailor, 62 Thompson's Alley, Silsbridge lane

Wiechus George R. manager (Kessler & Co.); house Hanover square

Wiggins David, boot and shoe maker, Back Duke street, Manchester rd.

Wigglesworth Abraham,[b] provision dealer, 43 Croft street, Manchester road

Wigglesworth Eli,[c] John street, Stott Hill

Wignall Eliza, milliner and dress maker, 52 Croft street, Manchester road

Wignall James,[b] provision dealer, 16 Fawcett court, Nelson street

Wignall Joseph, butter factor, 34 Bank street; house Keighley

Wignall Samuel, spindle and fly maker, Richard street, Leeds road

Wilcock, Bradley & Co. woollen cloth manufacturers, Union Mill, Shipley

Wilcock David, stuff manufacturer, New Piecehall; works Luddenden Foot, Halifax

Wilcock George, woollen cloth manufacturer, Windhill, Idle

Wilcock John, agent (Swaine and Wilcock); house Crowther street

Wilcock John,[b] [c] brazier and tinplate worker, 92 Manchester road

Wilcock Jonathan, deputy registrar for Horton district, 69 Fitzgerald street, Manchester road

Wilcock Joseph,[c] wool dealer and cloth manufacturer, Windhill, Idle

Wilcock Joseph, worsted inspector, Ebenezer street, Vicar lane

Wilcock William Butterfield,[b] [c] woolstapler, 2 Broadstones ; house Spring place, Manningham lane

Wild Benjamin,[b] manager, Edmund street, Little Horton lane

Wild John,[c] Brick-kiln, Manningham

Wildsmith Amelia, straw bonnet maker, 159 Wakefield road

Wilkinson Aaron,[b] beer retailer, Manchester road

Wilkinson & Bradley, painters, gilders , and paper hangers, 145 Brick lane

Wilkinson Charles, beer retailer, Thornton road

Wilkinson Charles, butcher, 52 Northgate

Wilkinson Christopher,[b c] letter-press and copper-plate printer, stationer and bookseller, Tyrrel street

Wilkinson Croft,[b c] woolstapler, 16 Union street; house Broomfield terrace

Wilkinson George,[b c] provision dealer, 101 Bridge street

Wilkinson George Carver,[b c] Leeds road

Wilkinson Isaac,[c] provision dealer, Little Horton

Wilkinson James,[c] Bowling Old lane

Wilkinson James, provision dealer, 196 Bolton road

Wilkinson James,[b] hat manufacturer, 25 Ivegate

Wilkinson John,[b] farmer, Beldon Hill, Horton

Wilkinson John, provision dealer, 21 Melbourne street, Leeds road

Wilkinson John, boot and shoe maker, 11 Wellesley street, Northwing

Wilkinson John, green grocer, 101 Bridge street

Wilkinson John, boot and shoe maker, Wellington street, Stott Hill

Wilkinson John, coal and provision dealer, 8 Providence street, White Abbey

Wilkinson Joseph,[b c] green grocer, 78 Westgate

Wilkinson Joseph,[b] cabinet maker and upholsterer, New Market place, and North Parade

Wilkinson Joseph, stuff manufacturer, Laycock's Mill, Thornton road; house Market street

Wilkinson Joseph, tailor, Dudley Hill, Bowling

Wilkinson Mary, draper and straw bonnet maker, 83 Timber street, Otley road

Wilkinson Rachael, earthenware dealer, 17 Hustlergate

Wilkinson Richard,[b] hardware and rag, rope and paper dealer, Lister's place, Silsbridge lane

Wilkinson Robert,[b] sizing and picker dealer, Exchange street, Kirkgate; house Hanover square

Wilkinson Robert, provision dealer, 17 Silsbridge lane

Wilkinson Sarah, bonnet maker, 59 Thornton street, Thornton road

Wilkinson Samuel,[b] farmer, Beldon Hill, Horton

Wilkinson Samuel,[c] machine maker, Westgrove street

Wilkinson Thomas, tailor and draper, 37 Kirkgate; house Illingworth's Court, Westgate

Wilkinson Thomas, tailor and draper, Leeds road ; house 4 George street

Wilkinson Thomas, tailor, 184 Keighley Old road, Mannningham

Wilkinson, William,[b c] spinner (Bottomley, Wilkinson & Co.); res. Hallfield House, Bowling

Wilkinson William, stuff manufacturer, 23 Old Piecehall; works and house Thornton

Wilkinson William,[b] farmer, Wakefield road

Wilks John,[c] Green lane, Manningham

Wilks Joseph,[c] Providence street, White Abbey

Willett Thomas,[b] spinner (Thomas Willett & Co.); house Park place, Manningham

Willett Thomas & Co. worsted spinners and manufacturers, Clarence street, Manchester road

Willey John, woolstapler, Hustler's Buildings, Market street; house Birkenshaw

Williams Ann, milliner and dress maker, North Parade, Christ Church

Williams E. G. merchant (John Haigh & Co.); house Drewton st.

Williams George,[c] provision dealer, Park square, Manningham

Williamson James,[b] Haughton place, Drewton street

Williamson John, stuff manufacturer, Old Market place; works and house Keighley

Williamson Priscilla, butcher, 24 Manchester road

Williamson Thomas,[b] North Parade

Williamson William Harrison,[b c] 4 Drewton street

Willis John, beer retailer, 42 Millbank, Thornton road

Willis Thomas, brass founder, Millbank, Thornton road

Willoughby Thomas, beer retailer, 114 Bolton road

Wilman Isaac,[b c] beer retailer, 7 Cross Wellington street

M 2

Wilman James,[b c] beer retailer, 147 Silsbridge lane

Wilman James, *Sun Hotel*, spirit vaults and posting house, Bridge street and Ivegate

Wilman John,[b] brush maker, 41 Westgate

Wilman Peter,[b] tailor and beer seller, 3 Longcroft place, Silsbridge lane

Wilsden Robert, tailor, Primrose terrace, Manningham

Wilson Benjamin,[b c] agent for wines, spirits, Scotch and Burton ales and London porter, Primrose Hill, Great Horton

Wilson David, clog and patten maker, 3 Toad lane, Nelson street

Wilson Edward,[bc] currier and leather cutter, 5 Hustlergate; house Victoria street, North Parade

Wilson & Fairbank, silversmiths, watch makers and jewellers, ornamental engravers and printers, 47 Kirkgate, and 18 Tabot Yard

Wilson Francis,[b] new & second-hand clothes dealer, New Market place; house Northgate

Wilson Francis, grocer and provision dealer, Northgate

Wilson George,[b] Temperance coffee house, 24 Southgate

Wilson James,[b c] joiner (James Wilson & Son); house Spring Row, Manningham

Wilson James, painter, colourer, &c. 85 Bedford street, Wakefield road

Wilson James, agent and dealer in silk and cotton yarns and warps, Hall Ings; house Frizing Hall, near Shipley

Wilson James,[b] clog & patten maker, 11 Charles street, Leeds road

Wilson James & Son, joiners and builders, Spring Row, Manningham

Wilson John, merchant (John Wilson & Co.); house Melbourne place

Wilson John & Co. stuff merchants, 4 Bridge street

Wilson John, manufacturer (John Wilson & Co.); house Crosshills, Keighley

Wilson John,[b c] agent to the Low Moor Company, Great Horton road

Wilson John & Co. stuff manufacturers, Dale street, Cheapside; works Dale End Mill, Crosshills, Keighley

Wilson Joseph,[b c] builder (James Wilson & Son); house Spring Row, Manningham

Wilson Joseph, boot and shoe maker, 16 Bower street, Manchester road

Wilson Joseph, boot and shoe maker, New Row, Manningham

Wilson Joshua,[b] silversmith (Wilson & Fairbank); house Kirkgate

Wilson Maria, dress and bonnet maker, 8 Park place, Little Horton

Wilson Rebecca, milliner and dress maker, Victoria street, North Parade

Wilson Richard, blacksmith, Halifax road, Bowling

Wilson Samuel,[b c] agent and commission stuff buyer, Hanover square

Wilson Samuel Thomas,[b] hairdresser, 3 Ivegate

Wilson Thomas, boot & shoe maker, Bradford Moor

Wilson Thomas,[c] Portland street

Wilson Thomas, chemist (Maud & Wilson), and agent for the British and Foreign Bible Society, 10 Bridge street

Wilson Mr. William,[b] Westgate

Wilson William,[c] Low Moor

Wilson William,[c] Boggart lane, Vicar lane

Winn William, tailor, 77 Bridge street

Winterhalder Severin, clock maker (Dilger, Winterhalder & Co.); house Hustlergate

Wiseman Henry, *Roebuck Inn*, and spirit vaults, Sun Bridge and Market street

Wittam James, waste dealer (Walton & Wittam); house Threadneedle street

Wittam John,[b c] dealer in new and second-hand clothes, jewellery, plate, &c. 26 Ivegate

Woller George, schoolmaster, 86 Providence street, White Abbey

Woller Joseph, general dyer, Brick la.

Woller Samuel, blacksmith, Bradford Moor

Womersley John, *White Bear Inn*, Bradford Moor

Wood Benjamin,[c] Back lane, Manningham

Wood Benjamin,[c] Thornton street, Thornton road

Wood Benjamin, merchant,[b] (Benj. Wood & Co.); house Southfield lane end, Little Horton

Wood Benjamin & Co. stuff merchants, 30 Pearson's Buildings, Bridge street

Wood George,[b] pawnbroker, top of Westgate

Wood George,[b] provision dealer, 26 Union street

Wood George,[c] provision dealer, Holme top, Little Horton

Wood Hannah, provision dealer, 9 Kirkgate

Wood Hannah, *Black Horse Inn*, Little Horton lane

Wood & Harrison, packing case makers, Duke street and Manchester road

Wood Henry, butcher, 167 Westgate; house White Abbey

Wood Isaac, china, glass and earthenware dealer, 10 Broadstones

Wood Isaac, butcher, 5 High street

Wood Isaac,[b c] provision dealer, 19 Green lane, Manningham

Wood Jacob,[b c] provision dealer, 10 School street

Wood James,[b] boot and shoe maker, 44 Northgate

Wood James,[b c] solicitor (Bentley & Wood); house Park place

Wood Mr. Job,[c] Manningham

Wood John,[c] Duckworth lane, Manningham

Wood John, district post office, Great Horton road

Wood John,[c] provision dealer, Little Horton lane

Wood John,[c] spinner (Walkers' and Co.); house Theddon Grange, Hampshire

Wood John, plasterer, colourer, &c. 4 Lumb lane

Wood John,[b c] butcher, 18 Wood st. Manningham

Wood Joseph,[b c] worsted spinner and manufacturer, Swaine street; works and house Shipley Fields

Wood Joseph, machinist (Wright, Wood & France); house Westbrook terrace

Wood Joseph,[c] Park square, Manningham

Wood Joseph, plasterer, colourer, and cement dealer, 4 Vicar lane

Wood Joseph, worsted spinner and manufacturer, Brook street; works Thornton road; house Allerton

Wood Joseph, tailor, 15 Brick row, Thornton road

Wood Joseph, hair dresser, 25 Broadstones

Wood Joseph,[b] merchant (Bottomley, Wood & Co.); house North Parade

Wood Joseph,[b] worsted spinner and manufacturer, Swaine street; works and house Shipley

Wood Joseph, *Red Lion Inn*, Wibsey bank foot

Wood Joseph,[b] provision dealer, Halifax road, Bowling

Wood Joseph,[c] Sterling street, Manchester road

Wood Joseph & Co. general carriers, wharfingers, &c. Canal road

Wood Joshua, general commission agent for grey goods, cotton warps, canvas, soaps, &c. 21 Market st.; house 3 Charles street

Wood Matthew,[c] *King's Arms Inn*, Heaton

Wood Samuel,[b] farmer, Legram's la.

Wood Samuel, worsted spinner and manufacturer, 14 New Piecehall; works and house Sowerby Bridge

Wood Mrs, Sarah, Springfield place, Manningham lane

Wood Susan, milliner and dress maker, Leeds road

Wood William[c] Parkfield, Lumb lane

Wood William,[b] reed and heald manufacturer, Tyrrel square

Wood William,[b c] *Talbot Hotel* and posting house, Kirkgate

Wood William, clogger, 619 Wakefield road

Wood William,[c] Peel street, Leeds rd.

Wood William,[c] Holme top, Little Horton

Woodcock Charles,[b] land and building agent and surveyor, and agent for the Great Britain and Royal Exchange Insurance Companies; office 4 Bridge street; house Broad street

Woodcock Joseph,[b] grocer, tea dealer and German and Italian warehouseman, Darley street; house Manor place, Cheapside

Woodcock Thomas,[c] manager, Low Moor

Woodhead James,[b] Back lane, Bowling

Woodhead Jane, provision dealer, Little Horton lane

Woodhead John,[c] Great Horton

Woodhead Joseph, whitesmith, Keighley street, Silsbridge lane

Woodhead Samuel,[b c] high bailiff of County court, Nutter's place, Northgate

Woodhead Mr. Thomas, cashier, Low Moor

Woodhead William,[c] Chapel Farm, Horton

Woodhead William,[b] provision dealer, Little Horton lane

Woodhead William Henry,[b] chemist and druggist, North Parade and 48 Westgate; house North Parade

Woodhouse Thomas,[c] dealer in tea, coffee, &c. 35 Providence street, White Abbey

Wooller Samson, stuff manufacturer, Brook street; works and house Manningham

Woolsorters' Public Gardens and Baths, Heaton road

Worsnop Ann, milliner and dress maker, 65 Tumblinghill street, Thornton road

Worsnop Joseph Benson,[c] iron founder, Providence Foundery, Manchester road

Worsnop Luke,[b] butcher, Manchester road

Worsnop Martha, milliner and dress maker, 236 Manchester road

Worsnop Nancy, milliner and dress maker, Seymour street, Leeds road

Worsnop Sarah Ann, dress maker, 12 Lower Thomas street, Manchester road

Worsted Committee (Borough); clerk Mr. Edward Hailstone, solicitor, Manchester road

Wrathmell Harriet, *Prince of Wales*, Bowling Old lane, Bowling

Wray Joseph,[bc] machine maker, and sole maker and fitter-up of John Hyde's patent improvements in the power-loom, Westholme Mill, Thornton road; house Drewton street

Wray Richard,[c] Little Horton lane

Wray William, butcher, 16 Nelson street, Chapel lane

Wright Edwin, pork dealer, 144 Manchester road

Wright Frances, milliner, 13 Union Passage, Kirkgate

Wright George,[b] tailor, 160 Bridge street

Wright George Anderson, reed and heald maker, 8 Back Quebec terrace, Thornton road

Wright George Royle,[b c] grocer, tea dealer, and coffee roaster, 72 Market street and 124 Westgate; house Manor street

Wright Isaac,[b c] merchant (Wright and Tillotson); house Bellevue, Manningham lane

Wright James, agent for silk, cotton and worsted yarns and warps, Hustlergate and Ivegate

Wright James,[b] wine, spirit and porter merchant, Hustlergate and Ivegate; house Richmond place, Horton road

Wright John, stuff manufacturer, New Piecehall; works and house Wibsey

Wright John,[c] Spring row, Manningham

Wright John,[b] boot and shoe maker, 96 Westgate

Wright John,[b c] beer retailer, Northbrook, Bolton road

Wright John, tailor, 44 Chandos st. Wakefield road

Wright Mr. Joseph,[b] Crowther st.

Wright Joseph,[b] tailor and draper, Bridge street

Wright Joseph, stuff manufacturer, 46 Old Piecehall; works and house Haworth

Wright Joseph,[b] farmer, Oaks Fold, Bowling

Wright Miss Lydia, Bolton place

Wright Misses, boarding and day school, Sawrey place, Little Horton

Wright Bobert, shuttle-maker (Robert Wright & Sons); house 3 Westbrook terrace

Wright Robert & Sons, shuttle makers, heald shafts, temples and double stocks, Thompson's Mill, Thornton road

Wright Rushworth, coal dealer, Victoria street, Manningham

Wright Thomas, provision dealer, Bowling lane

Wright Thomas,[b] officer of inland revenue (excise branch), Undercliffe

Wright & Tillotson, wool merchants, Bermondsey

Wright William, machinist (Wright, Wood & French); house Bower street, Manchester road

Wright William, worsted spinner and manufacturer, 11 Hartley's Buildings, Brook street; works and house, Silsden, near Keighley

Wright William, joiner and builder, Earl street, Manchester road; house Adelaide street

Wright William, provision dealer, 89 Adelaide street, Manchester road

Wright William,[b] *Regent Inn*, Leeming street, School street

Wright, Wood & French, machine makers, Thompson's Mill, Thornton road

Wroe Joseph,[b] farmer, Rooley lane, Bowling

Wroe Mr. Thomas,[b] Eastbrook terrace, Leeds road

Wynn Richard, officer of inland revenue (excise branch), Shipley

Wyrill Frances, general furnishing ironmonger & cutler, 8 Westgate; house Primrose Hill

Wyrill William,[b] William street, Little Horton lane

YATES Christopher,[b] *Old Red Lion Inn*, Little Horton lane

Yates Robert,[b] manufacturer (Anderson & Yates); house Hanover sq.

Yeadon William,[c] Bolton road

YEOMANRY CAVALRY,—Bradford D Troop; Captain, Thomas Hill Horsfall; lieutenant, Mr. George Addison, and cornet Mr. Frank Rouse

Yewdall John,[b c] *Woodman Inn*, and

joiner, Wibsey bank foot, Halifax road

Yewdall Abraham,[b c] Edward street, Croft street

YORKSHIRE BANKING COMPANY (Branch), Darley street; Mr. William Duckitt manager

YORKSHIRE FIRE AND LIFE ASSURANCE COMPANY; agents Mr. Dixon, Bridge Street Buildings, and Mr. Dewhirst, Union Passage

YORKSHIRE AND LANCASHIRE RAILWAY COMPANY; Passengers' Entrance on the Leeds and Wakefield roads; Goods' Warehouse Vicar lane

Young Hiram, colourer, &c. 60 Croft street, Bridge street

CLASSIFICATION

OF

MANUFACTURES, PROFESSIONS, & TRADES,

IN

THE FOUR TOWNSHIPS

OF

BRADFORD, BOWLING, GREAT & LITTLE HORTON, AND MANNINGHAM;

TOGETHER WITH

Places of Worship and other Public Buildings, Institutions, Offices, &c.

AND THE VARIOUS CONVEYANCE LISTS.

Academies & Public Schools.

Not otherwise described are Day Schools.
(See also Professors and Teachers.)

ABBOTT Robert, Brunswick place, Northgate

AIREDALE, Churchbank, High street; Archibald Dick master; Miss Davison mistress

Atkinson William Child, Manningham

Balme John, Great Horton road

Barker Thomas, Northgate

Beanland George, 30 Pearson's Buildings, Bridge street

Booth Elizabeth, 9 North Parade, Christ Church

BOROUGH WEST SCHOOL, Sterling st. Manchester road; George Drew master; Miss Barkley mistress

BRADFORD MOOR (old school), Wm. Postlethwaite master; Mrs. Mitchell mistress

Brown John, Gain lane, Laister Dyke

Burton Misses, Chapel street, Leeds road

Carey Sarah Ann, Little Horton lane

Carveth George, Chapel street, Leeds road

CATHOLIC SCHOOL, Stott Hill; Thos. Smythe master; Miss Wallace and Miss O'Shea (Sisters of Charity), conduct the girls' department

Child Messrs. Drewton street; house Manningham lane

CHRIST CHURCH SCHOOL, Westgate; Royal Atkins master; Miss Farrer mistress

Clough Thomas, Garden place, Silsbridge lane

Craven Elijah, Croft street, Bridge street

Cudworth Ann, Earl street, Manchester road

Douthwaite John, Queen street, Manchester road

Downing Caroline (day and boarding), Spring gardens
Fielding Elizabeth, King street, Manchester road
Foster Joseph, John street, Westgate
Furby Martha, Broom street, Wakefield road
Gamble Mrs. Stott Hill
GRAMMAR SCHOOL (FREE), Manor place; Rev. John Richards, M. A. head master; Mr. Hubert Lewis, B. A. and George Voigt, B. A. assistant masters
Haining Jane & Hannah (day and boarding), Hanover square
Haley Samuel, 13 Duke street, Manchester road
Hanson James, (day and boarding), Manor row
Harker Catherine, 8 Ebenezer street, Vicar lane
Harland Elizabeth, 43 Chandos st. Wakefield road
Harrison William, Prospect street, Silsbridge lane
Hartley Benjamin, Southgate, Great Horton
Heads Thomas, Great Horton road
Heap Mrs. Hannah Manor street, Manor row
Heath Sarah Elizabeth, Northrop square, Westgate
Holdsworth Miss, Fountain street, Manningham lane
Holdsworth Joseph, Back lane
INDUSTRY (SCHOOL OF) Northgate; Elizabeth Piper superintendent
INFANTS' SCHOOL, Chapel street, Leeds road; Miss Rhodes mistress
INFANTS' SCHOOL, Little Horton lane; Miss Green mistress
Kirby Amelia & Sister (day and boarding), Skinner lane, Manningham
Lamb John, Manchester road
Laycock George, Great Horton
Laycock John, West Parade, Brick lane
Lumb George, Hall lane, Bowling
Malim Margaret, 35 Victoria street, North Parade
Milnes John, 28 Manchester road
MODEL FACTORY SCHOOL (National Society's), Lumby street, Manchester road; Frederick Rowbotham master; Elizabeth Siggs mistress
NATIONAL SCHOOL, North Bierley; John Butler master; Rebecca Firth mistress
NATIONAL SCHOOL, Spinkwell, Bolton road; John Mitchell master
NATIONAL SCHOOL, Sticker lane, Bowling; Thomas Browning master
NATIONAL SCHOOL (St. Jude's), Lumb lane; John L. Robson master; Miss Revell mistress
NATIONAL SCHOOL (St. Paul's), Lillycroft, Manningham; Henry Heppinstall master; Mrs. Heppinstall mistress
Nesbit George (and commercial writing master), 17 Stone st. Manor row
Nesbit Susannah, seminary, 17 Stone street, Manor row
Nursey Mrs. Hanover square
PAROCHIAL SCHOOL, New Leeds; Luke Bland master; Sarah Louisa Booth mistress
Pattinson Ann & Jane Elizabeth, North Parade, Manningham lane
Pratt Mary Ann, Bradford Moor
Ramshaw Miss, Manor st. Manor row
Roberts Elizabeth, Great Horton road
Sargeant John, Preston place, Great Horton

Scholefield James, Regent street, White Abbey

Scott Miss (day and boarding), Lister terrace, Horton road

Smith Jane, Belgrave place, Lumb lane, Manningham

St. Hilaire's Educational Institute, Pearson's Buildings, Bridge street

St. James's School, James street, Manchester road; Samuel Batty master; Miss West mistress

St. John's School, Church Hill, Wakefield road; Thomas Briggs master; Elizabeth Briggs mistress

Taylor Mrs. Mary (boarding and day), Bellevue, Manningham lane

Walker Mary Ann, Sawrey place, Little Horton lane

Walker William, Back lane, Bowling

Waters Jane, 25 Westgrove street

Wesleyan Schools (Eastbrook), Chapel street, Leeds road; David John Crebbin master; Mrs. Crebbin mistress, — Infants' School, Miss Rhodes

Wesleyan School, Clayton lane, Manchester road; Edward M. Jaram master

Whiteley Priscilla, Drewton street

Wilks Mary (day and boarding), 4 Park place, North Parade

Wilson John, Bedford st. Bridge st.

Woller George, 88 Providence street, White Abbey

Wood Walter, Longcroft place, Silsbridge lane

Wright Elizabeth, Bolten place, Bridge street

Wright Hannah & Emma (day and boarding), Sawrey place, Little Horton lane

Accountants.

(See also Agents,—General and Miscellaneous).

Blackburn Henry William (for railway and other public companies, trustees' and receivers' accounts in chancery, or for any of the courts of equity or bankruptcy), Dispensary Buildings, 36 Darley street—(*See* advertisement)

Charlesworth Thomas Richard (and general agent, bankrupts' and insolvents' balance sheets, &c. made out), 49 Darley street, near Christ Church—(*See* advertisement)

Clayton James (and general agent), Charles street — (*See* advertisement)

Clough William (to the corporation of Bradford), Swaine street, Hall Ings

Haigh Thomas (and actuary), Savings' Bank, Kirkgate

Hammond James, Cheapside

Mason William, 3 Bridge street Buildings, Bridge street

Roberts John, 11 Harris street, Leeds road

Agents—Ale and Porter.

(See also Porter Merchants).

Brumfit Charles (Guinness & Co's. porter and Scotch, Burton and East India pale ales, cider, perry, &c.); office and stores 27 Bermondsey—(*See* advertisement)

Clough James (London porter, Burton ale, &c.), 20 Market street

Greenwood Frederick Smith (London porter, Burton ale, &c.), Duke street, Darley street

Hargreaves Sarah (and British wines, &c.), 30 Kirkgate

Holloway William Henry (London and Dublin porter, Burton and Scotch ales, cider, &c.), Exchange Vaults, Kirkgate

Kitcheman Samuel (London porter, Burton ale, &c.), Leeds road

Reaney James (Meux's London porter, Scotch and Burton ales, &c.), 6 Baldwin lane, James street

Roberts Joshua (Guinness & Co's. porter, Burton, Scotch and East India pale ales, &c.), 5 Manor row

Taylor Thomas (London porter and Burton ale), Brook street, Hall Ings

Town Edward Henry (London porter and Burton ale), 21½ Ivegate

Wilson Benjamin (Burton and Scotch ales, London porter, &c.), Primrose Hill, Great Horton

Wright James (London and Dublin porter, Scotch and Burton ales), Hustlergate and Ivegate

Agents—Commission Stuff Buyers.

(See also Agents—General and Miscellaneous).

Banks & Pollard, 28 Leeds road

Brigg Joshua, Booth street, Hall Ings

Clayton James, Charles street, Market street

Greenwood Thomas, Charles street, Market street

Haigh William Chapman, Swaine street, and Exchange street, Kirkgate

Halliday John, Hartley's Buildings, Brook street

Holmes Richard, Talbot Yard, Hustlergate and Kirkgate

Hutchinson Samuel, Charles street

Knapton James, 20 Market street

Preston John, 20 Bank street

Sugden John, Brook street, Hall Ings

Sutcliffe Jonas, Hope and Anchor Yard, Bank street

Sutcliffe Joseph, Hope and Anchor Yard, Bank street

Agents—Commission Wool and Tops.

(See Woolstaplers, and also Worsted Top Makers).

* Marked thus are Wool only.

Brooks Edward, Swaine street

Brown Joseph, Hustler's Buildings, Market street

Butterfield Samuel, Hustler's Buildings, Market street

Clayton James (tops), Charles street (*See advertisement*)

* Clayton Thomas, Thornton road

Denton William (tops), Swaine street

Donisthorpe Joseph, Tyrrel street

Forster & Fison, Hustler's Buildings, Leeds road

Haigh William Chapman, Exchange street and Swaine street

* Hall & Bankart, Bermondsey

* Hargreaves John, Union street, Bridge street

Holdsworth James, Cheapside

* Horsfall William and Brothers, Broadstones

Hudson John (tops), 98 Old Piecehall

* Illingworth & Kenion, Charles st. Hall Ings

* Margerison & Sutcliffe, Bermondsey

* Rochfort Valentine, 17 Union Passage, Kirkgate

* Selby Samuel, Cheapside

Sugden & Webster, Hustler's Buildings, Market street

Turner Charles Timothy, Charles st.

Agents—General and Miscellaneous.

INCLUDING SILK, COTTON and WORSTED YARN and WARPS, &c.

(See also preceding list, likewise the following Land and Building Agents, Coal Agents, Fire Office Agents, &c.)

(Marked thus * are General Agents.)

Anderton J. W. silk and cotton warps, 30 Pearson's Buildings, Bridge st.

Banks & Pollard, stuff goods, &c. 28 Leeds road

Bayldon William, cotton warps, &c. Swaine street

Bentham Joseph, French yarn, and stuff goods, Market street

Blamires Samuel, Bradford Flour Mill Co. Great Horton road

Bryar Joseph, tea, coffee, &c. Victoria street, Manningham lane

Charlesworth J. & J. Haigh Coal Company, Railroad street, Canal road

Clayton James, worsted tops and yarns, Charles street (*See advertisement*)

*Collinson Edward, emigration, packet, and soaps, oils, &c. Leeds road

Cressey William, house agent, 26 Bedford street, Bridge street

Dawson Mark, cotton warps, Booth street, Hall Ings

Denton John, flag and stone, Balme street, Bolton road

Denton William, worsted tops, Swaine street

Donisthorpe Joseph, worsted tops, Tyrrel street

Frank & Co. foreign agents for the Bowling Iron Works, Duke street, corner of Exchange street

Greenwood Thomas, stuff goods and yarn, Charles street

*Haigh William Chapman, silk and cotton warps, &c. Swaine street and Exchange street, Kirkgate

*Halcro Augustus John, 22 Piecehall Yard, Kirkgate

Halliday John, warps and yarns, stuff goods, paper, &c. Hartley's Buildings, Brook street

Hargreaves John, Lothersdale Lime Company, Union street, and Railroad street

* Hepper James, Leeds and Liverpool Canal Carrying Co. Thornton road, and Canal wharf, Shipley

Heselton J. A. silk warps, &c. Union street, Bridge street

Holmes Richard, worsted yarn and stuff goods, Talbot Yard

*Holt Benjamin, machine, washing leather, &c. Charles street, and Mawson street, Thornton road

*Hutchinson Samuel, yarn, warps, &c. Charles street, Market street

Ingham Joseph, silk and cotton warps, and stuff goods, Hope and Anchor Yard, Bank street

Knapton James, yarn, warps and stuff goods, 20 Market street

Leather George Henry, silk warps, &c. Charles street

Liebert Bernhard, stuff goods, yarn, &c. Hall Ings

*Lister George Thompson, house and land, 19 Drewton street, Westgate

Mills James William, silk and cotton yarn, and stuff goods, Hustler's Buildings, Market street

Mitton Henry and Co. oils, colours, varnish, &c. 20 Nag's Head Yard, Kirkgate

Mortimer William, silk and cotton warps and stuff goods, 21 Market street

Muller George, yarn, oils, &c. Charles street

Murgatroyd William, silk warps, &c. Charles street

Oddy William, sizing, leather skeps, and pickers, picking straps, &c. 65 Market street

*Phillipp Joseph, 60 Market street

Poole George, house agent, 85 Silsbridge lane

Preston John, stuff goods, cotton and worsted yarn, &c. 20 Bank street

Rhodes John, grey goods, canvas, paper, &c. 22 Nag's Head Yard

Selby Samuel, soaps, oils, &c. Cheapside

Stephenson David, house and land, Little Horton Green

Stephenson Thomas, soaps, oils, glue, &c. Charles street

Sugden John, stuff goods and worsted yarn, &c. Brook street

Sussmann Alfred, paper and packing materials, Court street, Leeds road

Sutcliffe Jonas, worsted and stuff goods, Hope and Anchor Yard, Bank street

Sutcliffe Joseph, yarn and stuff goods, Hope and Anchor yard, Bank street

Sutcliffe Joseph & Robert, cotton yarn and warps, Brook street

Swaine & Wilcock, yarn, warps and stuff goods, 40 Old Market place

Taylor James S. cotton warps, &c. Charles street

Turner Charles Timothy, cotton warps and worsted tops, Charles street

Wilson Benjamin, wines and spirits, ales and porter, Primrose Hill, Horton

Wilson James, silk and cotton yarn and warps, Hall Ings

* Wood Joshua, grey goods, cotton warps, soaps, oils, &c. 21 Market street

Wright James, silk, cotton and worsted yarn and warps, Hustlergate and Ivegate

Architects and Surveyors.

(See also Land and Building Agents).

Andrews & Delauney, Rennie's Buildings, Hall Ings

Dixon John (and builder), Swaine street

Dixon Thomas (surveyor), Bridge street Buildings, Bridge street

Fairbank John Tertius, 36 Darley st.

Mallinson & Healy (and valuers), Tyrrel street

Mawson David, 29 Westend Buildings, Lister Hills, Horton

Metcalf William, Bridge street Buildings, Bridge street

Rawsthorne William, North Parade, Christ Church

Thornton Henry, 10 Duke street, Cheapside

Artists' Colourmen and Depositories.

(See also Printsellers).

Gelderd Joshua, 140 Westgate

Robinson Dan, 20 Well street

Attorneys.

Barret Edward Alexander, Charles st.

Bentley Greenwood, junr. Regent place, Darley street

Bentley & Wood, Hall Ings

Berry John (and clerk to the deputy-lieutenant for Lower Agbrigg), Leeds road

Busfeild Johnson Atkinson (and treasurer of County Courts), Thornton's Buildings, Market street

Butterfield Francis, White Lion Yard, Kirkgate, and Bingley

Darlington John (and agent in the West Riding for the Guarantee Society), 12 Union Passage, Kirkgate

Dawson Joseph, Tyrrel square, Tyrrel street

Ecroyd Benjamin (conveyancer), 67 Market street

Foster Marmaduke, 70 Market st.

Fowler Edward (*see* Terry, Watson and Fowler) 9 Market street

Gant James Greaves Tetley, 3 Market street

Hailstone Samuel & Edward; Edwd. Hailstone clerk to the worsted committee, and to the Leeds and Halifax turnpike road; offices 37 Manchester road

Harrison John Seppings, Bridge street Buildings, Bridge street

Hodgson Joseph (and commissioner for taking affidavits for the county palatine of Lancaster), 12 Hustlergate

Lambert James (and clerk to the commissioners of taxes), 14 Exchange street, Kirkgate

Lee J. M. Pearson's Buildings, Bridge street

Lees Humble; Charles Lees commissioner for taking recognizances of insolvent debtors, and affidavits in the Irish courts; George Humble commissioner for taking acknowledgments of married women; offices 5 Albion Court, Kirkgate

Morris Joseph (and clerk to the North Bierley Union), 36 Darley street

Mossman George Robert (and clerk to the West Riding magistrates acting at Bradford, commissioner for taking bail in the Insolvent Debtors' Court, and for taking acknowledgments of married women), office Hall Ings

Northwood George, Darley street

Pickup Mark, 14 Union Passage, Kirkgate

Rawson & George; John Rawson town-clerk and clerk to the borough magistrates; office Swaine street, Hall Ings

Terry, Watson & Fowler, 9 Market street

Thompson & Clegg; Joseph Thompson clerk to the Bradford Water Works Company; John Clegg steward to the Ladies of the Manor; offices Bridge street Buildings, Bridge street

Thornton George, 10 Duke street, Darley street

Tolson, Clough & Taylor; Charles Clough clerk to the County Court, and to the Bradford and Wakefield turnpike trust; offices Rawson place, Darley street

Wagstaff John Reid (and clerk to the Board of the Bradford Poor Law Union, and superintendent registrar of Bradford and North Bierley districts), office Charles street

Wells & Ridehalgh (to the Bradford Banking Company); Richard Ridehalgh clerk to the gas works; offices Tyrrel court, Tyrrel street

Auctioneers and Appraisers.

(See also Furniture Brokers.)

Barraclough John (appraiser only), 68 Westgate

Bates William, 15 Union Passage, Kirkgate

Bryar Joseph, Victoria street, North Parade

Carr John, Tyrrel street, and Halifax
Driver Peter, Procter's Buildings, Leeds road
Firth James, 15 Broadstones, Well street
Grainge James, 7 Union Passage, Kirkgate
Halcro John Augustus, 22 Piecehall Yard, Kirkgate
Hardcastle George, 53 Westgate
Hartley James, Well street
Hepper Christopher, Old Post Office Buildings, Bridge street
Holt Benjamin (appraiser only), Bank street and Mawson street, Thornton road
Ingham Timothy, 34 Market street
Lister George Thompson, 19 Drewton street, Westgate
Poole George (appraiser only), 85 Silsbridge lane
Riley Matthew, 2 Keighley Old road, Manningham
Tetley Benjamin, Leeds road
Turner Jonas, 49 Kirkgate

Bacon and Ham Dealers,—Wholesale and Retail.

(See also Provision Dealers, Shopkeepers, and Pork Butchers.)

Cluderay William, 134 Westgate
Dennison Patrick, 88 Manchester rd.
Diggles James, 158 & 160 Westgate
Diggles John, 23 Ivegate
Dowling Michael, 51 Market street
Emsley James and John, 204 Manchester road, and 38 Bolton road
Farnell James, 150 Westgate
Harrison John, 49 Silsbridge lane
Morrell John (wholesale), 4 and 6 Tyrrel street
Morrell Robert & Co. 17 and 92 Westgate
Robertshaw Joshua, 77 Silsbridge lane
Robson John, 7 Wakefield road
Rooks George, 9 and 11 Broadstones
Rowntree Isaac, 146 Manchester rd.
Settle Samuel Ellick, West Parade, Brick lane
Smith Charles, 170 Manchester road
Waud & Co. (wholesale), 5 Market street
Waud William (wholesale), 1 and 21 Darley street

Bag and Sacking Dealers.

(See also Rope & Twine Manufacturers.)

Oddy George, 19 Kirkgate
Oddy Mark, 69 Market street

Bakers and Flour Dealers.

(See also Corn and Flour Dealers.)

Asquith William, 42 Greenaire place, Silsbridge lane, and 117 Westgate
Burrows John, Great Horton road
Burton Francis, 12 Nelson street, Chapel lane
Burton Robert, 6 Silsbridge lane
Butterfield James, 122 Longcroft st. Silsbridge lane
Butterfield William, 46 Sterling st. Manchester road
Cameron William, 57 Park place, Little Horton
Cansfield Isaac, 30 Gaunt street, Otley road
Carr Thomas, 4 Nelson street, Chapel lane
Carter Robert, 138 Manchester road
Casson John, Churchbank, High st.
Challand George, 20 Bowling lane, Manchester road
Child James, 94 Bolton road

Clark James, 163 George street, Leeds road
Clarke Joshua, Pit lane, Barkerend
Clarkson Richard, 45 Westgate
Clayton Matthew, Back lane. Bowling
Clough James, Ebor street, Little Horton lane
Clough Jane, Fitzgerald street, Manchester road
Clough John, High street, Great Horton
Cockson William, Mount street, Leeds road
Cole Benjamin, Church Hill, Wakefield road
Collier William, 85 Victoria street, North Parade
Collingwood Job, Great Horton
Collins George, 452 Wakefield road
Cooper John, 192 Manchester road
Copley Thomas, 37 Longlands street, Westgate
Crabtree Thomas, 121 Manchester road
Craven Benjamin, Daisyhill Top, Manningham
Critchley Henry, 7 Longcroft place, Silsbridge lane
Croft Benjamin, 597 Wakefield road
Crowther Rachael, 8 Nelson street, Chapel lane
Darling Benjamin, 101 Northwing, High street
Dawson John, 164 Croft street, Leeds road
Demain William, Upper North Parade
Denbeigh Elizabeth, 15 Thornton street, Thornton road
Dennison Patrick, 88 Manchester rd.
Dewhirst Thomas, Providence street, Silsbridge lane
Dilley Philip, Back lane, Bowling
Dixon John, 4 Duke street, Manchester road
Dobson Thomas, 300 Manchester rd.
Dracup Richard, High street, Great Horton
Drake Andrew, Clayton street, Thornton road
Eastwood George, 10 Silsbridge lane
Elliott William, 23 Nelson street, Chapel lane
Ellis John, 35 George street, Leeds road
Ellison Thomas, 65 High street, Well street and Chapel lane
Fearnley George, Otley road
Firth William, 169 Bolton road
Foster William, 26 Silsbridge lane
Fox William, 18 Providence street, White Abbey
Galloway John, 44 Sterling street, Manchester road
Gaukroger Samuel, 21 Silsbridge la.
Gelderd Robert, 88 Thornton road
Goggs Henry, 29 Wellington street, Stott Hill
Greenwood John Wilson, High street, Great Horton
Greenwood Joseph, Great Horton rd.
Haley William, 1 Fawcett Court, Nelson street
Halliday Richard, Ebenezer street, Vicar lane
Hamilton Mary, Church-steps, Bolton road
Hammond John, 4 Melbourne street, Leeds read
Hammond Joseph, Four Lane Ends, Manningham
Hanson Daniel, 43 Northgate
Hanson Joseph, 178 Wakefield road
Hardaker James, 18 Longlands st. Westgate

Harker John, Railroad street, School street
Harris James, Dudley Hill, Bowling
Harrison John, 49 Silsbridge lane
Harrison Miles, 10 Fawcett Court, Nelson street
Harrison William, Back lane, Bowling
Hartley Richard, 69 High street
Hartley William, Crown street, Thornton road
Hewitt William, 10 Prospect street, Thornton road
Hill Edmund, Little Horton lane
Hill Joshua, 49 Lumb lane
Hinchliffe Thomas, 29 Brook street, Leeds road
Hird John, 18 Providence street, Westgate
Hodgson Benjamin, 1 Nelson Court, Nelson street
Hodgson John, 60 Garnet street, Leeds road
Holdsworth James, Barkerend
Holdsworth Joseph, Great Horton
Holdsworth Thomas, 191 Wakefield road
Holdsworth William, 72 Bolton road
Hollings Abraham, Legrams lane, Horton
Holmes Joseph, 28 Joseph street, Leeds road
Holmes Richard, Wakefield road
Hopkinson William, 5 Wel street
Hornby Henry, Back lane, Bowling
Howard Joseph, 36 Manchester road
Jackson Abraham, 274 Manchester road
Jackson Samuel, 52 George street, Leeds road
Jackson Thomas, 26 Clarence street, Manchester road
Johnson William, 57 Regent street, Duke street
Jowett Nathan, 21 Ebor street, Little Horton lane
Jowett William, 88 Silsbridge lane
Kaye John, Leeds road
Kelley John, 132 Bridge street
Kennedy Richard, 132 Victoria street, Manchester road
Knowles William, Bavaria place, Manningham
Lapage John, Back lane, Bowling
Laycock Joshua, 16 King Charles st. Otley road
Lee William, Commercial street, Canal road
Lister Benjamin, High street, Great Horton
Lister James, Park place, Little Horton
Lister Robert, Wakefield road
Liversedge John, Great Horton road
Lonsdale Daniel, 3 James street, Manchester road
M'Kell William, Lillycroft, Manningham
M'Lean Thomas, Croft street, Manchester road
Mann James, 68 Hope street, Manchester road
Mann William, Manchester road
Markham Joseph, 129 Manchester road
Martin Joseph, 128 Wakefield road
Mason William, 2 Cropper lane, Westgate
Mawson Joseph, 149 Silsbridge lane
Maskell George, 43 Edward street, Bridge street
Midgley William, Bridge street
Mills Henry, 122 Manchester road
Mills Robert, 141 Manchester road
Moody Nathaniel, 216 Manchester road
Moorhouse Smith, 27 Silsbridge lane

Naylor William, New row, Manningham
Parker Henry, High street, Great Horton
Parker William, 131 Brick lane
Pearson Abraham, Primrose terrace, Manningham
Peel Edward, Southgate, Great Horton
Pickard Joseph, 2 Anngate, High st.
Pickard William, 189 Bridge street
Piercy John, 222 Manchester road
Pollard Maria, 20 Chapel lane
Poole Jacob, 53 Northwing, High st.
Preston William, 54 Manchester road
Priestley Joseph, 2 Castle street, Manchester road
Raistrick James, 80 Bolton road
Rayner Edward, 35 Portland street, Manchester road
Riley James, Sterling street, Manchester road
Roberts Jonathan, 106 Victoria street, Thornton road
Robertshaw Joshua, 77 Silsbridge lane
Robson John, 7 Wakefield road
Robson John, 74 George st. Leeds rd.
Rooks George, 9 and 11 Broadstones
Russell Joshua, 80 Northwing, High street
Shackleton Thomas, Gt. Horton road
Sharp Squire, 291 Manchester road
Sharp William, Broadstones
Shaw William, Wakefield road
Spence George, Broadstones
Starkey Edmund, 22 George street, Leeds road
Stocks Joseph, Southgate, Gt. Horton
Sunderland Simeon, 45 Bedford street, Bridge street
Swithenbank Joshua, 17 Prospect street, Thornton road
Swithenbank Sarah, 13 Broadstones
Taylor John, Birkshall, Bowling
Taylor Joseph, Church st. High st.
Taylor Thomas, 81 Otley road
Waddington Jonathan, 41 Hope street, Manchester road
Wade John, 463 Wakefield road
Wadsworth Thomas, Leeds road
Walls William, 38 Wellington street, Stott Hill
Walsh John, Victoria street, Manningham
Whittaker Jonas, 86 Bridge street
Wilkinson James, 196 Bolton road
Wilkinson Robert, 17 Silsbridge lane

Bankers.

(For Extended Banking Information see "BANKER'S LIST.")

BRADFORD BANKING COMPANY, Kirkgate; draw on Jones, Loyd & Co. Mr. Samuel Laycock manager

BRADFORD COMMERCIAL JOINT STOCK BANK, Market street; draw on Glyn & Co.—Mr. Joseph Hill manager

BRADFORD OLD BANK (Messrs. Harris); draw on Barnett, Hoares & Co.—Mr. Charles Heron and John Pawson cashiers.

YORKSHIRE BANKING COMPANY,—Darley street; draw on Williams, Deacon & Co.—Mr. William Duckitt manager

SAVINGS' BANK (Bradford and East Morley), Kirkgate; open on Thursdays from 2 to 4. afternoon, and on Saturdays from 6 to a quarter before 8 night—Thomas Haigh actuary

Barometer and Looking-Glass Dealers.

(See also Mathematical Instrument Makers.)

(Marked thus + are Looking-Glass only.)

Archer Edward, 5 Tyrrel street

+ Clough Joseph, 2 Manchester road
+ Constántine James, 76 Bridge street
+ Cowin James & Son, 59 Northgate
+ Craven Isaac, 34 Darley street
Franks Isaac (glass and other instruments for chemical experiments), 71 Market street, and Leeds
+ Hartley Samuel, Leeds road
Hepper Christopher, Old Post-Office Buildings, Bridge street
Mills Thomas, 45 Market street
+ Milnes Enoch, 28 Manchester road
Nutter Joseph, Nutter's place, North Parade
Rhodes Charles, 2 Cheapside
Rhodes Manoah, (barometer only), 6 Westgate
Robinson Dan, 20 Well street
+ Sutcliffe Samuel, 138 and 140 George street, Leeds road
+ Thornton John, 21 Westgate
+ Tyas John, 115 Westgate
+ Whitehead John, 14 Well street
+ Whitehead Richard, 24 Bridge st.
Wilkinson Joseph, New Market place, and 13 North Parade

Basket and Skep Makers.

Dobson Edward, 33 Westgate
German William, 4 Bridge street
Smith Samuel, 2 Market place, Darley street
Taylor James, 38 Market street
Walker James, Brumfit's Yard, Kirkgate and Regent place, Duke street
Walker James G. 25 James street, Northgate

Baths—Public.

Blackburn Henry (warm and cold), Great Horton road
Leach John and Son (cold), at the gardens, Manningham lane
Woolsorters' Gardens, (warm and cold), Heaton road

Beer Retailers

Follow Inns, Hotels and Taverns.

Berlin Wool Dealers,

AND FANCY WORSTEDS AND PATTERNS FOR NEEDLEWORK.

Hunton William, 8 Darley street
Simpson Elizabeth, 5 and 6 Market st.

Billiard Room

AND BAGATELLE KEEPERS.

EXCHANGE BUILDINGS (and Assembly Rooms), Exchange st. Kirkgate
BOWLING GREEN INN, Bridge street; Joseph Baxter proprietor
Edwin Patrick Duggan (bagatelle), Union street, Bridge street
Greenwood Frederick Smith (bagatelle), Duke street, Darley street

Birmingham and Sheffield Warehouses.

(See also Ironmongers—Furnishing).

Cannan James, Silsbridge lane
Denton Joseph, Bazaar, Kirkgate, and Lidget Green, Horton
Dilger Theodore, 15 Hustlergate
Dixon & Byrne, 77 Market street
Dove Thomas Pashley, 17 Ivegate
Flinn Edward, 14 Providence street, Westgate, and Bazaar, Kirkgate
Marshall William, 4 Kirkgate
Parratt Edward Hawksworth, 1 Broadstones, Well street
Pearson Henry, 30 and 32 Bridge st.
Read Henry, 29 Market street
Rhodes John, 18 Kirkgate
Rudd Robert (and agent for Ransome and Parsons' patent filterer), 35 Kirkgate

Scully Ambrose, 7 Ivegate
Shackleton William, 23 Broadstones
Smith Jonas, 40 Westgate
Stelling Thomas, 63 Kirkgate
Wyrill Francis, 8 Westgate—(*See* advertisement)

Blacking Makers.

Muldoon James, Market place, Kirkgate
Murgatroyd Charles, 56 Manchester road
Turner William, 166 Silsbridge lane

Bleachers.

Holroyd & Barstow, New road, Great Horton

Blacksmiths.

Marked thus + are also Farriers.
(See also Veterinary Surgeons.)

Appleyard James, Quebec terrace, Thornton road
Balmforth Joseph, Clayton street, Thornton road
+ Beanland Henry, Northgate
+ Bradley John, Thornton road
Brook Joseph, Silsbridge lane
Calvert John, Well street
Carter William, Vicar lane
Clark Joseph, Bradford Moor
+ Clayton John, Market street
Coates Ralph, Hardcastle lane, Well street
+ Denison Dyson & Thomas, Tyrrel street, Bridge street
+ Dewhirst Benjamin, Vicar lane
England Samuel, Thornton road
+ Evans James, Back Green lane, Manningham
Garthwaite John, High street, Great Horton
Gray John, 68 Manchester road
Haley Jonas, Dudley Hill, Bowling
Hargreaves Charles and Michael (general), Cropper lane, Westgate
Hillas Abraham, 213 Manchester rd.
Holdsworth & Raistrick, (general), Croft street, Manchester road
Kitchenman Charles, Bierley lane, North Bierley
+ Ludlam Benjamin, Spink'sBuildings, Black Abbey
Martin Benjamin, Manchester road
Mitchell Thomas (farrier only), Bradford Moor
+ Muff John, Cutlerheight-lane, Dudley Hill
+ Parker Samuel, Brook street
Rayner Joseph, 17 Mill street, Canal road
+ Robinson Francis, 240 Wakefield road
+ Scott William, Churchbank, Well street
+ Thompson George, Northgate
+ Turner Thomas, Cross street, Westgate
Tillotson Joseph (general), Pennyoaks Mill, Leeds road
Walton Joseph, Queen street, Manchester road
Wilson Richard, Halifax road, Bowling
Woller Samuel, Bradford Moor

Blanket Merchants.

(See also Stuff Merchants.)

Birchall Edwin & Sons, Leeds road
Holdsworth John & Co. Norfolk st. Bridge street
Scarf & Hanson, Hall Ings

Bobbin & Skewer Turners.

(See also Turners.)

Briggs Robert & Sons, Sugden's Mill, Black Abbey

Cowperthwaite Stephen, New Miller Dam, Thornton road

Boiler Makers.

Cliffe James & Joseph, Old Foundry, Tyrrel street

Crosland Robert, Union Foundry, Manchester road

Holdsworth & Raistrick (and gasometer), Croft street, Manchester road

Bookbinders.

(See also Booksellers and Stationers, and Pattern Card Makers.)

Byles Henry B. 17 Kirkgate

Dale John, 1 Thornton's Buildings, Bridge street

Drake & Fawcett, 21 Market street

Drake John, King's Court, Northgate

Ibbetson James (account-books, ledgers, &c. ruled and bound to any pattern), 20 Bridge street

Lumley Joseph, Hustler's Buildings, Leeds road

Lund Joseph, 82 Westgate

Mawson Henry Ogle, 43, Kirkgate

Morris Benjamin Gough, Swan Yard, Market street

Nicholson John, 1 Bermondsey

Parry Robert, 15 Market street

Spencer Richard & Thomas, Broadstones

Stanfield Charles, 5 Westgate

Watson Robert, James street

Wilkinson Christopher, Tyrrel street

Booksellers and Stationers.

(See also Stationers).

Blackburn William Howgill, 15 Market street

Boulton Samuel, 4 Lumb lane

Byles Henry, 17 Kirkgate

Cannan William, 149, Bridge street

Cooke William, Ebenezer street, Vicar lane

Dale John (Depository of the Religious Tract Society), 1 Thornton's Buildings, Bridge street

Hainsworth John, 32 Manchester rd.

Ibbetson James, 20 Bridge street

Lund Joseph, 82 Westgate (*see advertisement*)

Mawson Henry Ogle, 43 Kirkgate

Parker Mrs. (Catholic), Stott Hill

Pearce George, Tyrrell street

Smithson John (old and new), 218 Manchester road

Stanfield Charles (and Homily and Prayer Book Society's Depot), 5 Westgate

Umpleby Thomas, 2 Lumby street,

Walker Benjamin, 8 Market street

Waterhouse Thomas (old and new), 25 Darley street (*See advertisement*)

Wilkinson Christopher, Tyrrel street

Boot and Shoe Makers and Dealers.

Allison Sarah, 25 Market street

Anderson Joseph, Parkgate, High st.

Armitage George, Back lane, Bowling

Armitage George, 136 Providence st. White Abbey

Armitage Joseph, North street, Northwing

Ashworth Simeon, Old Gardens, Cropper lane

Aspinall Abraham, Bavaria place, Manningham

Atkinson Joseph, 4 Johnson Fold, Northwing

Baker Matthew, 87 John street, Stott Hill

Bell Thompson, 57 Providence street, White Abbey

Bell William, Greenhill place, Manningham

Bennett David, 176 Silsbridge lane
Bennett John, 21 Clayton street, Thornton road
Bennett Joseph, 3 King Charles st. Otley road
Blakebrough Joshua, High street, Great Horton
Bland Jonathan, 73 High street
Booth Thomas, Southgate, Great Horton
Bostock William, 29 Ivegate
Boulton Nathan, Mount street, Bowling
Bracewell John, Wood street, Manningham
Bradley Joseph, 13 Priestley street, Bolton road
Brearley David, 47 Westgate
Briggs Rawdon, Clayton street, Thornton road
Briggs Samuel, Low Green, Great Horton
Broadley & Taylor, 3 North Parade
Brown Edward, 2 Vicar lane
Burnley William, Little Horton lane
Calvert George, Castle street, Manchester road
Carr Sarah, High street, Great Horton
Cherry John, Stott Hill
Clarkson Abraham, 17 Cropper lane, Westgate
Clayton John, Cheapside
Clough Henry, Little Horton
Clough John, 176 Wakefield road
Cook David, Sticker lane, Bowling
Cotton Edward, 7 Westgate; George Roberts agent
Crabtree Matthew, High street, Great Horton
Crosland Francis, 5 Croft street, Bridge street
Dalby James, 9 Park place, Little Horton

Dawson Joseph, Chapel lane, Tyrrel street
Denison Emanuel, Swaine Green, Bowling
Dracup Squire, High street, Great Horton
Dunwell Jonathan, 46 Manchester road
Eastburn William, 10 Sterling street, Manchester road
Ellis Watson, 12 Manchester road
Eltoft Ann, 24 Darley street
Exley Joseph, Sticker lane, Bowling
Fairbank William, 132 Queen street, Manchester road
Fawbert James & John, 40 Barkerend
Fawcett John, North Parade and Tyrrel street
Feather Joseph, Manchester road
Fenton James, Uppercroft row, Bowling
Firth Constantine, 25 Oak street, Leeds road
Firth Joseph, 45 Bridge street
Fletcher Abraham, Albion Court, Kirkgate
Fletcher James, 79 Portland street, Manchester road
Forrest Samuel, 27 Otley road
Foulds Joseph, 20 Providence street, White Abbey
Foulds Thomas, 69 Manchester road
Fox Amos, Great Horton road, Horton
Fox Charles, Lidget green, Legrams, Horton
Fox Henry, High street, Great Horton
Franks Robert, 300 Leeds road
Galloway James, Halifax road, Bowling

Galloway John, Halifax road, Bowling
Gill Joshua, 126 Brown street, Manchester road
Goodchild James, Market place, Kirkgate
Gough John, 1 North street, Northwing
Greenlay Thomas, 22 Darley street
Haigh Richard, Westgrove street
Haigh William, Dudley Hill, Bowling
Haigh William, Mitchell's Buildings, Manchester road
Hardaker Thomas, 32 White Abbey
Hargreaves David, 212 Manchester road
Harpley John, Laister Dyke, Bradford Moor
Harrison Stephen, 96 Bedford street, Wakefield road
Hawley John, 27 Westgate
Heckley James, 23 Fitzgerald street, Manchester road
Heron William, Brown street, Wakefield road
Highmes John, Sunnyside, Lumb lane
Hill Edward, 5 Arundel street, Manchester road
Hill Edward, 27 Nelson street, Chapel lane
Hill Nott, 15 Burrow street, Manchester road
Hodgson James, 27 Nelson street, Chapel lane
Hollingworth William, Wadkin's Fold, Well street
Holmes James, Dudley Hill, Bowling
Holroyd Matthew, Sticker lane, Bowling
Hopper John, 2 King street, Manchester road
Hudson John, 87 Wakefield road
Huggan Thomas, 46 Kirkgate
Hurtley Thomas, 11 Green lane, Manningham
Hutchinson John, 53 Chapel lane, Tyrrel street
Imeson Matthew, 5 Melbourne street, Leeds road
Irving John, 210 Manchester road
Jones Morris, 4 Castle street, Manchester road
Josling William, 24 West street, Vicar lane
Keighley William, Great Horton road
Kellett Thomas, 106 Wapping road
Knowles Ezra, 32 York street, Bridge street
Knowles George, Dudley Hill, Bowling
Knowles Joseph, Halifax road, Bowling
Lund Richard, Uppercroft row, Bowling
Law James, 87 Bridge street
Laycock John, Victoria street, Manningham
Laycock Thomas, 20 Butterfield terrace, Manchester road
Lincey John, 90 Bedford street, Wakefield road
Liversedge Thomas (and registrar), 16 Ivegate
Liversedge William, 63 Hope street, Manchester road
Lockwood Edward, 48 Bedford street, Bridge street
Lucas Robert, 4 James street, Manchester road
Mann William, Belgrave place, Manningham
Margeson Isaiah, 29 Prospect street, Silsbridge lane
Marshall Thomas, 2 Gracechurch st. White Abbey
Marvell John, Silsbridge lane

Midgley John, 32 Prospect street, Thornton road
Moss William, 8 Leeds road
Nelson Richard, White Abbey
Newbould Thomas, 41 John street, Stott Hill
Nicholson John, 42 Bower street, Manchester road
Osborn William, 184 Bridge street
Parkinson John, 163 Whetley street, Manningham
Parkinson John, 39 York street, Bridge street
Parratt Charles, Green lane, Manningham
Parratt Robert, 28 Croft st. Bridge st.
Parratt Samuel, Bradford Moor
Parratt Samuel, 8 Lister street, Bermondsey
Pattison John, 13 John st. Northgate
Pawson Benjamin, 18 Victoria street, White Abbey
Peacock William, 2 North Street Court, North street
Peel Samuel, Great Horton road
Pickard John, 10 King street, Manchester road
Pilling Robinson, High street, Great Horton
Pollard James, 2 Threadneedle street, Vicar lane
Pollard John, 14 John st. Northgate
Pollard John, Back lane, Bowling
Pollard Joseph, 6 Hope street, Manchester road
Pollard Samuel, Wakefield road
Poole Thomas, Crown street, Thornton road
Prest William, 22 Well street
Punt William, 22 Bolton road
Raynes William, 10 Market street
Revell Emanuel, 51 Chandos street, Wakefield road
Richardson Benjamin, 68 Bolton road
Riley Alexander, Little Horton
Scholefield Michael, Back lane, Bowling
Sellers Eli, 19 Tumblinghill street, Thornton road
Settle Abraham, Four Lane Ends, Manningham
Shackleton Thomas, Holme Top, Little Horton
Sharp Mungo, 43 George street, Manchester road
Shuttleworth William, 13 Longcroft place, Westgate
Shuttleworth William, 82 Silsbridge lane
Simpson Christopher, Spring street, Bolton road
Simpson George, 2 Providence street, White Abbey
Simpson James, 76 Leeds road
Slater Paul, 9 Old Market, Hustlergate, and Hope street
Smith Eli, 12 Nutter's Buildings, Northgate
Smith Henry, 145 George street, Leeds road
Smith James, Thornton street, Thornton road
Smith John, 18 Nelson Court, Nelson street
Sowden Joseph, 25 Wharf street
Speight John, 34 Fitzgerald street, Manchester road
Speight William, Vicar lane
Stead Joseph Hitchin, 76 Manchester road
Steel Daniel, 31 Queen street, White Abbey
Steel Edward, 9 Bridge street; E. O. Cooke agent
Stott Jeremiah, 33 Black Abbey

Stoyles Jonathan, 6 Margerison street, Cheapside
Sugden George, 141 Leeds road
Sugden Samuel, 43 Vicar lane
Sutcliffe Robert, High street
Swift George, 46 Bower street, Manchester road
Swithenbank John, 31 Bedford street, Bridge street
Swithenbank Joseph, 28 Brook st. Leeds road
Swithenbank Samuel, 23 Chain st. Silsbridge lane
Sykes George, 524 Wakefield road
Teasdale John, 42 Thornton road
Thompson John, Tumblinghill st. Thornton road
Thompson Robert, 141 Longcroft place, Westgate
Thompson Thomas, 156 Westgate
Tordoff Squire, 16 Sterling street, Manchester road
Town Francis, 21 Ivegate and 50 Market street
Wallace Matthew, 12 Wellington st. Stott Hill
Wallis Joseph, 199 Bolton road
Walmsley James, 66 Market street
Watmuff Joe, 26 Northgate
Watson Levi, 268 Manchester road
Webster George, Dudley Hill, Bowling
Wells Joshua, 174 Manchester road
Wells Thomas Hollingworth, Wakefield road
West John, Longcroft place, Westgate
West Joshua, Tyrrel Court, Tyrrel st.
Wharton George, 33 Bank street
White Charles, 34 Chain street, Silsbridge lane
Whitley Squire, 98 Westgate
Wiggins David, Back Duke street, Manchester road
Wilkinson John, 11 Wellesley street, Northwing
Wilson Joseph, 16 Bower street, Manchester road
Wilson Joseph, New row, Manningham
Wilson Thomas, Bradford Moor
Wood James, 44 Northgate
Wright John, 96 Westgate

Bowling Greens.

Atkinson Thomas (subscription), Spotted House Inn, Manningham lane
Crabtree Elizabeth (public), Coach and Horses Inn, Shipley
Lumby John, (public), New Miller's Dam Inn, Thornton road

Brass Founders.

(See also Iron Founders.)

Cliffe James & Joseph, Old Foundry, Tyrrel street
Cole, Marchent & Co. Prospect Foundry, Wakefield road, Bowling
Crosland Robert, Union Foundry, Manchester road
Francis Thomas, Lumby street, Manchester road
Haley Christopher, Foundry street, Vicar lane
Haley Enoch, Thornton road
Halstead Isaac, Hope Foundry, Thornton road
Hargreaves & Kennedy, Waterloo Foundry, Adelaide street, Manchester road
Hopkinson Joseph, Millbank, Thornton road
Leeming John & Son, North Holme Mill, Railroad street, Canal road
Pease Richard (and lacquerer and finisher), 79 Chapel lane

Onion & Wheelhouse, Frederick st. Bridge street
Parker James, Hall lane, Bowling
Sturges John & Co. Bowling Works; office and wharf, Canal road
Waddington Richard, Railway Foundry, Manchester road
Walker James (and lacquerer and finisher), Northgate
Willis Thomas, Millbank, Wood st.
Worsnop Joseph Benson, Providence Foundry, Manchester road

Braziers and Tinplate Workers.

Calvert Michael, 13 Ivegate
Clough Benjamin, 8 White Abbey
Cooper William, 102 Manchester rd.
Denby Richard, 97 Bridge street
Dove Thomas Pashley, 17 Ivegate
Ellis Henry, 16 Triangle street, Manchester road
Graham Thomas, 29 Hope street, Manchester road
Grassington Job, 205 Bolton road
Marshall William, 4 Kirkgate
Pickard Henry, 282 Leeds road
Read Henry, 29 Market street
Rowbotham John, 113 Bridge street
Shackleton William, 22 Broadstones
Smith Jonas, 40 Westgate
Sowden Joseph, 63 Market street
Wardle Thomas, 43 Silsbridge lane
Wardle William, High street, Great Horton
Wilcock John, 92 Manchester road

Brewers—Ale and Porter.

Knowles Jonathan, Denholme Gate, Thornton; business attendance on Thursdays, New Inn, Tyrrel st.
Laycock Peter (executors of), and black beer, top of Ivegate
Pullan Joseph (Fountain Brewery) Manchester road
Singleton William & Co. Chapel lane and Brunswick Brewery, Leeds
Taylor Clement (Springhead Brewery), White Abbey (*See advertisement*)
Whittaker William & Co. (Old Brewery) Great Horton road

Brick Makers.

Balme Edward, 245 Manchester road, and Shipley
Craven William, Brick lane, Black Abbey
Foster William, Green Market, Rawson place
HUDSON BRICK WORKS, Leeds road; Messrs. Hudson proprietors

Bristle Merchant.

Waud William, 1 and 21 Darley st.

Brokers—Share and Stock.

Cooke John, 38 Bank street
Dewhirst Thomas, 10 Union Passage, Huslergate and Kirkgate
Haigh Thomas, Savings' Bank, Kirkgate
Holmes Thomas, 10 Exchange street, Kirkgate
Mason William, Bridge street Buildings, Bridge street
Scholefield Richard Mortimer, Roebuck Yard, Market street
Selby Samuel, Cheapside

Brush Makers and Dealers.

Brooke William, 17 High street
Farrar Joseph, Chapel lane
Greenwood John (and matting, &c.), 58 Market street

Waud William (wholesale and retail), 1 and 21 Darley street
Wilman John, 41 Westgate

Builders.

See Joiners and Builders.

Butchers.

Marked thus * have Shops in the Shambles.
(See also Pork Butchers.)

* Ackroyd Francis, Legrams lane, Great Horton
* Ackroyd John, 67 Westgate
* Ackroyd Jonathan, 1 Green lane, Manningham

Ackroyd Joseph, Bedford street, Wakefield road
* Ackroyd Robinson, Manningham
* Aldersley William, 2 White Abbey

Audsley William, 16 Hustlergate
Bairstow Paul, Little Horton lane
Bateson Samuel, 14 Market street
* Beanland Joseph, Whetley street, Manningham

Bentley Walter, Great Horton road
Berwick John, 14 Broadstones
Birkby James, 174 Silsbridge lane
* Bottomley James, Great Horton road

Bottomley Moses, 114 Manchester rd.
Bottomley Paul, Back lane, Bowling
* Bottomley William, Great Horton road

Bottomley William, 343 Wakefield road
* Bower Benjamin, Back lane, Bowling
* Bowker John, 191 Bolton road

Bramham Henry, 99 Tumblinghill street, Thornton road
* Branson William, 72 Manchester rd.

Brownbridge Robert, Wakefield road
* Bulmer William, 15 Silsbridge lane

Butler Joshua, 85 Bridge street
Casson Mary, 132 Brick lane
Casson William, Thornton road
Cheesebrough William, 30 King street, White Abbey
* Clarke Thomas, 76 White Abbey

Clarke William, Bradford Moor
* Crabtree Thomas, 39 Northgate
* Crabtree William, Heaton

Crampton John, 13 Hustlergate
Craven John, top of Greenhill, Manningham
* Cromack Charles, 152 George st. Leeds road

Darling Thomas, 23 Bower street, Manchester road
Dawson Charles, 84 Edward street, Wakefield road
Diggles James (pork), 158 Westgate
Diggles John (pork), 23 Ivegate
* Dixon William, Belgrave place, Manningham

Edmondson Abraham, High street, Great Horton
Edmondson Christopher, 27 Manchester road
* Edmondson John, Eccleshill
* Edmondson Richard, Eccleshill
* Edmondson Robert, Wibsey
* Edmondson Thomas, Eccleshill

Ellinthorpe Robert, 462 Wakefield rd.
Eshelby George, Dudley Hill, Bowling
Farrar Jonathan, Dudley Hill, Bowling
Farrar Richard (pork), 109 Bridge st.
Fenton John, 160 Manchester road
Forrest James, 25 Nelson street
Fox William, High st. Great Horton
Gibson Joseph, Well street
Greenwood Alfred, 79 High street
Greetham Joseph, 35 Bank street
Haigh Samuel, 256 Manchester road
Haley Dan, High st. Great Horton
Hammond John, 4 Melbourne street, Leeds road

Hobson Marmaduke (pork), 16 Manchester road
Howard Elizabeth, 191 Wakefield road
Ickringill Abraham, 63 Black Abbey
*Jennings John, Mill st. Canal road
Johnson Thomas, 12 Old Market
Johnson William, 7 Well street
* Law Richard, Brunswick place
Liversedge Jabez, Great Horton road
Long Charles, 35 George street, Leeds road
* Lund Luke, 6 White Abbey
Marsden Benjamin, Sticker lane, Bowling
Marshall John, 12 Barkerend
Middleton David, 52 Manchester road
Miller George, 108 Wakefield road
Mortimer David, Tyrrel street
Mudd Edward, 2 Wellington street, Stott Hill
*Muff Bentley, Halifax road, Bowling
Muff Charles, Back lane, Bowling
Munday James, Dudley Hill, Bowling
Murgatroyd John, Little Horton lane
Newbould Jacob, Tyrrel street
Newbould Michael, 12 Kirkgate
North John, Halifax road, Bowling
Oddy Joseph, 176 Manchester road
Peacock Harker, 179 Brick lane
Phillips George, 202 Manchester road
Prince Edward, 6 Well street
Ratcliffe John, 7 Bridge street
*Rhodes Isaac, Skinner lane, Manningham
* Robertshaw Job, Southgate, Great Horton
Rudd John, High street, Gt. Horton
*Ruddock Joseph, Belgrave place, Manningham
Sadler James (pork), 5 Kirkgate
Sagar John, Melville street, Great Horton
*Sagar Stephen, Belgrave place, Manningham
Sellers George, Dudley Hill, Bowling
Sharp Squire, 29 and 31 Mill street, Canal road
Shaw William, 129 Bridge street
Skirrow Thomas, Wakefield road
Smith Abraham, Sticker lane, Bowling
Smith Christopher (pork), 9 Ivegate
Smith Isaac, Silsbridge lane and 64 Westgate
*Smith John, Four Lane Ends, Manningham
Smith Prince, 11 Silsbridge lane
Smith William, 35 Silsbridge lane
Southwell Emanuel, Providence street Westgate
Southwell John, John st. Westgate
Sowden Benjamin, 71 Bolton road
Spencer Thomas, 7 York st. Bridge st.
Stephenson James, 2 North street, Northwing
Stephenson William, Queen street, White Abbey
* Suddards Samuel, High street, Great Horton
Sugden James, 77 Kirkgate
Sugden John, Tyrrel street
Sykes Samuel (pork), 87 Manchester road
Tainningcliffe Benjamin, Back lane, Bowling
Wardman Benjamin, Bolton road
* Watkins Thomas, 133 Bridge st.
Webster George, Dudley Hill, Bowling
Webster William, Bradford Moor
* Westwood Henry, 54 Westgate
Wharf Richard, 89 Manchester road
Wilkinson Charles, 52 Northgate
Williams Priscilla, 14 Manchester rd.
Wood Henry, 167 Westgate
Wood Isaac, 5 High street

Wood John, 18 Wood street, Manningham
Worsnop Luke, Manchester road
Wray William, 16 Nelson street
Wright Edwin (pork), 144 Manchester road

Butter Factors,

IMPORTERS AND WHOLESALE AND RETAIL DEALERS.

Alderson George, 7 Bridge street
Cluderay William, 134 Westgate
Denison Patrick, 88 Manchester rd.
Diggles James, 158 and 160 Westgate
Dowling Michael, 51 Market street
Emsley James & John, 204 Manchester road, and 38 Bolton road
Farnell James, 150 Westgate
Fawcett William, Regent place, Darley street
France Samuel, Well street, Bridge street and Tyrrel street
Hardy Henry, Market street, corner of Bridge street
Harrison John, 49 Silsbridge lane
Hodgson John, 60 Garnett street, Leeds road
Marsden James, 8 Ivegate
Midgley Thomas, 7 Providence street, White Abbey
Milner Thomas, 8 Well street, and 26 Ivegate
Morrell John, (wholesale), 4 and 6 Tyrrel street
Morrell Robert & Co. 17 and 92 Westgate
Rooks George, 9 and 11 Broadstones
Sagar Henry, 5 Broadstones
Smith Charles, 170 Manchester road
Smith Noah, 18 Old Market, and Pickles Hill, Keighley
Smith William, 40 Manchester road, and 48 Westgate
Stead William & Co. 20 Ivegate and 56 Market street
Waud & Co. (wholesale), 5 Market street
Waud William (wholesale), 1 and 21 Darley street
Whitham Thomas, 53 King street, Manchester road
Wignall Joseph, Bank street

Button Merchants and Dealers.

(See also Woollen Drapers.)

Bell & Prest, Tyrrel street
Brook, Grant & Co. 10 Westgate
Brown & Muff, 54 Market street
Chapman & Co. 26 Kirkgate
Dixon & Masser, 8 Bridge street
Farrar & Gillham, 20 Kirkgate
Hall Francis Stuart, 33 Kirkgate
Longfield William & Co. Kirkgate
Monies James & Co. 30 Kirkgate, and 2 Exchange street
Ogden Michael & Co. 29 Kirkgate
Parkinson & Clarke, 27 Kirkgate
Storey & Brook, 37 Kirkgate

Cabinet Makers.

(See also Upholsterers.)

Andrew George, Victoria street, Silsbridge lane
Annison Samuel, Church street, High street
Archer Edward, Tyrrel street
Atkinson Francis Whitley, Bolton road
Barraclough John, 68 Westgate
Beanland William, North Parade, Christ Church
Bentley Albert, Hope and Anchor Yard, Bank street
Booth Joseph, Dudley Hill, Bowling

Carter William, Thornton road
Clough Joseph, 2 Manchester road
Constantine James, 76 Bridge street
Cowin James & Son, 59 Northgate
Craven Isaac, 34 Darley street
Duckworth & Watson, Tyrrel Court, Tyrrel street
Dunn & Stoddart, Market street and Vicar lane
Emmott Samuel, 61 John street, Westgate
Ferrand Jonathan, 71 Frederick street, Wakefield road
Green James, Colliergate, Swaine street
Hartley Samuel, Leeds road
Heap Joseph, Brick lane
Hepper Christopher, Old Post Office Buildings, Bridge street
Ingham Benjamin, 172 Back lane, Bowling
Kershaw Samuel, Bowling lane, Bowling
Mills Thomas, 45 Market street
Milnes Enoch, 28 Manchester road
Mitchell John, 125 Westgate
Moore John, Wakefield road
Newell John, Broadstones
Nutter Joseph, Nutter's place, North Parade
Pearson Joseph, High street
Poole David, Bowling lane, Bowling
Poole Joseph, 22 Silsbridge lane
Pratt & Prince, 4 North Parade, Christ Church
Pyrah Joseph, Great Horton road
Robinson Michael, Smith street, Manchester road
Sedgwick John (and wood turner), Nelson street
Sedgwick Robert, King street, Manchester road
Sellers John, 162 George street, Leeds road
Sutcliffe Samuel, 138 & 140 George street, Leeds road
Thornton John, 21 Westgate
Tyas John, 115 Westgate
Ward William, King's Arms Yard, Westgate
Wardle William, 19 Bedford street, Bridge street
West Joseph, Sticker lane, Bowling
Wheater Henry, 62 King street, Manchester road
Whitehead John, 14 Well street
Whitehead Richard, 24 Bridge street
Whiteley Thomas, Bolton street, Barkerend
Wilkinson Joseph, New Market place and 13 North Parade

Calico and Stuff Fent Dealers.

Hey Joseph (stuff), Primrose terrace, Manningham
Hill Abraham (stuff), York street, Bridge street
Patchett William, 34 Manchester road
Preston Benjamin, 8 Manchester road
Sagar John, 1 Croft street, Bridge street
Sykes Abraham (stuffs, Orleans, &c.) Wakefield road

Canvass and Sacking Dealers.

Oddy Mark, 68 Market street.
Sussman Alfred (and packing materials), Court street, Leeds road

---

Cap Dealers.

See Fur and Cloth Cap Dealers.

Card Cutter.

(See also Jacquard Machine Makers.)

Foster Jonas, 50 Victoria street, Manchester road

Card Manufacturers.

Bateman Daniel & Sons (and wire drawers), Folly Hall, Wibsey

Bateman Samuel, Wibsey

Gomersall Jonathan, Dudley Hill, Bowling

Gomerall Joshua, Dudley Hill, Bowling

Law Ann, Dudley Hill, Bowling

Carpet and Floor Cloth Warehouses.

(See also Upholsterers.)

Archer Edward, Tyrrel street

Brumfit Joseph, 80 Market street

Cockin Joseph & James, 12 Cheapside, and Manchester

Hartley Samuel, Leeds road

Hepper Christopher, Toad lane, Bridge street

Mills Thomas, 45 Market street

Milnes Enoch, 28 Manchester road

Monies James & Co. 30 Kirkgate and 2 Exchange street

Nutter Joseph, Nutter's place, North Parade

Wilkinson Joseph, New Market and North Parade

Carriers and their Agents.

(See the Conveyance Lists.)

Carvers and Gilders.

Briggs Henry, 1 North Parade

Holmes Joseph, 53 Darley street

Lenham Thomas (carver only), 9 Reform street, Westgate

Mills Thomas, 45 Market street

Rhodes Charles, 2 Cheapside

Rhodes James, Chapel Court, Kirkgate (*See advertisement*)

Snow William, Brunswick place

Ward Edwin, 12 Wellington street, Stott Hill

White Charles, Bolton street, Barkerend

Cement Dealers.

See Plasterers and Colourers.

Cheese Factors and Dealers,

WHOLESALE AND RETAIL.

(See also Provision Dealers and Shopkeepers.)

Clarkson Richard, 45 Westgate

Denison Patrick, 88 Manchester road

Dowling Michael, 51 Market street

Emsley James & John, 204 Manchester road, and 38 Bolton road

Jagger Abraham, 44 Manchester rd.

Morrell John (wholesale), 4 and 6 Tyrrel street

Morrell Robert & Co. 17 and 92, Westgate

Rooks George, 9 and 11 Broadstones

Waud & Co. (wholesale), 5 Market street

Waud William (wholesale), 1 and 21 Darley street

Chemists and Druggists.

(See also Chemists—Manufacturing.)

Beanland Joshua, 30 Northgate

Blackburn Bailey, Top of Ivegate

Bolton Richard, Britannia street, Manchester road

Branson Thomas, Wakefield road

Cannan William, Wakefield road

Cockshott William (and dealer in British wines), 32 Westgate

Duckett John Broughton, 3 Tyrrel street

Ellis Thomas (druggist), Thornton lane, Little Horton,

Fanshaw Robert (and seedsman), High street, Great Horton

Fell Christopher, 36 White Abbey

Haley Richard (druggist), High street, Great Horton
Harland John, Brick lane
Hick Joseph, Broadstones, Well st.
Irving William, 20 Northrop's Buildings, Westgate
Kirk George, 94 Manchester road
Lister John (druggist), Wood street, Manningham
Maud & Wilson, 10 Bridge street
Naylor Joseph (druggist), Bradford Moor
Newby Richard, 10 Kirkgate, 1 Church Steps, and 94 Manchester road
Outhwaite William Thomas, 45 Kirkgate
Pratt John, Ivegate
Preston John, 45 Silsbridge lane
Raper Joseph (druggist), 175 Bridge street
Rawnsley Frederick, 16 White Abbey
Rimmington Felix Marsh, 6 Ivegate
Robinson Lund, 83 High street
Robinson William, 2 Silsbridge lane
Rogerson Michael, 2 Darley street and 31 and 33 North Parade
Savage William, 113 Westgate
Senier George & Co. 15 Westgate
Sharp John, 75 Westgate, and White Abbey
Stanley Samuel Haigh, 58 Kirkgate
Sutcliffe James, 26 Westgate
Swaine John, Manchester road
Thomas William Jacob, 110 Manchester road
Thorn Charles, 24 Britannia street, Manchester road
Topham Richard Busfeild, 36 Westgate
Wade John (druggist), 43 King st. Manchester road
Walker John, 106 Manchester road
Woodhead William Henry, 48 Westgate, and North Parade

Chemists—Manufacturing.

Holliday Read & Co. (and patentees of self-generating gas lamps) Well st. and Huddersfield; Thomas Cobb agent
Leather George Henry (vitriol), Northbrook Works, Canal side

Child-Bed and Ready-Made Linen Warehouses.

Hunton William, 8 Darley street
Simpson Elizabeth, 6 and 6 Market street

China Dealers.

See Glass and China Dealers.

Chocolate, Chicory and Cocoa Manufacturers.

Tordoff John & Son, 46 Kirkgate

Cigar Importers and Dealers.

(See also Tobacconists.)

Blackburn Samuel, 38 and 39 Tyrrel street
Broadley Henry, top of Ivegate
Gilderdale John, 28 Bridge street
Newby Richard, 10 Kirkgate
Parkinson Joseph, 2 Old Market place
Smithson, Sugden & Co. 53 Westgate, and High street
Swithenbank Samuel, 5 Chapel lane
Taylor Martha, 11 and 13 Bridge st.
Wigglesworth William, 79 Market st.

Circulating Libraries.

See Libraries—Circulating.

Clock Makers and Dealers,

GERMAN, DUTCH AND AMERICAN.

(See also Watch and Clock Makers).

Atkinson George, 87 George street, Leeds road
Barrow William, 2 Bank street, Market street
Bowes James, 8 Union Passage, and Leeds road
Brooksbank William, 64 Market st. —(*See advertisement.*)
Brumfit Joseph, 80 Market street
Dilger Theodore, 15 Hustlergate
Dilger, Winterhalder & Co. 18 Hustlergate
Freeman Ambrose, 28 Manchester rd.
Hardaker James, 12 Providence st. Westgate
Harker & Crabtree, 162 Manchester road
Hill John, Whetley street, Manningham
Knowles David, 19 Manchester road
Prest William, 22 Well street
Sykes Walter, Wakefield road, Bowling

Clog and Patten Makers.

Binns Joseph, Great Horton road
Blamires Joseph, White Abbey
Bullock John, 26 Brick lane
Cockcroft Thomas, Lidget Green, Great Horton
Crosland William, 630 Wakefield rd.
Dixon Joseph, 58 White Abbey
Dixon Robert, 102 Queen's Cut, Manchester road
Dracup Abraham, 18 Broadstones, and 76 Silsbridge lane
Ellis Sharp, Black Bull Yard, Westgate
Foulds John, 186 Manchester road
Foulds William, 74 Silsbridgs lane
Greenwood David, 24 Leeds road
Greenwood Thomas, 105 Bridge st.
Hardaker Henry, 12 White Abbey
Hartley Joseph, 25 Paperhall, Northwing
Heaton William, Manningham
Kelsall John, 197 Bridge street
Lancaster Robert, 1 Paperhall, Northwing
Nutton Lawrence, 7 Clayton lane, Manchester road
Raw Thomas, 164 Manchester road
Riley John, 109 Brick lane
Roberts Thomas, 26 Well street
Robinson Joseph, Wakefield road
Scott William, 314 Mount street, Stott Hill
Spencer John Sharp, Church Steps, Bolton road
Tankard Benjamin, 178 Silsbridge lane
Whittaker James, High street, Horton
Wilson David, 3 Toad lane, Bridge street
Wilson James, 11 Charles street, Leeds road
Wood William, 619 Wakefield road

Clothes Brokers—New and Second Hand.

Audsley John, 55 Bazaar, Kirkgate, and 1 Primrose terrace, Manughm.
Brumfit Joseph, 80 Market street
Dobson Mary, 2 Ivegate
Hewitt Benjamin, 33 John street, Westgate
M'Kay James, Well street
M'Nulty Edward, John street, Northgate
O'Hara Paul, 102 Westgate
Quinsey Mary, 36 Ivegate
Thackeray Henry William & James Robert, 47 and 48 Vicar lane (*See advertisement*)
Thompson & Co. 125 Westgate
Walker William, 3 Westgate

Waterhouse Richard, 67 New Market place, Kirkgate
Wilson Francis, New Market place, Kirkgate
Wittam John, 26 Ivegate

Coach Builders.

England & Walton, 54 Threadneedle street, Vicar lane
Harker Simon, Vicar lane
Procter Samuel, Leeds road
Rhodes John, Bray's Yard, Leeds rd.
Whitehead Joseph, Chapel lane

Coal Agents.

Charlesworth J. & J. (Haigh Coal Co.), Railroad street, Canal road
Clayton Isaac (Bradford and Calverley Colliery), 3 Market street
Falkingham Jeffrey (Fairbank William, Allerton), 59 Westgate
Hargreaves John (Whitewood Coal Company), Railroad street
Gomersal Coal Company, Railroad street; Joseph Knight agent
Hotchin Jonathan (Gomersall Co.), Thornton road
Roe Simeon (William Fairbank, Allerton), 103 Westgate
Sharp James (Crow Trees Colliery), 6 Darley street

Coal Merchants and Dealers.

Marked thus * are Coal Owners.

Balmforth Jabez, Victoria street, Silsbridge lane
Barraclough John, 125 Bridge street
Barrans Jonas, Back Tyrrel street
* Baxendale David, Bowling lane, Bowling
Berry Richard, 20 Keighley street, Silsbridge lane
BRADFORD AND CALVERLEY COLLIERY (Rawson, Clayton & Cousen) agent Mr. Isaac Clayton, 3 Market street
Brear James, Roundhill, Silsbridge ln.
Brown James, Victoria street, Thornton road
Brunt Joseph, Thomas street, Brick lane
Carter George, Back Fold, Northwing
Clark William, Tumblinghill street, Thornton road
Clayton, Marshalls & Co. North Bierley; wharf Canal road
* Clayton Thomas, Mireyshay, Bunker's Hill
Clegg John, Broomfields, Wakefield road
Cowling John, 237 Wakefield road
Dobson Thomas, 300 Manchester rd.
*Fairbank William, Crossley Hall Colliery, Allerton
Falkingham Jeffrey, Brick row, Thornton road
Flather Emanuel, Smith street, Manchester road
Foster Jonathan, Manchester road
Frear Bryan, Wakefield road
*GOMERSALL COAL CO.; office and wharf Railroad street, School street
*HAIGH COAL COMPANY (Lofthouse and Rothwell); office Railroad st. School street, J. & J. Charlesworth agents
Hardwick Thomas, 29 Thompson's Alley, Silsbridge lane
Hardy Joseph, High street, Black Abbey
Hartley William, Brick lane
Heyworth Samuel, Bradford Moor
* Hird, Dawson & Hardy, Canal road and Low Moor
Hotchin William, Broomfields, Wakefield road
Howson Eccles, 214 Manchester rd.

Hutton Bartholomew, 12 Fawcett's Court, Nelson street
Illingworth Jeremiah, Park square, Manningham
* Kaye Thomas, Bierley lane, North Bierley
* Knight Joseph, Little Horton lane
Lambert David, Summer street, White Abbey
Maden Samuel, 74 White Abbey
Mallinson Joseph, Bolton road
Mellor Mary, 28 Portland street, Manchester road
Mitchell Henry, 32 Queen street, White Abbey
Muscham William, Cropper lane, Westgate
* Pollard George (Crow Trees Colliery), Bradford Moor
Procter John, Silsbridge lane
Punt William, 202 Bolton road
Ramsden Joseph, Wood street, Manningham
Shields George, Crowther street, Manchester road
Shields Richard, Lumby street, Manchester road
Simpson William, top of Park square, Manningham
Simpson William, Bradford Moor
Smith John, King street, Manchester road
Smith Joseph, Foundry street, Vicar lane
* Sturges John & Co. Manchester rd.
Sugden George, 3 Providence street, Silsbridge lane
Sykes Sarah, 1 Chandos street, Wake field road
Thornton John, Victoria street, Manningham
*Tommis William, Wakefield road
Waddington Samuel, Victoria street, Silsbridge lane
Walker Sarah, Wildboar street, Bolton road
* WHITEWOOD COAL COMPANY, Railroad street; John Hargreaves agent
Whittaker William, Bolton road
Wilkinson John, 8 Providence street, White Abbey
Wright Rushforth, Victoria street, Manningham

Coffee and Tea Rooms.

(See also Eating Houses.)

Ambler Sarah, Market street
Chatterton Frederick, 34 Ivegate
Gill Ann, 75 Thornton road
Goodchild James (temperance), New Market place, Kirkgate
Hartley James (temperance), Well street
Lynn James, 7 Kirkgate
Mawson Sarah, 21 Kirkgate
Mitchell Joseph (temperance), 46 Union street, Bridge street
Poole Benjamin (commercial), 1 Tyrrel street
Walker Jas. (temperance), Northgate
Waterhouse Robert (commercial), 4 Bank street
Wilson George (temperance), 24 Southgate

Comb Manufacturers.

HORN, BOXWOOD AND SHELL, &c.

Dobson John, John street, Leeds road, and 87 Thornton road
Hustler Isaac & Son, 84 Manchester road
Poole William, 100 Silsbridge lane

Simonett & Freeman, Spence's Mill, Chapel lane

Confectioners.

Bartle Timothy, 26 and 28 Market st.
Binns Eleanor, 25 Hustlergate
Binns Richard, 47 Silsbridge lane
Braint William, 10 Nelson street, Chapel lane
Carter John, 124 Manchester road
Chatterton Frederick, 34 Ivegate
Crowther John, 17 Market street
Edmondson Christopher, 23 Westgate
Greenhough Thomas Lister, 157 Wakefield road
Hardcastle Sarah Ann, 53 Westgate
Hargreaves Sarah, 30 Kirkgate
Harker Thomas (wholesale), Wakefield road
Hutton William, 166 Stott Hill
Shires Mary, 13 Duke st. Darley st.
Smith Alfred, 93 Westgate
Smith Mary, 88 Westgate
Stenton William, Wakefield road
Thompson Ann & Mary, North Parade, Christ Church
Townend Martha, Wakefield road
Townend William, 82 Manchester rd.
Walker Rachel, 60 Market street

Contractors—Excavating, Building, &c.

(See also Joiners and Builders.)

Bray James & Sons (building), New Leeds and Harrogate
Brayshaw William (building), Westgate, corner of Lumb lane
Dixon John (building), Swaine street
Foster William (excavating), Green Market, Rawson place
Gibson Jonathan (excavating), Chapel street, Leeds road
Gledhill William (building), 72 Leeds road
Leach John (building), Drewton street, Westgate

Coopers.

Atkinson Richard, 120 Manchester road, and Leeds road
Mountain William (and sieve maker), 111 Westgate
Smith Abraham, Darley street, and Leeds road
Taylor Richard, 23 Hustlergate
Watson John, King's Arms Yard, Westgate

Cork Manufacturer.

Lawson James, Chapel lane, Bridge street

Cork Leg Maker.

Swithenbank John, 100 Bridge street

Corn and Flour Dealers.

(See also Bakers and Flour Dealers.)

Asquith William, 42 Greenaire place, and 117 Westgate
Beanland Geo. Joseph & John, Beckside, Horton
Bell Martin, 17 Chapel lane, Bridge st.
Blamires Samuel, agent for the Bradford Flour Mill Co. Gt. Horton road
Booth John, 4 Manchester road
Booth John, 4 Leeds road
BRADFORD FLOUR MILL SOCIETY, Gordon street, Manchester road; T. D. Tarbottom manager
Burrows John, Great Horton road
Clarkson Thomas, Back lane, Bowling
Clough James, Ebor street, Little Horton lane
Clough John, High street, Gt. Horton
Clough Joseph, Halifax road, Bowling
Cluderay John, Ivegate
Cluderay William, 134 Westgate

Cockson William, 1 Mount street
Cordingley John, Edward street, Bridge street
Denison Patrick, 88 Manchester road
Dewhirst Thomas, Providence street, Silsbridge lane
Eastwood George, 10 Silsbridge lane
Ellis & Priestman, 1 Manchester road and Queen's Mill, Millbank
Ellison Thomas, 65 High street, and Well street and Chapel lane
Emsley James & John, 204 Manchester road, and 38 Bolton road
Farnell James, 150 Westgate
Greenwood William Watson (Bankfoot Mill), Halifax road, Bowling
Harrison John, 49 Silsbridge lane
Hartley Richard, 69 High street
Jagger Abraham, 44 Manchester road
Jowett William, 88 Silsbridge lane
Knapton Abraham, corner of Bermondsey, Kirkgate
Mason William, 2 Cropper lane, Westgate
Mitchell John, Dudley Hill, Bowling
Morrell Robert & Co. 17 and 92 Westgate
Muscham Thornton, Gt. Horton road
Robson John, 7 Wakefield road
Rowntree Isaac, 146 Manchester road
Settle Samuel Ellick, West Parade, Brick lane
Sharp William, Silsbridge lane
Shaw William, Southfield place, Manningham
Shepherd Robert, Southgate, Great Horton
Smith Charles, 170 Manchester road
Spence George, Broadstones
Spence Samuel, 5 Nelson street
Sutcliffe John, 109 Northwing
Taylor John, Birkshall, Bowling
Taylor Peter, 226 Leeds road
Taylor Philip, 61 Manchester road
Wilkinson George, 101 Bridge street
Wilson Francis, Northgate

Corn Millers.

Beanland George Joseph & John, Beckside, Great Horton
Bradford Flour Mill Company, Gordon street, Manchester road; T. D. Tarbottom manager
Ellis & Priestman, Queen's Mill, Millbank, and 1 Manchester road
Greenwood William Watson, Bankfoot Mill, Halifax road, Bowling
Mitchell John, Bowling Old Mill, Manchester road
Pilling William & Joseph, Manchester road

Cotton Twine and Banding Manufacturers.

(See also Rope & Twine Manufacturers.)

Farrar Joseph, Chapel lane, Tyrrel street
Oddy George, 19 Kirkgate
Oddy Mark, 69 Market street

Cotton Warp Manufacturers and Dealers.

(See also Agents—General and Miscellaneous.)

Anderton Jonathan William, 30 Pearson's Buildings, Bridge street
Booth Thomas, (manufacturer), Great Horton
Burrows John, agent, High street, Great Horton
Crompton Charles, (double and single), Charles street, Market street
Farrar David (doubler), Thompson's Mill, Thornton road
Haigh William Chapman, Swaine st. and Exchange street, Kirkgate

Ingham Joseph, Hope and Anchor Yard, Bank street
Lancaster Judith, 32 Hustlergate
Lister Joshua Brook (manufacturer), Booth street, Hall Ings
Mills James William, Hustler's Buildings, Market street
Mortimer William, 21 Market street
Preston John, 20 Bank street
Sutcliffe Joseph & Robert (manufacturers), Brook street; works Idle
Sutcliffe, Rawson & Co. (manufacturers), Laycock's Mill, Thornton road
Taylor James S. Charles street, Leeds road
Towle Thomas John and Benjamin, (manufacturers), 12 Union Passage, Kirkgate; works Borrowash Mill, near Derby
Turner Charles Timothy, Charles street, Market street
Wilson James, Hall Ings
Wright James, Ivegate and Hustlergate

Curled Hair and Bagging Manufacturer.

Ambler Jeremiah, Skinner lane, Manningham

Curriers and Leather Cutters.

(See Gutta-Percha Dealers, and also Leather Dressers and Dealers.)

Ackroyd Thomas, 5 Bridge street
Atherton William, Hope street, Manchester road
Dove William & Jacob, 16 Darley street, and Leeds
Fairbank Alice, Westgate
Fairbank Thomas, 75 Westgate
Hanson Thomas, Westbrook place, Thornton road

Lupton John, 38 Chapel lane
Rawnsley John, 35 Market street
Rhodes Joseph & Son, 18 Well street
Seed Edward, Well street
Skirrow John, 4 Well street, and John street, Westgate
White John, Albion Court, Kirkgate; Mondays and Thursdays only
Wilson Edward, 5 Hustlergate, Unicorn Yard

Cutlers, and Truss and Surgical Instrument Makers.

Hall John (and truss maker), 40 Market street
M'Intyre Michael, Poole's Alley, Silsbridge lane
Rhodes Manoah, 6 Westgate
Roberts Benjamin (and truss maker), 5 Darley street
Wyrill Frances, 8 Westgate—(*see advertisement*)

Dentists.

Drury Rupert Alexander, 45 North Parade, Manningham lane—(*See advertisement*)
Gallen John Jardine, M. D. Drewton street, Manningham lane; Thursdays only—(*See advertisement*)
Le Dray Mons. 34 Darley street,
Matthews Alfred M. 6 North Parade
Parsons J. H. Mrs. Pattinson, Manningham lane; Thursdays only
Ramsden Henry, 29 Darley street
Roberts Benjamin, 42 Darley street

Drysalters.

Senier George & Co, 15 Westgate

Dyers.

Marked thus * are Stuff Dyers and Finishers.

Akroyd William (warp), Mawson st Thornton road

*Armitage George & Co. Water Lane Dye Works, Thornton road
Bowker John, 148 Westgate, and Ship Alley, Well street (*See advertisement*)
* Butterworth Sidney Aquilla, Hall Ings; works Shelf, near Halifax
Chapman William, 57 Chapel Lane and 8 Northgate—(*See advertisement*)
* Haigh Thomas, Charles street; works Newlay, near Leeds
* Holdsworth Joseph, Old Market, Market street; works Wakefield
Holroyd & Barstow (and bleachers), New road, Great Horton
Murgatroyd Charles, 56 Manchester road
* Ripley Edward & Son, Old Dye House, Bowling
* Smith Samuel & Brothers, Charles street; works Field Dyehouse, Thornton road
* Sutcliffe William, New Dyehouse, Bowling
Trees Thomas & Co. 8 Bower street, Manchester road—(*See advertisement*)
Walsh Jeremiah, 45 George street, Leeds road
Woller Joseph S. Brick lane

Earthenware Dealers.

(See also Glass and China Dealers).

Beanland Martin, 146 Westgate
Cawfield Owen, Millbank
Collins George, 452 Wakefield road
Dawson Hannah, 42 Market street
Goodwin James, 133 Manchester road
Harrison Thomas, 118 Manchester rd.
Laycock Abraham, Wakefield road
Lister Robert, Wakefield road
Naylor & Co. 152 Bridge street
Rhodes Charles, 2 Cheapside
Silson Jonas, 24 Silsbridge lane
Silson Joseph & John, Reform street, Westgate
Wilkinson Rachel, 17 Hustlergate
Wood Isaac, 10 Broadstones

Eating Houses and Temperance Hotels.

• (See also Coffee and Tea Rooms.)

Ambler Sarah, Market street
Goodchild James (temperance), New Market place, Kirkgate
Gill Ann, 75 Thornton road
Hardisty David (late Peckitt's), Market place, Kirkgate
Hartley James (temperance), Well street
Lynn James, 7 Kirkgate
Mawson Sarah, 21 Kirkgate
Poole Benjamin (commercial), 1 Tyrrel street
Shackleton Benjamin, Bowergate, Chapel lane
Turner Jonas, 49 Kirkgate
Walker James (temperance), Northgate
Waterhouse Robert (commercial), 4 Bank street
Wilson George (temperance), 24 Southgate

Egg, Fruit and Dried Fish Dealers.

(See also Fruiterers.)

Barraclough James, Broadstones
Barraclough John, 125 Bridge street
Bolton Elizabeth, 65 Westgate
Brooks James, 87 Birks st. Leeds rd.
Calvert William, 128 Manchester road
Carter William, 3 Nelson street, Chapel lane
Chadwick John, 47 Westgate

Clough William, High street, Great Horton
Cook William, 248 Manchester road
Denison Patrick, 88 Manchester road
Denton Joshua, Silsbridge lane
Farrand Henry, 70 Manchester road
Hall Joseph, Northgate
Hoadley Thomas, Northgate
Holdsworth Edward, High street, Great Horton
Hollings John, Bowling Green, Bridge street
Lister Benjamin, 91 Manchester road
Lofthouse William, 1 Market place, Darley street
Mann Joseph, 199 Wakefield road
Muldoon James, Northgate
Newby William, Tyrrel street
Renwick William, 37 Darley street
Simpson John, 30 Well street
Wilkinson John, 101 Bridge street
Wilkinson Joseph, 78 Westgate

Embroiderer and Shawl Fringer

Smith Elizabeth, 53 Chapel lane

Engravers, Copper-plate and Lithographic Printers.

Baxter Charles, 4 Markst street
Brown James, 2 Market street
Burton George, Leeds road
Masser & Bailey, Hustler's Buildings, Leeds road (*See advertisement*)
Parratt Thomas Williamson (engraver only) Bridge street Buildings, Bridge street
Ratcliffe Thomas & Co. Butterworth's Buildings, Ivegate
Topham Maria Dorothy, 24 Hustlergate
Walker Benjamin (wood only), 8 Market street
Wilkinson Christopher, Tyrrel street
Wilson & Fairbank, 46 Kirkgate and 18 Talbot Yard

Fancy Waistcoating and Woollen Warehouses.

(See also Woollen Drapers.)

Bell & Prest, Tyrrel street
Brook, Gant & Co. 10 Westgate
Brown & Muff, 54 Market street
Chapman & Co. 26 Kirkgate
Dixon & Masser, 8 Bridge street
Farrar & Gillham, 20 Kirkgate
Hall Francis Stuart, 33 Kirkgate
Hindle Thomas, 23 Darley street
Hunter John, 2 Market street
Hunter Thomas, 4 Westgate
Longfield William & Co. 30A Westgate
Milner Joshua, 3 Bridge street
Monies James & Co. 30 Kirkgate and 2 Exchange street
Ogden Michael & Co. 29 Kirkgate
Parkinson & Clarke, 27 Kirkgate
Storey & Brook, 37 Kirkgate

Excise Officers.

See Inland Revenue Officers.

Fellmongers.

Cordingley John & Samuel, Jacob's Fold, Manchester road
Cordingley William (and leather dresser), Old Market place, and Little Horton
Whittom William, Brumfit's Yard, Westgate

File Makers and Dealers.

(See also Tool Makers and Dealers.)

Dixon & Byrne, 77 Market street
Dove Thomas Pashley, 17 Ivegate
Marshall William, 4 Kirkgate
Parratt E. H. 1 Broadstones
Pearson Henry, 30 and 32 Bridge st.

Rhodes John, 18 Kirkgate
Rudd Robert, 35 Kirkgate
Scully Ambrose, 7 Ivegate
Speight Jonas (maker), Salem street and 13 North street
Stelling Thomas, 12 Kirkgate
Wyrill Frances, 8 Westgate

Fire and Life Assurance Offices and Agents.

Alfred Home and Foreign; Mr. Josh. Thompson, Bridge street Buildings, Bridge street
Alliance; Mr. Greenwood Bentley, jun. Regent place, Duke street
Architects' and Engineers'; Ingle and Smith, 1 Albion Court
Atlas; Mr. George Humble, 5 Albion Court, and Mr. E. A. Barret, Charles street
Caledonian; Mr. Thomas Stephenson, Charles street
Christian Mutual; Mr. John Cooke, 39 Bank street
Church of England; Mr. T. R. Charlesworth, 49 Darley street
City of London; Mr. Marmaduke Foster, solicitor, 70 Market street, (*See advertisement*)
Clerical, Medical and General (life); Mr. E. H. Parratt, Broadstones
County Fire, and Provident Life; Mr. John Berry, Leeds road, and Mr. Alfred Sussmann, Court street, Leeds road
Edinburgh; Mr. Edward Fowler, 9 Market street
Equity and Law; Mr. Charles Lees, 5 Albion Court
Experience; Dixon & Byrne, 77 Market street
Farmers' and Graziers'; Mr. George Thornton, 10 Duke street, and Mr. G. T. Lister, Drewton street
Friends' Provident Institution; Mr. Benjamin Ecroyd, Thornton's Buildings, Market street
Globe; Mr. Alfred Sussmann, Court street, Leeds road, and Mr. W. Clough, Swaine street
Great Britain Mutual; Mr. H. Neumann, Charles street, and Mr. C. Woodcock, 4 Bridge street
Guarantee Society; Mr. John Darlington, 12 Union Passage, Kirkgate (*See advertisement*)
Guardian; Mr. Benjamin Ecroyd, Thornton's Buildings, Market st.
Halifax, Bradford and Keighley; Mr. Joseph Farrar, 1 Market street (*See advertisement*)
Imperial; Mr. J. R. Wagstaff, Charles street, Leeds road
Leeds and Yorkshire; Mr. Henry Thornton, 10 Duke street, and Terry, Watson & Fowler, 9 Market street
Life Association of Scotland; Mr. Gant, 3 Market street
London Assurance; Mr. R. Ridehalgh, Tyrrel Court
London Indisputable; Mr. John Berry, Leeds road
Manchester Fire; Mr. John Darlington, 12 Union Passage, and Mr. Thomas Holmes, 10 Exchange st.
Medical, Invalid and General; Mr. E. H. Parratt, 1 Broadstones
Metropolitan and General; Mr. A. Sussmann, Court street, Leeds road
Minerva; Mr. H. O. Mawson, 43 Kirkgate
National Provident; Mr. John Dale, Thornton's Buildings, Bridge st.

Newcastle-on-Tyne; Mr. William Mason, Bridge street Buildings
Pelican (Life); Mr. Darlington, 12 Union Passage, and Mr. Holmes, 10 Exchange street
Professional; Mr. John M. Whiteley, Observer Office, 17 Kirkgate
Protestant Dissenters' and General; William George, Swaine street
Royal Exchange; Mr. Alfred Sussmann, Court street, Leeds road, and Mr. C. Woodcock, 4 Bridge st.
Scottish Equitable; Mr. Chas. Heron, Old Bank, Kirkgate
Scottish Provident; Mr. Thomas Massey Pearce, Messrs. Walkers' and Co. Bridge street
Scottish (Widows' Fund) Life; Mr. George Rogers, Charles street
Scottish Union; Mr. John Cooke, 38 Bank street
Sheffield; Mr. E. H. Parratt, 1 Broadstones
Star; Mr. Selby, Cheapside, and Mr. Alfred Sussman, Leeds road
Sun (Life); Mr. Charles Stanfield, 5 Westgate
West of England; Mr. Wm. Clough, Swaine street
Western; Mr. Charles Lees, Albion Court, Kirkgate
Yorkshire; Mr. Thos. Dixon, Bridge street, and Mr. Dewhirst, 10 Union Passage

Filtering Machine Dealers.

THE FOLLOWING ARE AGENTS FOR RANSOME & PARSON'S PATENT.

Dixon & Byrne, 77 Market street
Newington S. T. & Co. Tyrrel street
Rudd Robert, 35 Kirkgate

Fishing Tackle Dealers.

Blackburn Henry, 29 Hustlergate
Cousen Samuel, 13 Kirkgate
Dale George, 37 Market street
Deighton John, 18 Market street
Hall John, 40 Market street
Roberts Benjamin, 5 Darley street

Fishmongers.

Binns Joseph, Bridge street
Field John, Bridge street
Hebden John, Bull's Head, Westgate
Hebden William, Rawson place, Darley street
Hollings John, Bowling Green, Bridge street
Laycock Thomas, Wharf st. Bolton rd.

Flag Merchants.

See Stone Merchants and Quarry Owners

Floor Cloth Dealers.

Archer Edward, Tyrrel street
Brumfit Joseph, 80 Market street
Clough Joseph, 2 Manchester road
Cockin Joseph & James, 12 Cheapside, and Market st. Manchester
Cowin James & Son, 59 Northgate
Hepper Christopher, Old Post Office Buildings, Bridge street
Mills Thomas, 45 Market street
Milnes Enoch, 28 Manchester road
Nutter Joseph, Nutter's place, North Parade
Thornton John, 21 Westgate
Wilkinson Joseph, New Marketplace and North Parade

Fruiterers and Greengrocers.

Barraclough James, Broadstones
Barraclough John, 125 Bridge street
Bolton Elizabeth, 65 Westgate
Brooks James, 87 Birk st. Leeds road
Calvert William, 128 Manchester road

Carter William, 3 Nelson street, Chapel lane
Chadwick John, 47 Westgate
Clough William, High street, Great Horton
Cook William, 248 Manchester road
Denton Joshua, Silsbridge lane
Farrand Henry, 70 Manchester road
Hall Joseph, Northgate
Hoadley Thomas, Northgate
Holdsworth Edward, High street, Great Horton
Hollings John, Bowling Green, Bridge street
Lister Benjamin, 91 Manchester road
Lofthouse William, 1 Market place, Darley street
Longbottom Thomas, 44 Market st.
Mann Joseph, 199 Wakefield road
Muldoon James, Northgate
Newby William, Tyrrel street
Renwick William, 37 Darley street
Simpson John, 30 Well street
Wilkinson John, 101 Bridge street
Wilkinson Joseph, 78 Westgate

Fur and Cloth Cap Dealers.

(See also Hatters.)

Chapman & Co. 26 Kirkgate
Farrar & Gillham, 20 Kirkgate
Holmes Edward Stephen, 36 Bridge st.
Johnson William & Co. 30 Ivegate
Lowe Thomas, 22A Kirkgate
Moses & Son, 19 Bridge street
Ogden Michael & Co. 29 Kirkgate
Patchett James, 48 Kirkgate
Pearson Henry, 30 and 32 Bridge st.
Unwin Samuel, Tyrrel street
Waddington Thomas & William, 23 Ivegate
Wilkinson James, 25 Ivegate

Furniture Brokers.

Barker Thomas, 232 Northgate
Bates William, 15 Union Passage, Kirkgate
Bentley Abraham, 48 Market street
Briggs Michael, 149 Bridge street
Brook Thomas, 78 White Abbey
Brumfit Joseph, 80 Market street
Dawson George, 3 Stone street, Manor row
Grainge James, 7 Union Passage, Kirkgate
Hartley James, Well street
Hepper Christopher, Old Post Office Buildings, Bridge street
Ingham Timothy, 34 Market street
Jackson John, 61 Westgate, and Silsbridge lane
Marshall Joseph, Bolton road
Mills Edward, 2 Bower street, Manchester road
Pearson Joseph, High street
Poole Joseph, 22 Silsbridge lane
Porter William, 76 High street
Rendle Thomas (and machine), Ivegate, and 260 Manchester road
Shackleton Joseph, Longcroft place, Westgate
Sharp Abraham, White Abbey
Sharp Henry, Wakefield road
Smithson John, 218 Manchester road
Stoner Christopher, 154 Westgate, and Cropper lane
Sutcliffe John, Leeds road
Thompson Thomas, 95 Bedford st. Bridge street
Whitehead Richard, 24 Bridge street

Fustian Manufacturers and Dealers.

Brown & Muff, 54 Market street
Cunliffe Thomas, (manufacturer), 31 Darley street, Thursdays and Fridays only; works Hawksclough, Hebden Bridge
Russell Joseph, 8 Bank street

Game Dealers and Poulterers.

Cousen Samuel, 13 Kirkgate
Hollings John, Bowling green, Bridge street
Lofthouse William, 1 Market place, Darley street
Newby William, Tyrrel street

Gas Fitters and Apparatus Dealers.

Armitage Samuel, 52 Market street
Atkinson Robert, Vicar lane
Bolland William, Church bank, High street
Bowles John Holdsworth, 2 Black Abbey
Clarkson & Walton, 5 Manchester road
Colburn John, 7 Croft street, Leeds road
Cookson John, Well street
Dewhirst William, Beckside, Great Horton
Guthrie William, 4 Chapel lane, Bridge street
Hargreaves Charles & Michael, Cropper lane, Westgate
Hunter William, 1 Kirkgate
Keighley James, Chapel Court, Kirkgate
Leach William, Leeds road
Pearson John, Albion Yard, Ivegate
Pease Richard, 79 Chapel lane
Ridley George, 19 Westgate
Rhodes William, 99 Westgate
Taylor Charles, Church bank, High st.
Thornton George, 94 Northgate
Thwaites Thomas, 12 Tyrrel street

Ginger Beer and Soda-Water Makers.

Firth Nathan, near the Church, Manningham
Hartley William (and lemonade), Thornton street, Thornton road

Glass, China and Earthenware Dealers.

Beanland Martin, 146 Westgate
Dilger Theodore (ornamental china), 15 Hustlergate
Goodwin James, 133 Manchester road
Harrison Thomas, 118 Manchester rd.
Newington S. T. & Co. (Staffordshire warehouse), Tyrrel street
Rhodes Charles (Staffordshire warehouse), 2 Cheapside
Watkins William, 133 Bridge street
Wood Isaac, 10 Broadstones

Glass Painters and Gilders.

Briggs Henry, 1 North Parade
Byrom James, Townhill, Wakefield road
Goodchild Robert, 223 Manchester road
Harland Brothers, 14 Hustlergate
Hird William, 92 Northgate
Maud Jos & John, Hustler's Buildings, Leeds road
Oddy Sam, 19 Market street
Peel John, 64 Bridge street
Rhodes Charles, 2 Cheapside
Rhodes James, Chapel Court, Kirkgate

Glue Manufacturer.

Walker Benjamin (manufacturer), Shipley; business attendance on Thursdays, at the Wellington Inn, High street (*See advertisement*)

Grindery Warehouses.

(See also Curriers and Leather Cutters.)

Ackroyd Thomas, 5 Bridge street

Atherton William, Hope street, Manchester road
Blakeney Richard, 1 Toad lane, Bridge street
Dove William & Jacob, 16 Darley st. and Leeds
Fairbank Thomas, 75 Northgate
Gale Septimus, 11 Toad lane, Bridge street
Rhodes Joseph & Son, 18 Well street
Skirrow John, 4 Well street, and John street, Westgate

Grocers and Tea Dealers.

Marked thus * are also Wholesale.

Ackroyd William, 142 Manchester rd.
*Alderson George, 1 Bridge street
Arnold John, 41 Bridge street
Atkinson Nathan, 107 Wakefield rd.
Beanland John, 1 Victoria street, North Parade
Bell Thomas, 104 Manchester road
Binns George, 151 George street, Leeds road
Booth William, 38 White Abbey
Branson Thomas, Wakefield road
Britton Robert, 10 Bridge street
Collier William, 85 Victoria street, North Parade
Cowgill Thomas, 107 Bridge street
Cure William, 24 Westgate
Diggles James, 158 and 160 Westgate (*See advertisement*)
Emsley James & John, 204 Manchester road and 38 Bolton road
Firth Samuel, 80 Westgate
Fox Thomas, 56 Westgrove street
France Samuel, Well street, 141 Bridge street, and 7 Tyrrel street
Furnell George, 35 Lumb lane, Manningham
Gamble Sarah, 90 Westgate
Gibson George, 180 Manchester rd.
Hall Thomas, 42 Leeds road
Hardy Henry, Market street, corner of Bridge street
Harrison Joseph, 55 Westgate
Hesling John, North street, Stott Hill
Hill John, 254 Manchester road
Hill Joseph, 41 Market street
Hodgson Michael, 73 Westgate
Irving Christopher, 42 Westgate
Isitt George, 61 Kirkgate
Kaye John, Leeds road
Learoyd Abraham, 50 Manchester rd.
Lister John, Wood street, Manningham
M'Taggart William, 3 Silsbridge lane
Malim George, 140 Westgate
Marsden Ann, 1 Union street, corner of Bridge street
* Marsden James, 8 Ivegate
Mason Christopher, 537 Wakefield rd
Milner Thomas, 8 Well street and 26 Ivegate
Mitchell John, Dudley Hill, Bowling
Morrell John, 4 and 6 Tyrrel street
Morton Matthew, 84 Westgate
Neesom James, 43 Market street
Parker William, Tyrrel street
Parkinson Edward & William, 2 Kirkgate
Peacock James, 246 Leeds road
Peacock John, 63 Northgate
Raper Joseph, 175 Bridge street
Ripley William, 8 North st. Northwing
Roberts Benjamin, 308 Leeds road
Roberts John, 25 Westgate
Rooks George, 9 and 11 Broadstones
Rowntree Isaac, 146 Manchester road
Sagar Henry, 5 Broadstones
Sharp Joshua, Wakefield road
Sharp Simon, Green lane, Manningham
Shaw William, Southfield place, Manningham

Shaw William, Wakefield road
Smith George, Tyrrel street
Smith & Tuke (wholesale), 37 Bridge street
Smith William, 40 Manchester road and 48 Westgate
Smith William, Wood st. Manninghm.
Stead William & Co. 20 Ivegate and 56 Market street
Steel Henry, 99 Brick lane
Stocks Brothers, 27 Ivegate
Stocks Henry, 58 Kirkgate
Swaine John, 176 Northbrook street, Bolton road
Trigg Edwin, Broadstones
Waddington George, 45 Silsbridge a.
Waddington Joseph, 76 Westgate
Wade John, 43 King street, Manchester road
Wadsworth Eli, 108 Manchester road
Walker James, 24 Otley road
Waller Charles, 14 Kirkgate
Walmsley John, 66 Kirkgate
Wardman Martha, 2 Nelson street, Chapel lane
Whipp Robert, 42 Vicar lane
Wilson Francis, Northgate
Woodcock Joseph, 18 Darley street
Wright George Royle, 72 Market st. and 124 Westgate

Gun Makers.

Boykett Charles, 73 Chapel lane, Tyrrel street
Egan William, 21 Hustlergate
Jessop Joseph, Albion Court, Kirkgate

Gutta Percha Dealers.

(See also Curriers and Leather Cutters.)

Ackroyd Thomas, 4 Bridge street
Atherton William, Hope street, Manchester road

B.

Dove William & Jacob, 16 Darley st. and Leeds
Fairbank Alice, Westgate
Fairbank Thomas, 75 Northgate
Rawnsley John, 35 Market street
Rhodes Joseph & Son, 18 Well street
Skirrow John, 4 Well street, and John street, Westgate
Wilson Edward, 5 Hustlergate, Unicorn Yard

Haberdashers.

(See also Linen Drapers, &c.)

Abbs James, 43 Market street
Barritt John, 38 Leeds road
Bowman John, Wakefield road
Brook, Gant & Co. 10 Westgate
Byrd Thomas, 31 Kirkgate
Cummins John, 24 Market street
Edgar Robert, 27 Market street
Greenwood Sharp, 48 White Abbey, and Black Horse Yard, Thornton
Heron Peter, 69 Westgate
Holmes Thomas & Son, 36 Kirkgate, and Darley street
Hunton William, 8 Darley street
Illingworth John, 80 and 66 Westgate
Jardine Ann & Son, Ivegate
Lawson William Watson, 22 Ivegate
Laycock Henry, 17 Westgate
Longfield William & Charles, 30 Kirkgate
Lord William & John, 52 Kirkgate
M'Croben John, 41 Kirkgate
Maud Timothy, 42 Kirkgate
Maud & Co. 65 Westgate
Monies James & Co. 30 Kirkgate and 2 Exchange street
Murgatroyd Joseph, 6 Tyrrel street
Newell Frederick Henry, 34 Kirkgate
Newton & Duckett, 55 Manchester road

Parkinson & Clark, 27 Kirkgate
Procter & Holgate, 67 Kirkgate
Simpson Elizabeth, 5 and 6 Market street
Sugden William, 4 Broadstones
Watson William and Stephen, 6 Kirkgate

Hackney Coach and Cab Owners.

Andrew George, Victoria street, Silsbridge lane
Atkinson Thomas, Sun Hotel Yard, Bridge street
Clemitshaw John, Stone street, Manor row, and Lister st. Bermondsey
Emmott James, Nelson square, Great Horton road
Gledhill Thomas, Prince of Wales Yard, Leeds road
Harker Simon, Vicar lane
Hey Joseph, King street, Leeds road
Holt & Scaife (and omnibus), West street, Vicar lane
Hudson William, Victoria street, Silsbridge lane
Ibbetson John, Thompson's Buildings, Silsbridge lane
Lewty John, 43 North Parade, Manningham lane
Rhodes William, Quebec terrace, Thornton road
Ripley James, 178 Bridge street
Scaife John, Quebec terrace, Thornton road

Hair Dressers and Perfumers.

Bairstow Andrew, 12 Queen's Cut, Manchester road
Beetham James, 68 White Abbey
Blackburn Henry, 29 Hustlergate
Bradford Joseph, Chapel lane, Kirkgate
Broadley Henry, top of Ivegate
Clayton John, 40 White Abbey
Clough Maxwell, 178 Bridge street
Cook James, 127 Bridge street
Cousen Samuel, 13 Kirkgate
Dale George, 37 Market street
Deighton John, 18 Market street
Earnshaw David, 167 Wakefield road
Foster Jonathan, 3 Nelson street, Chapel lane
Gosling Lee, 252 Manchester road
Gosling Matilda, 266 Manchester road
Gould Thomas, 73 Bridge street
Hanson John, 29 Westgate
Hirst Edward, 42 Silsbridge lane
Holgate Robert, 19 Bank street
Holgate William, 10 Market street
Humphries Samuel, 81 High street
Hutchinson William, 119 Park square, Manningham
Lofthouse William, Gt. Horton road
Longstaff John Dixon, 13 High street
Marchbank John, 136 Westgate
Medley David, 98 Manchester road
Metcalf John, 14 Manchester road
Milner John, Laister Dyke
Moorhouse Robert, Chapel lane
Pickles Henry, 27 Northgate
Pickles John, 52 Westgate
Pickles Thomas, Brick lane
Pye Reuben, Leeds road
Sagar John, 86 Manchester road
Shackelton Benjamin, Bowergate, Chapel lane
Shackelton Ellis, 15 Providence st. Westgate
Sharp William, Wakefield road
Talbot James, 58 Manchester road
Taylor Martha, 11 and 13 Bridge st.
Taylor Thomas, 86 Silsbridge lane
Teal John, Back lane, Bowling
Thresh James, 13 Manchester road
Virr Alfred, 42 Northgate
Virr William, 15 Well street

Wade Thomas, 16 Westgate
Waterhouse Joseph, 119 Manchester road
Webster James, Silsbridge lane
Wigglesworth William, 79 Market st.
Wilson Samuel Thomas, 3 Ivegate
Wood Joseph, 25 Broadstones

Hair Seating and Curled Hair Dealers.

(See also Upholsterers.)

Archer Edward, Tyrrel street
Clough James, 2 Manchester road
Cowin James & Son, 59 Northgate
Craven Isaac, 34 Darley street
Duckworth & Watson, Tyrrel Court
Hartley Samuel, Leeds road
Mills Thomas, 45 Market street
Milnes Enoch, 28 Manchester road
Nutter Joseph, North Parade
Sutcliffe Samuel, 138 and 140 George street, Leeds road
Thornton John, 21 Westgate
Tyas John, 115 Westgate
Whitehead John, 14 Well street
Wilkinson Joseph, New Market place and North Parade

Ham Dealers.

See Bacon and Ham Dealers.

Hardware Dealers.

See Birmingham & Sheffield Warehouse s

Hat and Bonnet Box Maker.

Buckley Mrs. 39 Sterling street, Manchester road

Hat Lining and Trimming Dealer.

Holmes Edward Stephen, 36 Bridge street

Hatters.

(Marked thus * are Hat Manufacturers.)

See also Fur and Cloth Cap Dealers.

Blackburn Samuel 38 and 39 Tyrrel street
Chapman & Co. 26 Kirkgate
Farrar & Gillham, 20 Kirkgate
Farrar Joseph, 1 Market street
* Hird Joseph, 82 Queen street, White Abbey
* Holmes Edward Stephen, 36 Bridge street
Jenkins James, 123 Manchester road
Johnson William & Co. 29 Ivegate
* Lowe Thomas, 22A Kirkgate
Moses & Son, 19 Bridge street
Ogden Michael & Co. 29 Kirkgate
* Patchett James, 5 and 48 Kirkgate
Pearson Henry, 30 and 32 Bridge st.
Thompson George (dresser), 9 John street, Stott Hill
* Unwin Samuel, Tyrrel street
* Waddington Thomas & William, 23 Ivegate
Wilkinson James, 25 Ivegate

Hay and Straw Dealers.

Laycock John, 28 Well street
Parker George, Thornton road
Spence Samuel, 5 Nelson street, Chapel lane

Hop Merchants.

Alderson George, 1 Bridge street
Britton Robert, 10 Bridge street
Hodgson Michael, 73 Kirkgate
Irwing Christopher, 42 Westgate
Neesom James, 43 Market street
Parkinson Joseph, 2 Old Market place
Roberts Joseph, 50 Westgate
Smith William, 40 Manchester road and 48 Westgate

Horse Breakers.

Duggan Edwin Patrick, 42 Union st. (*See advertisement*)
Mawson Robert, Nelson Inn, Northgate

Hosiers and Glovers.

(See also Haberdashers and Linen Drapers.)

Auty Squire, 101 Manchester road and Bazaar, Kirkgate
Barrit John, 38 Leeds road
Beanland Robert, 195 Bridge street
Booth Jonas, High street, Great Horton
Bowman John, Wakefield road
Brook, Gant & Co. 10 Westgate
Brown & Muff, 54 Market street
Byrd Thomas 31 Kirkgate
Clough Charles, Little Horton lane
Crowther Eli, Black Abbey
Cummins John, 24 Market street
Edgar Robert, 27 Market street
Falls Thomas, Preston place, Great Horton
Farnell John, 138 Westgate
Farrar & Gillham, 20 Kirkgate
Frank & Davy, 63 High street
Greenwood Sharp, 48 White Abbey, and Black Horse Yard, Thornton
Hall John (manufacturer), 61 Northgate
Harrison Eden, 104 Westgate
Heron Peter, 69 Westgate
Hird James, 35 Westgate
Holmes Thomas & Son, 36 Kirkgate, and Darley street
Hunton William, 8 Darley street
Illingworth John, 80 and 66 Westgate
Jackson William, Manchester road
Jaram Edward N. 302 Manchester rd.
Jardine Ann & Son, Ivegate
Lawson William Watson, 22 Ivegate
Laycock Henry, 17 Westgate
Leach Elizabeth, 81 Westgate
Longfield William & Charles, 30 Kirkgate
Lord William & John, 52 Kirkgate
Lumb Samuel, 89 Brick lane
Lumb Samuel, 140 Manchester road
M'Croben John, 41 Kirkgate
Maud Timothy, 42 Kirkgate
Maud & Co. 65 Westgate
Monies James & Co. 30 Kirkgate and 2 Exchange street
Moss Dennis Topham, 48 Manchester road
Murgatroyd Joseph, Tyrrel street
Newell Frederick Henry, 34 Kirkgate
Newton & Duckett, 55 Manchester road
Ogden Michael & Co. 29 Kirkgate
Parkinson & Clarke, 27 Kirkgate
Pickles John, 43 Westgate
Pratt James (hosier), Bradford Moor
Procter & Holgate, 67 Kirkgate
Rochfort Valentine, 17 Union Passage, Kirkgate
Russell Peter, 56 Kirkgate
Shackleton John, Southgate, Great Horton
Shaw John, 97 Manchester road
Shaw William, 44 Vicar lane
Simpson Elizabeth, 5 and 6 Market street
Sugden William, 4 Broadstones
Sykes Sarah, 96 Manchester road
Thomas Henry, Southgate, Great Horton
Walker John, Wakefield road
Wallis Brothers, 22 Westgate
Walton Robert, 196 Manchester road
Watson William & Stephen, 6 Kirkgate
Whewall James (wholesale), 44 Kirkgate, and Halifax

Hydraulic Press Makers.

Cliffe James & Joseph, Old Foundry, Tyrrel street

Crosland Robert, Union Foundry, Manchester road

Thwaites & Co. Albion Works, Thornton road

Inland Revenue Officers,

(EXCISE BRANCH.)

Roberts John (supervisor), 24 Victoria street, North Parade

Bostock John, Manchester road

Davy William, 34 Westgrove street

Dixon John, Dudley Hill, Bowling

Penket John, 42 Canal terrace, Bolton road

Wright Thomas, Undercliffe

Wynn Richard, Shipley

Inns, Hotels and Taverns.

Airedale, Joseph Prince, Otley road

Albion Inn, Henry Dooley, Leeds rd.

Albion Hotel, Isaac Walmsley, Ivegate

Angel, William Hemingway Lister, 51 Westgate

Barley Mow, James Blakey, Wakefield road

Bee Hive, Joseph Foster, Westgate

Bermondsey Hotel, Mary Dunn, Lister street, Bermondsey

Barrack Tavern, William Sugden, Bradford Moor

Bishop Blaize, Mary Barraclough, Westgate

Black Bull, Thomas Swaine, Wood street, Westgate

Black Bull, Hiram Moulson, Little Horton lane

Black Horse, Hannah Wood, Little Horton lane

Black Swan, William Scholefield, Thornton road

Blue Lion, John Nowell, Manchester road

Boar's Head, Joseph Blamires, Market street

Bowling Green, (posting house and billiard room), Joseph Baxter, Bridge street

Britannia, Richard Tate, George st. Wakefield road

Brown Cow, Charles William Bradford, Kirkgate

Brunswick, Joseph Stead, Thornton road

Bull's Head, Joseph Sugden, Westgate

Church Steps, Charles Lightowler, Bolton road

Coach and Horses (and bowling green), Elizabeth Crabtree, Shipley Lane End

Coach and Horses, Samuel Ellison, Bradford Moor

Cock and Bottle, James Thornton, High street

Commercial, John Bell, Tyrrel street

Craven Heifer, George Knight, Four Lane Ends, Manningham

Craven Heifer, Sarah Steel, Bowling lane

Durham Ox, William Stephenson, Queen street, White Abbey

Farm Yard, Joseph Roberts, Back la.

Fleece, William Galloway, 208 Manchester road

Fleece, Robert Shackleton, Bank st. and Hustlergate

Fleece, William Bakes, Great Horton road

Four Ashes, Jeremiah Rudd, High st. Great Horton

Fox and Hounds, James Briggs, Northwing

Fox and Pheasant, David Bottomley, Little Horton lane

George Hotel (and posting house), Margaret Reaney, Market street

George and Dragon, Leah Swaine, High street, Great Horton

Golden Lion, James Lightowler, Leeds road

Granby Hotel, James Grainge, Union street, Bridge street

Hare and Hounds, Mary Tordoff, Banktop, Great Horton

Hit or Miss, James Hepworth, Sticker lane, Bowling

Hope and Anchor, Abraham Priestley, Bank street

Horse and Jockey, Jonas Jowett, Low Moor

Horse and Trumpet, William Greaves, Manchester road

Horse Shoes, William Baxter, Tyrrel street

Ivy Hotel, John Stephenson, Barker-end, High street

Junction, Thomas Outhwaite, Leeds road

Junction, John Stephenson, Laister Dyke

King's Arms, Matthew Wood, Heaton

King's Arms, John Rudd, High st. Great Horton

King's Head, Joseph Thornton, Buttershaw, North Bierley

Lister's Arms, William Shaw, Manchester road

Lower Globe, Jeremiah Parker, Manningham

Malt Shovel, Joshua Denison, Kirkgate

Manor House, Thomas Barber, Darley street

Market Tavern, James Hammond, Rawson place, Darley street

Moulders' Arms, Squire Marsden, Sticker lane, Bowling

Nag's Head, Elizabeth Crampton, Kirkgate

Nelson, Paul Rhodes, Northgate

New Inn, Elizabeth Wade, Tyrrel street

New Miller Dam (and bowling green) John Lumby, Thornton road

Odd Fellows' Arms, Henry Milnes, Manchester road

Odd Fellows' Hall, Joseph Smith, Thornton road

Old Crown, Elizabeth Lumb, 11 Ivegate

Old Globe, John Ledgard, Manningham

Old King's Arms, Charles Bradford Baxter, Westgate

Old King's Head, John Tordoff, Westgate

Old Red Gin, Thomas Mitchell, Bowling lane

Old Red Lion, Christopher Yates, Little Horton lane

Pack Horse, John Blamires, Westgate

Prince of Wales, Henry Gledhill, Leeds road

Prince of Wales, Harriet Wrathmell, Bowling Old lane

Prince of Wales (tap), Thomas Housoncroft, Leeds road

Prospect Inn, Thomas Hodgson, Bolton road

Queen's Arms, Thomas Walton, 135 Manchester road

Ram's Head, James Sadler, Silsbridge lane

Regent, William Wright, Leeming street, School street
Rawson's Arms, Elizabeth Ingle, Market street
Red Lion, Joseph Wood, Wibsey Bankfoot
Reservoir Inn, John Chadwick, Lady's Walk, Manningham
Ring O'Bells, Moses Sugden, Bolton road
Roebuck, Henry Wiseman, Sun Bridge
Rose and Crown, George Mortimer, New road, Great Horton
Royal Engineer, John Scholefield, Dudley Hill
Royal Oak, James Forrest, Kirkgate
Seven Stars, Robert Meynell, Wakefield road
Ship, Timothy Rhodes, 12 Well st.
Shoulder of Mutton, William Crampton, Kirkgate
Spotted House, Thomas Atkinson, Manningham lane
Star, Isaac Myers, Westgate
Sun Hotel (and posting house), James Wilman, Bridge street
Talbot Hotel (and posting house), William Wood, Kirkgate
Turf Tavern, John Hammond, Heaton road
Unicorn, Ann Reynolds, Ivegate
Victoria, Clement Taylor, White Abbey
Wellington, Hannah Pickles, High street
Wellington, Joseph Gummersall, Lister Hills, Little Horton
Wheat Sheaf, John Briskham, Wakefield road
White Bear, John Womersley, Bradford Moor
White Hart, William Whittaker, Thornton road
White Hart, John Firth, Dudley Hill, Bowling
White Horse, William Moorhouse, Great Horton
White Horse, George Lambert, 23 Kirkgate
White Lion, Maria Wheatley, Kirkgate
White Swan, Richard Gott Fox, Market street
Woodman, William Ingle, 157 George street, Leeds road
Woodman, John Yewdall, Halifax road, Bowling
Wool Packs, Ann Midgley, Well street

Beer Retailers.

Ackroyd Abraham, Little Horton lane
Ackroyd William, 24 Croft street, Leeds road
Ambler Eliza, 116 Bridge street
Athea John, 4 Longcroft place, Silsbridge lane
Atkinson Thomas, 15 Nelson street, Chapel lane
Bainbridge James, 110 Northwing, High street
Baines John Kirby, Britannia street, Manchester road
Barker James, 58 Smith street, Manchester road
Barker Squire, 224 Manchester road
Bartle George, 16 Croft street, Wakefield road
Bateman Charles, 12 Greenaire place, Silsbridge lane
Beck Benjamin, 14 Southgate
Beecroft John, 1 Duke street, Manchester road
Bentley Walter, Great Horton road
Binns Ogden, 53 Victoria street, Thornton road

Boats James, 40 Silsbridge lane
Boyle Joseph, 83 Westgate
Bradbury John, Lumb lane
Briggs Joseph, 12 Castle street, Manchester road
Brightman William, 93 Birk street, Leeds road
Broscomb Joseph, 49 Black Abbey
Brown Sarah, 18 Southgate
Brunt Jacob, 10 Longlands place, Westgate
Carrol Moses, Broomfield, Wakefield road
Carter Joseph, 209 Bolton road
Clair John, 88 Adelaide street, Manchester road
Clapham Thomas, 2 Duke street, Manchester road
Clark Robert, New road, Gt. Horton
Clough James, 20 Market street
Cockcroft Samuel, Lidget Green, Great Horton
Copley William, Manningham
Couldwell John, 52 Vicar lane
Coulson John, Wood st. Manningham
Crabtree George, 15 Peel street, Leeds road
Crabtree John, 95 Bolton road
Croft James, 111 Back lane, Bowling
Daker John, Mill street, Canal road
Daly Michael, 71 Westgate
Dickinson George, Well street
Drake Andrew, Clayton street, Thornton road
Dugdale Robert, Ivegate
Duggan Edwin Patrick, 42 Union st. Bridge street—(*See advertisement*)
Ellis John, 35 George st. Leeds road
Ellis Joseph, Leeds road
Facer John, 177 Wakefield road
Fearnley George, Otley road
Fearnley Robert, Stott Hill
Fell Mary, Providence street, White Abbey
Fieldhouse Thomas, Bradford Moor
Firth Charles, Uppercroft row, Bowling
Firth Henry, 44 Westgate
Forrest Francis Hanson, Westgate
Foster Abraham, 100 Westgate
Fox Sarah, Southgate, Great Horton
Francis Joseph, 80 Manchester road
Fryer John, 100 Manchester road
Geoghegan James, Hope street, Manchester road
Gibson Jabez, Dudley Hill, Bowling
Gilliard John, 112 Manchester road
Goodyear Richard, Canal road, Well street
Graham Joseph, Back lane, Bowling
Grainge John, 20 Brick lane, Black Abbey
Greenwood Frederick Smith, Duke street, Darley street
Grimshaw John, 32 Providence street, White Abbey
Haigh James, 201 Bridge street
Haley Abraham, Diamond street, Vicar lane
Hanson John, 81 Wapping road
Harrison Alfred, Bradford Moor
Harrison Joseph, 68 Bedford street, Wakefield road
Harrison Robert, 39 Westgate
Harrison Samuel, 41 Lumb lane
Harrison William, Back lane, Bowling
Hartley John, 460 Wakefield road
Hayes Michael, Poole's Alley, Silsbridge lane
Haywood James, Churchbank, Well street
Hill John, 32 Melbourne street, Leeds road
Hinchliffe Mary, 1 Melbounre street, Leeds road

Hoadley Ann, Northgate
Holden William, 42 Northwing, High street
Holmes Joseph, 28 Joseph street, Leeds road
Holroyd Esther, 18 Silsbridge lane
Hopkinson William, 7 Wapping road
Hudson James, Wakefield road
Ingham Nancy, Back lane, Bowling
Ingham William, Back lane, Bowling
Jenkinson Rachel, Silsbridge lane
Johnson John, 62 Duke street, Wakefield road
Jones Elizabeth, Wakefield road
Jones Samuel, 23 Bower street, Manchester road
Jordan William, Broom street, Wakefield road
Jowett Ellen, Cross street, Westgate
Jowett William, Lumby street, Manchester road
Kaye John, 1 Silsbridge lane
Keighley James, 38 Silsbridge lane
Kell Matthew, 18 Longcroft place, Westgate
Kellett James, 178 Manchester road
Kitcheman Samuel, Leeds road
Knowles Squire, Greenaire place, Silsbridge lane
Lacy John Womersley, 3 Churchbank, Well street
Laycock Joshua, 16 King Charles street, Otley road
Ledgard John, Manningham
Leng William, Paperhall, Northwing
Leyland Francis, Beckside, Horton
Lister James, Park place, Little Horton lane
Liversedge Jabez, Great Horton road
Lockwood William, 64 Bolton road
Long James, Hardcastle lane, Well street
Long Thomas, 97 Gracechurch street, White Abbey
Lonsdale Robert, Mount street, Bowling
Lowndes James, 57 Croft street, Manchester road
Marsden James, Bradford Moor
Midgley John, Broomfield, Wakefield road
Millett James, 2 Mason street, Thornton road
Moran Michael, 84 Thornton road
Muff Charles, Back lane, Bowling
Murgatroyd Joshua, Thornton road
Murphy Martin, 10 Providence street, Westgate
Parker James, Hall lane, Bowling
Peacock John, 41 Vicar lane
Pearson Hannah, 23 High street
Pickles John, Swaine Green, Bowling
Pilling John, 39 King street, Manchester road
Pitts Samuel, Back lane, Bowling
Poole William, 81 Thornton road
Porter Sarah, 46 Longlands street, Westgate
Rendle Thomas, 260 Manchester road
Riddihough John, 4 Toad lane, Chapel lane
Roberts William, Bradford Moor
Roberts William, Broomfield, Wakefield road
Robinson Charles, 67 York street, Bridge street
Robinson John, Spink place, Black Abbey
Robson William, 33 Wellington st. Stott Hill
Rodley John, 13 George street, Leeds road
Russell Mary, 82 Northwing
Sanderson George, Lidget Green, Horton

Sedgwick Ellen, 42 Westend street, Silsbridge lane
Sewell William, 6 Bedford street, Bridge street
Shackleton Benjamin, Bowergate, Chapel lane
Sharp Frederick, 24 White Abbey
Smith John, 4 Silsbridge lane
Smith John, High street
Smith John, 95 Bridge street
Smith Ruth, 71 Westgate
Smith Thomas, Hardcastle lane, Well street
Speak Jonas, 3 Burrow street, Manchester road
Speight Jonas, 13 North street, Northwing
Stead Joseph, 7 Prince street, Manchester road
Steel George, 11 Wellington street, Stott Hill
Stell Ann, Bridge street
Stephenson John, Barkerend
Swaine William, Thornton road
Taylor Joseph, Brook street, Hall Ings
Thomas Samuel, 10 Brick row, Thornton road
Thornton John, Vicar lane
Topham John, 39 Black Abbey
Town Edward Henry, 21½ Ivegate
Unwin David, Lillycroft, Manninghm.
Uttley William, 24 Sedgwick street, White Abbey
Waddilove Richard, 41 Victoria street, Manchester road
Waddilove Thomas, 4 Nelson Court, Nelson street
Waddington William, Broomfields, Wakefield road
Wainwright John Wilson, Bridge st.
Walker William, Hill Top, Manningham
Walton Thomas, 103 George street, Leeds road
Wheater Joshua, 38 Queen street, Manchester road
Whitehead James, 60 Westgate
Whittaker Clough, 15 Barkerend
Wilkinson Aaron, Manchester road
Wilkinson Charles, Thornton road
Willis John, 42 Millbank, Wood st.
Willoughby Thomas, 114 Bolton road
Wilman Isaac, 7 Cross Wellington street, Stott Hill
Wilman James, 147 Silsbridge lane
Wilman Peter, 3 Longcroft place, Silsbridge lane
Wright John, Northbrook, Wharf st. Bolton road

Irish and other Linen Merchants.

Abbs James, 43 Market street
Brook, Gant & Co. 10 Westgate
Brown & Muff, 54 Market street
Byrd Thomas, 31 Kirkgate
Cummins John, 34 Market street
Edgar Robert, 27 Market street
Heron Peter, 69 Westgate
Holmes Thomas & Son, 36 Kirkgate
Illingworth John, 66 Westgate
Jardine Ann & Son, Ivegate
Lawson William Watson, 22 Ivegate
Laycock Henry, 17 Westgate
Longfield William & Charles, 30 Kirkgate
M'Croben John, 41 Kirkgate
Maud Timothy, 42 Kirkgate
Monies James & Co. 30 Kirkgate
Murgatroyd Joseph, Tyrrel street
Newell Frederick Henry, 34 Kirkgate
Parkinson & Clarke, 27 Kirkgate
Procter and Holgate, 67 Kirkgate

Iron Fencing and Palisade Manufacturers.

Cliffe James and Joseph, Old Foundry, Tyrrel street
Cole, Marchent & Co. Prospect Foundry, Wakefield road, Bowling
Crosland Robert, Union Foundry, Manchester road
Hargreaves Charles & Michael, Cropper lane, Westgate
Hargreaves & Kennedy, Waterloo Foundry, Adelaide street, Manchester road
Leeming John & Son, Northolme Mill, Railroad street, Canal road
Waddington Richard, Railway Foundry, Manchester road
Wyrill Frances, 8 Westgate (*See advertisement*)

Iron Founders.

(See also Brass Founders.)

Berry Benjamin & Sons, Prospect Mill, Wakefield road
Clayton, Marshalls & Co. Bierley Works, and Canal road
Cliffe James & Joseph, Old Foundry, Tyrrel street
Cole, Marchent & Co. Prospect Foundry, Wakefield road, Bowling
Crosland Robert, Union Foundry, Manchester road
Haley Christopher, Foundry street, Vicar lane
Haley Enoch, Thornton road
Haley Joseph, Mill street, Manchester road
Halstead Isaac, Hope Foundry, Thornton road
Hargreaves & Kennedy, Waterloo Foundry, Adelaide street, Manchester road
Hird, Dawson & Hardy, Low Moor, and Canal road
Leeming John & Son, Northolme Mill, Railroad street, Canal road
Naylor & Merrall, Providence Mill, Manchester road
Onion & Wheelhouse, Frederick st. Bridge street
Sturges John & Co. Bowling Works; wharf and office, Canal road
Thwaites & Co. Albion Works, Thornton road
Waddington Richard, Railway Foundry, Manchester road
Worsnop Joseph Benson, Providence Foundry, Manchester road

Iron Manufacturers.

Hird, Dawson & Hardy, Low Moor Works; office and wharf, Canal road
John Sturges & Company, Bowling Works; iron wharf, Canal road

Iron and Steel Merchants.

Beecroft, Butler & Co. Leeds road; works, Kirkstall, near Leeds: David Thornton agent
Clayton, Marshalls' & Co. Bierley Works; office Canal road
Dixon Thomas (railway tire-bars, &c.), Thornton road
Hird, Dawson & Hardy, Low Moor Works; office Canal road

Ironmongers—Furnishing, &c.

Calvert Michael, 13 Ivegate
Clough Benjamin, 8 White Abbey
Dixon & Byrne (and stove-grate manufacturers), 77 Market street
Dove Thomas Pashley, 17 Ivegate
Marshall William, 4 Kirkgate
Parratt Edward Hawksworth, 1 Broadstones

Pearson Henry, 30 and 32 Bridge st.
Read Henry, 29 Market street
Rhodes John, 18 Kirkgate
Rudd Robert (and agent for Ransome and Parson's patent filterer), 35 Kirkgate
Scully Ambrose, 7 Ivegate
Shackleton William, 23 Broadstones
Smith Jonas, 40 Westgate
Stelling Thomas, 62 Kirkgate
Wyrill Frances, 8 Westgate (*See advertisement*)

Italian Warehousemen and Foreign Fruit Dealers.

Britton Robert, 10 Bridge street
Woodcock Joseph (and German provisions), 18 Darley street

Jacquard Machine Makers.

Dracup Samuel, Cliffe lane, Great Horton
Foster Jonas (and card cutter), 50 Victoria st. Manchester road
Sharp John, Victoria Mill, Wakefield road, Bowling

Jewellers—Working, &c.

Barrow William, 2 Bank street, Market street
Bowes James, 8 Union Passage, and Leeds road
Brooksbank William, 64 Market street (*See advertisement*)
Brumfit Joseph, 80 Market street
Dilger Theodore, 15 Hustlergate
Freeman Ambrose, 98 Manchester rd.
Hardaker James, 12 Providence st. Westgate
Harker & Crabtree, 162 Manchester road
Hill John, Whetley street, Manningham
Knowles David, 19 Manchester road
Prest William, 22 Well street
Renton James, 16 Well street
Rhodes Manoah, 6 Westgate
Snow Nicholas Mason, 24 Piecehall Yard, Kirkgate
Wilson & Fairbank, 47 Kirkgate

Joiners and Builders.

(See also Cabinet Makers.)

Andrew George, Victoria street, Silsbridge lane
Annison Samuel, Church street, High street
Armitage Thomas, King's Court, Northgate
Aspinall Samuel, Duke street, Cheapside
Atkinson Francis Whitley, Bolton road
Barraclough John, 68 Westgate
Bartle David, High street, Great Horton
Bartle John & Brothers, Great Horton road
Baxter & Johnson, Diamond street, Vicar lane
Beanland John & William, Little Horton lane
Beecroft Joseph (executors of), Toad lane, Bridge street
Booth Joseph, Dudley Hill, Bowling
Brayshaw William (builder), corner of Lumb lane, Westgate
Brunton William, Keighley street, Silsbridge lane
Crabtree John Anthony, Salem street, Manor row
Demain & Johnson, Manor row, Cheapside
Dixon John (builder), Swaine street, Hall Ings

Dunn & Stoddart (joiners), Market street and Vicar lane
Fox Kelitah (joiner), Greenhill place, Manningham
Gledhill William (builder), 72 Leeds road
Green James, Colliergate, Swaine st.
Green John, Mill lane, Little Horton
Haigh Henry (joiner), Little Horton lane
Heap Joseph (joiner), Brick lane
Hewitt & Knowles, School street
Hill Jonas and Thomas, Church bank, Well street
Horsfall George, Cure's Court, Westgate
Illingworth Booth & Thomas, Southgate
Illingworth Jonas, Southgate
Illingworth Jonas jun. Mawson st. Thornton road
Ingham William, Back lane, Bowling
Kershaw Samuel, Bowling lane, Bowling
Marshall Joseph (joiner), Bolton rd.
Mitchell John (joiner), 125 Westgate
Myers David (joiner), 113 Queen street, Manchester road
Nowell John (joiner), Broadstones
Pearson Joseph (joiner), High street
Pickard & Ogden, Silsbridge lane
Pickard William, Bradford Moor
Poole David (joiner), Bowling lane, Bowling
Ramsden Joseph, High street, Great Horton
Read Joseph (joiner), Fitzgerald st. Manchester road
Scholefield John, Great Horton
Scholefield John, Low Green, Horton
Sharp Abraham, White Abbey
Shaw & Neal, Arundel street, Manchester road

S

Smith George, Thornton road
Stephenson David, Little Horton Green
Stephenson John & Sons, Great Horton road
Stephenson Moses (joiner), Clayton lane, Manchester road
Stoner David, Churchbank, Well st.
Sugden Samuel, Dudley Hill, Bowling
Taylor Thomas, Salem street, Manor row
Thompson Thomas (joiner), 95 Bedford street, Bridge street
Wardle William (joiner), 19 Bedford street, Bridge street
Waugh William, Four Lane Ends, Manningham
Weatherhill Joseph, Eastbrook lane, Leeds road
West Joseph, Sticker lane, Bowling
Wheater Henry (joiner), 62 King street, Manchester road
Whitehead Samuel, Albion Yard, Ivegate
Whiteley Thomas (joiner), Bolton street, Barkerend
Wilson James & Son, Spring row, Manningham
Wright William, Manchester road

Lace Warehouses.

Abbs James, 43 Market street
Brook, Gaunt & Co. 10 Westgate
Cummins John, 24 Market street
Edgar Robert, 27 Market street
Heron Peter, 69 Westgate
Holmes Thomas & Son, 36 Kirkgate
Hunton William, 8 Darley street
Illingworth John, 66 Westgate
Jardine Ann & Son, Ivegate
Lawson William Watson, 22 Ivegate
Laycock Henry, 17 Westgate
M'Croben John, 41 Kirkgate

Maud Timothy, 42 Kirkgate
Monies James & Co. 30 Kirkgate and 2 Exchange street
Parkinson & Clark, 27 Kirkgate
Simpson Elizabeth, 5 and 6 Market street

Land and Building Agents and Surveyors.

(See also Architects and Surveyors.)

Andrews & Delauney (for the South Lancashire Building Association), Rennie Buildings, Hall Ings
Dixon Thomas, Bridge street Buildings, Bridge street
Hardcastle George (surveyor), 53 Westgate
Ingle & Smith, 1 Albion Court, Kirkgate
Lister George Thompson (and valuer), 19 Drewton street, Westgate
Mallinson & Healy (and valuers), Tyrrel street
Martin Samuel Dickinson (and valuer), 51 Darley street, and Albion place, Leeds
Robertshaw Joshua (valuer only), 77 Silsbridge lane
Smith Joseph, Thornton's Buildings, Market street
Tuke William (and valuer), Darley street, and Blake street, York
Woodcock Charles, 4 Bridge street

Last and Boot Tree Makers.

Blakeney Richard, 1 Toad lane, Bridge street
Gale Septimus, 11 Toad lane, Bridge street

Lathe and Tool Makers.

(See also Tool Makers and Dealers.)

Hattersley Samuel & Son, Westbrook Works, Thornton road
Thwaites & Co. Albion Works, Thornton road

Law Stationers.

Halliday Richard, Goodmansend
Hansom Richard, 12 Parkgate, High street

Lead Merchant.

Thwaites Thomas, 12 Tyrrel street

Leather Dressers and Dealers.

Ackroyd Thomas, 5 Bridge street
Cordingley William (white), Hustlergate, Mondays and Thursdays; house Park place, Little Horton
Fairbank Thomas, 75 Northgate
Hanson Thomas, Westbrook terrace, Thornton road
Rawnsley John, 35 Market street
Skirrow John, 4 Well street, and John street, Westgate
Walker Richard, 17 and 19 Darley st.
Wilson Edward, 5 Hustlergate, Unicorn Yard

Leather Skep, and Picking Strap, &c. Dealers.

Oddy William, 65 Market street
Wilkinson Robert, Exchange street

Libraries.

SUBSCRIPTION AND CIRCULATING.

Boulton Samuel, 4 Lumb lane, Westgate
Brown Jacob, John street, Northgate
Conservative, Albion Court, Kirkgate
Cooke William, 1 Ebenezer street, Vicar lane
Hainsworth John, 32 Manchester rd.
Ibbetson James, 20 Bridge street
Lund Joseph, 82 Westgate (*See advertisement*)

Mechanics' Institute, Leeds road; Edward Starkey librarian
Oddfellows' Literary Institution, Darley street
Subscription, Exchange Buildings, Kirkgate; open from ten till five summer, winter closes at four; Miss Mason librarian
Umpleby Thomas, 2 Lumby street, Manchester road
Waterhouse Thomas, 25 Darley street

Lime Dealers.

BRADFORD LIME WORKS, Canal road; Joseph Wood proprietor
Hepper James, Thornton road, and Canal wharf, Shipley
LOTHERSDALE LIME Co. (William Spencer & Sons); office and wharf Railroad street, Canal road; John Hargreaves agent

Linen Drapers, Silk Mercers, &c.

Abbs James, 43 Market street
Barritt John, 38 Leeds road
Beanland Robert, 195 Bridge street
Bennett John, 77 Westgate
Bird Samuel, 10 White Abbey
Booth Jonas, High street, Great Horton
Bowman John, Wakefield road
Brook, Gant & Co. 10 Westgate
Brown & Muff, 54 Market street
Byrd Thomas, 31 Kirkgate
Calvert Mary, Wakefield road
Carr Mary, Dudley Hill, Bowling
Clayton Henry, Arcadia street, Lumb lane
Clough Charles, Little Horton lane
Crowther Eli, Brick lane
Cummins John, 24 Market street
Edgar Robert, 27 Market street
Falls Thomas, Preston place, Great Horton
Farnell John, 138 Westgate
Franks and Davy, 63 High street
Greenwood Sharp, 48 White Abbey, and Black Horse Yard, Thornton
Harpley John, Laister Dyke
Harrison Eden, 104 Westgate
Heron Peter, 69 Westgate
Hird James, Westgate
Holmes Thomas & Son, 36 Kirkgate
Illingworth John, 66 and 80 Westgate
Illingworth Thomas, 2 Black Abbey
Jackson William, Manchester road
Jaram Edward N. 302 Manchester rd.
Jardine Ann & Son, Ivegate
Lawson William Watson, 22 Ivegate
Laycock Henry, 17 Westgate
Leach Elizabeth, 81 Westgate
Longfield William and Charles, 30 Kirkgate
Lord William and John, 52 Kirkgate
Lumb Samuel, 89 Brick lane
Lumb Samuel, 140 Manchester road
M'Croben John, 41 Kirkgate
Mason Christopher, 537 Wakefield rd.
Maud and Co. 65 Westgate
Maud Timothy, 42 Kirkgate
Monies James & Co. 30 Kirkgate and 2 Exchange street
Moss Denis Topham, 48 Manchester road, and Leeds
Murgatroyd Joseph, Tyrrel street
Newell Frederick Henry, 34 Kirkgate
Newton and Duckett, 55 Manchester road
Parkinson and Clark, 27 Kirkgate
Pickles Joseph, 43 Westgate
Procter and Holgate, 67 Kirkgate
Russell Peter, 56 Kirkgate
Scholey Stephen, Thornton road
Shackleton John, Southgate, Great Horton
Sharp Simon, Green lane, Manninghm.
Shaw John, 97 Manchester road

Shaw William, 44 Vicar lane
Simpson Elizabeth, 5 and 6 Market street
Sugden William, 4 Broadstones
Swaine John, 176 Northbrook street, Bolton road
Sykes Sarah, 96 Manchester road
Thomas Henry, Southgate, Great Horton
Walker John, Wakefield road
Wallis Brothers, 22 Westgate
Walton Robert, 196 Manchester road
Watson William & Stephen, 6 Kirkgate, and Bermondsey
Wilkinson Mary, 83 Timber street, Otley road

Linen Drapers and Tea Dealers —Travelling.

Beard Hugh, Victoria street, North Parade
Brear William, Brick lane
Clarkson George (tea), Smith street, Manchester road
Cockcroft John, Brick lane
Douglas Robert, 114 Westgate
French Adam, Northgate
French John, Northgate
Gourlay Andrew, Southfield place, Lumb lane
Gourlay James, Victoria street, North Parade
Gourlay Thomas, Fountain street, Manningham lane
Graham Edward, 116 Westgate
Graham James, 16 Victoria street, North Parade
Graham James, 3 Victoria street, North Parade
Heron James, Hanover square
Heron Thomas, Broad street, Manor row
Hope John, 7 Victoria street, North Parade
Johnstone John, 23 Westgrove street
Lund William (tea), Westgrove street
M'Clennan William Johnstone, 30 Westgrove street
M'Math James, Victoria street, North Parade
M'Meeking Gilbert, 38 Westgrove street
M'Michan James, Victoria street, North Parade
M'William James, 17 Green lane, Manningham
Middleton Thomas, Brunswick place
O'Leary Randall (silk goods, &c.) Great Cross street, George street
Robison William & Co. Regent place, Duke street
Smith Robert Kerr, Apperley Bridge
Sproat John, Westgate
Sproat John, Victoria street, North Parade
Steel Henry, Brick lane
Thompson James, Victoria street, North Parade
Vernon Samuel, Victoria street, North Parade
Wadsworth William, Broomfield terrace, Wakefield road
Wood Thomas, Northgate
Woodhouse Thomas, Providence st. White Abbey

Livery Stable Keepers.

Atkinson Thomas, Sun Hotel Yard, Bridge street
Gledhill James, Prince of Wales Yard, Leeds road
Lewty John, 43 Manningham lane
Roberts Joseph, Back lane
Scott George, Thornton road

Locksmiths and Bellhangers.

(See also Whitesmiths.)

Campbell Richard, Reform street, Westgate
Cowman William, Mawson street, Thornton road
Dixon & Byrne, 77 Market street
Dove Thomas Pashley, 17 Ivegate
Fell James, 17 Nelson street
Fenton Sarah, 15 Market street
Hargreaves Peter, Ship Alley, Well street
Midgley Thomas, 1 Cure's Court, Westgate
Pearson John, Albion Yard, Ivegate
Rhodes William, 99 Westgate
Richardson Henry, 5 Bedford street, Bridge street
Rudd Robert, 35 Kirkgate
Shackleton William, 123 Broadstones
Smith John, Portland street, Manchester road
Smith Thomas, Bowergate, Chapel lane
Wyrill Frances, 8 Westgate (*See advertisement*)

Looking Glass and Picture Frame Makers.

(See also Carvers and Gilders.)

Archer Edward, Tyrrel street
Briggs Henry (picture frames), 1 North Parade, Christ Church
Briggs Joseph, 92 Leeds road
Clough Joseph, 2 Manchester road
Constantine James, 76 Bridge street
Cowin James & Son, 59 Northgate
Craven Isaac, 34 Darley street
Holmes Joseph, 53 Darley street
Mills Thomas, 45 Market street
Rhodes James (picture frames), Chapel court, Kirkgate (*See advertisement*)
Robinson Dan, 20 Well street
Snow William, Brunswick place
Ward Edwin, 12 Wellington street, Stott Hill
White Charles, Bolton street, Barkerend, High street

Machine Makers.

(See also Millwrights and Engineers.)

Berry Benjamin & Sons, Prospect Mill, Wakefield road
Child Daniel, Spence's Mill, Chapel lane
Crabtree William, Laycock's Mill, Thornton road
Dodsworth William, Thornton road
Donisthorpe & Co. (top machine patentees), Tyrrel street
Dracup Samuel (jacquard), Cliffe lane, Great Horton
Eastwood Jonathan, Portland street, Manchester road
Foster Jonas (jacquard), 50 Victoria street, Manchester road
Hattersley George, Charles street; works Keighley
Hattersley Samuel & Son, Westbrook Works, Thornton road
Hill John & Co. (weighing), 8 Cheapside
Leeming John & Son, Northolme Mill, Railroad street, School street
Naylor & Merrall, Providence Mill, Manchester road
Onion & Wheelhouse, Frederick st. Bridge street
Sharp John (jacquard), Victoria Mill, Wakefield road
Smith John, Albion Works, Thornton road

Thwaites & Co. Albion Works, Thornton road

Tillotson Joseph, Pennyoak's Mill, Melbourne street, Leeds road

Wells Joseph, Back lane, Bowling

Wray Joseph (sole maker and fitter-up of John Hyde's patent improvements in the power loom), Westholme Mill, Thornton road

Wright, Wood & French, Thompson's Mill, Thornton road

Machine Rulers.

(See also Bookbinders, &c.)

Dale John, 1 Thornton's Buildings, Bridge street

Drake John, 2 Market street

Drake John, King's Court, Northgate

Lumley Joseph, Hustler's Buildings, Leeds road

Morris Benjamin Gough, Market st.

Parry Robert, Market street

Spencer Richard & Thomas, Broadstones

Stanfield Charles, 5 Westgate

Watson Robert, James st. Northgate

Machinery Brokers.

Brown Joseph, Hustler's Buildings, Market street

Ellis John, Roebuck Yard, Ivegate

Greenhough John, Roebuck Yard, Ivegate

Holt Benjamin, Bank street, and Mawson street, Thornton road

Lee George, Roebuck Yard, Ivegate

Lister Joseph, Thornton road

Rendle Thomas, Ivegate, and 260 Manchester road

Makers-Up and Packers.

Banks & Pollard, 28 Leeds road

Cooper & Wainwright, Dale street, Kirkgate

Howitt George, 1 Churchbank, Well street

Maltsters.

Butler James, Dudley Hill, Bowling

Hill Elizabeth, 20 Manchester road

Hill John, 57 Westgate

Mason William, 2 Cropper lane, Westgate

Thompson Benjamin, Old Brewery, Horton road

Map Publisher.

Ibbetson James, 20 Bridge street

Marble Masons.

Ruddock Edward Harris (and sculptor), Leeds road

Tattersall John (and cement dealer), Leeds road

Mathematical Instrument Makers, &c.

(See also Barometer Dealers & Opticians.)

Franks Isaac (and glass apparatus for chemical tests and experiments), 71 Market street, and Leeds

Rhodes Manoah, 6 Westgate

Rimmington Felix (glass apparatus for chemical tests), 6 Ivegate

Mattress and Cushion Makers.

(See also Upholsterers.)

Archer Edward, Tyrrel street

Brumfit Joseph, 80 Market street

Cockin Joseph & James, 12 Cheapside

Cowin James & Son, 59 Northgate

Duckworth and Watson, Tyrrel Court, Tyrrel street

Edmondson Jacob, Bowergate, Chapel lane

Hartley Samuel, Leeds road

Hepper Christopher, Old Post Office Buildings, Bridge street
Mills Thomas, 45 Market street
Milnes Enoch, 28 Manchester road
Nutter Joseph, Nutter's place, North Parade
Sutcliffe Samuel, 138 and 140 George street, Leeds road
Thornton John, 21 Westgate
Tyas John, 115 Westgate
Ward William, King's Arms Yard, Westgate
Whitehead John, 14 Well street
Wilkinson Joseph, New Market place, and 13 North Parade

Merchants—Commission.

(See also Stuff and Yarn Merchants.)

Frank John Philip & Co. Duke street, Darley street
Henry A. & S. and Co. Bermondsey, and Manchester
Hiller Harry, 16 Dale street, and 7 Hall st. St. Peter's, Manchester
Liebert Bernhard, Hall Ings
Passavant Philip Jas. & Co. Cheapside
Steinthal & Co. Hall Ings

Milliners and Dress Makers.

Ackroyd Rachel, 13 Green lane, Manningham
Anderson Emma, Wakefield road
Anderson Ruth, 26 Croft street, Manchester road
Archer Hannah, 8 Providence street, Silsbridge lane
Barker Sarah, 217 Bolton road
Barraclough Rachel & Margaret, 56 John street, Stott Hill
Barratt Elizabeth, 70 John street, Stott Hill
Barrett Misses, 302 Leeds road
Bates Mary Ann, 53 Manchester rd.
Bates Sarah, 6 Sharp street, Manchester road
Batley Ann, Northwing, High street
Beanland Eliza, Keighley Old road
Bedford Rebecah, 17 North Parade, Christ Church
Boddy Elizabeth, 39 Mill lane, Manchester road
Booth Ann & Sarah, 38 Manchester road
Boville Sarah, 31 Prospect street, Thornton road
Bradley Catherine, Laister Dyke
Brayshaw Elizabeth, 298 Leeds road
Brear Maria, 134 Silsbridge lane
Brown Frances, 45 Croft street, Manchester road
Brown Harriet, Swaine Green, Bowling
Brown Margaret, 53 Thornton road
Brown Mary Ann, 97 Westgate
Brown Sarah, 32 Britannia street, Manchester road
Burgess Susannah, 1 George street, Manchester road
Carritt Ann, 97 Brick lane
Carter Jane, Park square, Manningham
Chapel Sarah, 18 School street, Manchester road
Clayton Mary, Wakefield road
Clayton Mary Ann, Barkerend
Coates Sarah Ann, 8 Northgate
Dalton Margaret, 17 Manchester rd.
Dean Ellen & Christiana, 21 Manchester road
Deighton Mary Ann, 86 Leeds road
Denton Elizabeth, 48 Sterling street, Manchester road
Dewhirst Sarah, Belgrave place, Manningham
Edwards Mrs. 10 Wellington street, Stott Hill

Ellis Ellen,' Arcadia street, Lumb lane, Manningham
Ellis Rebecah, Wakefield road
English Mrs. 44 Wellington street, Stott Hill
Fawcett Mary Ann, Croft street, Manchester road
Featherstonehaugh Martha & Jane, Upper North Parade, Manningham lane
Fielden Mary Ann, William street, Little Horton lane
Fowler Elizabeth, Belgrave place, Manningham
Fox Theodosia, 153 Manchester road
Gaunt Fanny, Belgrave place, Manningham
Gibson Mrs. 8 Chapel street, Leeds road
Gill Tamar, Spring street, Manningham
Gouldsbrough Hannah, 10 James st. Northgate
Haley Ellen, 25 Thornton road
Hannay Mary Ann, 10 John steeet, Northgate
Harker Mary, Railroad street, School street
Harrison Eden, 104 Westgate
Harrison Elizabeth, 40 Northgate
Hartley Elizabeth, Thornton road
Hartley Jane & Margaret, 78 John street, Stott Hill
Hellewell Mary Ann, Broomfield terrace, Wakefield road
Henry Elizabeth, 32 Earl street, Manchester road
Hill Oliva & Eliza, 30 Westgate
Hodgson Mrs. North Parade, Christ Church
Holdsworth Elizabeth, 79 Westgrove street
Holdsworth Ellen, 2 Portland street, Manchester road
Holgate Misses, Spring Gardens, Manningham lane
Hopkinson Elizabeth, 8 Parkgate, High street
Hornby Mary, Garnett's Yard, Union street
Horne Charlotte, 125 Bolton road
Hotchin Sarah, 121 Bridge street
Hudson Jane, 120 Park square, Manningham
Hutchinson Eliza, 3 Illingworth's Court, Westgate
Illingworth Martha, Broadstones
Illingworth Mazeppa, 23 Queen st. White Abbey
Illingworth Rachel, 1 Keighley Old road
Irving Harriet, King street, White Abbey
Johnson Mary, Burrow street, Manchester road
Jones Alice, 4 John street, Westgate
Jowett Jane Elizabeth, 23 Great Horton road
Kershaw Sarah, 31 Green lane, Manningham
Kitson Jane, 72 Hope street, Manchester road
Levee Maria, 52 Vicar lane
Lewty Clara, 59 Fitzgerald street, Manchester road
Lincey Sarah, 90 Bedford street, Bridge street
Lindley Sarah, 182 Manchester road
Lowe Mary Ann, 5 Stone street, Manor row
Lupton Ann, 156 Bridge street
Marriott & Brearley, 62 Earl street, Manchester road
Mawson Mary Elizabeth, Primrose terrace, Manningham

Medley Elizabeth, 73 Manchester rd.
Metcalf Elizabeth, Thornton road
Mortimer Ann, 185 Wakefield road
Moxon Emma, Manchester road
Nichols Sarah Elizabeth, 1 Fitzgerald street, Manchester road
Oddy Mary Ann, Wakefield road, Bowling
Ogden Elizabeth, 54 Northgate
Oldfield Elizabeth, 22 School street, Manor row
Parker Elizabeth, 4 Southgate
Parker Hannah & Mary (Friends' bonnets, &c.), Tyrrel street
Parker Mrs. 74 John street, Stott Hill
Parker Mrs. Chapel street, Leeds rd.
Parkin Caroline, 63 Bower street, Manchester road
Peacock Eliza and Sarah, 244 Leeds road
Pemberton Catherine, 18 Queen st. White Abbey
Peyton Miss, Lumb lane, Manningham
Porter Mary Ann, Arcadia street, Manningham
Pyrah Maria, 37 Providence street, White Abbey
Ramsden Mary Ann, 2 Nelson Court, Nelson street
Rawnsley Mrs. 17 Peel street, Northwing
Ray Sarah, 40 Adelaide street, Manchester road
Revell Elizabeth, 324 Bowling lane, Manchester road
Reynolds Mrs. 12 Westgate
Rhodes Ann, 120 Westgate
Rhodes Ann & Mary, 66 Greenaire place, Silsbridge lane
Rigg Martha, 6 Sterling street, Manchester road
Rushworth Mary, 40 Garnet street, Leeds road
Rycroft Mary, Little Horton lane
Scholefield Ann Martha, 52 Fitzgerald street, Manchester road
Scholey Mary Ann, 83 Westgrove st.
Seed Anne, 94 Westgate
Shackleton Ann & Mary, Tyrrel st.
Shackleton Betty, 183 Manchester rd.
Shackleton Hannah, 34 Westgate
Sharp Mary, Primrose terrace, Manningham
Shaw Martha, Bradford Moor
Shreeve Mary Ann, 29 North Parade, Christ Church
Skelton Jane, 9 Ebor street, Little Horton lane
Smedley Ann, 9 Westgrove street
Smith Hannah, 2 Sedgwick street, White Abbey
Smith Margaret & Isabel, 37 Green lane, Manningham
Smith Mary, 40 Wakefield road
Smithies Hannah, Hall lane, Bowling
Spencer Mrs. Well street
Spencer Mrs. 7 High street
Spurr Nancy, Church Hill, Wakefield road
Standeavens Sarah, 1 Lumb lane, Westgate
Stapleton Harriet, Belgrave place, Lumb lane
Sugden Emma Jane, 25 Manchester road
Sutcliffe Mary, 7 Peel st. Northwing
Swaine Jane, 29 Wakefield road
Sykes Ellen, 253 Manchester road
Sykes Sarah, 5 Vicar lane
Tankard Elizabeth, 7 Ebor street, Little Horton lane
Tate Dinah and Mary, 14 King street, White Abbey
Tennant Elizabeth, 15 Westgrove st.

Tetley Ann, Uppercroft row, Bowling
Townend Ann, 2 Portland street, Manchester road
Varley Martha, 167 Whetley street, Manningham
Verity Mary, 79 Bolton road
Virr Harriet, 58 Bedford street, Manchester road
Walker Mary and Harriet, 43 Arundel street, Manchester road
Walmsley Sarah Ann, 45 Arundel st. Manchester road
Walsh Alice, 14 White Abbey
Walton Miriam, 58 Greenhill place, Manningham
Warburton Hannah, 55 Silsbridge la.
Ward Henrietta, 53 Victoria street, North Parade
Wardman Elizabeth, 19 Chapel lane
Watmuff Emma, 147 George street, Leeds road
Webster Ann, 19 Barkerend, High st.
Webster Frances and Elizabeth, Leeds road
Whitehead Eliza, 16 Kirkgate
Whitley Sarah Ann, Simes street, Westgate
Wignall Eliza, 52 Croft street, Manchester road
Wilkinson Sarah, 59 Thornton road
Williams Ann, North Parade, Christ Church
Wilson Maria, 8 Park place, Little Horton
Wilson Rebecah, Victoria street, North Parade
Wood Susan, Leeds road
Worsnop Ann, 65 Tumblinghill street, Thornton road
Worsnop Martha, 236 Manchester rd.
Worsnop Nancy, Seymour street, Leeds road
Worsnop Sarah Ann, 12 Lwr. Thomas street, Manchester road
Wright Frances, 13 Union Passage, Kirkgate

Millwrights and Engineers.

Boader John, Great Horton road
Clayton, Marshalls' & Co. Bierley Works; office Canal road
Cliffe James & Joseph, Old Foundry, Tyrrel street
Cole, Marchent & Co. Prospect Foundry, Wakefield road, Bowling
Crosland Robert, Union Foundry, Manchester road
Hargreaves & Kennedy, Waterloo Foundry, Adelaide street, Manchester road
Hattersley Samuel & Son, Westbrook Works, Thornton road
Hird, Dawson & Hardy, Low Moor Works; office Canal road
Leeming John & Son, Northolme Mill, Railroad st. Canal road
Sagar Tubal (agent for W.C. Mathers, of Manchester, patent metallic pistons), 56 Longcroft place, Westgate
Smith John, Albion Works, Thornton road
Sturges John & Co. Bowling Works; office Canal road
Thwaites & Co. Albion Works, Thornton road
Tillotson Joseph, Pennyoak's Mill, Melbourne st. Leeds road
Waddington Richard, Railway Foundry, Manchester road

Mourning Coach Owners.

Andrew George, Victoria street, Silsbridge lane
Gledhill Thomas, Prince of Wales' Yard, Leeds road
Holmes Thomas & Son, 36 Kirkgate
Rhodes William, Thornton road

Music Sellers and Piano-Forte, &c. Dealers.

Marked thus * are Sheet Music Sellers Only.

(See also Organ Builders.)

* Blackburn William Howgill, 15 Market street
Bower Jonas, Victoria street, North Parade
Brear William (tuner), Belgrave place, Manningham
Brown Henry (organs), Leeds road
Brumfit Josph. (various instrumental) 80 Market street
Holt John & William (organs), Preston place, Great Horton
* Ibbetson James, 20 Bridge street
Leach John, Westgrove street
* Lund Joseph, 82 Westgate (*See advertisement*)
Metcalf James (tuner), Spring Gardens, Manningham lane
Misdale Frederick, 1 Grammar School street, Manor row
Nicholson John (organs), 6 Melburne street, Leeds road
* Stanfield Charles, 5 Westgate
* Walker Benjamin, Market street

Nail Manufacturers.

Dowson John, Wakefield road, Bowling
Parkin John, top of Westgate

Newspaper.

The "Observer," published at 17 Kirkgate, every Thursday morning, with a second edition (giving reports of the day's market), early in the afternoon.—Mr. Wm. Byles proprietor

Newspaper Agents.

Boulton Samuel, 4 Lumb lane Westgate
Brown Jacob, John street, Northgate
Byles Henry, 17 Kirkgate
Cannan William, Wakefield road
Child John, 137 Brick lane
Cook Jabez, 28 White Abbey
Cooke William, Ebenezer street, Vicar lane
Cousen Samuel, 13 Kirkgate
Dale John, 1 Thornton's Buildings, Bridge street
Ibbetson James (The Times, Daily News, Morning Herald, Chronicle, &c. received by express daily, and punctually supplied to subscribers immediately after the arrival of the trains), 20 Bridge street
Lund Joseph, 82 Westgate (*see advertisement*)
Mawson Henry Ogle, 43 Kirkgate
Parkinson John, 2 Union street
Stanfield Charles, 5 Westgate
Umpleby Thomas, 2 Lumby street, Manchester road
Walker Benjamin, Market street
Wilkinson Christopher, Tyrrell street

Nursery and Seedsmen,

AND LANDSCAPE GARDENERS.

Blakey Samuel, Kelvin Grove public gardens, and 8 Union Passage, Kirkgate
Clark Walter, public gardens, Manningham lane
Ely Benjamin, Northgate
Fanshaw Robert (seedsman), High street, Great Horton
Hutchinson John, Well street
Jowett Ann, Manningham lane

Leach John & Son, public gardens, Manningham lane
North William, public gardens, Low Moor
Pape Thomas, Undercliffe
Pilkington William, Victoria street, Manningham
Stead William & Co. (seedsmen), 56 Market street
Taylor Thomas, public gardens, Manningham lane
Topham John, Great Horton road

Oil and Colour Dealers.

(See also Druggists.)

Briggs Henry, 1 North Parade and Northgate
Haley & Edwards, 60 Market street
Hallpike William, Great Horton road, Horton
Harland Brothers, 14 Hustlergate
Hird William, Northgate
Mitton Henry & Co. 20 Piecehall Yard, Kirkgate
Oddy Sam, 19 Market street
Peel John, 64 Bridge street
Rhodes Charles, Cheapside
Rhodes James, Albion Court, Kirkgate
Tate Richard, Fair ground, Darley st.

Oil Merchants.

Bartle Thomas, High street, Great Horton
Crompton Charles, Charles street, Market street
Harrison Joseph, 55 Westgate
Mitton Henry & Co. 20 Piecehall Yard, Kirkgate
Rimmington Felix Marsh, 6 Ivegate
Senier George & Co. 15 Westgate
Stephenson Thomas, Charles street, Leeds road

Opticians.

Barrow William, 2 Bank street
Brooksbank William, 64 Market st.
Franks Isaac (and lecturer on the human eye), 71 Market street, and Leeds
Rhodes Manoah, 6 Westgate

Organ Builders.

Brown Henry, Leeds road
Holt John & William, Preston place, Great Horton
Nicholson John, 6 Melbourne street, Leeds road

Ornamental Letter Manufacturers and Dealers.

Brown James (gold and silver), 2 Market street
Rhodes Charles (porcelain), 2 Cheapside, Kirkgate
Rhodes James (china, &c.), Chapel Court, Kirkgate
Topham Maria Dorothy (gold and silver), 24 Hustlergate
Wyrill Frances (porcelain, &c.), 8 Westgate

Packers.

See Makers-Up and Packers.

Packet Office.

Collinson Edward, Hustler's Buildings, Leeds road

Packing Case and Rolling Board Makers.

(See also Timber Merchants.)

Beecroft Joseph (executors of), Toad lane, Bridge street

Hartley Brothers, Bridge street, and Leeds
Hewitt & Knowles, School street, Manor row
Rhodes James, Wharf street, Bolton road
Thorpe, Scholefield & Co. John st. Leeds road, and Prospect Mill, Wakefield road, Bowling
Wood & Harrison, Duke st. Cheapside, and Manchester road

Painters.

LANDSCAPE, HISTORICAL, & PORTRAIT.

Bird Isaac Faulkner (portrait), Hustler terrace, High street
Richardson Joseph (landscape, historical and portrait), Canal terrace, Bolton road
Thompson John (portrait), Lumb lane, Manningham

Painters—House, Sign and Decorative, Gilders, &c.

(See also Paper Hangers.)

Barker Thomas Lister, Ivegate
Bocock John, Black Bull Yard, Westgate
Briggs Henry, 1 North Parade
Byrom James, Townhill House, Wakefield road
Ellis John, Dudley Hill, Bowling
Gelderd Joshua, 140 Westgate
Goodchild Robert (and animal), 223 Manchester road
Greenhough John, Garden place, Westgate
Haley & Edwards, 60 Market street
Hallpike William, Great Horton road, Horton
Hargreaves Richard, Tyrrel Court, Tyrrel street

Harland Brothers, 14 Hustlergate
Hird William, 92 Northgate
Maud Joe & John, Hustler's Buildings, Leeds road
Oddy Sam, 19 Market street
Peel John, 64 Bridge street
Pickard James, 2 Melbourne street, Leeds road
Rhodes Charles, 2 Cheapside
Rhodes James, Chapel Court, Kirkgate (*See advertisement*)
Tate Richard, Fair Ground, Darley street
Walton George, North Parade, Christ Church
Walton John, 11 Lumby street, Manchester road
Warburton William, Brunswick place
Wilkinson & Bradley, 145 Brick lane
Wilson James, 85 Bedford street, Bridge street

Paper Dealers and Warehouses.

(See also Stationers.)

Blackburn William Howgill, 15 Market street
Boulton Samuel, 4 Lumb lane, Westgate
Brown Jacob, John street, Northgate
Byles Henry, 17 Kirkgate
Cannan William, Bridge street
Cooke William, 1 Ebenezer street, Vicar lane
Dale John, 1 Thornton's Buildings, Bridge street
Glover Henry, 5 Bermondsey
Ibbetson James, 20 Bridge street, (*See advertisement*)
Lund Joseph, 82 Westgate (*See advertisement*)
Mawson Henry Ogle, 43 Kirkgate

Milthorp William (maker), Swaine street, Hall Ings
Pearce George, 46 Tyrrel street
Stanfield Charles, 5 Westgate
Sussmann Alfred, Court street, Leeds road
Walker Benjamin, 8 Market street
Wardman Henry, 18 Chapel lane
Wilkinson Christoper, Tyrrel street

Paper Hangers and Dealers.

Archer Edward, Tyrrel street
Beanland William, North Parade, Christ Church
Briggs Henry, 1 North Parade, Christ Church
Brown Jacob, John street, Northgate
Byrom James, Townhill House, Wakefield road
Clough Joseph, 2 Manchester road
Constantine James, 76 Bridge street
Cowin James & Son, 59 Northgate
Duckworth & Watson, Tyrrel Court, Tyrrel street
Ellis John, Dudley Hill, Bowling
Greenhough John, Garden place, Westgate
Hallpike William, Great Horton road, Horton
Harland Brothers, 14 Hustlergate
Hird William, 92 Northgate
Holmes Joseph (and stainer), 53 Darley street
Maud Joe & John, Hustler's Buildings, Leeds road
Mills Thomas, 45 Market street
Morton George & Son (manufacturers), 39 Market street, and Leeds
Nutter Joseph, Nutter's place, North Parade
Oddy Sam, 19 Market street
Peel John, 64 Bridge street
Rhodes Charles, 2 Cheapside
Rhodes James, Chapel Court, Kirkgate (*See advertisement*)
Sellers John, 162 George street, Leeds road
Walton George, North Parade, Christ Church
Walton John, 11 Lumby street, Manchester road
Ward William, King's Arms Yard, Westgate
Wilkinson & Bradley, 145 Brick lane
Wilkinson Joseph, New Market and 13 North Parade

Pattern-Card and Book Makers

Bray Joseph, Wadkin's Fold, Well street
Byles Henry B. 17 Kirkgate
Dale John, 1 Thornton's Buildings, Bridge street
Drake John, King's Court, Northgate
Drake John, 21 Market street
Lumley Joseph, Hustler's Buildings, Leeds road
Morris Benjamin Gough, Swan Yard, Market street
Nicholson John, 1 Bermondsey
Parry Robert, 15 Market street
Ratcliffe Thomas & Co. Butterworth's Buildings, Ivegate
Spencer Richard & Thomas, Broadstones
Stanfield Charles, 5 Westgate

Pawnbrokers.

Brown William King, 10 Vicar lane
Hudson Joseph, 9 Portland street, Manchester road
Lumb Abraham, Old Market, Market street
Senior John, 14 Darley street
Thackeray Henry William & James Robert, 47 and 48 Vicar lane

Webster Robert, 29 Chapel lane
Wood George, top of Westgate

Perfumers.

See Hair Dressers and Perfumers.

Periodical Publications,—Agents and Dealers.

(See also News Agents.)

Blackburn William Howgill, 15 Market street
Boulton Sam. 4 Lumb lane, Westgate
Brown Jacob, John street, Northgate
Cannan William, 149 Bridge street
Child John, 137 Brick lane
Cook Jabez, 28 White Abbey
Cooke William, 1 Ebenezer street, Vicar lane
Hyslop Robert, (agent for Scottish and English), Thornton st. Thornton rd.
Ibbetson James (agent for Punch), 20 Bridge street
Lund Joseph, 82 Westgate—(*see advertisement*)
Mawson Henry Ogle (agent for Journal of Design, &c.) 43 Kirkgate
Umpleby Thomas, 2 Lumby street, Manchester road
Wilkinson Christopher, Tyrrel street

Pewter Measure Dealers.

Calvert Michael, 13 Ivegate
Clough Benjamin, 8 White Abbey
Dixon & Byrne, 77 Market street
Dove Thomas Pashley, 17 Ivegate
Marshall William, 4 Kirkgate
Parratt Edward Hawksworth, 1 Broadstones
Pearson Henry, 30 and 32 Bridge st.
Read Henry, 29 Market street
Rhodes John, 18 Kirkgate
Rudd Robert, 35 Kirkgate
Scully Ambrose, 7 Ivegate
Smith Jonas, 40 Westgate
Stelling Thomas, 62 Kirkgate
Wyrill Frances, 8 Westgate

Physicians.

(See also Surgeons.)

Cryer William, Hanover square
Farrar William, Darley street, and Richmond place, Great Horton rd.
Hornell James, Rawson place
M'Turk William, 27 Manor row
Taylor William, Eldon place

Picture Dealers and Restorers.

Briggs Henry, 1 North Parade, Christ Church
Gelderd Joshua, 140 Westgate
Holmes Joseph, 53 Darley street
Pearce George, 46 Tyrrel street
Rhodes James, Chapel Court, Kirkgate—(*see advertisement*)
Richardson Joseph, Canal terrace, Bolton road
Robinson Dan, 20 Well street

Plane Maker.

Watkins William (and tool), Cure's Court, Westgate

Plasterers and Colourers.

INCLUDING CEMENT DEALERS.

Bolton John, 78 Bridge street
Bolton William, Southgate, Great Horton
Clayton Charles, High street
Cordingley & Raistrick, Thornton rd.
Dixon John (and builder), Swaine street
Firth Thomas, Manningham
Hargreaves Henry, Swaine street
Howroyd & Duckworth, Smith street, Manchester road

Laycock James, 2 Longcroft place, Westgate
Merton Lupton, 70 Northgate
Pickles William, 69 York street, Bridge street
Rothwell Benjamin, Wakefield road
Simpson William, Chapel street, Leeds road
Stead & Brook, Back Tyrrel street
Tattersall John (and cement dealer), Leeds road
Wood John, 4 Lumb lane, Westgate
Wood Joseph, 4 Vicar lane
Young Hiram, 60 Croft street, Bridge street

Plate and Crown Glass Dealers.

Armitage Samuel, 52 Market street
Atkinson Robert, Vicar lane
Bolland William, Churchbank, High st
Bowles J. H. 2 Black Abbey
Clarkson & Walton, 5 Manchester rd.
Colburn John, 7 Croft st. Leeds road
Cookson John, Well street
Dewhirst William, Beckside, Horton
Guthrie William, 4 Chapel lane
Hunter William, 1 Kirkgate
Keighley James, Chapel Court, Kirkgate
Leach William, Leeds road
Rhodes Charles, 2 Cheapside
Ridley George, 19 Westgate
Taylor Charles, Churchbank, High st.
Thornton George, 94 Northgate
Thwaites Thomas, 12 Tyrrel street

Plumbers and Glaziers.

(See also Gas Fitters.)

Armitage Samuel, 52 Market street
Atkinson Robert, Vicar lane
Bolland William, Churchbank, High street
Bowles John Holdsworth, 2 Black Abbey
Clarkson & Walton, 5 Manchester rd.
Cookson John, Well street
Dewhirst William, Beckside, Great Horton
Guthrie William, 4 Chapel lane, Bridge street
Hunter William, 1 Kirkgate
Keighley James, Chapel Court, Kirkgate
Leach William, Leeds road
Ridley George, 19 Westgate
Taylor Charles, Churchbank, High street
Thornton George, 94 Northgate
Thwaites Thomas, 12 Tyrrel street

Pork Butchers.

[See also Bacon and Ham Dealers.]

Diggles James, 158 and 160 Westgate
Diggles John, 23 Ivegate
Farrar Richard, 109 Bridge street
Hobson Marmaduke, 16 Manchester road
Sadler James, 5 Kirkgate
Smith Christopher, 9 Ivegate
Sykes Samuel, 87 Manchester road
Wright Edwin, 144 Manchester road

Porter Merchants.

Brumfit Charles (and Scotch and Burton ales, perry, cider, &c.), Bermondsey—(*see advertisement*)
Clough James (and ale), 20 Market street
Crampton John, Manchester road
Greenwood Frederick Smith (and ale), Duke street, Darley street
Hargreaves Sarah (and ale and British wines), 30 Kirkgate
Holloway William Henry (and Bur-

ton and Scotch ales, cider, &c.) Exchange Vaults, Kirkgate

Kitcheman Samuel (and Burton and Scotch ales), Leeds road

Laycock Peter (executors of) (and ale and black beer), top of Ivegate,

Reaney James (and Burton and Scotch ales), 6 Balwin lane, James street, Westgate

Roberts Joshua (and East India pale and Scotch and Burton ales), 5 Manor row

Taylor Joseph (and Scotch and Burton ales, &c.), Brook street, Hall Ings

Town Edward Henry (and Burton ales, &c.) 21½ Ivegate

Wright James (and East India pale, Scotch and Burton ales), Hustlergate and Ivegate

Portmanteau, Trunk, and Travelling Bag Makers.

Bonnell Joseph Fearnley, 22 Bridge street

Brown and Muff, 54 Market street

Brumfit Joseph, 80 Market street

Dawson Daniel, 1 Bermondsey

Farrar and Gillham, 20 Kirkgate

Harrison John, Halifax road, Bowling

Longbottom Thomas, 111 Bridge st.

Loveday Willm. Dudley Hill, Bowling

North Wm. Halifax road, Bowling.

Ogden Michael and Co. 29 Kirkgate

Phillips Mary, 8 Old Market place

Rhodes James, 1 Leeds Old road

Stephenson Frederick, 14 Market st.

Tiplady Samuel, 73 Chapel lane

Walker Richard, 17 and 19 Darley st.

Potato Merchants.

Barraclough James, Broadstones

Barraclough John, 125 Bridge street

Bolton Elizabeth, 65 Westgate

Brooks James, 87 Birk st. Leeds road

Calvert William, 128 Manchester road

Carter William, 3 Nelson st. Chapel la.

Chadwick John, 47 Westgate

Clough William, High st. Gt. Horton

Cook William, 248 Manchester road

Crabtree Mark, Paperhall, Northwing

Denton Joshua, Silsbridge lane

Farrand Henry, 70 Manchester road

Hall Joseph, Northgate

Hoadley Thomas, Northgate

Holdsworth Edward, High street, Great Horton

Hollings John, Bowling Green, Bridge street

Lister Benjamin, 91 Manchester road

Lofthouse William, 1 Market place, Darley street

Mann Joseph, 199 Wakefield road

Newby William, Tyrrel street

Rooks George, 9 and 11 Broadstones

Sagar William, 49 Duke street, Manchester road

Simpson John, 30 Well street

Wilkinson John, 101 Bridge street

Wilkinson Joseph, 78 Westgate

Pressers and Finishers.

WOOLLEN AND STUFF.

Anderton Sarah, Mawson street, Thornton road

Howitt George, 1 Churchbank, Well street

Lowden & Robertons', Westbrook terrace, Thornton road

Pulman Samuel, 18 James street, Northgate

Roberts Joshua, Keighley street, Silsbridge lane

Walton Joseph, Westbrook terrace, Thornton road

Printers' Joiners.

Jowett Jonas, Southgate
Sanders Edward (and wood letter cutter), Prospect street, Silsbridge lane

Printers—Letter-Press.

Blackburn William Howgill, 15 Market street
Burton Daniel, 16 Ivegate
Byles William (and newspaper publisher), 17 Kirkgate
Copley John, 4 Market street
Dale John, 1 Thornton's Buildings, Bridge street
Ibbetson James (and Directory publisher), 20 Bridge street
Mawson Henry Ogle, 43 Kirkgate
Moore William, Park Cottage, Little Horton Green
Parkinson John, 2 Union street
Scarlet Samuel Wharton, King's Court, Northgate
Stanfield Charles, 5 Westgate
Walker Benjamin, 8 Market street
Wardman Henry, 18 Chapel lane
White Walter, 22 Piecehall Yard, Kirkgate
Wilkinson Christopher, Tyrrel street

Printers—Lithographic.

Baxter Charles, 4 Market street
Bray Joseph, Wadkin's Fold, Well st.
Brown James, 2 Market street
Copley John, 4 Market street
Masser & Bailey (maps, plans, &c.), Hustler's Buildings, Leeds road—(*see advertisement*)
Ratcliffe Thomas & Co. Butterworth's Buildings, Ivegate
Topham Maria Dorothy, 24 Hustlergate
Wilson & Fairbank, 47 Kirkgate and 18 Talbot Yard

Printer—Woollen Stuffs and De Laines.

Butterworth Sidney Aquilla & Co. Hall Ings

Print Sellers.

(See also Artists' Colourmen.)

Briggs Henry, 1 North Parade, Christ Church
Byles Henry Beuzeville, 17 Kirkgate
Dale John, 1 Thornton's Buildings, Bridge street
Gelderd Joshua, 140 Westgate
Holmes Joseph, 53 Darley street
Ibbetson James (and map publisher), 20 Bridge street (*See advertisement*)
Mawson Henry Ogle, 43 Kirkgate
Pearce George, 46 Tyrrel street
Rhodes Charles, 2 Cheapside
Robinson Dan, 20 Well street
Stanfield Charles, 5 Westgate
Walker Benjamin, 8 Market street

Professors and Teachers

OF MUSIC, DRAWING, LANGUAGES, &c.

(See also Painters—Landscape, &c.)

Bird Isaac Faulkner (drawing), Hustler terrace, High street
Borissow Christian Ignatius (French, German, Italian and Spanish languages), 2 Victoria street, North Parade
Bower Jonas (piano-forte and organ), 48 Victoria street, North Parade
Brear William (piano-forte), Belgrave place, Manningham
Burton Daniel (piano-forte and organ, Laura place, Leeds road
Burton Francis (violin), Laura place, Leeds road
Clark William Oswald (drawing), 12 Wellington street, Stott Hill

Clayton Solomon (piano-forte and organ), Victoria street, North Parade
Coates Joseph (singing), Thornton road
Hardaker Benjamin (singing), Frederick street, Bridge street
Hick Joseph (piano-forte and organ), Drewton street
Hill Thomas (singing and double bass), Cropper lane
Le Blanc John (gymnastics), Church Institution Rooms, Charles street
Marsden William (singing and double bass), School street, Cheapside
Metcalfe James (piano-forte and organ), Spring Gardens
Nesbit George (commercial writing), 17 Stone street, Manor row
Priestley Samuel (violincello), Green lane, Manningham
Richardson Joseph (drawing, &c.) Canal terrace, Bolton road
Robinson Jonas (flute), Greenaire place, Silsbridge lane
Scholey Stephen (violin), Thornton road
Shackleton Benjamin (violincello), Bowergate, Chapel lane
Simpson Joseph (piano-forte and organ), High street
Sutcliffe John (drawing), 25 Ivegate

Provision Dealers—Wholesale and Retail.

[See Shopkeepers, and also Bacon and Ham Dealers.]

Cluderay William, 134 Westgate
Denison Patrick, 88 Manchester rd.
Diggles James, 158 and 160 Westgate (*See advertisement*)
Dowling Michael, 51 Market street
Emsley James & John, 204 Manchester road, and 38 Bolton road
Farnell James, 150 Westgate
Morrell John (wholesale), 4 and 6 Tyrrel street
Morrell Robert & Co. 17 and 92 Westgate
Robson John, 7 Wakefield road
Rooks George, 9 and 11 Broadstones
Rowntree Isaac, 146 Manchester road
Waud & Co. (wholesale) 5 Market street
Waud William (wholesale), 1 and 21 Darley street

Public Houses.

See Inns, Hotels and Taverns.

Rag, Rope and Old Metal Dealers.

Berry Richard, 20 Keighley street, Silsbridge lane
Boyd James, Leeds road and Chapel lane
Cawfield Owen, Millbank
Naylor & Co. 152 Bridge street
Parker Henry, Wharf street, Bolton road
Silson Joseph & John, Reform street, Westgate
Sugden John, Back Tyrrel street
Wilkinson Richard, Lister's place, Silsbridge lane
Wood Isaac, 10 Broadstones

Railway Turn-Table Manufacturers.

Cliffe James & Joseph, Old Foundry, Tyrrel street
Cole, Marchent & Co. Prospect Foundry, Wakefield road, Bowling
Crosland Robert, Union Foundry, Manchester road

Waddington Richard, Railway Foundry, Manchester road

Railway Waggon, Wheel and Axle Manufacturers.

Cliffe James & Joseph, Old Foundry, Tyrrel stret.
Cole, Marchent & Co. Prospect Foundry, Wakefield road
Crosland Robert, Union Foundry, Manchester road
Holdsworth & Raistrick, Croft street, Manchester road
Waddington Richard, Railway Foundry, Manchester road

Ready-Made Linen Warehouses.

(See also Hosiers, Glovers, &c.)

Abbs James, 43 Market street
Barritt John, 38 Leeds road
Brook, Gant & Co. 10 Westgate
Brown & Muff, 54 Market street
Cummins John, 24 Market street
Edgar Robert, 27 Market street
Farrar & Gillham, 20 Kirkgate
Hunton William, 8 Darley street
Ogden Michael & Co. 29 Kirkgate
Rochfort Valentine, 17 Union Passage, Kirkgate
Simpson Elizabeth, 5 and 6 Market street
Whewall James, 44 Kirkgate, and Halifax

Reed and Heald Makers.

Dawson James, 60 Croft street, Manchester road
Denby Jonathan, 7 Southgate
Harrowby John, Little Horton lane
Ramsden John, Waterloo Mill, Brook street
Wood William, Tyrrel Square, Tyrrel street
Wright George Anderson, 8 Back Quebec terrace, Thornton road

Register Offices for Servants.

Bryar Mrs. Victoria st. North Parade
Eltoft Ann, 24 Darley street
Greenlay Mrs. 22 Darley street
Hartley Ann, 19 James st. Northgate
Leach Elizabeth, 81 Westgate
Mitchell Mrs. 2 Lumb lane, Westgate
Newby William, Tyrrel street
Turley Mrs. 18 High street

Registrars of Births, Deaths and Marriages.

See Public Buildings, Offices. &c.

Repositories.

See Artists' Colourmen and Repositories.

Roman, &c. Cement and Plaster of Paris Dealers.

See Oil and Colourmen, and Plasterers.

Rope and Twine Manufacturers

Farrar Joseph, Chapel lane, Tyrrel st.
Oddy George, 19 Kirkgate
Oddy Mark, 68 Market street
Reynolds Benjamin, Bradford Moor

Saddlers and Harness Makers.

Bonnell Joseph Fearnley, 22 Bridge street
Dawson Daniel, 1 Bermondsey
Harrison John, Halifax road, Bowling
Longthorn Thomas, 111 Bridge street
Loveday William, Dudley Hill, Bowling
North William, Halifax road, Bowling

Phillips Mary, 8 Piecehall Yard, Hustlergate
Procter Samuel (harness), Leeds rd.
Rhodes James, 1 Leeds Old road, Well street
Stephenson Frederick, 14 Market st.
Tiplady Samuel, 73 Chapel lane
Walker Richard, 17 and 19 Darley st.

Salt Dealers—Wholesale.

Sutcliffe Robert (and whiteing), 157 Leeds road
Tillotson William, Fawcett Court, Nelson street

Saw Mills.

(See also Packing Case and Rolling Board Makers.)

Beecroft Joseph (executors of), Toad lane, Bridge street
Briggs Robert & Sons, Black Abbey
Hewitt & Knowles, School street, Manor row
Rhodes James, Wharf street, Bolton road
Thorpe, Scholefield & Co. John street, Leeds road, and Prospect Mill, Wakefield road, Bowling
Wilson James & Son, Spring row, Manningham

Scale-Beam and Weighing Machine Makers.

Crosland Robert, Union Foundry, Manchester road
Hill John & Co. 8 Cheapside
Rhodes William, 99 Westgate
Richardson Henry, 5 Bedford street, Bridge street

Screw Bolt Manufacturers.

Cliffe James & Joseph, Old Foundry, Tyrrel street
Coates Ralph, Hardcastle lane, Well street
Crabtree William, Laycock's Mill, Thornton road
Crosland Robert, Union Foundry, Manchester road
Gray John, 68 Manchester road
Hargreaves Charles and Michael, Cropper lane, Westgate
Holdsworth and Rastrick, Croft street, Manchester road
Rayner Joseph, 17 Mill street, Canal road
Tillotson Joseph, Pennyoak's Mill, Melbourne street, Leeds road
Walton Joseph, Queen street, Manchester road
Wilson Richard, Halifax road, Bowling
Woller Samuel, Bradford Moor

Sharebrokers.

See Brokers—Share and Stock.

Sheriff's Officer.

Ingham Timothy, 34 Market street

Shopkeepers,

AND DEALERS IN GROCERIES AND SUNDRIES.

(See also Bakers and Flour Dealers.)

Abbey John, Clayton lane, Manchester rood
Ackroyd Elijah, Bower street, Manchester road
Ackroyd John, 189 Manchester road
Ackroyd William, 24 Croft street, Leeds road
Adams George, Halifax road, Bowling

Adams Joseph, 17 Broomfield terrace, Wakefield road
Allen Matthew, Croft street, Manchester road
Ambler Elizabeth, Manningham
Anderson John, 121 Tumblinghill street, Thornton road
Arnold Tubal-Cain, Longlands street, Cropper lane
Ashley Ascough Leonard, 128 Broom street, Wakefield road
Ashley Nathaniel, Bradford Moor
Aspinall John, Hope street, Manchester road
Asquith William, Greenaire place, Silsbridge lane
Atkinson James, 274 Wakefield road
Atkinson Nathan, 187 Wakefield rd.
Auty Squire, 101 Manchester road
Baldwin Dan, Sticker lane, Bowling
Banks Matthew, Bradford Moor
Barker Benjamin, 52 White Abbey
Barker Thomas Lister, George street, Leeds road
Barnes John, 37 Black Abbey
Barons James, Green lane, Manningham
Barraclough John, Little Horton la.
Barraclough Mary, Upper West st. Silsbridge lane
Bartle David, High street, Great Horton
Barton James, 73 Brick lane
Barton James, Thornton road
Bastow James, Whetley street, Manningham
Bastow Jonathan, Great Horton rd.
Baxter Moses, Mill street, Canal rd.
Baxter William, 59 North street, Stott Hill
Beanland John, 1 Victoria street, North Parade
Beanland Joseph, Bradford Moor
Bearder John, 89 Sticker lane, Bowling
Beetham William, Swaine Green, Bowling
Bell William, Greenhill place, Manningham
Bennett William, Great Horton road
Benson Joseph, Manningham
Berry Thomas, 21 Park street, High street
Bielby William, 1 Westgrove street
Binns Mills, Albert street, Bolton rd.
Blackburn Thomas, Back lane, Bowling
Blamires Joseph, Spring row, Manningham
Bland James, Church Hill, Bowling
Bland James, Shearbridge, Great Horton
Bland John, 133 Wakefield road
Bland Luke, 286 Manchester road
Bocock Jane, 8 Cannon street, Cheapside
Bolton Joseph. Wapping, Northwing
Bolton Richard, Great Horton
Bonwell John, 3 Kirkgate
Booth Thomas, Southgate, Great Horton
Bottomley Eli, 24 Croft street, Wakefield road
Bowes Hannah, 78 Silsbridge lane
Bowker Susannah, 144 White Abbey
Boyes Richard, Laister Dyke
Bradley John, Laister Dyke
Branson Thomas, Wakefield road
Brightman William, 93 Birk street, Leeds road
Broadley William, 37 Vicar lane
Brook John, Sticker lane, Bowling
Brooke Richard, 19 Queen street, White Abbey
Brooks James, 87 Birk street, Leeds road

Brown Joseph, Leach's Square, Laister Dyke
Burke John, 54 Nelson Court, Nelson street
Burton Francis, 620 Wakefield road
Burton Francis, 12 Nelson street, Chapel lane
Burton Robert, 6 Silsbridge lane
Bussey Eleanor, Bradford Moor
Butterfield James, 122 Longcroft place, Silsbridge lane
Butterfield William, 46 Sterling street, Manchester road
Cameron William, 57 Park place, Little Horton
Cansfield Isaac, 30 Gaunt street, Otley road
Carr Thomas, 4 Nelson street, Chapel lane
Carter Robert, 138 Manchester road
Casson John, Churchbank, High st.
Cawfield Owen, Millbank
Cawthara John, Park square, Manningham
Challand George, 20 Bowling lane, Manchester road
Charlesworth John, Bowling lane, Bowling
Charlesworth Thomas, Manningham
Child James, 94 Bolton road
Clark James, 163 George street, Leeds road
Clark John, Four Lane Ends, Manningham
Clarke Joshua, Pit lane, Barkerend
Clark Thomas, 11 Mill street, Manchester road
Clarkson Richard, 45 Westgate
Clayton Matthew, Back la. Bowling
Clegg John, 31 Hayworth street, White Abbey
Clough Ann, 66 Bolton road
Clough James, Ebor street, Little Horton lane
Clough Jane, Fitzgerald street, Manchester road
Clough John, High street, Gt. Horton
Clough Joseph, Halifax road, Bowling
Cocks Thomas, Manningham
Cockson William, 1 Mount street, Leeds road
Cole Benjamin, Church Hill, Wakefield road
Collier William, 85 Victoria street, North Parade
Collingwood Job, Great Horton
Collins Edward, Bradford Moor
Collins George, 452 Wakefield road
Cooper John, 192 Manchester road
Copley Thomas, 37 Longlands street, Westgate
Cowgill Thomas, 107 Bridge street
Cowling John, 237 Wakefield road
Crabtree Thomas, 121 Manchester rd.
Craven Benjamin, Daisyhill Top, Manningham
Critchley Henry, 7 Longcroft place, Silsbridge lane
Croft Benjamin, 597 Wakefield road
Croft James, 111 Back lane, Bowling
Crowther Rachel, 8 Nelson street, Chapel lane
Darling Benjamin, 101 Northwing
Dawson John, 164 George street, Leeds road
Demain William, Upper North Parade, Manningham lane
Denbeigh Elizabeth, 15 Thornton street, Thornton road
Denison Patrick, 88 Manchester road
Dewhirst Thomas, Providence street, Silsbridge lane
Dilley Philip, Back lane, Bowling
Dixon Jeremiah, 4 Duke street, Manchester road

Dobson Christopher, Swaine Green, Bowling
Dobson Thomas, 300 Manchester road
Dovener William, Milton street, Wakefield road
Dracup Richard, High street, Great Horton
Drake Sarah, 54 Clayton street, Thornton road
Dunn John, Wakefield road
Eastwood George, 10 Silsbridge lane
Elliott William, 23 Nelson street, Chapel lane
Ellis John, Dudley Hill, Bowling
Ellis John, 35 George street, Leeds road
Ellis Joseph, Leeds road
Ellis Manasseh, Dudley Hill, Bowling
Ellis Thomas, Thornton lane, Little Horton
Elsworth Joseph, 555 Wakefield road
Falkingham Jeffrey, 59 Westgate
Farrar Squire, 2 High street
Fearnley George, Otley road
Fell Mary, Providence street, White Abbey
Fieldhouse Benjamin, Southgate, Great Horton
Fieldhouse William, Bradford Moor
Fieldsend William, 17 Brick row, Thornton road
Firth Betty, Leach's Square, Laister Dyke
Firth Elizabeth, 30 Mill lane, Manchester road
Firth William, 169 Bolton road
Foster Joseph, 28 Longlands street, Westgate
Foster William, 26 Silsbridge lane
Fox Peter, High street, Great Horton
Fox Thomas, 56 Westgrove street
Fox William, 18 Providence street, White Abbey
Franks Robert, 300 Leeds road
Furnell George, 35 Lumb lane
Furness Joseph, Back lane, Bowling
Galloway John, 44 Sterling street, Manchester road
Gamble Richard, Swaine Green, Bowling
Gaukroger Samuel, 21 Silsbridge lane
Gelderd Robert, 88 Thornton road
Gillett Henry, 86 Victoria street, North Parade
Goggs Henry, 29 Wellington street, Stott Hill
Goodair Joseph, 183 Whetley street, Manningham
Green Thomas, Undercliffe
Greenhough Benjamin, 47 Victoria, street, North Parade
Greenwood John Wilson, High street, Great Horton
Greenwood Joseph, Great Horton rd.
Haley Dan, High street, Gt. Horton
Haley Richard, High street, Great Horton
Haley William, 1 Fawcett Court, Nelson street
Halliday Richard, Ebenezer street, Vicar lane
Hamilton Mary, Churchsteps, Bolton road
Hammond John, 4 Melbourne street, Leeds road
Hammond Joseph, Four Lane Ends, Manningham
Hanson Daniel, 43 Northgate
Hanson Joseph, 178 Wakefield road
Hardaker James, 18 Longlands street, Westgate
Harker John, Railroad street, School street
Harris James, Dudley Hill, Bowling
Harrison John, 49 Silsbridge lane

Harrison Miles, 10 Fawcett Court, Nelson street
Harrison William, Back lane, Bowling
Hartley John, Cross lane, Gt. Horton
Hartley Peter, Little Horton lane
Hartley Richard, 69 High street
Hartley William, Crown street, Thornton road
Hay Abraham, Butterfield's row, Manningham
Helliwell Joseph, 300 Wakefield road
Hesling John, North st. Stott Hill
Hewitt William, 10 Prospect street, Thornton road
Heyworth Samuel, Bradford Moor
Hill Edmund, Little Horton
Hill James, Little Horton
Hill Joshua, 49 Lumb lane
Hill Thomas, Dudley Hill, Bowling
Hinchliffe Thomas, 29 Brook street, Leeds road
Hird John, 18 Providence street, Westgate
Hodgson Benjamin, 1 Nelson Court, Nelson street
Hodgson John, 60 Garnett street, Leeds road
Holdsworth James, Barkerend
Holdsworth Joseph, Great Horton
Holdsworth Thomas, 191 Wakefield rd.
Holdsworth William, 72 Bolton road
Hollings Abraham, Legrams lane, Horton
Holmes Ellen, Wakefield road
Holmes Joseph, 28 Joseph street, Leeds road
Holmes Richard, Wakefield road
Hopkinson William, 5 Well street
Hornby Henry, Back lane, Bowling
Howard Joseph, 36 Manchester road
Jackson Abraham, 274 Manchester rd.
Jackson John, Legrams lane, Horton
Jackson Samuel, 52 George street, Leeds road
Jackson Thomas, 26 Clarence street, Manchester road
Jarratt William, top of Green lane, Manningham
Johnson Richard, Swaine Green, Bowling
Johnson William, 57 Regent street, Duke street
Jones Elizabeth, Wakefield road
Jowett Ann, Great Horton road
Jowett Nathan, 21 Ebor street, Little Horton lane
Jowett William, 88 Silsbridge lane
Kaye John, Leeds road
Keighley James, 38 Silsbridge lane
Kellett John, High street, Gt. Horton
Kelley James, Great Horton road
Kelley John, 132 Bridge street
Kelley William, Shearbridge, Horton
Kennedy Richard, 132 Victoria street, Manchester road
Knowles William, Bavaria place, Manningham
Lapage John, Back lane, Bowling
Laycock Abraham, Wakefield road
Laycock Joshua, 16 King Charles st. Otley road
Lee William, Commercial street, Canal road
Lever John, Broom street, Wakefield road
Lister Benjamin, High street, Great Horton
Lister James, Park place, Little Horton
Lister Robert, Wakefield road
Liversedge John, Great Horton road
Longbottom Thomas, 579 Wakefield road
Longbottom William, Milton street, Wakefield road

Lonsdale Daniel, 3 James street, Manchester road
M'Kell William, Lillycroft, Manningham
M'Lean Thomas, Croft street, Manchester road
Mann James, 68 Hope street, Manchester road
Mann William, Manchester road
Markham Joseph, 129 Manchester road
Marsden Benjamin, Sticker lane, Bowling
Martin Joseph, 128 Wakefield road
Maskell George, 43 Edward street, Bridge street
Mason William, 2 Cropper lane, Westgate
Massa John, Ellis street, Bermondsey
Mawson Joseph, 149 Silsbridge lane
Middleton Christopher, Hannahgate, Manchester road
Middleton Joseph, Bradford Moor
Midgley William, Bridge street
Mills Henry, 122 Manchester road
Mills Robert, 141 Manchester road
Milnes John, Back lane, Bowling
Mirfield John, Bradford Moor
Mitchell John, Dudley Hill, Bowling
Mitchell William, 2 Lumb lane, Westgate
Moody Nathaniel, 216 Manchester road
Moorhouse Smith, 27 Silsbridge lane
Moss William, 8 Leeds road
Myers David, 113 Queen street, Manchester road
Myers Susannah, Uppergreen, Horton
Naylor Joseph, Bradford Moor
Naylor William, New row, Manningham
Nicholson Richard, 10 Cross Wellington street, Stott Hill
Northorp William, 13 Tumblinghill street, Thornton road
Nowell John, High street
Oddy William, Bradford Moor
Overend James, Sticker lane, Bowling
Parker Henry, High street, Great Horton
Parker Lydia, Great Horton road
Parker William, 131 Brick lane
Parratt Richard, Bradford Moor
Peacock James, 246 Leeds road
Pearson Abraham, Primrose terrace, Manningham
Pearson William, Halifax rd. Bowling
Peel Alfred, Great Horton
Peel Edward, Southgate, Great Horton
Peel William, 51 Lumb lane
Petty Henry, 598 Wakefield road
Pickard Joseph, 2 Anngate, High st.
Pickard William, 189 Bridge street
Pickles John, Manningham
Piercy John, 222 Manchester road
Pollard Maria, 20 Chapel lane
Pollard Samuel, Millbank, Thornton road
Poole Jacob, 53 Northwing, High st.
Preston Nanny, 152 Westgate
Preston William, 54 Manchester road
Priestley James, Dudley Hill, Bowling
Priestley John, High street, Great Horton
Priestley Joseph, 2 Castle street, Manchester road
Raistrick James, 80 Bolton road
Raistrick Martha, 29 Croft street, Leeds road
Ratcliffe John, Badger's Square, Bowling
Rayner Edward, 35 Portland street, Manchester road

Rhodes Thomas, 2 Providence street, White Abbey
Riley Francis, Uppercroft row, Bowling
Riley James, Back lane, Bowling
Riley John, 39 Melbourne street, Leeds road
Ripley William, North street, Northwing
Roberts Benjamin, 308 Leeds road
Roberts Jonathan, 106 Victoria street Thornton road
Robertshaw John, Belgrave place, Manningham
Robertshaw John, Southgate, Great Horton
Robertshaw Joseph, Belgrave place, Manningham
Robertshaw Joshua, 77 Silsbridge lane
Robinson Esther, Sticker lane, Bowling
Robinson John, Little Horton
Robinson Josiah, Greenhill place, Manningham
Robson John, 74 George street, Leeds road
Robson John, 7 Wakefield road
Roe Simeon, 103 Westgate
Rooks George, 9 and 11 Broadstones
Rusby Richard, Little Horton
Rushton George, Belgrave place, Manningham
Rushworth Jonas, Park square, Manningham
Rushworth William, 3 Queen street, White Abbey
Russell Joshua, 80 Northwing, High street
Sagar Samuel, White Abbey
Sanderson George, Lidget Green, Horton
Saville Jonas, 135 Crown street, Thornton road
Scott Patience, Southgate, Gt. Horton
Settle Samuel Ellick, West Parade, Brick lane
Sewell William, Bradford Moor
Shackleton Thomas, Great Horton rd.
Sharp James, 10 Chain street, Silsbridge lane
Sharp Squire, 291 Manchester road
Sharp Thomas, 254 Manchester road
Sharp William, Silsbridge lane
Sharp William, Broadstones
Sharp William, School street, Cheapside
Shaw Edward, 8 Wellesley street, North street
Shaw William, Smiddles, Bowling lane, and Bazaar, Kirkgate
Shepherd John, Back lane, Bowling
Shepherd Robert, Southgate, Great Horton
Shires Mary Ann, 7 Nelson street
Shoesmith Joseph, Dudley Hill, Bowling
Silson John, Victoria street, White Abbey
Silson William, Green lane, Manningham
Silverwood Richard, 109 Providence street, White Abbey
Simpson William, Green lane, Manningham
Smith Charles, 170 Manchester road
Smith Edward, George street, Leeds road
Smith John, 21 Gracechurch street, White Abbey
Smith Thomas, Thornton street, Thornton road
Sowden Joseph, Four Lane Ends, Manningham
Sowden William, 193 Bridge street
Speight Benjamin, Preston place, Great Horton
Spence George, Broadstones

Spencer Grace, 1 Spring street, Northwing
Spencer William, Bradford Moor
Starkey Edmund, 22 George street, Leeds road
Stead James, White Abbey
Stead John, 29 Three street, Silsbridge lane
Stephenson William, Little Horton
Stirk George, 43 Lumb lane
Stirk Martha, 1 Bower street, Manchester road
Stocks Joseph, Southgate, Gt. Horton
Stott Joseph, 37 Smith street, Manchester road
Sugden George, 3 Providence street, Silsbridge lane
Sugden Zacheus, Peel st. Leeds road
Sunderland Simeon, 45 Bedford street, Bridge street
Sunderland Thomas, Great Horton
Sutcliffe Aaron, 104 Silsbridge lane
Sutcliffe Martha, Little Horton lane
Sutcliffe Saville, 143 Manchester road
Swaine John, 176 Northbrook street, Bolton road
Swaine William, Great Horton
Swire Samuel, Dudley Hill, Bowling
Swithenbank Joshua, 17 Prospect st. Thornton road
Swithenbank Sarah, 13 Broadstones
Sykes James, Wakefield road
Sykes Sarah, 1 Chandos street, Wakefield road
Tate Robert, Manchester road
Taylor Gideon, 1 Black Abbey
Taylor John, Birkshall, Bowling
Taylor Joseph, Church st. High st.
Taylor Richard Goodchild, 15 Cannon street, Cheapside
Taylor Thomas, 81 Otley road
Taylor Thomas, 38 Thornton street, Thornton road
Tennant Jonathan, 15 Westgrove st.
Tetley Mark, Cutlerheight lane, Dudley Hill
Tetley Samuel, Wakefield road
Thomas Henry, Southgate, Gt. Horton
Thorpe James, Wakefield road
Tomlinson Christopher, Roundhill place, Silsbridge lane
Tommis Mary, Bowling lane, Bowling
Tommis William, Wakefield road
Towers Thomas, Clayton lane, Manchester road
Townson Richard, 36 Bolton road
Turner Charles, 84 Croft street, Manchester road
Waddington George, 45 Silsbridge la.
Waddington Jonathan, 41 Hope street, Manchester road
Wade John, 463 Wakefield road
Wadsworth Thomas, Leeds road
Wainwright Grace, Swaine Green, Bowling
Walker George, Clarence street, Manchester road
Walker James, 24 Otley road
Walker John, Hill Top, Manningham
Walker Robert, 56 Frederick street, Bridge street
Walls William, Wellington street, Stott Hill
Walsh John, Victoria street, Manningham
Walton William, Lidget Green, Horton
Ward Elizabeth, King street, Manchester road
Waters John, 48 Nelson Court, Nelson street
Watson James, 13 Brick row, Thornton road
Watson Jeremiah, 20 Prospect street, Thornton road
West Thomas, Otley road
Wheater Thomas, 125 Silsbridge lane,

Whitehead John, 29 Sterling street, Manchester road
Witham Thomas, 53 King street, Manchester road
Whittaker Jonas, 86 Bridge street
Whitworth Hannah, 188 Bridge street
Wigglesworth Abraham, 43 Croft st. Manchester road
Wignall James, 16 Fawcett Court, Nelson street
Wilkinson George, 101 Bridge street
Wilkinson Isaac, Little Horton
Wilkinson James, 196 Bolton road
Wilkinson John, 21 Melbourne street, Leeds road
Wilkinson John, 8 Providence street, White Abbey
Wilkinson Robert, 17 Silsbridge lane
Williams George, Park Square, Manningham
Wilson Francis, Northgate
Wood George, 26 Union street
Wood George, Holme Top, Little Horton
Wood Hannah, 9 Kirkgate
Wood Isaac, 19 Green lane, Manningham
Wood Jacob, 10 School street
Wood John, Little Horton lane
Wood Joseph, Halifax road, Bowling
Woodhead William, Bowling
Woodhead William, Little Horton lane
Wright Thomas, Bowling lane
Wright William, 89 Adelaide street, Manchester road

Shuttle, Temple, Heald Shaft, and Double Stock Makers.

Clayton Charles & John, Thornton road
Dracup Edward, Great Horton road
Dracup Nathaniel, High street, Great Horton
Dracup Samuel (and jacquard machine), Cliffe lane, Great Horton
Firth William, New row, Manningham
Sharp John, Victoria Mill, Wakefield road, Bowling
Wright Robert & Sons, Thompson's Mill, Thornton road

Silk Mercers.

See Linen Drapers and Silk Mercers.

Silk Warp Dealers.

(See also Agents—General and Miscellaneous.)

Anderton J. W. 30 Pearson's Buildings, Bridge street
Crompton Charles, Charles street, Market street
Haigh W. C. Swaine street and Exchange street
Heselton J. A. Union street, Bridge street
Ingham Joseph, Hope and Anchor Yard, Bank street
Leather George Henry, Charles st.
Mills James William, Hustler's Buildings, Market street
Mortimer William, 21 Market street
Murgatroyd William, Charles street
Wilson James, Hall Ings
Wright James, Hustlergate and Ivegate

Silversmiths and Jewellers.

(See also Watch and Clock Makers.)

Brooksbank William, 64 Market st. (*see advertisement*)
Brumfit Joseph, 80 Market street
Rhodes Manoah, 1 Westgate
Wilson & Fairbank, 47 Kirkgate

Size Manufacturers & Dealers.

(See also Leather Skep, &c. Dealers.)

Hainsworth William, Hustler's Buildings, Market street

Oddy William (and leather skeps, picking straps, laces, &c.) 65 Market street

Whittaker Edmund, Thornton road

Wilkinson Robert, Exchange street, Kirkgate

Slaters and Slate Merchants.

Hill J. & W. and Sons, Vicar lane

Hill, Smithies & Nelson, Well street (*see advertisement*)

Hill & Sutcliffe, Canal Side, Bolton rd.

Thompson Joseph, Canal Side, Bolton road

Smallware Dealers.

[See also Haberdashers, &c.]

Garvey Francis (girths, brace-webs, &c.) 24 Silsbridge lane

Harrison Eden, 104 Westgate

Hunton William, 8 Darley street

Illingworth John, 66 Westgate

Jardine Ann & Son, Ivegate

Lawson William Watson, 22 Ivegate

Laycock Henry, 17 Westgate

Leach Elizabeth, 81 Westgate

Lumb Samuel, 140 Manchester road

M'Croben John, 41 Kirkgate

Maud Timothy, 42 Kirkgate

Maud & Co. 65 Westgate

Monies James & Co. 30 Kirkgate and 2 Exchange street

Moss Denis Topham, 42 Manchester road, and Leeds

Murgatroyd Joseph, Tyrrel street

Newell Frederick Henry, 34 Kirkgate

Newton & Duckett, 55 Manchester road

Parkinson & Clark, 27 Kirkgate

Pickles John, 43 Westgate

Procter & Holgate, 67 Kirkgate

Rochfort Valentine, 17 Union Passage, Kirkgate

Russel Peter, 56 Kirkgate

Shaw John, 97 Manchester road

Shaw William, 44 Vicar lane

Simpson Elizabeth, 5 and 6 Market street

Sugden William, 4 Broadstones

Sykes Sarah, 96 Manchester road

Wallis Brothers, 22 Westgate

Watson William & Stephen, 6 Kirkgate

Soft Soap Manufacturer.

Gott John, Wharf street, Bolton road

Spindle and Fly Makers.

Hattersley George, Charles street and Keighley

Hattersley Samuel & Son, Westbrook Works, Thornton road

Holmes & Carter, Victoria Mill, Wakefield road, Bowling

Wignall Samuel, Richard street, Leeds road

Spirit Dealers, and Wine and Spirit Vaults.

Barraclough Mary, Westgate

Baxter Joseph, Bridge street

Bell John, Tyrrel street

Brumfit Charles (wholesale), 27 Bermondsey—(*See advertisement*)

Foster Joseph, Westgate

Greaves John, Tyrrel street

Holloway William Henry, Exchange Vaults, Kirkgate

Laycock Peter (executors of), top of Ivegate

Lee Hannah, 11 Westgate
Popplewell Benjamin Briggs, 43 Market street
Richardson Francis (late Wells), Westgate
Wade Elizabeth, Tyrrel street
Wilman James, Ivegate
Wiseman Henry, Sunbridge
Wright James, Hustlergate and Ivegate

Starch & Blue Manufacturers.

Tordoff John & Son, 46 Kirkgate

Stationers.

[See also Booksellers and Stationers, and Printers—Letter-press.]

Blackburn William Howgill, 15 Market street
Boulton Samuel, 4 Lumb lane, Westgate
Brown Jacob, John street, Northgate
Byles Henry, 17 Kirkgate
Cannan William, Bridge street
Cooke William, 1 Ebenezer street, Vicar lane
Dale John, 1 Thornton's Buildings Bridge street
Glover Henry, 5 Bermondsey
Ibbetson James, 20 Bridge street—(*see advertisement*)
Lumley Joseph, Hustler's Buildings, Leeds road
Lund Joseph, 82 Westgate (*See advertisement*)
Mawson Henry Ogle, 43 Kirkgate
Parkinson John, 2 Union street
Pearce George, 46 Tyrrel street
Stanfield Charles, 5 Westgate
Walker Benjamin, 8 Market street
Wardman Henry, 18 Chapel lane
Wilkinson Christopher, Tyrrel street

Stay Makers.

Audesley John, 55 Bazaar, Kirkgate, and 1 Primrose terrace, Manningham
Beanland Frances, 42 Manchester road
Eltoft Ann, 24 Darley street
Rochfort Valentine (wholesale), 17 Union Passage, Kirkgate
Smith George, 81 Bedford street, Bridge street
Smith Joseph (wholesale), 27 Darley street

Steam-Engine Makers.

See Millwrights and Engineers.

Stone Masons.

Marked thus * are also Marble Masons.

(See also Marble Masons.)

Ackroyd Abraham, Little Horton lane
Burnley James, Black Abbey
Gledhill William, 72 Leeds road
Greenwood Luke, Great Horton
Moulson Miles, Great Horton road
Rhodes John, Legrams lane, Horton
* Ruddock Edward Harris (and sculptor), Leeds road
Stead John, Broad street, Manor row
Sugden John, Upper Globe, Manningham
* Tattersall John, Leeds road
Turner Jonas, Parkgate, High street
Webster Geo. Stickers lane, Bowling

Stone Merchants and Quarry Owners.

Booth Benjamin, Bolton road
Bottomley, Wood & Co. Canal road
Brayshaw William, corner of Lumb lane, Westgate

Clough James, Little Horton lane
Cousen & Thackray, Brunswick place, Northgate
Crabtree Richard, Lower Globe, Manningham
Hill, Hardaker Hill & Co. Balme street, Bolton road
Hill, Smithies & Nelson, Well street (*See advertisement*)
Jagger Thomas & John, Canal Side, Bolton road
Murgatroyd Benjamin, Whetley st. Manningham
Rhodes John, Legrams lane, Horton
Rogerson & Thackray, Canal road
Vint George & Brothers, Canal side, Bolton road

Straw Hat and Bonnet Makers.

Anderson Emma, Wakefield road
Atkinson Alice, Crown street, Thornton road
Bairstow Sarah Ann, Laister Dyke
Barker Sarah, 217 Bolton road
Bateman Mrs. 49 High street
Bell Mary, 153 Silsbridge lane
Bentley Mrs. 58 Kirkgate
Booth Ann & Sarah, 38 Manchester rd.
Botterill Mary Ann (late Pearson), 48 Kirkgate
Brown Frances, 45 Croft street, Manchester road
Brown Sarah, 82 Britannia street, Manchester road
Carter Jane, Park square, Mannghm.
Clayton Mary Ann, Barkerend
Coates Ann, 284 Leeds road
Colley Maria, 25 Silsbridge lane
Connell Sarah, 93 Manchester road
Daniel Mary Ann, 36 Vicar lane
Dodgson Mary, 24 Hustlergate
Elsworth Ann, 555 Wakefield road
Farrar Sarah Ann, Frederick street, Wakefield road
Fox Theodosia, 153 Manchester road
Harrowby Sarah, 12 John street, Westgate
Hartley Elizabeth, Thornton road
Hartley Jane & Margaret, 78 John street, Stott Hill
Hawksworth Esther, 18 Cropper lane, Westgate
Henry Elizabeth, 32 Earl street, Manchester road
Holgate Mary, 5 Cannon street, Cheapside
Hornby Mary, Garnett's Yard, Union street, Bridge street
Hudson Martha, Church Hill, Wakefield road, Bowling
Illingworth Martha, Broadstones
Ingham Martha, 99 Brick lane
Johnson Mary, 135 Vicar lane
Kellett Maria, 5 Churchbank, Well st.
Kitson Jane, 72 Hope street, Manchester road
Lumb Misses, 1 Westgate
Mathers Mary Ann, 173 Back lane, Bowling
Mountain Eliza, 6 Lister street, Bermondsey
Nichols Sarah Elizabeth, 1 Fitzgerald st. Manchester road
Noble Elizabeth, 117 Park square, Manningham
Oddy Mary Ann, Wakefield road
Ogden Elizabeth, 54 Northgate
Parker Hannah & Mary (Friends' bonnets), Tyrrel street
Phelps Jane, 139 Gracechurch street, White Abbey
Robertshaw Ann, Mortimer row, Bradford Moor
Roe Martha, Arcadia street, Manningham

Routh Mrs. 29 Gaunt street, Otley road
Seed Anne, 94 Westgate
Sellers Ann, 102 George street, Leeds road
Senior Mary, Church Hill, Wakefield road
Shackleton Ann & Mary, Tyrrel st.
Shackleton Hannah, 34 Westgate
Sharp Mary, Primrose terrace, Manningham
Sharp Misses, 6 Darley street
Siddall Mary Ann, 6 George street, Leeds road
Sidney Mary, 103 Manchester road
Smith Martha, 157 Manchester road
Smithies Hannah, Hall lane, Bowling
Spurr Nancy, Church Hill, Wakefield road
Standeavens Sarah, 1 Lumb lane, Westgate
Steel Mary Ann, Wakefield road
Sykes Sarah, 5 Vicar lane
Terry Sarah Ann, Laister Dyke
Thackwray Martha, 20 Darley street
Turley Mrs. 18 High street
Varley Caroline, 5 Keighley Old road
Webster Ann, 19 Barkerend, High street
Webster Frances & Elizabeth, Leeds road
Whitehead Eliza, 16 Kirkgate
Whittaker Harriet, Bavaria place, Manningham
Wildsmith Amelia, 159 Wakefield rd.
Wilkinson Mary, 83 Timber street, Otley road
Wilkinson Sarah, 59 Thornton road

Stuff Manufacturers.

See Worsted Stuff Manufacturers.

Stuff Merchants.

(See also Yarn Merchants, and Worsted Stuff Manufacturers.)

Abercrombie David & Co. Leeds road
Akroyd James & Son, Booth street, Hall Ings
Anderson & Yates, Leeds road
Bannerman Henry & Sons, Union st.
Behrens Jacob, Leeds road
Behrens Solomon Levi, Swaine st.; Mr. J. A. Unna manager
Berwick Brothers & Jamieson, Swaine street
Birchall Edwin & Sons, Leeds road
Birkbeck Morris & Co. 52 Cheapside
Broadbent John & Co. Swaine street
Brook & Knowles, Crossley's Buildings, 10 Westgate
Browne James & John, Court street, Leeds road
Burghardt, Aders & Co. Bermondsey
Butterfield Brothers, 1 Norfolk street, Bridge street
Butterworth Sidney Aquilla, Hall Ings
Clayton John Son & Co. Exchange street, Kirkgate
Crafts & Stell, Butterworth's Buildings, Ivegate
D'Hauregard Henry, Leeds road; Mr. Errel manager
Dewhirst William & Co. Leeds road
Douglas John & Co. Hall Ings
Douglas, M'Candlish & Co, Butterworth's Buildings, Ivegate
Ellissen Philip David, Booth street; manager Mr. Weil
Emanuel & Son, Exchange street, Kirkgate; Mr. J. F. Reickmann manager
Fugill Joseph, Chapel lane, Tyrrel street

Furst Bernard & Co. Hall Ings; manager Mr. Louis Goldstein
Garner Joseph & Co. 30 Pearson's Buildings, Bridge street
Goldstein Martin, Swaine street, Hall Ings
Greenwood George Oates, Hall Ings
Gumpel Gustavus & Co. Chapel lane, Tyrrel street; Mr. Louis Becher manager
Haigh John & Co. Hall Ings
Hammond Turner & Sons, Charles street and Manchester
Hanson Thomas Anderson, Leeds road
Henry A, & S. & Co. Bermondsey
Hertz Heinrich D. Brook street, and Bond street, Leeds
Hertz Martin & Co. Tyrell street
Heymann & Alexander (late A. J. Saalfeld & Co.), Charles street
Holdsworth John & Co. Norfolk street, Bridge street, and Halifax
Howatt E. & W. and Co. 16 Dale st.
Jennings & Hargrave, Leeds road
Kessler & Co. Bermondsey and Manchester; Mr. Wiechus manager
Liebert Bernhard, Hall Ings and Manchester
Luccock, Lupton & Co. Bridge street
M'Kean, Tetley & Co. Leeds road
M'Laurin A. S. & Co. Tyrrel street
Mann Thomas & John & Co. White Lion Yard, Kirkgate
Meyer George Solomon, 7 Lister st. Bermondsey
Milligan, Forbes & Co. 4 Exchange street, Kirkgate
Milligan, Hunter & Co. Exchange street, Kirkgate
Milligan John Son & Co. Leeds road
Mills James William, Hustler's Buildings, Market street
Mitchell Edmund Johnson, 11 Manor row
Nathan N. P. & H. Bermondsey; manager Mr. J. Philips
Patterson Robert & Co. 38 Bridge street
Peel William & Co. 40 Bridge street
Pregel George & Co. Swaine street, Hall Ings
Rennards Thomas, Union st. Bridge street
Rennie, Tetley & Co. Leeds road
Reuss, Kling & Co. Colliergate, Hall Ings; manager Mr. G. Kerstein
Russell, Douglas & Co. Leeds road
Russell Joseph, 8 Bank street
Sampson & Leppoc, Hall Ings; manager Mr. Anton Engelmann
Scarf & Hanson, Hall Ings
Schonfeld Michael, Hall Ings
Schunk, Souchay & Co. Brook street; Mr. C. Lockwood manager
Schuster Leo Brothers & Co. Charles street
Schwann Frederick, Hall Ings
Semon, Siltzer & Co. 76 Chapel lane, Tyrrel street
Sichel Augustus Sylvestro, Leeds rd.
Speyer Charles G. & Co. Swaine st.
Steinthal & Co. Hall Ings
Stow Brothers & Co. Hall Ings
Thornton, Firth, Ramsden & Co. Thornton road
Tobler, Amschel & Co. Tyrrel street; manager Mr. Samuel Webster
Wilson John & Co. 4 Bridge street
Wood Benjamin & Co. 30 Pearson's Buildings, Bridge street

Surgeons.

(See also Physicians.)

Beach John, Rawson place, Darley st.

Beaumont Thomas, Laura place, Leeds road
Bennet James Heaton (late Caton), 37 Manningham lane
Buckley William Halstead, 22 Portland place, Manchester road
Casson Edwin, 1 High street
Coates William, Rawson place, Darley street
Croser William, 42 Darley street
Cryer Willson, M. D. Hanover square
Douglas James, Drewton street, Manningham lane
Farrar William, M. D. 10 Darley street, and Richmond House, Great Horton road
Field William, Dudley Hill, Bowling
Gordon John, 27 Bridge street
Greenwood Benjamin, 51 Portland place, Manchester road
Holmes Samuel, 40 Darley street
Hornell James, M. D. Rawson place, Darley street
Illingworth Henry, 26 James street, Westgate
Illingworth Jonathan, 14 Westgate
M'Michan John Little, 23 Thornton's Buildings, Leeds road
Meade Richard Henry, Manor row
Parkinson William, Well street
Poppleton Joe, Bridge street
Roberts John Walker, 9 Rawson place, Darley street
Smith George Priestley, Wakefield rd.
Steel John, 86 Westgate
Taylor Christian Henry, 12 Darley st.
Thomas Abraham, Cross lane, Great Horton

Surveyors.

(See Architects and Surveyors, and also Land and Building Agents.)

Tailors.

Marked thus * are also Woollen Drapers.

(See also Woollen Drapers.)

Alderson Joseph, Ivegate
Anderson Richard, 1 Quecec terrace, Thornton road
* Askwith Joseph, 91 Westgate
* Atkinson George, 103 Manchester rd.
Barraclough Thomas, Primrose terrace, Manningham
Barrett Job, Leach's Square, Laister Dyke
Barrett William, 2 Illingworth's Court, Westgate
Boyce Thomas, Stott Hill
Boyd William, Bradford Moor
Brewer Abel, Dudley Hill, Bowling
Briggs John, High street, Gt. Horton
Brook Luke, Sticker lane, Bowling
Brown George, Sedgwick street, Lumb lane
* Brown & Muff, 54 Market street
Brown William, Whetley street, Manningham
* Buckanan Andrew, 3 Paperhall, Northwing
Burrows John, 35 Heber street, Little Horton lane
* Calvert Brothers, 73 Market street
Carter William, 7 Three street, Silsbridge lane
* Chapman & Co. 26 Kirkgate
Clark William, Wakefield road
Clarke Benjamin, Cherrytree row, Manningham
Clayton & Son, Wakefield road
Cordingley William, 34 Reform street, Westgate
Crabtree Cornelius, Southgate, Great Horton
Crabtree Samuel, Greenhill, Manningham

Crabtree William, Southgate, Great Horton
Crossley James, 12 School street, Manchester road
Darnbrough William, Walmsley's Buildings, Prospect street, Silsbridge lane
Davison William, 10 King street, Silsbridge lane
* Dewhirst John, 47 High street
Dewhirst Simon, Great Horton road
Dixon John, 54 Earl street, Manchester road
* Dixon & Masser, 8 Bridge street
England William, 14 School street, Cheapside
* Farrar & Gillham, 20 Kirkgate
Fawthorp Thomas, 10 Croft street, Bridge street
Firth Thomas, Dudley Hill, Bowling
Gill William, 257 Manchester road
Gornall Thomas, Church Hill, Wakefield road
Halliday Joseph, 46 George street, Manchester road
Handby Cornelius, 3 Ivegate
Hanrahan John, 21 Longcroft place, Westgate
Hanson Joseph, 178 Wakefield road
Hardaker Benjamin, 20 Hustlergate
Hawkins Thomas, 83 Wakefield road
Heaton Peter, 48 King street, Manchester road
* Hewitt Edward Smith, 10 Manchester road
Hewitt James, 82 Bedford street, Bridge street
Hillas Samuel, Wakefield road
* Hindle Thomas, 23 Darley street
* Hinds & Walmsley, 36 Market st.
Hodgson William, Mary Farrar's Yard, Westgate
Hodgson William, 106 Silsbridge la.
Holdsworth John, 36 Wellington st. Stott Hill
Holgate William, 16 Union Passage, Kirkgate
Holroyd John, 41 High street
Horrocks James, 3 Hayworth street, White Abbey
* Hunter John, 2 Market street
* Hunter Thomas, 4 Westgate
Hustler Joseph Oddy, 3 Castle st. Manchester road
Illingworth Charles, Four Lane Ends, Manningham
Illingworth Herr, Brick lane, Manningham
Illingworth Titus, Spring row, Manningham
Jardeen Richard,. 122 Bridge street
Jarvis George, 41 George street, Leeds road
Jenkins James, 123 Manchester road
Jenkinson Robert, 62 Joseph street, Leeds road
Joyce John, Longlands street, Westgate
Kaye Miles, Tumblinghill street, Thornton road
Keighley John, Frederick street, Wakefield road
Kyme Thomas, 22 Croft street, Bridge street
Lauckland Joseph, 48 Chapel lane
Leachman Robert Gilchrist, 25 Prospect street, Silsbridge lane
Lee George & Son, 43 John street, Westgate
Lee Joshua, 26 High street
* Lewis Benjamin, 2 Kirkgate
Lightowler Jonas, Southgate, Great Horton
Long Joseph, Temperance terrace, Spring street

*Lumb Luke, Little Horton lane
Milner Joshua, 3 Bridge street
* Moses & Son, 19 Bridge street
* Nalton Thomas, 12 Cheapside
Newton Reuben, 304 Mitchell's Buildings, Manchester road
Parkinson George, Wood street, Manningham
Patchett Joshua, Otley road
Pattison William, Uppercroft row, Bowling
Pattison William, Swaine Green, Bowling
Pellet Emanuel Lines, 49 Queen st. Manchester road
Pittam Samuel, 30 Chapel lane
Pitts Joseph, Dudley Hill, Bowling
Pitts Mark, Dudley Hill, Bowling
Poulter William, Belgrave place, Lumb lane
Proud William, 32 Park street, High st.
Raistrick James, 232 Manchester rd.
Rennard Ambrose, 27 Victoria street, North Parade
Reynolds Patrick, Regent street, White Abbey
Rhodes William, 153 Bridge street
* Rhodes William, High street
Robinson Ralph, 60 Manchester road
Robinson Thomas, 13 Albion Court, Kirkgate
Rowntree Thomas, 1 Burnley Fold, Black Abbey
Rowntree Thomas, jun. 3 Saltpie st. Black Abbey
Rowntree William, York st. Bridge st.
Sharp Samuel, 10 Longlands street, Westgate
Shaw William, Little Horton
Sheard John, Spring street, Wharf street
Slatery John, Park square, Manningham

V

* Smallpage & Son, 10 Darley street, and Leeds
Smith Michael, Great Horton road
Stapleton William, 230 Leeds road
Stead Joseph, Bradford Moor
Stelling Robert, 13 Bedford street, Bridge street
* Thackeray W. & J. R. 47 and 48 Vicar lane (*See advertisement*)
Todd John, 19 Manchester road
Uttley William, 46 Union street, Bridge street
Walker William, 60 Chapel lane
*Waterhouse Richard, 67 New Market place
Waterhouse Robert, Bank street
White Thomas, Low Green, Horton
Widdop William, 62 Thompson's Alley, Silsbridge lane
Wilkinson Joseph, Dudley Hill
* Wilkinson Thomas, 37 Kirkgate
Wilkinson Thomas, Leeds road
Wilkinson Thomas, 184 Keighley Old road
Wilman Peter, 3 Longcroft place, Silsbridge lane
Wilsden Robert, Primrose terrace, Manningham
Winn William, 77 Bridge street
Wood Joseph, 15 Brick row, Thornton road
Wright George, 160 Bridge street
Wright John, 44 Chandos street, Wakefield road
* Wright Joseph, 53 Bridge street

Tallow Chandlers.

Ackroyd William, 142 Manchester road
Harker John, Wakefield road
Harrison Joseph, 55 Westgate
Mitchell Joshua, 30 Ivegate
Smith and Tuke, 37 Bridge street

Stephenson Thomas (and glue and soaps), Charles street
Waddington Joseph, 76 Westgate

Tanner.

Freeman Joseph, Thornton road

Tarpauling and Cart Cover Manufacturer.

Leeming William, 7 Old Market place, Market street

Tea Dealers & Coffee Roasters.

[See also Grocers and Tea Dealers.]

Alderson George, 1 Bridge street
Arnold John, 41 Sun Bridge, Bridge st.
Atkinson Nathan, 187 Wakefield road
Bartle Timothy, 26 and 28 Market street
Beaumont William, 29½ Kirkgate
Bell Thomas, 104 Manchester road
Binns Eleanor (tea), 25 Hustlergate
Binns George, 151 George street, Leeds road
Booth William, 38 White Abbey
Britton Robert, 10 Bridge street
Carter John, 124 Manchester road
Clarance & Co. 34 Kirkgate (*see advertisement*)
Cowgill Thomas, 107 Bridge street
Crossley Henry William, 31 Ivegate
Cure William, 24 Westgate
Diggles James, 158 and 160 Westgate (*see advertisement*)
Elmsley James and John, 204 Manchester road and 38 Bolton road
Firth Samuel, 80 Westgate
France Samuel, Well street, 141 Bridge street and 7 Tyrrel street
Furnell George, 35 Lumb lane
Gamble Sarah, 90 Westgate
Gibson George, 180 Manchester road
Gilderdale John, 28 Bridge street, and Wakefield
Hall Thomas, 42 Leeds road
Hardy Henry, Market street, corner of Bridge street
Harrison Joseph, 55 Westgate
Hesling John, North st. Stott Hill
Hill John, 254 Manchester road
Hill Joseph, 41 Market street
Hodgson Michael, 73 Westgate
Irving Christopher, 42 Westgate
Irving William, 20 Northrop's Buildings, Westgate
Isitt George, 36 Kirkgate
Kaye John, Leeds road
Learoyd Abraham, 50 Manchester road
Lister John, Wood st. Manningham
M'Taggart William, 3 Silsbridge lane
Malim George, 140 Westgate
Marsden Ann, 1 Union st. Bridge st.
Marsden James, 8 Ivegate
Marshall James, 185 Bridge street
Milner Thomas, 8 Well street and 26 Ivegate
Morrell John, 4 and 6 Tyrrel street
Mortimer William Dawson, 68 Market street
Morton Matthew, 84 Westgate
Neesom James, 43 Market street
Newby Richard, 10 Kirkgate
Parker William, Tyrrel street
Parkinson Edward and William, 2 Kirkgate
Parkinson Joseph, 2 Old Market place
Peacock James, 246 Leeds road
Peacock John, 63 Northgate
Raper Joseph, 175 Bridge street
Roberts John, 25 Westgate
Roberts Joseph, 50 Westgate
Sagar Henry, 5 Broadstones
Sharp Joshua, Wakefield road
Smith George, Tyrrel street
Smith & Tuke, 37 Bridge street

Smith William, 40 Manchester road, and 48 Westgate

Stead William & Co. 20 Ivegate and 56 Market street

Stocks Brothers, 27 Ivegate

Stocks Henry, 58 Kirkgate

Tordoff John & Son (and chocolate and cocoa manufacturers), 46 Kirkgate

Trigg Edwin, Broadstones

Waddington Joseph, 76 Westgate

Wadsworth Eli, 108 Manchester rd.

Waller Charles, 14 Kirkgate

Walmsley John, 66 Kirkgate

Woodcock Joseph, 18 Darley street

Woodhouse Thomas, 35 Providence street, White Abbey

Wright George Royle, 72 Market st. and 124 Westgate

Timber Merchants.

(See also Packing Case and Rolling Board Makers, and Saw Mills.)

Barraclough John, North Parade, Christ Church

Beanland William, Northgate

Beecroft Joseph (executors of), Toad lane, Bridge street

Briggs Robert & Sons (hardwood), Sugden's Mill, Black Abbey

Cowperthwaite Stephen (hardwood), New Miller Dam, Thornton road

Green James, Colliergate, Swaine st.

Harrison & Singleton, Canal road, and Leeds

Hartley Brothers, Bridge street, and Leeds

Hewitt & Knowles, School street, Cheapside

Hill Jonas & Thomas, Churchbank, Well street

Ramsden Joseph, High street, Great Horton

Rhodes James, Wharf street, Bolton road

Smith George, Thornton road

Stephenson John and Sons, Great Horton road

Thorpe, Scholefield & Co. John street, Leeds road, and Prospect Mill, Wakefield road, Bowling

Wilson James & Son, Spring row, Manningham

Tobacco Pipe Maker.

Jolly Joshua, 21 Albion street, Silsbridge lane

Tobacconists.

Marked thus * are Manufacturers.

Blackburn Samuel, 38 and 39 Tyrrel street

Broadley Henry, top of Ivegate

Gilderdale John, 28 Bridge street and Wakefield

Newby Richard, 10 Kirkgate

* Parkinson Joseph, 2 Old Market, Market street

* Smithson, Sugden & Co. 53 Westgate, and High street

Swithenbank Samuel, 3 Chapel lane, Bridge street

Taylor Martha, 11 and 13 Bridge st.

Wade Thomas, 16 Westgate

Wigglesworth William, 79 Market st.

Tool Makers and Dealers.

[See also File, and Lathe & Tool Makers.]

Dixon & Byrne, 77 Market street

Dove Thomas Pashley, 17 Ivegate

Hattersley Samuel & Son, Westbrook Works, Thornton road

Marshall William, 4 Kirkgate

Parratt Edward Hawksworth, 1 Broadstones

Pearson Henry, 30 and 32 Bridge st.

Rhodes John, 18 Kirkgate
Rudd Robert, 35 Kirkgate
Thwaites & Co. Albion Works, Thornton road
Scully Ambrose, 7 Ivegate
Stelling Thomas, 62 Kirkgate
Watkins William (and plane), Cure's Court, Westgate
Wyrill Frances, 8 Westgate

Toy Warehouses and Dealers.

Marked thus + are Importers of Foreign Fancy articles and Perfumery.

Broadley Henry, top of Ivegate
Dale George, 37 Market street
+ Dilger Theodore, 15 Hustlergate
Hanson John, 29 Westgate
+ Rhodes Charles, 2 Cheapside
Taylor Martha, 11 and 13 Bridge st.

Truss Makers.

(See also Cutlers.)

Hall John, 40 Market street
Roberts Benjamin, 5 Darley street

Turners in Wood, Ivory and Metal.

(See also Bobbin and Skewer Turners.)

Barraclough John, Spence's Mill, Chapel lane
Barraclough William, Spence's Mill, Chapel lane
Briggs Robert & Sons, Sugden's Mill, Black Abbey
Cowperthwaite Stephen, New Miller Dam, Thornton road
Leavens Robert, 212 Bolton road
Lenham Thomas, 9 Reform street, Westgate
Oxtoby Thomas, 6 Cross street, Westgate
Sedgwick John, Nelson street
Sedgwick Robert, King street, Manchester road

Umbrella Makers.

Flinn Edward, 14 Providence street, Westgate, and Bazaar, Kirkgate
Hird Alexander, 28 Hustlergate
Metcalf John, 14 Manchester road
Pickles Henry, 27 Northgate
Wade Thomas, 16 Westgate

Undertakers.

Andrew George, Victoria street, Silsbridge lane
Baxter Benjamin, 27 North street, Stott Hill
Farrand Jonathan, 71 Frederick st. Wakefield road
Holmes Thomas & Son, 36 Kirkgate
Monies James & Co. 30 Kirkgate, and 2 Exchange street
Sellers John, 162 George street, Leeds road
Thompson Thomas, 95 Bedford st. Bridge street

Upholsterers.

(See also Cabinet Makers.)

Archer Edward, Tyrrel street
Beanland William, North Parade
Clough Joseph, 2 Manchester road
Cockin Joseph & James, 12 Cheapside, and Manchester
Constantine James, 76 Bridge street
Cowin James & Son, 59 Northgate
Craven Isaac, 34 Darley street
Duckworth & Watson, Tyrrel Court, Tyrrel street
Ferrand Jonathan, 71 Frederick st. Wakefield road
Hartley Samuel, Leeds road
Mills Thomas, 45 Market street
Milnes Enoch, 28 Manchester road

Nutter Joseph, Nutter's place, North Parade

Pratt & Prince, 4 North Parade, Christ Church

Sutcliffe Samuel, 138 and 140 George street, Leeds road

Thornton John, 21 Westgate

Tyas John, 115 Westgate

Ward William, King's Arms Yard, Westgate

Whitehead John, 14 Well street

Wilkinson Joseph, New Market place and 13 North Parade

Veterinary Surgeons.

Byron Robert, Hall Ings

Collins Thomas, Bee Hive Yard, Westgate

Drake William, Leeds road

Mitchell Thomas, Bradford Moor

Warp Sizer.

Whittaker Edmund, Thornton road

Watch and Clock Makers.

(See also Silversmiths and Jewellers.)

Atkinson George, 87 George street, Leeds road

Barrett James, 1 Wellington street, Stott Hill

Barrow William, 2 Bank street, Market street

Bowes James, 8 Union Passage, and Leeds road

Brooksbank William, 64 Market st.—(*see advertisement*)

Brumfit Joseph (dealer), 80 Market street

Freeman Ambrose, 98 Manchester rd.

Hardaker James, 12 Providence st. Westgate

Harker & Crabtree, 162 Manchester road

Hill John, Whetley street, Manningham

Knowles David, 19 Manchester road

Prest William, 22 Well street

Renton James, 16 Well street

Rhodes Manoah, 6 Westgate

Sewell Christopher, 37 Westgate

Snow Nicholas Mason, 24 Piecehall Yard, Kirkgate

Sykes Walter, Wakefield road, Bowling

Wilson & Fairbank, 47 Kirkgate

Wharfingers and Canal Companies.

Bradford and Selby Fly Boats' Company (Pearson & Co.), Canal road; John Adamson manager

Leeds and Liverpool Canal Company; principal agent Robert Nicholson, Salem street, Manor row; carrying agent James Hepper, Thornton road, and Canal Wharf, Shipley

Wood Joseph & Co. Canal road

Wheelwrights.

Bower John, Bunker's Hill, Barkerend

Bower Samuel, Thornton road

Clapham William, Manchester road, Bowling

Clarke Christopher, High street, Great Horton

Driver John, Cutlerheight lane, Dudley Hill

England Samuel, Thornton road

Fearnley John, Thornton road

Green Benjamin, 49 Leeds road

Green John, top of Westgate

Naylor Abraham, Bowling lane, Bowling

Pratt John, Sedgwick street, White Abbey

Ramsden Thomas, High street, Great Horton
Thompson Thomas, High street, Great Horton
Thornton Benjamin, High street
Whittaker William, Dudley Hill, Bowling

Whitesmiths.

(See also Locksmiths and Bellhangers).

Campbell Richard, Reform street, Westgate
Cowman William, Mawson street, Thornton road
Dixon & Byrne, 77 Market street
Dove Thomas Pashley, 13 Ivegate
Fell James, 17 Nelson street
Hargreaves Charles & Michael, Cropper lane, Westgate
Hargreaves Peter, Ship Alley, Well street
Hill John & Co. 8 Cheapside
Holdsworth & Raistrick, Croft street, Manchester road
Martin Benjamin, Manchester road
Pearson John, Albion Yard, Ivegate
Rhodes William, 99 Westgate
Richardson Henry, 5 Bedford street, Bridge street
Smith Thomas, Bowergate, Tyrrel st.
Woodhead Joseph, Keighley street, Silsbridge lane
Wyrill Frances, 8 Westgate (*see advertisement*)

Wine and Spirit Merchants.

Marked thus ‡ are British Wine Dealers Only.

‡ Bartle Timothy, 26 and 28 Market street
‡ Binns Eleanor, 25 Hustlergate
‡ Britton Robert, 10 Bridge street
Brumfit Charles, 27 Bermondsey (*see advertisement*)
‡ Carter John, 124 Manchester road
‡ Cockshott William, 32 Westgate
‡ Crowther John, 17 Market street
Greaves John, Tyrrel street
‡ Hargreaves Sarah, 30 Kirkgate
Holloway William Henry, Exchange Vaults, Kirkgate
Laycock Peter (executors of), top of Ivegate
Lee Hannah, 11 Westgate
Popplewell Benjamin Briggs, 43 Market street
Richardson Francis (late Wells), Westgate
‡ Smith Mary, 88 Westgate
‡ Thompson Ann and Mary, 17 North Parade
‡ Walker Rachel, 69 Market street
Wright James, Hustlergate & Ivegate

Wire Drawers, and Window Blind, &c. Makers.

Bateman Daniel & Sons, Folly Hall, Wibsey
Rhodes Henry & Charles, Old Post Office Buildings, Bridge street
Rhodes William, 11 Northgate

Wool-Combers—(Machine.)

Collier John, Duckitt's Mill, Nelson street, Bridge street
Collier William & Co. Duckitt's Mill, Nelson street
Donisthorpe & Co. Thornton road
Lister Samuel Cunliffe (and combing machine patentee), Mill street, Canal road
Todd David, Albion Works, Thornton road
Todd John & Son, Duckitt's Mill, Nelson street

Wool-Comb Makers.

Bates Miles, Silsbridge lane
Binns William, Bolton road
Clark James, Southgate
Crook William, Fawcett's Court, Nelson street
Day John, 3 Thomas street, Manchester road
Hammond Joseph, Ship Abbey, Well street
Smith & Speed, Westbrook terrace, Thornton road
Waddington William, Albion street, Silsbridge lane

Woollen Cloth Manufacturers.

Coates Henry, Bradford Moor
Coates James, Bradford Moor
Hudson George, Bradford Moor
Mirfield John, Bradford Moor
Roberts William, Bradford Moor
Wilcock Bradley & Co. Union Mill, Shipley
Wilcock George, Windhill, Idle
Wilcock Joseph (and wool dealer), Windhill, Idle

Woollen Drapers.

Bell & Prest, Tyrrel street
Brook, Gant & Co. 10 Westgate
Brown & Muff, 54 Market street
Chapman & Co. 26 Kirkgate
Dixon & Masser, 8 Bridge street
Farrar & Gillham, 20 Kirkgate
Hall Francis Stuart, 33 Kirkgate
Hewitt Edward Smith, 10 Manchester road
Hindle Thomas, 23 Darley street
Hunter John, 2 Market street
Hunter Thomas, 4 Westgate
Longfield William & Co. 30A Kirkgate
Milner Joshua, 3 Bridge street
Monies James & Co. 30 Kirkgate, and 2 Exchange street
Moses & Son, 19 Bridge street
Ogden Michael & Co. 29 Kirkgate
Parkinson & Clark, 27 Kirkgate
Storey & Brook, 37 Kirkgate

Woollen Flock Dealers.

See Cabinet Makers, & also Upholsterers

Woolstaplers.

Marked thus * are also Foreign Wool Dealers.

(See likewise Agents—Commission Wool and Top.)

* Adamson John & Son, Well street
Adcock John & Son, 60 Bridge street
*Aked & Robertshaw, Cheapside
Aked Thomas, Brook street
Anderton John Ashworth, Hardcastle lane, Well street
*Atkinson John, Cheapside
Aykroyd Jonathan & Son, Swaine st.
Baines Thomas, Swaine street
Barker James, 38 Cheapside
Barrans James, Hustler's Buildings, Market street
Bates Joshua, 23 Well street
Beanland Joseph, 16 Union street, Bridge street
Beaver William, 13 Cheapside
Bingham George, 20 Balm street and 9 Bolton road
* Booker Robert Alfred, Swaine st.
Bottoms James, Back Tyrrel street
Brown Joseph, Hustler's Buildings, Market street
Brown Matthew, Cheapside
Buck Bolland, 14 Cheapside
Buck & Holmes, 1 Exchange street, Duke street
Butterfield George, Swaine street
* Butterfield John & Son, Swaine st.

Butterfield Robert, Swaine street
Butterfield Samuel, Hustler's Buildings, Market street
*Cheesebrough John, 16 Exchange street, Kirkgate
* Cheesebrough William, Cheapside, Dale street and Exchange street
Clarkes & Ingham, 8 Broadstones, Well street
Clayton John Son & Co. Exchange street, Kirkgate
Clayton Thomas, Thornton road
Clough James, Bermondsey
Cockcroft Joseph, Commercial street, Canal road
Cook William, 44 Cheapside
Davidson Joseph, 13 Exchange street, Kirkgate, and London
Denby John, Cheapside
* Denton William, Swaine street, Hall Ings
Dibb & Co. Commercial street, Canal road
Elgey George Allison, Swaine street
Elgey Joseph Bowron, Swaine street
Emmett Emanuel, Bermondsey
*Exley John, Chespside
Fawcett Richard, Cheapside
Firth Daniel, Bermondsey
Flatman John & Samuel, Wood's Court, Cheapside, and Westgate, Wakefield
Forster & Fison, Hustler's Buildings, Leeds road
Fox Edmund & William, Roebuck Yard, Market street
Fryer John, Commercial street, Canal road
Haigh William Chapman, Swaine st and Exchange street, Kirkgate
Hainsworth John & Son, 47 Union street, Bridge street
Haley Joshua, 6 Broadstones, Well street
Hall & Bankart (agents), 39 Bermondsey
Hall Joshua, Cheapside
Halstead John, Bermondsey
* Hardcastle Joseph & Co. 256 Bolton road
Hardy Squire, Hustler's Buildings Market street
Hargreaves Benjamin, Charles street
Hargreaves John, Union street, Bridge street
Harrison James, Bermondsey
Harrison John, Liverpool street, Bank street
Harrison & Laycock, Cheapside
Heaton Robert, Cheapside
Helliwell Benjamin, Commercial st. Canal road
Helliwell Henry, Commercial street, Canal road
Hill Luke Crosby, Broadstones, Well street
Hirst J. & W. H. Leeds road
Holdsworth James, Cheapside
* Horsfall William & Brothers, Broadstones, Well street
Hubbard James & Son, Hall Ings and Leeds
* Illingworth & Kenion, Charles st. Hall Ings
Ingham & Taylors, Booth street, Hall Ings
Jowett Edmund, Union Passage, Kirkgate, and Upper North Parade
Light John, 39 Darley street
Lister John, Swaine street, Hall Ings
Lister Joshua Brook, Booth street, Hall Ings
Lupton Richard & Son, 24 Cheapside
Mahony Michael Joseph, Booth st.

Margerison & Sutcliffe (agents), Bermondsey
Marshall James, Bermondsey
Marten William, 28 Cheapside
* Morren John, 32 Cheapside
Mortimer Richard Polycarp, 62 Commercial street, Canal road
* Murgatroyd William, Charles st.
Musgrave Samuel & Simeon, Swaine street
Oddy James & Sons, Brook street, and Tong
Parkinson Samuel & Thomas, Exchange street, Kirkgate
Peckover & Ferrand, Dale street and Duke street
Pennington John, Cheapside
Perfect Henry Goodwin, Hall Ings
Pollard Richard, Bermondsey
Renton Thomas, 9 Well street
Rhodes John, Ship Alley, Well street
Rhodes John & Joseph, junrs. Brook street
Robinson John Thomas, 4 Commercial street, Canal road
Rushworth Joseph Taylor, 1 Well st.
+ Schafer John Henry & Co. (importers), Hustler's Buildings, Market street
Scholefield William, 8 Duke street and Leeds
Shackleton James, School street, Cheapside
Shepherd & Foster, Swaine street
Snowden & Alderson, Swaine street
Speight John, Bermondsey
Sugden Jonas, Cheapside
Sugden & Webster, Hustler's Buildings, Market street
Taylor James Somerville, Charles st.
Tetley Robert, 66 Bridge street
Thistlethwaite John & Co. 42 Cheapside
Townend John, Bank street
Turner Charles Timothy, Charles street
Twycross James & Son, Commercial street, Canal road
Walker William, Bermondsey
White Stephen, Commercial street, Canal road
Whitley Richard, Hustler's Buildings, Market street
* Whitley William, Cheapside
Wilcock William Butterfield, 2 Broadstones
Wilkinson Croft, 16 Union street, Bridge street
Willey John, Hustler's Buildings, Market street
Wright & Tillotson, Bermondsey

Wool (Short) & Waste Dealers.

Ambler Illingworth, Albion Yard, Ivegate
Blackburn Abraham, Liverpool street, Bank street
Cooper Jane, Hope and Anchor Yard, Bank street
Denton John, Hope and Anchor Yard, Bank street
Edmondson Thomas, Albion Yard, Ivegate
Hardy Squire, Hustler's Buildings, Market street
Hirst Joseph, Roebuck Yard, Ivegate
Holmes John & Hartley, Back Tyrrel street
Horsfall Joshua, Hope and Anchor Yard, Bank street
Longbottom Thomas, Hope & Anchor Yard, Bank street
Metcalf John, Brumfit's Yard, Kirkgate
Moorhouse William, Great Horton
Newsholme Thomas, Albion Yard, Ivegate

Robinson John Thomas, 4 Commercial street, Canal road
Rudd Jeremiah, High street, Great Horton
Simpson Joseph, Oak st. Leeds road
Suddards Edward, Hope and Anchor Yard, Bank street
Thresh Abraham, 36 Bank street
Waddington Henry, Hope and Anchor Yard, Bank street
Walton & Wittam, Albion Yard, Ivegate
Whitley Joseph, Hustler's Buildings, Market street
Whittaker & Hartley, Roebuck Yard, Ivegate

Wool-Washer.

Crabtree William, Mill street, Manchester road

Worsted Spinners and Manufacturers.

Marked thus + are Spinners only.

Ackroyd Cowling, Charles street; works Great Horton
Ackroyd Thomas & Sons, Dale st. Kirkgate; works Birkenshaw
Ackroyd William & Co. 5 Dale street, Kirkgate; works Otley
+Addison George Wilson & Sons, Hall Lane Mill, Bowling
Akroyd James & Son, Booth street, Hall Ings
Ambler Henry, Schuster's Buildings, Brook street; works Ovenden
Anderson George, Mill's Yard, Brook street; works Wilsden
Anderson Joshua & Co. Brook street; works Wilsden
Anderson & Yates, Leeds road; works Wilsden
+Anderton George & Sons, Bank st.; works Cleckheaton
+Anderton Swithin & Sons, Eastbrook Mills, Peel street, Leeds rd.
Anderton William, Brook street; works Bingley
Appleyard William & Son, Schuster's Buildings, Brook street; works Wainstalls and Hebble Mills, near Halifax
Arnold Solomon, 13 Bank street; works Eastburn, near Halifax
Baines Samuel, New Piecehall; works Brighouse
Bairstow Thomas & Matthew, Charles street; works Sutton Mill, Keighley
Bentley Nathan & Sons, Piecehall Yard; works Legrams, Horton
Billingsley, Tankard & Co. Market st.; works Bradford Moor
+Blackburn John, Laister Dyke Mill, Laister Dyke; house New Drop, Leeds road
+Bottomley Jonathan, Marshall's Mill, Manchester road; house Portland street
Bottomley Moses & Son, Brook st.; works Shelf, near Halifax
Bottomley Samuel & Brothers, Swaine street; works Low Moor
Bottomley, Wilkinson & Co. Portland street, and Marshall's Mill, Manchester road
Bower William & Henry, Charles street; works Drighlington, near Leeds
+Braithwaite Samuel, Marshall's Mill, Manchester road
Brigg John & Co. Charles street; works Keighley
Broadbent James Sutcliffe, Hartley's Buildings, Brook street; works Roundhill, Cleckheaton

Brown George & Co. Charles street; works Thornton road

+ Buck and Holmes, Pennyoak's Mill, Melbourne street, Leeds road

Calvert Lodge and Son, 30 Bank st.; works Thornton road

Clapham and Whittaker, Schuster's Buildings, Brook street; works Baildon

Clough John, Charles street; works Ingrow, near Keighley

+ Corless George, Uppercroft Mill, Bowling

+ Corless Thomas, Uppercroft Mill, Bowling

+ Corless William, Uppercroft Mill, Bowling

+ Cousen William, Old Piecehall; works Great Horton

Dalby Joseph, George Hotel Yard; works Laister Dyke

Dalby Samuel, Old Market, Market street; works Bradford Moor

Denby William and Sons, Court st. Leeds road; works Shipley

Denton Richard, New Piecehall; works Great Horton

+ Dewhirst Thomas, Piecehall Yard, Kirkgate; works Laister Dyke

Ecroyd William and Son, Brook st.; works Lomeshaye, near Burnley

Ellis John, Charles street; works Dudley Hill, Bowling

Fawthorp Joseph, New Piecehall; works Brow Mill, Clayton

Field Samuel, Brook street; works Millbank, Bridge street

Firth Isaac and Son, 22 Bank street; works Lilly lane, Halifax

+ Firth Thomas and Co. Caledonia Mill, Manchester road

Fison William, Charles street; works Foundry Mill, Manchester road

Foster John and Sons, Piecehall Yard, Kirkgate; works Black Dyke Mills, Clayton

Foster William and Henry. New Piecehall; works Denholme, Thornton

+ Garnett James and William, Barkerend, and Union st. Bridge st.

Green Robert Fletcher and Sons, Hartley's Buildings, Brook street; works Burley, Leeds

Greenwood Joseph and Benjamin, 38 Liverpool st. Bank st.; works Thornton road

Gregory Thomas and Brothers, 23 Old Market place; works Shelf, Halifax

Haggas William, Hustler's Buildings, Market street; works Oakworth, Keighley

Hargreaves Joseph, Booth street; works Shipley

Harker William, Brook street; works Victoria Mill, Bowling

+ Hartley William, Thompson's Mill, Thornton road

Hattersley George, Charles street; works Keighley

Hill and Drummond, Booth street; works Manningham

+ Hird Isaac, 97 Old Piecehall; works Keighley

Holdsworth John and Co. Norfolk st. Bridge st.; works Shaw Lodge Mills, Halifax

Holland Samuel and Co Charles st.; works Slade Syke, Halifax

Horsfall J. G. and Co. Charles street; works Northwing

Illingworth Daniel, Providence Mill, Thornton road

Illingworth William, Schuster's Buildings, Brook street; works Halifax

Isles John, 1 and 7 Old Piecehall; works Illingworth, Halifax

Jennings William and Son, 4 Hartley's Buildings, Brook street; works Windhill, Idle

Jowett Edmund, Union Passage, Kirkgate; works North Parade

Keighley G. W. and S. and Co. Charles street; works Keighley

Kershaw Samuel and Henry, Charles street; works Allerton

+ Lea Henry, Victoria Mill, Wakefield road

+ Lea Henry, jun. Babk lane, Bowling

Leach George Henry, Charles street; works Phœnix Mill, Thornton road

+ Leather George Henry, Charles st.; works Mill street, Canal road

Lister Thomas, 79 Old Piecehall; works Idle

Lupton John, Charles street; works Laister Dyke

M'Crea and Shephard, Charles st.; works Crosshills Mill, Halifax

Mason Henry and George, Market street; works Cliffe Mill, Horton

Merrall Brothers, 3 Hartley's Buildings, Brook street; works Haworth, near Keighley

Milner John and Co. 11 Exchange street, Kirkgate; works Clayton

Mitchell Francis and John, Unicorn Yard Hustlergate; works Manchester road

Mitchell James, New Piecehall; works Lane Ends, Keighley

Normington Isaac, George Hotel Yard; works Laister Dyke

+ Padgett William, Waterloo Mill, Victoria street, Manchester road

Parkinson, Mitchell & Co. Swaine street; works Fulneck, Pudsey

+ Pilling and Boulton, Westholme Mill, Thornton road

+ Popplewell Benjamin, Greenwood's Mill, Portland street

Porritt Jonathan, 10 Old Piecehall; works Birkenshaw

+ Raine Thomas, Spence's Mill, Chapel lane

Rand John and Sons, 22 Nag's Head Yard; works Horton road

Rishworth Henry, 13 Hartley's Buildings, Brook street; works Castle Mill, Keighley

Roberts Henry, Bank street; works Bailiff Bridge

Roberts James, Charles street; works Uppercroft Mill, Bowling

+ Robinson James and Co. Phœnix Mill, Thornton road

Robinson William, 31 Bank street; works Keighley

Rogers George, Charles street; works Beehive Mill, Thornton road

Rouse William and Co. Market street; works Bradford Mill, Canal road

Salt Titus (mohair and alpacca), Brook street; works Union street

Sharp David Wilkinson, 24 Exchange street, Kirkgate; works Bingley

Sharp Jonas, Brook street; works Bingley

+ Shaw and Mitchell, Northolme Mill, Leeming street, Canal road

Shuttleworth William and Co. Charles street; works North Bierley

Smith Benjamin, Market street; works Farnhill, Kildwick

+ Smith and Booth, Leeming's Mill, Southgate

Smith, Clough and Co. Brook street; works Globe Mill, White Abbey

+ Smith James, Pennyoaks Mill, Leeds road

† Smith Jonas, Uppercroft Mill, Bowling

†Smith and Shephard, Alland's Mill, Thornton road

Speak Paul, 18 Hartley's Buildings, Brook street; works Clayton

Sugden Jonas and Brothers, Piece-hall Yard; works Dobroyd

† Sugden William and John, 44 Old Market; works Keighley

Sutcliffe John, Bank street; works Low Moor

Sutcliffe William, Bank street; works Dudley Hill, Bowling

† Tankard Matthew, Uppercroft Mill, Bowling

† Taylor James, Greenwood's Mill, Portland street, Manchester road

Taylor John and Co. Old Market; works Fawcetholme Mill, Thornton road

Taylor Thomas and Sons, Old Piece-hall; works Hey Mill, near Halifax

Terry William and John, Hope and Anchor Yard; works Dudley Hill

Tetley Charles, Cannon Mill, Great Horton road

† Tetley Richard and Co. Caledonia Mill, Duke street, Manchester road

Titherington Eli, New Piecehall; works Midgley, near Halifax

Townend George and Brothers (heald and genappe yarn), Brook street; works Cullingworth, near Bingley

Townend Simeon, Charles street; works Thornton

Tremel Adolphus and Co. Hall Ings; works Fieldhead Mills, Thornton road

Turner and Mitchell, Unicorn Yard, Hustlergate; works Manchester rd

Varley John, Piecehall Yard; works Stanningley

W

Wade Joseph and Sons, Old Market; works Victoria Mill, Canal road

Walkers' and Co. Bridge street

Wall, Cockshott & Wall, Old Piece-hall; works Grassington, near Skipton

Waud Christopher and Co. (and mohair and alpaca), Brook street; works Britannia Mills, Portland street

† Webster Isaac, Greenwood's Mill, Portland street

† Wells William, Laycock's Mill, Thornton road

Whitehead, Goddard and Co. Charles street; works Canal road

Whitley Isaac, 19 Hartley's Buildings, Brook street; works Thornton road

Whitley Nathan, George Hotel Yard; works Dudley Hill

Whitworth Robert and Co. New Piece-hall; works Lee Mill, Halifax

Willett Thomas and Co. Clarence street, Manchester road

Wood Joseph, Swaine street; works Shipley Fields

Wood Joseph, Brook street; works Thornton road

Wood Samuel, 14 New Piecehall; works Sowerby Bridge

Wright William, 11 Hartley's Buildings, Brook street; works Silsden, near Keighley

Worsted Stuff Manufacturers.

See also Worsted Spinners and Manufacturers, and Stuff Merchants.

☞ Many manufacturers from the country, having warehouses in the town, attend on Mondays and Thursdays only, and many others attend the Inns; for which refer to Index.

Akroyd James and Son, Booth street, Hall Ings; works Copley & Halifax

Allen Edward and Robert and Co. Charles street; works Melbourne street, Leeds road

Appleyard Henry, Booth street; works Ibbotroyd, Hebden Bridge

Bartle John, Hustler's Buildings, Market street; works Great Horton

Binns John, 170 Old Piece hall; works Wilsden

Bottomley John, 8 Cheapside; house Cross School street, Cheapside

Briggs Thomas, Market street; works Birstal, Dewsbury

Briggs Jonathan, Old Piecehall; works Clayton

Butterfield Brothers, 1 Norfolk street, Bridge street; works Prospect Mill, Keighley

Chapman and Lofthouse, 48 Bridge street

Clapham William, Swaine street; works Wilsden

Clapham William and John, Holmefield Mill, Thornton road

Cockcroft John and Son, Brook st.; works Ovenden, near Halifax

Cockcroft Thomas, 24 Old Market, Market street; works Heaton

Coulters Jonathan, 14 Hartley's Buildings, Brook street; works Thornton road

Cousen Samuel, 22 Nag's Head Yard, Kirkgate; works Great Horton

Cousen Thomas, Cross lane, Great Horton

Craven Benjamin (moreen), Old Piecehall, works Allerton

Craven and Harrop, Brook street; works Waterloo Mill, and Thornton

Craven John & Joseph, Booth street; works Keighley

Craven Joshua, Old Piecehall; works Allerton

Craven Joshua, Charles street; works Thornton

Dalby James, Schuster's Buildings, Brook street; works Thornton road

Dean Henry & Son, 15 Old Market; works Colne

Denby John (moreen), 87 Old Piecehall; works Manningham

Dickinson & Barraclough, Charles street; works Hope Mill, Hunslet, Leeds

Eckroyd Thomas & Sons, Charles street; works Thornton road

Ellis & Holmes, Charles street; works Dub Mill, Bingley

Emsley George, New Piecehall; works Queen's Head, Clayton

Fawcett James, Charles street; works Greenfield, near Halifax

Foster John, New Piecehall; works Lower Heywood, Midgley

Fox Jabez, Industry Mill, Dudley Hill, Bowling

Greenwood William, junior, Brook street; works Oxenhope, near Keighley

Haigh George & Co. Brook street; works Holme Mill, Canal road

Hanson Thomas Anderson, Leeds road

Harris & Fison, Charles street; works Victoria Mill, Manchester road

Harrison John, 13 Old Piecehall; works Shelf, near Halifax

Harrop William, Charles street; works Cullingworth, Bingley

Hartley Henry, Brook street; works Trawden, near Colne

Hartley James and Son, Hope and Anchor Yard, Bank street; works Skipton

Hindle Edmund (and damask), Victoria Buildings, Cheapside
Hoadley & Pridie (and damask), 20 Nag's Head Yard, Kirkgate; works Archer street, Halifax
Hodgson John, Brook street; works Sunderland, Halifax
Holdsworth John & Co. Norfolk street, Bridge street; works Shaw Lodge Mill, Halifax
Holdsworth & White, Prospect Mill, Wakefield road, Bowling
Holmes Richard, 19 Talbot Yard, Kirkgate; works Heaton
Illingworth Armitage (moreen), 178 Old Piecehall; works Allerton
Illingworth Samuel (moreen), 59 Old Piecehall; works Allerton
Jagger Jonas, Hope and Anchor Yard, Bank street; works Clayton-Heights
Jennings Jonathan, Bank street; works Hewnden, Wilsden
Jowett Jonathan, Hope and Anchor Yard, Bank street; works Clayton
Jowett Thomas & Co. Old Market; works Bingley
Kitchen John, (moreen), Old Piecehall; works Clayton
Lambert James, 14 Old Market, Market street; works Haworth
Lund William, Hope and Anchor Yard, Bank street; works Keighley
Lythall & Haigh, Swaine street; works Caledonia Mill, Manchester road
M'Crea & Shephard (damask, &c.), Charles street; works Crosshills Mill, Halifax
Micklethwaite James, Hustler's Buildings, Market street; works Wakefield
Milligan Robert & William, Charles street; works Thornton road
Milligan Walter & Son, Brook street; works Harden, Bingley
Mitchell Henry, 16 Hartley's Buildings, Brook street; works Hebden Bridge
Moore John & Son, Brook street; works Morton, Bingley
Moore Thomas & James, New Piecehall; works Shibden Head, near Halifax
Murgatroyd John, Swaine street; works Midgley, near Halifax
Oddy Micah, Hope and Anchor Yard; works Northowram
Overend Richard, New Piecehall; works Crosshills, Keighley
Pearson Gent, 18 Old Piecehall; works North Bierley
Pease Henry & Co. Hall Ings; works Railway Mill, Darlington
Peel Thomas, Market street; works Cononley, Skipton
Peel William & Co. 40 Bridge street
Preston James, 20 Bank street; works Trawden, Colne
Priestley Job (moreen), 103 Old Piecehall; works Allerton
Priestley John, Bank street; works Wibsey
Priestley Simeon (damask), 22 Nag's Head Yard; works Illingworth Moor, near Halifax
Priestman John & Co. Brook street; works Ashfield Mill, Thornton road
Procter James, 10 Hartley's Buildings, Brook street; works Leeds road
Ramsden John & Co. Charles street; works Waterloo Mill, Brook street
Ratcliffe James & Son, Charles street; works Ovenden, Halifax

Rhodes Benjamin, 108 Old Piecehall; works Heaton

Ridings Edwin, Charles street; works Cannon Mill, Great Horton

Rigg James, New Piecehall; works Manchester road

Rigg Samuel, Sterling street, Manchester road

Robertshaw Isaac (moreen), 142 Old Piecehall; works Allerton

Robertshaw James, George Hotel Yard; works Allerton

Robinson Charles, 22 Nag's Head Yard; works Spence's Mill, Chapel lane

Robinson Joseph, Old Market place, Market street

Robinson Joseph, 22 Nag's Head Yard; works Spence's Mill, Chapel lane

Rogers George, Charles street; works Beehive Mill, Thornton road

Salt Titus, Brook street; works Union street

Smith Briscoe, Market street; works Crosshills, Keighley

Smith Joseph & Co. George Hotel Yard; works Dudley Hill

Smith Michael & Samuel, Brook street; works Dudley Hill

Smith Noah, 18 Old Market; works Pickles Hill, Keighley

Smith Thomas, Old Market; works Crosshills, Keighley

Smith William, Brook street; works Shelf, Halifax

Spencer John, 50 Old Market place; works Hainsworth, Keighley

Spiro Ferdinand, Booth street; works Westholme Mill, Thornton road

Stocks James, 12 Hartley's Buildings, Brook street; works Queen's Head, Halifax

Stowell, Sugden & Co. Bank street; works Holmetop, Little Horton

Sugden John, Brook street; works Dudley Hill

Sudgen Jonas & Brothers, Piecehall Yard; works Dobroyd

Sugden Thomas, 17 Old Market; works Lane End, near Keighley

Sutcliffe Abraham, 106 Old Piecehall; works Great Horton

Taylor C. & F. Booth street; works Shipley

Taylor John & Co. Old Market; works Fawcetholme Mill, Thornton road

Thompson Thomas (moreen), Old Piecehall; works Allerton

Thornton Benjamin, Charles street; works Gomersall, near Leeds

Topham Edward, Victoria Mill, Wakefield road, Bowling

Townend George & Brothers, Brook street; works Cullingworth, near Bingley

Townend Simeon, Charles street; works Thornton

Turner John, 25 New Piecehall; works Cononley, Skipton

Turner John & Robert, Booth street; works Holmetop Mill, Little Horton

Unwin Joshua, Queen's Mill, Millbank, Thornton road

Wade & Bairstow, Market street; works Laneclose Mill, Great Horton

Walbank Nathaniel, Old Piecehall; works Keighley

Waterhouse Thomas, Old Piecehall; works Keighley

Waud Brothers & Co. Brook street; works Britannia Mills, Portland street

Whalley John Henry, Brook street; works Trawden, Colne
White Samuel, George Hotel Yard; works Allerton
White Thomas (moreen), Old Piecehall; works Allerton
Wilcock David, New Piecehall; works Luddenden Foot, near Halifax
Wilkinson Joseph, Laycock's Mill, Thornton road
Wilkinson William, 23 Old Piecehall; works Thornton
Williamson John, Old Market; works Keighley
Wilson John & Co. Dale street, Kirkgate; works Crosshills, Keighley
Woller Samson, Brook street; works Manningham
Wright John, New Piecehall; works Wibsey
Wright Joseph, Old Piecehall; works Haworth

Worsted Top Makers.

Allen Edward & Robert and Co. Charles street
Baines Thomas, Swaine street
Bingham George (English & foreign), 9 Bolton road, Broadstones
Brown Joseph, Hustler's Buildings, Market street
Butterfield Samuel, Hustler's Buildings, Market street
Dalby Thomas, 16 Old Piecehall
Denton William, Swaine street, Hall Ings
Donisthorpe & Co. (and top machine patentees), Tyrrel street, and Thornton road
Fawcett Richard, Cheapside
Hartley Jarvis, Hustler's Buildings, Market street
Hudson John, 98 Old Piecehall

2 W

Lister Samuel Cunliffe, Mill street, Canal road
Marshall James, Bermondsey
Sugden & Webster, Hustler's Buildings, Market street
Watkinson Henry, Commercial street, Canal road

Yarn Merchants and Dealers.

Marked thus * are also Stuff Merchants.

Barthelmes & Pickup (linen and worsted), Dale street, Kirkgate
*Birkbeck, Morris & Co. 52 Cheapside
* Burghardt, Aders & Co. Bermondsey
* Butterfield Brothers, 1 Norfolk street, Bridge street
* Emanuel & Son, Exchange street, Kirkgate
Fawcett Richard, Cheapside
Firth James, Commercial street, Canal road.
Frank & Co. Duke street, Darley st.
* Hertz Martin & Co. Tyrrel street
* Heymann & Alexander (late A. J. Saalfeld & Co.), Charles street
Hiller Harry, 16 Dale street, and Hall street Manchester
* Liebert Bernhard, Hall Ings, and Manchester
Passavant Philip Jacob & Co. Cheapside
* Pregel George & Co. (linen and worsted), Swaine street
Quitzow, Schlesinger & Co. Bermondsey
* Schunck, Souchay & Co. Brook st.
*Semon, Siltzer & Co. 76 Chapel lane, Tyrrel street
* Steinthal & Co. Booth street, Hall Ings
Watkinson Henry, Commercial street, Canal road

COUNTRY MANUFACTURERS, MERCHANTS, SPINNERS, WOOLSTAPLERS, ETC.

Attending the Bradford Markets;

The Days of Attendance, Places of Residence, and the Inns they put up at—the generality of whom have no warehouses in the town.

The Merchants, Manufacturers, &c. who attend the Exchange will be found in a separate List.

Ackroyd T. & S. quarry owners, of Manningham, Packhorse, Westgate, —Thursdays

Addison Mr. (G. W. Addison & Sons), George Hotel, Market street— Thursday.

Aked Mr. of Halifax, New Inn, Tyrrel street—Thursdays.

Anderton Mr. of Cleckheaton, New Inn, Tyrrel street—Thursdays.

Anderton John, manufacturer, of Harden, Bull's Head, Westgate—Thurs.

Appleby Benjamin, corn miller, of Farnley, Swan, Market street—Thurs.

Barff William & Sons, woolstaplers, of Wakefield, Talbot, Kirkgate—Thurs.

Barker Exley, maltster, of Bramley, Packhorse, Westgate—Thursday.

Barker John, pattern designer, &c. of Thornton, Packhorse, Westgate— Thursdays.

Barker Robert and Sons, fellmongers, of Otley, Rawson's Arms, Market street, Thursday.

Barrett Mr. seedsman, of Wakefield, Bowling Green, Bridge street—Thurs.

Bastow Joshua, butter factor, of Wilsden, Packhorse, Westgate—Thurs.

Bateman James, card maker, of Wibsey, Bowling Green, Bridge street— Thursdays.

Bateman Samuel, card maker, of Wibsey, Bowling Green, Bridge street— Thursday.

Bean Mr. drysalter, of Colne, Packhorse, Westgate—Thursday.

Beattie Mr. corn miller, of Heckmondwike, Angel Inn, Westgate—Thurs.

Beck Mr. of Halifax, New Inn, Tyrrel street—Thursdays.

Bentley Thomas, dyer, Halifax, New Inn, Tyrrel street—Thursdays.

Blackburn Mr. of Brighouse, New Inn, Tyrrel street—Thursdays.

Bland Mr. maltster, &c. of Carlton, Junction Inn, Leeds road—Thursday.

Booker Mr. commission agent, of Leeds, Nag's Head, Kirkgate—Thursdays.

Botterill John, dyer, of Leeds, Swan, Market street—Thursday.

Bracewell John, butter factor, of Keighley, Hope and Anchor, Bank street—Thursdays.

Brear William, corn miller, of Shipley, Packhorse, Westgate—Thursdays.

Briscall Mr. manufacturer, of Leeds, Rawson's Arms, Market st.—Thurs.

Brook Mr. woolstapler, of Mirfield, Shoulder of Mutton, Kirkgate—Thurs.

Brook Mr. stuff merchant, Boar's Head, Market street—Mons. and Thurs.

Brunskill William, stuff merchant, of Manchester, Fleece, Bank street— Thursdays.

Burr & Weatherhead, solicitors, of Bingley, Brown Cow, Kirkgate—Thursdays.
Buster Mr. drysalter, of Leeds, New Inn, Tyrrel street—Thursdays
Carr Mr. of Halifax, New Inn, Tyrrel street—Mondays and Thursdays.
Cawlishaw Mr. of Manchester, New Inn, Tyrrel street—Thursdays.
Chew & Ferguson, stuff merchants, of Manchester, New Inn, Tyrrel street—Thursdays.
Chippendale John, timber merchant, of Otley, Rawson's Arms, Market street—Thursdays.
Clough Mr. manufacturer, of Keighley, Rawson's Arms, Market street—Thursdays.
Cousens Mr. (for Nathan Jennings), quarry owner, of Thornton, Packhorse, Westgate—Thursdays.
Crabtree Samuel, overseer of Heaton, Packhorse, Westgate—Thursdays.
Craven Jonathan, quarry owner, of Thornton, Packhorse, Westgate—
Crossley & Harper, dyers, of Wheatley, Boar's Head, Market street—Mondays and Thursdays.
Crossley Henry, dyer, of Brighouse, Boar's Head, Market street—Mondays and Thursdays.
Crossley James, shuttle and picker maker, of Todmorden, Fleece, Bank street—Mondays and Thursdays.
Curtis Mr. farmer, of Hawksworth, Packhorse, Westgate—Thursdays.
Davis Mr. of Huddersfield, New Inn, Tyrrel street—Thursdays
Dawson Joseph, woollen cloth manufacturer, of Yeadon, Shoulder of Mutton, Kirkgate—Thursdays.
Dawson Mr. lime burner, of Bingley, Packhorse, Westgate—Thursdays.
Dawson Samuel, woolstapler, of Wakefield, Bull's Head, Westgate—Thurs.
Dobson John, overseer of Thornton, Packhorse, Westgate, Thursdays.
Drake John, veterinary surgeon, Angel Inn, Westgate.
Eastburne Robert, dyer, of Halifax, New Inn, Tyrrel street—Thursdays
Ellis Mr. woolstapler, of Keighley, Shoulder of Mutton, Kirkgate—Thurs.
England William and Son, corn millers, of Bingley, Packhorse, Westgate—Thursdays.
Fairbank William, coal owner, of Allerton, Packhorse, Westgate—Thurs.
Farrar Samuel, fellmonger, of Horsforth, Rawson's Arms, Market street—Thursdays.
Farmery George, fancy shawls, Fayley, Eccleshill, Wool Packs, Well street—Mondays and Thursdays.
Firth John, of Heckmondwike, Commercial Inn, Tyrrel street—Monday and Thursdays.
Fielding Mr. drysalter, of Hebden Bridge, Boar's Head, Market street—Mondays and Thursdays.
Foster Mr. of Queenshead, Halifax, New Inn, Tyrrel street—Thursdays.
Gaukroger James, cotton warp dealer, of Hebden Bridge, Fleece, Bank street—Thursday.
Gelderd John, quarry owner, of Thornton, Packhorse, Westgate—Thurs.
Goldthorp Mr. of Cleckheaton, New Inn, Tyrrell street—Thursday.
Greenwood William, butter factor, of Colne, Packhorse, Westgate—Thurs.
Greenwood Mr. corn miller, Wibsey Bankfoot, Fleece Inn, Bank street—Thursday.
Haigh Charles, woolstapler, of Halifax, Rawson's Arms, Market st—Thurs.

Haigh Thomas, dyer, of Newlay, Swan, Market street—Thursdays.
Hardy Abraham, corn miller, of Thornton, Packhorse, Westgate—Thurs.
Hardy Richard, cattle dealer, of Tong, Fleece, Bank street—Thursday.
Hardy Thomas, top maker, of Heaton, Packhorse, Westgate—Thursdays.
Hartley James, draper, of Thornton, Packhorse, Westgate—Thursdays.
Hartley Mr. of Halifax, New Inn, Tyrrel street—Thursday,
Harvey Mr. of Halifax, New Inn, Tyrrel street—Thursday.
Heaton John, stuff merchant, of Leed, Talbot, Kirkgate—Thursday.
Heaton Mr. (Akroyd and Son, of Halifax), George Hotel, Market street—Thursdays.
Heaton Mr. woolstapler, of Silsden, Packhorse, Westgate—Thursdays.
Helliwell and Dibb, cattle dealers, of Manningham, Packhorse, Westgate, —Thursdays.
Helliwell Thomas, auctioneer, &c. of Halifax, Fleece, Bank street—Mondays and Thursdays.
Higginbottom James, spinner, of Halifax, Fleece, Bank street—Thursdays.
Hill John, quarry owner, of Thornton, Packhorse, Westgate—Thursdays.
Hindle Mr. woolstapler, of Haslingden, Shoulder of Mutton, Kirkgate—
Hird Mr. of Huddersfield, New Inn, Tyrrel street—Thursday.
Hirst and Roper, quarry owners, of Allerton, Packhorse, Westgate—Thursdays.
Hirst John, land agent, Bull's Head, Westgate—Thursday.
Hirst Mr. of Halifax, New Inn, Tyrrel street—Thursday.
Hobkin Daniel, malster, of Clayton, Bull's Head, Westgate—Thursday.
Holdsworth John, quarry owner, of Allerton, Packhorse, Westgate—Thursdays.
Holdsworth Joseph and John, woolstaplers, of Halifax, Boar's Head, Market street—Thursdays.
Holdsworth Mr. of Cleckheaton, New Inn, Tyrrel street—Thursday.
Holdsworth Mr. of Halifax, New Inn, Tyrrel street—Thursday.
Holmes Abraham, agent, of Cottingley, Packhorse, Westgate—Thursdays.
Holroyd Henry and Co. dyers, of Leeds, Swan, Market street—Thursdays.
Hudson John, grocer, of Thornton, Packhorse, Westgate—Thursdays.
Hudson Mr. Bromby, near Leeds, New Inn, Tyrrel street—Thursdays,
Huntriss Mr. woolstapler, of Halifax, New Inn, Tyrrel street—Thursday.
Jowett Henry, contractor, of Leeds, Boar's Head, Market street—Mondays, Thursdays and Saturdays.
Kay John, quarry owner, of Heaton, Packhorse, Westgate—Thursdays.
Kaye Mr. tanner, of Burley, Bowling Green, Bridge street—Thursday.
Keighley John & Brothers, stuff manufacturers, Bowling Green, Bridge street—Thursday.
Kelley George, woolstapler, of Heckmondwike, George Hotel, Market street—Thursdays.
Kershaw Mr. corn miller, of Halifax, Fleece Inn, Bank street—Thursday.
Knowles David, quarry owner, of Queen's Head, Bowling Green, Bridge street—Thursday.
Knowles Jonas, tanner, of Cottingley Bridge, Bull's Head, Westgate—Thursday.

Knowles Jonas & John, corn millers, of Shipley, Packhorse, Westgate—Thursdays.

Land Mr. cotton band manufacturer, of Dewsbury, Fleece, Bank street—Thursdays.

Lassey & Hullah, woollen cloth manufacturers, of Dewsbury, Shoulder of Mutton, Kirkgate—Thursday

Laycock Richard, spirit merchant, of Bingley, Brown Cow, Kirkgate——Thursday.

Lewis Mr. of Halifax, New Inn, Tyrrel street—Thursday.

Lowe & Gommersall, card makers, of Tong, Shoulder of Mutton, Kirkgate—Thursday.

Lund James, cotton band manufacturer, of Lee Moorgate, Nag's Head, Kirkgate—Thursdays.

Mariner B. & W. worsted spinners, of Keighley, Talbot, Kirkgate—Thurs.

Marshall Mr. New Inn, Tyrrel street—Thursday.

Mitchell James, cotton warp dealer, of Oldham, Fleece, Bank street—Mondays and Thursdays.

Musgrave Mr. maltster, of Kirkstall, Hope and Anchor, Bank street—Thursdays.

Newsholme William, woolstapler, of Haworth, Shoulder of Mutton, Kirkgate—Thursdays.

North John, fellmonger, of Bailiff Bridge, Rawson's Arms, Market street—Thursdays.

Oates Mr. of Huddersfield, Nag's Head, Kirkgate—Thursdays.

Oates Mr. reed and heald maker, of Armley, Swan, Market st.—Thurs.

Oates Ingham and Sons, dyers, of Halfax, Fleece, Bank street—Mondays and Thursdays.

Ormrod Mr. merchant, of Brighouse, New Inn, Tyrrel street—Thursdays

Parker Hugh, woollen cloth manufacturer, of Windhill, Shoulder of Mutton, Kirkgate—Thursday.

Parker John, woollen cloth manufacturer, of Windhill, Shoulder of Mutton, Kirkgate—Thursdays.

Parkin Mr. Wood, merchant, of Apperley Bridge, Bowling Green, Bridge street—Thursday.

Pearson James, corn miller, of Horton, Packhorse, Westgate—Thursdays

Pearson Nathan, relieving officer for Shipley, &c. Packhorse, Westgate—Thursdays.

Penny Mr. corn miller, of Mirfield, Brown Cow, Kirkgate—Thursdays

Pickles Henry, overseer, of Shipley, Packhorse, Westgate—Thursday.

Pighills Mr. corn miller, of Apperley Bridge, White Lion, Kirkgate—Thurs.

Pilling Messrs. corn millers, Bull's Head, Westgate—Thursdays.

Pitchforth Henry, drysalter, of Brighouse, Boar's Head, Market street—Thursdays.

Popplewell Mr. of Birstall, Commercial Inn, Tyrrel street—Thursdays

Priestley Midgley (for Jonathan Priestley), quarry owner, of Thornton, Packhorse, Westgate—Thursday.

Rayner John, drysalter, of Pudsey, Swan, Market street—Thursday.

Rayner William, cotton band manufacturer, of Wakefield, Swan, Market street—Thursday.

Rhodes Mr. farmer, of Shipley, Packhorse, Westgate—Thursday.

Robertshaw Joseph, clogger, of Thornton, Packhorse, Westgate—Thurs.

Robertshaw Joseph, maltster and farmer, of Allerton, Packhorse, Westgate—Thursday.
Robertshaw Joshua, land agent, of Allerton, Packhorse, Westgate—Thurs.
Roper Messrs. manufacturers, of Keighley, Rawson's Arms, Market street—Mondays and Thursdays.
Rowntree Mr. corn miller, of Kirkstall, Hope and Anchor, Bank street—Thursday.
Sargeant Mr. (for Hird, Dawson & Hardy, Low Moor Iron Works), Talbot Kirkgate—Thursdays.
Scott George, corn miller, of Pudsey, Junction Inn, Leeds road—Thurs.
Sellers Godfrey, card maker, of Wike, Boar's Head, Market street—Thursdays.
Shaw Mr. of Huddersfield, New Inn, Tyrrel street—Thursday.
Silson Benjamin, farmer, of Heaton, Packhorse, Westgate—Thursdays.
Slack Mr. manufacturer, of Keighley, Boar's Head, Market street—Thurs.
Smallpage Mr. tailor, of Leeds, New Inn, Tyrrel street—Thursdays.
Smith Jonathan, dyer, of Halifax, New Inn, Tyrrel street—Thursday.
Smith Joseph, reed and heald maker, of Keighley, Nag's Head, Kirkgate—Thursdays.
Smith Isaac Skirrow, cattle dealer, &c. of Cottingley, Packhorse, Westgate—Thusdays.
Smith Mr. machine maker, of Keighley, Packhorse, Westgate—Thursdays
Smith N. butter factor, of Keighley, Hope and Anchor, Bank street—Thurs.
Smith & Son, machine makers, of Keighley, Rawson's Arms, Market street—Thursdays.
Stead Thomas, cotton spinner, of Huddersfield, Fleece, Bank street—Thursdays.
Sugden Joseph, drysalter, Boar's Head, Market street—Thursdays.
Sugden Mr. of Brighouse, New Inn, Tyrrel street—Thursday.
Sugden Thomas & Son, corn millers and maltsters, of Brighouse, Brown Cow, Kirkgate—Thursdays.
Sutcliffe Jonas, commission agent, of Cottingley, Swan, Market street—Thursdays.
Sykes George, maltster, of Driglington, Nag's Head, Kirkgate—Thursday.
Thackray Thomas, fellmonger, currier, &c. of Otley, Rawson's Arms, Market street—Thursdays.
Thomas William, stationer, of Thornton, Packhorse, Westgate—Thurs.
Thomas William, manufacturer, of Windhill, Shoulder of Mutton, Kirkgate—Thursdays.
Thomas William, spirit merchant, of Haworth, Packhorse, Westgate—Thursdays.
Thurles Mr. dyer, of Huddersfield, Swan, Market street—Thursday.
Townend Mr. of Thornton, New Inn, Tyrrel street—Thursdays.
Traughton James, maltster, of Drighlington, Roebuck, Ivegate—Thurs.
Umpleby Mr. farmer and grazier, of Hawksworth, Packhorse, Westgate—Thursday.
Varley Messrs. Nag's Head, Kirkgate—Thursday.
Vickers Mr. drysalter, of Leeds, New Inn, Tyrrel street—Thursday.
Waddington Joseph, dyer, of Leeds, Swan, Market street—Thursday.
Waddington Joseph, grocer, of Thornton, Packhorse, Westgate—Thurs.
Wade Jesse, corn miller, of Thornton, Packhorse, Westgate—Thursday

Wade Jonas, (for the Clayton Co-Operative Provision Company), Bull's Head, Westgate—Thursday.
Wallbank Mr. manufacturer, of Keighley, Shoulder of Mutton, Kirkgate, Thursday.
Walker Mr. Nag's Head, Kirkgate—Thursday.
Walker Mr. of Stainland, New Inn, Tyrrel street—Thursday.
Walker Mr. of Halifax, New Inn, Tyrrell street—Thursday.
Walker Thomas, fellmonger, of Baildon, Rawson's Arms, Market street—Thursdays.
Walton James, size dealer, of Halifax, Rawson's Arms, Market street—Monday and Thursday.
Walton John, size dealer, of Halifax, Rawson's Arms, Market street—Monday and Thursday.
Watson Joseph, fellmonger, &c. of Leeds, Rawson's Arms, Market street—Thursdays.
Whitley Thomas, farmer, of Allerton, Packhorse, Westgate—Thursdays.
Whitworth Messrs. manufacturers, of Halifax, New Inn, Tyrrel street—Thursday.
Wignall Joseph and John, butter factors, of Keighley, Hope and Anchor, Bank street—Thursdays,
Wilson Mr. leather cutter, of Low Moor, Roebuck, Ivegate—Thursdays.
Wilson Samuel, waste dealer, of Pudsey, Shoulder of Mutton, Kirkgate—Monday, Wednesday and Thursday
Wilson Thomas, cotton warp dealer, of North Bierley, Fleece, Bank street—Thursdays.
Winter John, grocer, of Thornton, Packhorse, Westgate—Thursdays.
Wood Isaac, farmer, of Thornton, Packhorse, Westgate—Thursdays.
Wood & Son, manufacturers, of Allerton, Packhorse, Westgate—Thurs.
Wood Mr. manufacturer, of Sowerby Bridge, New Inn, Tyrrel street—Thursday.
Wright John & Son, corn millers and paper makers, of Shipley, Bull's Head, Westgate—Thursday
Wright Joseph, grocer, of Wilsden, Packhorse, Westgate—Thursdays.
Wright Mr. woolstapler, of Silsden, Packhorse, Westgate—Thursdays.
Yates Mr. cotton warp manufacturer, of Manchester, New Inn, Tyrrel street—Thursday

---

FOR CARRIERS, &c.

See next Page.

CARRIERS, COACHES, ETC.

CARRIERS BY RAILWAY.

LANCASHIRE AND YORKSHIRE RAILWAY COMPANY, General Carriers, in connexion with other railway companies, to all parts of England and Scotland.—GOODS' RECEIVING WAREHOUSE, Vicar lane—CARVER & Co. agents to the company.

MIDLAND COUNTIES RAILWAY, General Carriers, in connection with other railway companies, to all parts of England and Scotland.—GOODS' RECEIVING WAREHOUSE, Railroad street, School street,—Mr. Robert Boyes head clerk.

CARVER, Chaplin & Horne, to Bristol, London, &c. Hall Ings; Mr. Saml. Harrison agent.

CARRIERS BY WAGGON.

FROM THE VARIOUS INNS AND TAVERNS, &c.

To ALLERTON, thrice a week, Thomas Leach, Pack Horse, Westgate.
To BATLEY CAR, Huddersfield, &c. twice a week, William Lister, Brown Cow, Kirkgate.
To BINGLEY daily, Enoch Bailey, Nag's Head, Kirkgate.
To Bingley, daily, Thompson Foulds, Brown Cow, Kirkgate.
To BRAMLEY and Leeds, Thursday only, William Boyne, Rawson's Arms, Market street.
To BRIGHOUSE, Monday and Thursday, Thomas Crowther, New Inn, Tyrrel street.
To BURLEY, Otley, &c. twice a week, John Barrett, Nelson Inn, Northgate
To COLNE, Bingley, Keighley, Crosshills, &c. Thurs. only, James Turner, King's Head, Westgate.
To DEWSBURY, Thursday, James Armitage, Hope and Anchor, Bank st.
To FARSLEY, Thurs. only, Isaac Allerton, Ship, and the Woolpacks, Well street.
To GUISELEY and Leeds, Mon. and Thurs. George Whittaker, Rawson's Arms, Market street.
To GOMERSALL, Heckmondwike, Dewsbury, &c. Mon. and Thurs. Edwd. Butler, Brown Cow, Kirkgate.
To Gomersall, Monday and Thursday, Crispin Smith, Hope and Anchor, Bank street
To HALIFAX, and from thence forwarded to Sowerby Bridge, Hebden Bridge, Todmorden, Rochdale and Manchester; George Clough, Thornton road.
To Halifax, Elland, Huddersfield, and from thence forwarded to Todmorden, Rochdale, and other parts of Lancashire; Joseph Farrar, Back Tyrrel street

To HARDEN and Bingley, twice a week, John Foster, Royal Oak, Kirkgate

To HAWORTH and Halifax, twice a week, William Todd, Bull's Head, Westgate

To HECKMONDWIKE, Mon. and Thurs. J. Riddlesworth, Brown Cow, Kirkgate.

To Heckmondwike, twice a week, John Firth, Commercial Inn, Tyrrel st.

To HIGHTOWN, Robertown and Cleckheaton, Mon. and Thurs. Samuel Lee, Fleece, Bank street.

To HUDDERSFIELD, and from thence forwarded to Honley, Holmfirth, Lockwood, and various parts of Lancashire; George Armitage, Thornton road.

To IDLE, Thurs. only, James Spence, Malt Shovel, Kirkgate.

To Idle, Thurs. and Sat. Benjamin Greaves, Wool Packs, Well street.

To Idle, daily, William Illingworth, Wool Packs, Well street.

To KEIGHLEY, daily, William Walker, Brown Cow, Kirkgate.

To Keighley, four days a week, Thomas Wilcock, Nelson, Northgate

To Keighley, Kendal, and Lancaster, Mon. and Thurs. Richard Peckover, Royal Oak, Kirkgate.

To LEEDS, and from thence by the Aire and Calder Co. to Goole, Hull, London, Norwich, Yarmouth, Aberdeen, Glasgow, and various parts of of Scotland; Mary Firth, Thornton road.

To Leeds, twice a week, James Walker, Prince of Wales, Leeds road

To Leeds, doily, and from thence forwarded to Harrogate, Ripon, Knaresbro', Thirsk, Northallerton, and the northern parts of Yorkshire John Humble, Illingworth's Court, Westgate.

To Leeds, Harrogate, Ripon, and Snaith, Thursdays only, John Jackson, Wool Packs, Well street.

To Leeds, Keighley, and Bingley, four times a week, Joseph Bastow, Bull's Head, Westgate.

To LOW MOOR, once a week, John Wood, Fleece Inn, Bank street

To MYTHOLMROYD, Halifax, &c. twice a week, David Taylor, Brown Cow, Kirkgate.

To OAKENSHAW, Thursday and Saturday, John Sugden, Hope and Anchor, Bank street.

To OTLEY, Skipton &c. three times a week, John Robinson, White Lion, Kirkgate.

To OVENDEN, Monday and Thursday, Peter Ambler, Hope and Anchor, Bank street.

To QUEENSHEAD, Halifax, Mon. and Thurs. John Yates, Fleece Inn, Bank street.

To SETTLE, Keighley, &c. thrice a week, William Driver, Shoulder of Mutton, Kirkgate.

To SHIPLEY and Baildon, daily, George Taylor, Shoulder of Mutton Kirkgate.

To Shipley, and Windhill, Mon. and Thurs. Joseph Pitts, Malt Shovel, Kirkgate.

To Shipley, twice a week, William Hall, Malt Shovel, Kirkgate.

To Shipley, twice a week, Samuel Crabtree, Malt Shovel, Kirkgate.

To SKIPTON, Kendal, Settle, &c. Mon. and Thurs. William Farrar, Royal Oak, Kirkgate.

To SUTTON, Keighley, twice a week, James Briggs, Fleece, Bank street.

To **Thornton**, daily, Jonathan Craven, Brown Cow, Kirkgate.
To Thornton, thrice a week, Samuel Bentham, Packhorse, Westgate.
To **Uppertown**, Thornton and Halifax, three times a week, Jonathan Whittaker, Bull's Head, Westgate.
To **Wakefield**, Mon. and Thurs. Thomas Rennard, Rawson's Arms, Market street.
To **Wilsden**, daily, William Anderson, White Swan, Market street.
To **Yeadon**, daily, William Holmes, Ship Inn, Well street.

CARRIERS BY WATER.

Bradford and **Selby Fly Boats' Company** (Pearson & Co.), to Leeds, Selby, &c. Canal road; John Adamson agent.

Leeds and **Liverpool Canal Carrying Company**; fly boats in connection with the Union Company's Vessels, to and from Liverpool, Leeds, &c.; Goods' Receiving Warehouse Thornton road; Jas. Hepper agent.

Wood Joseph & Co. to Goole, and in connection with steam vessels to London, Hull, and Newcastle; also with fly boats to Leicester, Nottingham, Gainsbro', and other intermediate towns; office Canal road.

COACHES, RAILWAY TRAINS, OMNIBUSES, &c.

TO THE VARIOUS PLACES SPECIFIED.

COACHES.

To **Halifax** twice a day—at quarter-past ten and one o'clock, from the Bowling Green, Bridge street; Joseph Baxter proprietor.
To **Leeds** once a day—at nine o'clock, from the Bowling Green, Bridge street; Jacob Wood proprietor.
To **Harrogate**, during the season, every day, Sunday excepted, from the Bowling Green, Bridge street.
To **Ilkley**, during the season, on succeeding Sundays, Mondays, Wednesdays, and Fridays, from the Bowling Green, Bridge street.

OMNIBUS.

To **Heckmondwike**, on Mondays and Thursdays, at four o'clock, from the Commercial Inn, Tyrrel street.

LEEDS AND BRADFORD RAILWAY.

Station—bottom of Kirkgate.

To **Leeds** fifteen times a day
To Manchester, six do.
To Liverpool, five do.
To Ingleton, four do.
To Skipton, seven do.

To Keighley, seven times a day
To Colne, do.
To Shipley, fifteen times a day.
To Lancaster, four ditto.

Passengers can be booked at this office for Stations on the *East Lancashire* and *North Western* Railways.

An *Omnibus* attends every train at the Skipton station to convey passengers to any part of the town.

LANCASHIRE AND YORKSHIRE RAILWAY.

STATION—Leeds and Wakefield Road.

To MANCHESTER, eight times daily	To Dewsbury, seven times daily
To Liverpool, five ditto	To Cleckheaton, nine ditto
To Bury, six ditto	To Preston, five ditto
To Doncaster, five ditto	To Normanton, eight ditto
To Fleetwood, three ditto	To Wakefield, nine ditto

Also to Wigan, Pontefract, Goole, Lincoln, &c.

GOODS and PARCELS conveyed (in connection with other Railway Companies, to all parts of England and Scotland.

*** The above is not intended as a Railway Time Table, but merely gives the average *number* of trains to each place daily.

MERCHANTS, MANUFACTURERS, SPINNERS, WOOL-STAPLERS, &c.

RESIDENT IN BRADFORD AND THE CLOTHING DISTRICTS,

WHO ATTEND THE BRADFORD EXCHANGE ON THE MARKET DAYS.

Mr. Isaac Wright, *Treasurer.*
— E. Preller
— William Foster
— Cowling Ackroyd
— John Thistlethwaite
— H. W. Saches
— M. Meyertien
— J. Knowles
— JohnTwycross
— Maud Stead
— Henry Forbes
— George Taylor
— Joshua Illingworth
— Edward Ripley
— Henry Smith
— Francis Beswick
— William L. Bunting
— Jacob Arnold Unna
— B. Buck
— Joseph Oddy
— John Parkinson

Mr B. Harrison
— Edmund Hall
— Joseph Dawson
— Henry Haigh
— Joseph Hollings
— A. M. Goldschmidst
— N. Joseph
— Henry Harris
— Alfred Harris
— M. Harris
— John Light
— R. M. Scholefield
— Thomas Murgatroyd
— Richard Ridehalgh
— David Rouse
— Edward A. Barret
— James Firth
— R. G. Aked
— Thomas Lockwood
— R. H. Robinson

Mr Manoah Rhodes
— J. A. Enipper
— Richard Fawcett
— Samuel Storey
— John Gough
— James Wood
— J. E. Taylor
— Julius Schlesinger
— J. Morren
— William Milnes
— Thomas Holmes
— William Cooke
— John Atkinson
— Edward Allen
— J. L. M'Michan
— Marten Schlesinger
— J. Gibson
— Robert Allen
— S. M. Pein
— James Douglas
— Joseph Hill
— William Garnett
— Louis Becher
— William Duckett
— John Clayton
— C. A. T. Muller
— James Lambert
— C. Speyer
— W. C. Haigh
— George Alderson
— William Marten
— Harrison Milligan
— William Horsfall
— Timothy Horsfall
— C. Clough
— Joshua Lupton
— Alfred Bankart
— Charles Walker
— G. R. Wiechus
— Alfred Illingworth
— W. E. Forster
— H. W. Blackburn
— Jonathan Knowles
— Jacob Behrens
— W. H. Birchall
— John Rand
— William Rand
— M. Hertz
— George Rogers
— Thomas Beaumont
— J. P. Frank
— Richard Wrigley

Mr James Hammond
— J. S. Harrison
— Thomas Willett
— Frederick Hattersley
— Richard Newby
— James Leeming
— John Clegg
— George Turner, jun.
— Samuel Laycock
— H. Frankel
— John Taylor
— William Cheesebrough
— S. L. Tee
— George Brown
— William Peel
— J. A. Busfeild
— S. Anderton
— Richard Haigh
— Benjamin Wild
— D. Peckover
— M. Schonfeld
— John Lowenthal
— M. Birkbeck
— Christopher Waud
— John Cooke
— Charles Semon
— Henry Michael Steinthal
— Samuel Hutchinson
— Thomas Dewhirst
— Julius Kolfsen
— A. Quitzow
— C. T. Turner
— Frank Rouse
— G. Kerstein
— E. Casson
— M. Mahony
— John Darlington
— William George
— Alfred Cheesebrough
— J. F. Reickmann
— H. Schutt
— S. Bergel
— Thomas Renton
— Charles Lockwood
— Thomas Sutcliffe
— James Monies
— L. Fulda
— Thomas Dixon
— Samuel Margerison
— Joshua Mann
— William Rouse
— Joseph Cheesebrough

Mr E. Barthelmes
— Thomas Harrison
— Josh. Smith
— William Hick
— William Lythall
— R. A. Booker
— William Wells
— D. Illingworth
— J. Hurter
— H. Neumann
— Henry Perfect
— Archibald M'Nought
— S. Lassan
— Thomas Buck
— William Coates
— Dr. Farrar
— J. V. Godwin
— Dr. Godwin
— Thomas Ambler
— R. P. Harris
— David Ramsden
— Edward Behrens
— W. P. Whitfield
— James Hodson
— P. Passavant, jun.
— E. Waud
— William Millthorp
— William Firth
— Joseph Fugill
— Miles Tillotson
— Henry Brown
— James Wilson
— William Dewhirst
— George S. Meyer
— James Green
— Robert Heaton Sutton
— Edward Hailstone
— Thomas Clayton
— Isaac Hollings
— John Buckup
— Joseph Holmes
— Mark Dawson
— L. Weil
— George Turner
— A. Kolfsen
— Thomas Dewhirst
— F. Spiro
— John Greaves
— N. Briggs
— M. Goldstein
— C. E. Parkinson
— Samuel Selby

Mr Edward Fowler
— William Walker
— J. D. Marten
— Murgatroyd
— John Siltzer
— A. Engelmann
— Thomas Hollings
— Thomas Rennards
— Thomas Haigh
— John M. Hustler
— George Knowles
— Robert Milligan
— H. O. Mawson
— William Fison
— R. Goldthorp, Cleckheaton
— W. H. Bilbrough, Menston
— Edward Williams, Manchester
— F. Sykes, Cleckheaton
— J. Appleyard, Halifax
— E. Atkinson, Cleckheaton
— William Huntriss, Halifax
— J. W. Youd, Halifax
— John Clough, Keighley
— William Booker, Leeds
— Robert Sutcliffe, Idle
— Joseph Smith, Keighley
— Joseph Morris, Halifax
— J. H. Mills, Leeds
— Samuel Walker, Halifax
— Joseph Hirst, Leeds
— Thomas Williamson, Cleckheaton
— John Holland, Brighouse
— William Oldenbaurg, Leeds
— J. B. Dewhirst, Skipton
— G. Anderton, Cleckheaton
— W. Ackroyd, Birkenshaw
— Thomas Ackroyd, Birkenshaw
— T. M. Horsfall, Hawksworth Hall
— William Lister, Halifax
— Thomas Fison, Rawden
— William Dawson, Wakefield
— Henry Birchall, Leeds
— S. Clapham, Esholt
— H. C. M'Crea, Halifax
— John Foster, Queen's Head
— Henry Whitaker, Otley
— P. L. Wolf, Leeds
— S. Johnson, Halifax
— C. Bairstow, Sutton
— William Marriner, Keighley
— John Holdsworth, Halifax
— James Hubbard, Leeds
— W. H. Greaves

PLACES OF PUBLIC WORSHIP.

List of the ESTABLISHED CHURCHES in Bradford, Bowling, Horton, Manningham, with their Situations, Names and Residences of the Clergy, and Times of Service.

The Days of Service at the respective Places of Worship are Sundays, when not otherwise named.

NAMES OF CHURCHES.	SITUATION.	MINISTERS AND THEIR RESIDENCES.	TIME OF SERVICE.
St. Peter's (parish church)	High street, Stott Hill	Rev. John Burnett, LL.D. vicar; Greenhill House, Leeds road Rev. W. F. Black, M.A. senior curate, Hillside. Rev. Nathaniel Cooper, B.A. assistant curate; house Brunswick place	Sunday morning at quarter past ten, three in the afternoon, summer; half-past two, winter; evening service, half-past six: morning prayers daily at nine, and full service every Wednesday evening.
Christ Church	Top of Darley street	Rev. Wm. Morgan, B.A. incumbent, Snow Hill	Morning quarter past ten, three afternoon, and quarter past six evening; service every Tuesday evening.
St. James's	Manchester road	Rev. Wm. Sherwood, A.M. incumbent; St. James's Square Rev. John Richards, M. A. curate, Manor Row	Morning half-past ten, and evening half-past six.

St. John's	Manchester road	Not appointed	Morning half-past ten, half-past two, and half-past six.
St. John's	Wakefield road, Bowling	Rev. Joseph Loxdale Frost, A.M. incumbent, Wakefield road Rev. Geo. Tolson Cotham, curate, Wakefield road	Morning quarter past ten, three afternoon, and half-past six evening.
St. Judes's	Lumb lane, Manningham	Rev. James Cooper, M.A. incumbent, Belle Vue Rev. J. W. Adams, B.A. curate, Hanover Square	Morning half-past ten, three afternoon, and half-past six evening.
Bierley Chapel	Bierley lane, Bowling	Rev. John Barber, M. A. incumbent, Parsonage, Bierley	Morning half past ten, three afternoon, and half-past six evening.
St. Matthew's	Bankfoot, Bowling	Not appointed	Morning half-past ten, and afternoon at three.
St. Paul's	Manningham	Rev. Welbury Mitton incumbent, house Manningham	Morning half past ten, and three afternoon.
Episcopal Chapel	Great Horton	Rev. J. C. Boddington, incumbent, Great Horton Rev. J. H. Edmonds, B.A. curate, High street, Great Horton. Rev. W. P. Bennett, Southgate, Great Horton	Morning half-past ten, afternoon three, evening half-past six.
Divine Service in the National School Rooms	Daisy-hill, Manningham, and at New Leeds	Rev. Peter Henderson, B.A. and other Ministers	Morning, afternoon, and evening.

A LIST OF THE ROMAN CATHOLIC & DISSENTING CHAPELS

In Bradford, Bowling, Horton, and Manningham.

Their Names, Situations, and Ministers' Names and Residences.—The hours of divine service are for Sundays, unless otherwise stated.

BAPTIST CHAPELS.

Zion—Bridge street, Rev. J. P. Chown, Little Horton lane—Service in the morning half-past ten, afternoon three, and half-past six evening.

Prospect Street, Thornton road, Rev. Henry Rose, Westgrove street—Service in the morning at half-past ten, afternoon half-past two, and six evening.

Westgate, Rev. Henry Dowson, Brick lane—Service in the morning half-past ten, afternoon half-past two, and half-past six evening.

CATHOLIC CHAPEL.

Stott Hill, Rev. Thomas Harrison and Rev. Wm. Arnold, adjoining the chapel—Service in the morning at eight, nine, and half-past ten; evening at half-past six; daily morning service at eight.

FRIENDS' MEETING HOUSE.

Bridge street—Meet in the morning at ten, afternoon three, winter; summer, half-past five; and on Wednesday mornings at ten o'clock.

INDEPENDENT CHAPELS.

Parkgate, High street, Rev. Walter Scott and Rev. Danl. Fraser—Service in the morning half-past ten, afternoon three, and half-past 6 evening.

Little Horton Lane, Rev. Jonathan Glyde, Melbourne place—Service in the morning half-past ten, and the afternoon at two.

Salem, Manor Row, Rev. J. G. Miall, Brunswick Place—Service in the morning half past ten, and half-past six evening.

WESLEYAN METHODIST CHAPELS.

Eastbrook, Leeds road, (various ministers)—Service in the morning half-past ten, afternoon half past two, and evening six.

Kirkgate, (various ministers)—Services as last.

Great Horton Road, (various ministers)—Services as last.

Black Abbey, (various ministers)—Services as last.

Bradford Moor, (various ministers)—Services as last.

Clayton Lane, (various ministers)—Service in the morning half-past ten, afternoon at two, and six evening.

Spring street, Wharf street, (various ministers)—Service in the morning half past ten, and evening six.

Dudley Hill, (various ministers)—Service in the morning half-past ten, afternoon two, and evening, six.

WESLEYAN ASSOCIATION CHAPELS.

Bridge street and top of Westgate, (ministers various),—Service in the morning half-past ten, afternoon half-past two, evening half-past six.

WESLEYAN NEW CONNEXION CHAPEL.

Horton lane, (ministers various).—Service in the morning half-past ten, afternoon half-past two, evening six.

PRIMITIVE METHODIST CHAPELS.

Great Horton road, (various ministers)—Service in the morning half-past ten, afternoon, two, and evening at six.

Eudley Hill, (various ministers)—Service as last.

Manchester road, (various ministers—Service as last.

Laister Dyke, (various ministers)—Service as last.

Daisy Hill, Manningham, (various ministers)—Service as last.

MORAVIAN CHAPEL.

Little Horton Lane, Rev. John Carey, adjoining the chapel.—Service in the morning half-past ten, afternoon half-past two.

UNITARIAN CHAPEL.

Chapel Lane, Tyrrel street, Rev. John Howard Ryland, Hanover Square—Service in the morning quarter before eleven, evening half-past six.

UNITED PRESBYTERIAN CHURCH.

Drewton street, Rev. Alexander Wallace, Hanover Square—Service in the morning half-past ten, evening half-past six.

PUBLIC BUILDINGS, OFFICES, INSTITUTIONS,

&c. &c.

WITH THE SEVERAL OFFICERS ATTACHED TO EACH ESTABLISHMENT.

BRADFORD INFIRMARY AND DISPENSARY.

SITUATE IN LUMB LANE AND WESTGATE.

PATRONS :

George Baron, Esq. Clock House, Manningham
Right Hon. Earl of Rosse, Heaton Hall
Robert Milligan, Esq. Acacia House, near Rawden

President—Rev. S. Sharp

Vice-Presidents—All Individual Donors of £50. or upwards.

Treasurer—Henry Harris, Esq.

Medical Officers.

John Onthwaite, M. D. Consulting Physician
William Macturk, M. D. and William Taylor, M. D. Physicians
Mr. Illingworth Consulting Surgeon, assisted by Mr. Casson, Mr. Douglas, Mr. Roberts and Mr. Holmes.

Honorary Secretary—Mr. Mossman
House Surgeon and Apothecary—Mr. Knowles
Matron—Miss Rowley | *Collector*—Mr. Charles Woodcock
Finance Committee—Mr. J. Light, Mr. C. Semon and Mr. J. Wade.

AUXILIARY BIBLE SOCIETY

OF BRADFORD AND ITS VICINITY.

President—Rev. William Morgan, B. D.
Treasurer—Henry Harris, Esq.

Secretaries—Rev. Thomas Taylor, Rev. Jonathan Glyde, Mr. T. Aked, and Mr. T. Wilson.

The Ministers who support the Society, and twelve Gentlemen, form the Committee; and 23 Bible Associations are connected with it in the villages.

LADIES' BRANCH BIBLE SOCIETY.

President—Mrs. Rand | *Secretary*—Miss Taylor.
Assisted by a Committee of Ladies.

CHURCH SOCIETIES AND ASSOCIATIONS, &c.

Missionary Association.

President—Rev. John Burnett, L. L. D.
Treasurer—John Rand, Esq. *Secretaries*—Rev. W. Mitton and Mr. Hall.

Pastoral Aid Society.

President—Rev. Dr. Burnett | *Treasurer*—William Fison, Esq.
Secretary—Rev. James Cooper.

Prayer-Book and Homily Society.

DEPOSITORY—Mr. Charles Stanfields, 5 Westgate

Society for the Propagation of the Gospel.

President—John Burnett, L. L. D. | *Secretary*—Rev. James Cooper.

Society for Promoting Christianity amongst the Jews.

Secretary—Mr. J. Hollings.

Society for Promoting Christian Knowledge.

DEPOSITORY—ALBION COURT, KIRKGATE.

President—Rev. John Burnett, L. L. D. *Treasurer*—E. J. Mitchell, Esq.
Secretaries—J. Morris, Esq. and Rev. James Cooper.

Botanical and Horticultural Society.

Two Exhibitions in each year; Spring Show at the Exchange Buildings; Midsummer, at the Cricket Ground, Great Horton.

Bradford Tradesmens' Protection Society (Branch).

TO PROTECT PERSONS IN TRADE AGAINST SWINDLERS.

Secretary—Mr. Henry Farrar, 20 Kirkgate.

BRADFORD POOR LAW UNION.

Comprising Bradford, Bowling, Great and Little Horton and Manningham.

Inspector—A. Austin, Esq. *Assistant Inspector*—J. Mainwaring, Esq.
Chairman—Mr. John Hill *Clerk*—J. R. Wagstaff, Esq.
Auditor—Thomas Barker, Esq. Halifax.

☞ The MEETINGS of the GUARDIANS are held every Friday, at the Board Room, Charles street, at ten o'clock in the morning.

RELIEVING OFFICERS.

Bradford East District—Mr. Jonas Booth, Charles street
Bradford West and Manningham—Mr. Amos Bairstow, Lumb lane
Horton and Bowling—Mr. Jonas Jennings.

ASSISTANT OVERSEERS.

Bradford—Mr. W. W. Barlow | *Great and Little Horton*—Mr. T. Myers
Bowling—Mr. J. Ellis | *Manningham*—Mr. G. B. Crowther

REGISTRARS OF BIRTHS AND DEATHS

FOR THE SEVERAL DISTRICTS IN THE UNION.

Superintendent Registrar—John Reid Wagstaff. Esq Charles street
Deputy Superintendent—Mr. W. H. Hodson
Bradford East District—Mr. Richard Spencer, Church Steps
Bradford West—Mr. Thomas Liversedge, Ivegate
Horton District—Mr. James Reaney, Great Horton Road
Bowling—Mr. James Ellis, Hall lane
Manningham—Mr. Edward Firth, Eastsquire lane

REGISTRARS OF MARRIAGES.

Mr. William W. Barlow, Bridge street, and Mr. James Reaney, Great Horton road

Information Necessary for the Public.

As to Births.—Births may be registered within six weeks from the time of birth *without any charge whatever.* After forty two days the charge for registering a birth will be seven shillings and sixpence; and, after the expiration of six months, cannot be registered at all. The father or mother, or the occupier of the house in which the child is born, is bound to give the necessary information to the Registrar of the District. The information required will be, when born—name (if any)—name and surname of the father—name and maiden name of the mother. *The child need not be brought to the Registrar's office.*

As to Deaths.—Before burial, every death *must* be *registered,* and a *certificate* obtained from the Registrar of the District, for neither of which can any charge be made. Some person present at the death, or in attendance during the last illness, or the occupier of the house in which such death shall have happened, is bound to give the necessary information. The information required will be—when died—the name and surname—the age—the business or occupation—and the cause of death.

NORTH BIERLEY POOR LAW UNION,

Comprising Allerton, Bolton, Calverley, Clayton, Cleckheaton, Drighlington, Heaton, Hunsworth, Idle, North Bierley, Pudsey, Shipley, Thornton, Toug, Wike and Wilsden.

Inspector—Alfred Austin, Esq.
Assistant-Inspector—J. Manwaring, Esq. *Clerk*—J. Morris, Esq.
Superintendent Registrar—J. R. Wagstaff, Esq. Charles street, Hall Ings
Auditor—Mr. Thomas Barker.

RELIEVING OFFICERS.
William Wilson, Joseph Boothroyd and Nathan Pearson.

COLLECTORS.
John Tordoff, Samuel Crabtree, Joseph Lister, Abraham Craven, Henry Jowett, John Mallinson, Joseph Newell, and John Dobson.

The MEETINGS of the GUARDIANS are held on Thursdays, at the Board Rooms, 36 Darley street

---

Baptist College, Little Horton Lane.

President and Professor of Theology—Rev. James Acworth, L. L. D.
Classical Tutor—Rev. F. Clowes | *Treasurer*—W. Murgatroyd, Esq.
Secretaries—Rev. H. Dowson and T. Aked, Esq.

Baths—Public.

Henry Blackburn, Great Horton Road; John Leach & Son, Manningham lane, and Woolsorters' Gardens, Keighley road.

Bazaar for General Merchandise,

MARKET PLACE, KIRKGATE.

Open for Business on Mondays, Thursdays and Saturdays.

Billiard and Assembly Rooms.

EXCHANGE BUILDINGS, KIRKGATE.

Superintendent—Mr. Samuel Lord.

London Missionary Auxiliary Society,

SALEM CHAPEL, MANOR ROW.

Treasurer—James Garnett, Esq. | *Secretary*—Rev. J. G. Miall.
Depository of the Society—1 Thornton's Buildings, Bridge street.

Borough Conservative News Room and Library,

ALBION COURT, KIRKGATE.

The Library is open three nights in each week, viz.—Monday, Thursday and Saturday, from eight till half-past nine. The news Room every day (Sundays excepted), from nine in the morning till ten in the evening.

Borough Coroner's Offices.

COURT HOUSE, HALL INGS.

CORONER for the Honour of Pontefract—Mr. Christopher Jewison; Residence Rothwell, near Leeds.

Borough Operative Conservative Association,

NEW INN, TYRREL STREET.

President—James Wade, Esq.
Treasurer—Mr. Robert Webster
Secretary—Mr. W. Greenwood
Assist. Secretary—Mr. W. W. Procter.

Bradford Anti-State Church Association.

Secretary—Mr. James Hanson, Manor row.

Bradford Coursing Club,

BULL'S HEAD INN, WESTGATE.

President—Joshua Mann, Esq.

Treasurer—Mr. Joseph Sugden | *Secretary*—Mr. Thomas Hirst.

The Gentlemen composing this Club meet every Thursday evening at the above Inn.

Bradford Gas Works.

STATIONS—MILL STREET AND THORNTON ROAD.

Superintendent—Mr. David Swallow. *Engineer*—Mr. Joseph Bean.

Bradford Reform Club, Registration Society & Reading Rooms,

4 BRIDGE STREET.

This News Room and Library are open every day (Sunday excepted), from eight to ten, and are supplied with the leading Daily and Weekly Papers, and many of the most sterling and popular Magazines of the day.

Managing Secretary—Mr. William German.

Bradford School of Design,

MECHANICS' INSTITUTE, LEEDS ROAD.

The object of this branch of study is an extension of the Fine Arts and Principles of Design applicable to Manufactures.

Members—5s. per quarter——Non-Members—7s. 6d.

Bradford Subscription Library,

EXCHANGE BUILDINGS, KIRKGATE.

Open from ten till five in summer,—winter closes at four o'clock.

Librarian—Miss Mason.

Bradford Water Works Company,

RENNIE'S BUILDINGS, HALL INGS.

Manager—Mr. Adam Beattie.

Building and Investment Society,

VICTORIA BUILDINGS, CHEAPSIDE.

Secretary—Mr. William Clough.

Choral and Philharmonic Society,

ODD FELLOWS' HALL, THORNTON ROAD.

Collectors of Taxes Office,

SWAINE STREET, HALL INGS.

Highways—Mr. Thomas Driver Heaton
Lighting and Watching—Mr. William Clough
Poors' Rate—Mr. W. Barlow, Court House, Hall Ings

County Court of Bradford.

This court, established in 1847, has superseded the Court of Requests and the Court Baron of the Honor of Pontefract, formerly held here. The court sits thrice a month, and the fees for the recovery of small debts are very moderate, and its jurisdiction extends to, and includes, Bradford, Bowling, Manningham, and Horton townships.

The Costs of obtaining Verdicts in the above Court are as follows :—

	Where the debt or damages do not exceed—														
	£1		£2		£5		£10		*£20			‡£20		
	s.	d.	s.	d.	s.	d.	s.	d.	£.	s.	d.	£.	s.	d.
Summons and Service (within 1 mile)...	0	9	1	10	7	6	14	10	1	7	0	1	8	0
Hearing, Judgment, and Order........	3	1	4	11	8	10	19	0	1	8	0	1	18	6

*Founded on contract. ‡ Founded on tort.

Judge—C. H. Elsley, Esq.

Clerk—Mr. Charles Clough. — *High Bailiff*—Mr. Samuel Woodhead.

Cavalry and Infantry Barracks,

BRADFORD MOOR.

These commodious Barracks were erected in 1843-4, partly at the expense of Government and partly by Subscription.

Barrack Master—Mr. Jackson Midgley.

Depository of the Religious Tract Society,

1 Thornton's Buildings, Bridge street.

Freeholders' Land and Building Association,

4, BRIDGE STREET.

Secretary — Mr. William German.

Fruit, Egg, Butter and Potato Market,

RAWSON PLACE, DARLEY STREET.

Market Collector and Constable—Mr. Richard Webster.

Income and Assessed Taxes Office,

10 Exchange street, Kirkgate.

Clerk to the Commissioners—Mr. James Lambert, solicitor.

Ladies of the Manor.

Misses Mary and Elizabeth Rawson.

Residence—Nidd Hall, near Knaresborough.

Manor Court.

MANOR HOUSE INN, DARLEY STREET.

Stewart—John Clegg, Esq. solicitor.

Principal Bailiff—Mr. Timothy Ingham.

Established for the recovery of debts under 40s. The trial of causes are fixed by the Steward, as occasion may require, and the various processes issued by the Court are served and executed by the appointed bailiffs, and are returnable twenty-one days after the dates of issue. The jurisdiction of the Court extends to and comprises the townships of Bradford, Bowling, Manningham, Horton, Heaton, Haworth, Thornton, Allerton-cum-Wilsden and Wike.

Manor Office,

BRIDGE STREET BUILDINGS, BRIDGE STREET.

Clerk—John Clegg, Esq. Solicitor.

Agent—Mr. Jonas Knowles | *Bailiff*—Mr. Timothy Ingham.

Mechanics' Institute,

LEEDS ROAD.

Committee of Management, for 1849-50.

President—Rev. James Acworth, L. L. D.

Vice-Presidents.

Mr. Alderman Beaumont
W. E. Forster, Esq.
John Rawson, Esq.
Rev. W. Scott

Treasurer—Mr. Alderman Rogers

Secretaries—Mr. John Dale and Mr. James Hanson

Directors.

Mr. Alderman Brown
Rev. J. P. Chown
" J. H. Ryland
Mr. Joseph Cockin
" John Cooke
" W. Dunning
" Councillor German
" E. Harland
Mr. Booth Illingworth
" E. Kenion
" James Law
" Thomas Murgatroyd
" V. Rochfort
" S. E. Sichel
" S. Smith
" G. Taylor

Mr. Alexander Walker.

Mechanics' Institute, Great Horton.

Established 1839.

Members and friends of this establishment meet in the Church School, where classes are formed, superintended by the various teachers, and aided by the acquisition of a Library, Lectures, &c.

Medical Society and Library,

HELD AT THE INFIRMARY AND DISPENSARY, LUMB LANE.

Natural History Society and Museum,

MECHANICS' INSTITUTE, LEEDS ROAD.

This local Museum has lately had many valuable additions, and is being constantly enriched from various prolific sources.

Nuisance Office,

POLICE STATION, SWAINE STREET.

Inspector of Meat, Hackney Coaches, &c.—Mr. W. Bakes.

Scavengers, Road, and Street Obstructions—Mr. Isaac Rowntree.

Odd Fellows' Literary Institution and Library,

DARLEY STREET, KIRKGATE.

President—John Gordon, Esq.

Treasurer—Mr. Samuel Woodhead | *Secretary*—Mr. Ralph Fawcett.

Overseers' Offices.

Bradford District—Court House, Hall Ings

Horton (Great and Little)—Cross lane, Horton

Bowling District—Hall lane, Bowling

Manningham—Lumb lane.

Railway Stations, Offices, &c.

Lancashire and Yorkshire.—Passengers' New Station and Offices on the Leeds and Wakefield road.—Goods' Warehouse, Vicar lane—Engineer Mr. Wm. Eckersley.

Midland Counties and Leeds.—Booking Office and Passengers' Station, bottom of Kirkgate.—Goods' Warehouse, Railroad street, Canal road—Engineer, Mr. F. M. Young.—Superintendent, Mr. Matthew Crabtree.

Savings' Bank (Bradford and East Morley),

33 KIRKGATE.

Actuary—Mr. Thomas Haigh.

Open every Thursday from two to four o'clock in the afternoon, and every Saturday from six to a quarter before eight in the evening.

School of Industry,

NORTHGATE.

Superintendent—Miss Elizabeth Piper.

Situations of Fire Engines.

FOR BRADFORD.

Borough—Police Station, Swaine street; Mr. Richard Collinson, superintendent.

HALIFAX, BRADFORD, AND KEIGHLEY INSURANCE Co's.—Rennie, Tetley & Co's. Yard, opposite the Court House; John Gill superintendent, Vicar lane.

LEEDS AND YORKSHIRE INSURANCE Co's.—No. 10 Exchange street, Kirkgate; Mr. Edwin Olivant, superintendent, 36 Ebor street, Little Horton lane.

☞ In cases of fire occuring in the neighbourhood of a Plug, application should be instantly made at the Police Station House for the fire-plug apparatus before other steps are taken.

Staff Officers' and Pensioners' Pay Office,

COURT HOUSE, HALL INGS.

Acting Officer—Major John Edward Orange.

Stamp Office, 5 Westgate,

Sub-Distributor—Mr. CHARLES STANFIELD.

Surveyors of the Highways' Office.

POLICE STATION, SWAINE STREET.

Collector—Mr. Thomas Driver Heaton.

Inland Revenue Officers (Excise Branch).

Supervisor—Mr. John Roberts, 24 Victoria street, North Parade

Officers—John Bostock, Manchester road; William Davy, 34 Westgrove street; John Penket, 12 Canal Terrace, Bolton road; Thomas Wright, Undercliffe; John Dixon, Dudley Hill, and Richard Wynn, Shipley.

Temperance Hall, Leeds Road.

Treasurer—Mr. John Dale.

☞ Adapted for Public Meetings, Festivals, Soirees, &c.

Temperance (Teetotal) Hall, Southgate.

Hall Keeper—Mr. George Wilson.

Theatre Royal, Duke Street,

DARLEY STREET.

Proprietor—Mr. John Moseley.

Town Clerk's Offices,

SWAINE STREET, HALL INGS.

Town Clerk (and Clerk to the Borough Magistrates), John Rawson, Esq.

Town's Office for Lighting, Watching, Highways, &c.

SWAINE STREET, HALL INGS.

Union Club House,

MANOR ROW, CHEAPSIDE.

Steward—Mr. Ulas Selix.

United Independent Order of Odd Fellows.

District Head Offices—Odd Fellows' Hall, Thornton road.

Vagrant Office for Bradford Union,

TOAD LANE, BRIDGE STREET.

Vagrant Master—Mr. William Booth.

Washing Establishing for Domestic Linen, &c.

RAILROAD STREET, SCHOOL STREET.

Proprietor—Mr. Edmund Johnson Mitchell.

Weights and Measures Adjusting Office,

COURT HOUSE, HALL INGS.

Adjuster—Mr. William Baxter.

Wesleyan Missionary Societies.

KIRKGATE—William Walker, Esq. *Treasurer.*—Mr. W. Whitaker *secretary.*

EASTBROOK—Lodge Calvert and W. Cheesebrough, Esqs. *Treasurers.* Mr. William Whittaker, *Secretary*

Woolsorters' Gardens and Baths.

KEIGHLEY ROAD.

Worsted Committee (Borough).

Clerk—Edward Hailstone, Esq. Solicitor.—*Offices* Manchester road.

Yeomanry Cavalry—Bradford D. Troop.

Captain—(not appointed.)

Lieutenant—Mr. George Addison | *Cornet*—Mr. Frank Rouse.

CORPORATION OF BRADFORD.

1849-50.

JUSTICES OF THE BOROUGH.

THE MAYOR.

Robert Milligan, Esq.
William Cheesbrough, Esq.
Henry Fotbes, Esq.
Samuel Laycock, Esq.
William Rand, Esq.
H. W. Ripley, Esq.
Samuel Smith, Esq.

THE COUNCIL.

Comprises the Mayor, fourteen Aldermen, and forty-two Councillors.

Clerk to the Justices—Mr. John Rawson, Swaine street.

Mayor's Auditor—Mr. William Clough.

THE COMMITTEES.

The Committees are those for GENERAL PURPOSES, WATCH, FINANCE, SANATORY, &c. and are generally convened at the COUNCIL CHAMBERS, Court House, Hall Ings, on fixed days in each week.

Borough Court and Justices,

COURT HOUSE, HALL INGS.

THE FOLLOWING GENTLEMEN CONSTITUTE THE BOROUGH JUSTICES:

THE MAYOR.

Robert Milligan, Esq.
Wm. Cheesebrough, Esq.
Henry Forbes, Esq.
Samuel Laycock, Esq.
William Rand, Esq.
Henry William Ripley, Esq.
Samuel Smith, Esq.

The West-Riding Magistrates having concurrent jurisdiction.

The BOROUGH JUSTICES meet at the Court House every day (Thursday and Sunday excepted), at eleven o'clock in the morning, for the hearing of cases and despatch of business.

PUBLIC HOUSE LICENSES.

A Special Sessions for the Transfer of Public House Licenses, within the Borough, are held on the first Thursday in the months of February, March and June, and the last Friday in August, at the Court House, at eleven o'clock, a. m.

SPECIAL SESSIONS for Highways, and for hearing Appeals against Poor Rates, are held on the last Wednesday in every month, at the Court House, Hall Ings

COURT HOUSE, HALL INGS.

WEST RIDING MAGISTRATES ACTING IN THE DIVISION IN WHICH THE BOROUGH IS SITUATED.

E. C. L. Kaye, Esq. Manningham Hall
Col. J. P. Tempest, Tong Hall
H. W. Wickham, Esq, Lightcliffe
B. Thompson, Esq. Park Gate
L. W. Wickham, Esq. Lightcliffe
John Rand, Esq. Whetley
Charles Hardy, Esq. Odsal
Joshua Pollard, Esq. Scarr Hill
Robert Milligan, Esq. Acacia House
T. G. Clayton, Esq. Bierley Hall
William Walker, Esq. | Alfred Harris, Esq.

Borough Police Station,

SWAINE STREET, HALL INGS.

Chief Constable—Mr. William Leveratt
Superintendent of Night Police—Mr. Richard Collinson
Detective Officers—Joseph Field and John Shuttleworth
Process Server—John Andrew.

Magistrates' Clerk (West Riding), Geo. Robt. Mossman, Esq.
Constables to the West Riding Magistrates—Messrs. Ingham and Jowett
Inspector of Weights and Measures—Mr. William Baxter.

The Petty Sessions for this District (exclusive of the Borough) are held in the Court House, Hall Ings, every Thursday morning at eleven o'clock, and all precepts must be delivered to the officer in court before that time, otherwise discharged without any allowance for expenses.

Magistrates are in attendance on Mondays, also, at twelve o'clock, to grant processes, deliver the goal, &c.

Persons having business in this Court should attend at nine o'clock, a. m. to give instructions to the clerks.

NAMES AND BOUNDARIES OF THE MUNICIPAL WARDS

Bradford, since the grant of a Charter of Incorporation, has been divided into *eight* wards, presided over and represented by a mayor, 14 aldermen, and 42 councillors, which constitute the corporate body. Twenty-four councillors are divided among the four wards comprising the Bradford township—three each for Manningham and Great Horton, and six each for Bowling and Little Horton.

No. 1.—EAST WARD.

Which comprise Leeds New road, Garnett street, and the Leeds Old road, to the extent of the township of Bradford, thence along the eastern and northern boundaries of the township, till the intersection of the Eccleshill and Idle turnpike road, thence in a southerly direction along the said Eccleshill and Idle road, commonly known by the name of Bolton road, to its junction with Broadstones, thence along the centre of Broadstones, Well street, and Kirkgate, to Market street, thence along the centre of Market street and Bridge street to the termination in Leeds New road.

No. 2—NORTH WARD.

Beginning at the intersection of the township boundary with the Eccleshill and Idle road, along the centre to its junction with Broadstones, thence along the centre of Broadstones, Well street, and Kirkgate, to the bottom of Darley street, thence along the centre of Darley street, North Parade, and Manningham lane, to the boundary of the township, and along the north-western and northern boundaries to the intersection of theEccleshill and Idle road.

No. 3—SOUTH WARD.

Commencing at the point where the Bowing beck crosses Chapel lane, thence along Chapel lane to and along the centre of Norfolk street, thence along the centre of the Leeds New road to Garnett street, along the centre of Garnett street, to the Leeds Old road, thence along the centre of the Leeds Old road to the extent of the township, and along the eastern and southern boundaries of the township to the said point in Chapel lane.

No. 4—WEST WARD.

Comprises that part from where Manningham lane intersects the boundary of the township of Bradford, along the centre of Manningham lane, North parade, Darley street, Kirkgate, Market street, Bridge street, Norfolk street, to Chapel lane, thence along the southern, western, and northern boundaries of the township to where the same intersects Manningham lane.

Nos. 5, 6, 7, AND 8.

Being Bowling, Great and Little Horton, and Manningham, the boundaries of which are the townships' limits.

AN ALPHABETICAL LIST

OF THE

STREETS, LANES, COURTS, PLACES, SQUARES, ETC.

IN THE

BOROUGH AND VICINITY OF BRADFORD,

WITH REFERENCE TO THE NEXT PRINCIPAL OR ADJOINING STREETS.

A

ABRAHAM GATE, Bower street, Manchester road
Adelaide street, Manchester road
Adelaide street, Manningham
Albert street, Bolton road
Albert street, Bermondsey
Albion Court, 34 Kirkgate
Albion Hotel Yard, Ivegate
Albion Square, Manchester road
Albion street, Manchester road
Albion street, Silsbridge lane
Anne street, High street
Ann's Place, Little Horton lane
Ashfield Place and Terrace, Great Horton road
Aspinall's Yard, Westgate
Aycliffe Hill, Great Horton
Aycliffe lane, Great Horton

B

BACK FOLD, Great Horton
Back George street, Vicar lane
Back lane, Bowling
Back lane, Leeds road
Back lane, Manningham
Back lane, Northgate
Back School street, Cheapside
Back Tyrrel street, Tyrrel street
Balme's Buildings, Bolton road and Charles street
Balme street, Bolton road
Bankbottom, Great Horton
Bankfoot, Bowling
Banktop, Great Horton
Bank street, Market street
Barkerend, High street
Barker street, Wharf street, Bolton road
Bazaar, Market Place, Kirkgate
Beanland's Yard, Silsbridge lane
Beckbotton, Little Horton
Beckside, Great Horton
Beck street, Croft street, Leeds road
Beddoe & Brook's Yard, 10 Westgate
Bedford street, Bridge street
Beehive Yard, Westgate
Beetham street, Spring row, Manningham
Beldon Hill, Great Horton
Belgrave place, Lumb lane, Manningham
Belgrave street, Leeds road
Bellevue, Manningham lane
Bermondsey, Kirkgate
Birks, Great Horton
Birks Hall, Bowling
Birksland, Leeds road
Birk street, Birksland, Leeds road
Black Abbey, Brick lane, top of Westgate
Bolton place, Bridge street
Bolton Royd, Manningham
Bolton road, Well street
Booth street, Hall Ings
Bower's Buildings, Tyrrel street
Bowergate, Tyrrel street
Bower street, Manchester road
Bowling Green Yard, Tyrrel street
Bowling Hall, Bowling
Bowling street and lane, Manchester road
Bracken Hill, Great Horton
Bradford Moor, Leeds road
Brick lane, Black Abbey, top of Westgate
Brick row, Thornton road

Bridge street, Wakefield road
Britannia street, Manchester road
Broadstones, Well street
Broad street, Manor row
Brook street, Hall Ings
Brook street, George street, Leeds rd.
Broomfield terrace, Wakefield road
Broom street, Wakefield road
Brow, Daisyhill, Manningham
Brumfit's Yard, 47 Kirkgate
Brunswick place, Northgate
Bunker's Hill, Barkerend, High st.
Burnett Field, Bowling
Burnley Fold, Black Abbey
Burrow street, Manchester road
Butler street, Otley road, High street
Butterfield row, Manningham
Butterfield's terrace, Manchester rd.
Butterworth's Buildings, Ivegate

C

CANAL road, Well street
Canal terrace, Bolton road
Cannon street, Cheapside
Cannon street, Wakefield road
Captain street, Wharf street
Carlton place, Little Horton
Castle street, Manchester road
Cavalier street, Otley road, High st.
Chain street, Silsbridge lane
Chandos street, Wakefield road
Chapel Court, 44 Kirkgate
Chapel lane, Bridge street
Chapel street, Leeds road
Chapel street, High street
Charles street, Market street
Cheapside, 22 Kirkgate
Church bank, Well street
Church Buildings, Manchester road
Church steps, Bolton road
Church street, High street
Clarence street, Manchester road
Clayton lane, Manchester road
Clock House, Manningham
Close Top, Lidget Green, Gt. Horton
Club Houses, Longlands st. Westgate
Cobourg street, Otley road, High st.
Colliergate, Swaine street, Hall Ings
Commercial street, Canal road, Well st.
Cooper street, Thornton road
Court street, Brook street, Leeds road
Crackhill, Silsbridge lane
Croft st. Manchester rd. & Bridge st.
Croft street, Birksland, Leeds road
Cropper lane, top of Westgate
Crossley's Buildings, Westgate
Cross street, Westgate, Stott Hill, and Canal road
Crow Nest, Legrams, Horton
Crow Trees, Bradford Moor
Crow Trees, Manningham
Crown street, Brick lane
Crowther street, Manchester road
Cure's Yard, Westgate

D

DAISYHILL, Manningham
Dale street, Kirkgate
Darley street, Kirkgate
Day lane, Great Hörton
Diamond street, Vicar lane
Diana street, Manchester road
Dirkhill, Great Horton
Dodgson Hill, Kirkgate
Down street, Middleton Field
Drewton street, Manningham lane
Drop, Great Horton
Duckworth lane, Manningham
Dudley Hill, Bowling
Duke street, Darley street
Duke street, Manchester road
Duke street, Wapping

E

EARL street, Manchester road
East street, George street, Leeds road
Eastbrook lane, Vicar lane
Eastbrook Terrace and sq. Vicar lane
Ebenezer street, Vicar lane
Ebor street, Little Horton lane
Edmund street, Little Horton lane
Edward street, Croft street, Bridge st.
Eldon place, North Parade
Elizabeth street, Little Horton lane
Exchange street, Kirkgate

F

FAWCETT Court and Row, Nelson st.
Fearnley's row, Eastbrook lane
Fieldhead, Thornton road
Field House, Manningham
Fitzgerald street, Manchester road
Foundry street, Diamond street
Foundry street, School street
Fountain street, Manchester road

Fountain street, Manningham lane
Four Lane Ends, Manningham
Frederick street, Bridge street
Furnace lane, Bowling

G

Garden place, Providence street,
Garnettstreet, Leeds road
Gaunt street, Otley road, High street
George Hotel Yard, Market street
George street, Leeds road
George street, Manchester road
Goodmansend, Bridge street
Gothic Buildings, Hanover Square
Gracechurch street, White Abbey
Great Cross st. George st. Leeds road
Greenaire place, Silsbridge lane
Greenfield Place, Lumb lane,
Green lane, Lumb lane, Manningham
Green row, Brick lane, Black Abbey

H

Hall Ings, Bridge street
Hall Field and Lane, Bowling
Hall street, Croft street, Bridge street
Hannah gate, Manchester road
Hanover Square, NorthParade
Harris street, Leeds road
Harrogate road, High street
Hayworth street, White Abbey
Haworth road, Westgate
Heap lane, High street
Herring row, Brick lane, BlackAbbey
High street, Churchbank, Well st.
High street, Black Abbey
High street, Great Horton
High street terrace, Barkerend
Hill End, Great Horton
Hillside Villas, Otley road
Hill Top, Daisyhill, Manningham
Holland's Yard, Kirkgate
Hollinwood lane, Great Horton
Holme, Thornton road
Holmegate, Horton road
Holme lane, Little Horton
Hope and Anchor Yard, Bank street
Hope street, Manchester road
Houghton Place, Drewton street
Hudson's Fold, Manchester road
Hustler's Building, Leeds road and Market street
Hustlergate, Ivegate
Hustler's Terrace, Barkerend, Highst.

I

Illingworth's Yard, Ivegate
Ivegate, Bridge street

J

Jacob's lane, Manchester road
James street, Northgate, Northwing and Manchester road
Jer lane, Great Horton
John street, Northgate and Stott Hill
John street, Manchester road
Jonasgate, Bower st. Manchester road
Joseph street, Leeds road
Junction Mill, Laister Dyke

K

Keighley street, Silsbridge lane
King street, Silsbridge lane
King street, Manchester road
King Charles street, Otley road
Kirkgate, Well street

L

Lady Royd, Four Lane Ends, Manningham
Lady's Walk, Daisyhill, Manningham
Laister Dyke, Bradford Moor
Laura Place, Leeds road
Leeds road, Bridge street
Leeming street, School street
Legrams and Legrams lane, Great Horton
Lidget Green, Legrams, Gt. Horton.
Lillycroft, Manningham
Little Horton lane, Tyrrel street
Lister Place, Silsbridge lane
Lister Terrace, Great Horton road
Little Cross street, Vicar lane
Longcroft Place, Silsbridge lane
Low Green, Great Horton
Low street, Black Abbey
Lowclose House, Cross lane, Great Horton
Lower Globe, Spring row, Manngham.
Lower West street, Prospect row, Silsbridge lane
Lumb lane, Westgate
Lumby street, Manchester road
Lyndhurst street, Leeds road

M

Mab street, Otley road
Manchester road, Tyrrel street
Manchester Buildings, Tyrrel street
Manningham lane, North Parade
Manor place and row, Cheapside
Manor street, Manor row, Cheapside
Manville, Great Horton road
Manville terrace, Great Horton road,
Margerison street, Cheapside
Market place (Old), Market street
Market place (New), Kirkgate
Market street, Bridge street
Marygate, Manchester road
Mawson street, Thornton road
Medley's Yard, Westgate
Melbourne place, North Parade and Little Horton lane
Melbourne street, Leeds road
Middle street, Manor row, Cheapside
Middleton Field, Silsbridge lane
Millbank, Bridge street
Millgate, Manchester road
Mill lane, Bowling
Mill lane and street, Manchester road
Mill street, Canal road
Milton street, Broomfield Terrace
Mount Pleasant, Manchester road and Manningham
Mount street, Stott Hill
Myrtle Grove, Bower street, Manchester road

N

Nag's Head Yard, Kirkgate
Nelson Square, Great Horton
Nelson street, Chapel lane
New Leeds, Leeds road
New Road, Great Horton
New Road, Bowling
Norcliffe road, Great Horton road
Norfolk street, Bridge street
Northbrook Place, Bolton road
Northgate, Westgate
Northolme Mill, Foundry street
North Parade, Manningham lane
North street, Wellington st. Stott Hill
Northwing, High street
Northrop's Buildings, Westgate
Nurser lane, Little Horton
Nutter's Place, Northgate

O

Oakhouse, Manningham lane
Oakfield, Manningham
Oaksfold, Bowling
Oastler's Court, Manchester road
Old lane, Bowling
Old King's Head Yard, Westgate
Old Market place, Market street

P

Paperhall and street, Otley road
Paradise Green, Great Horton
Parkgate, High street
Park Place, Little Horton lane and North Parade
Park lane, Little Horton lane
Park Square, Lumb lane
Park street, High street & Barkerend
Peckover Walk, High street
Peel street, North st. and Leeds road
Pennyoaks Mill, Melbourne street, Leeds road
Philadelphia street, Wapping, Bolton road
Pickles Hill, Great Horton
Piecehall and Yard, Kirkgate
Pit lane, Barkerend
Priestley street, Wharf st. Bolton rd.
Popplewell's Buildings, Market street
Portland Blace, Manchester road
Portland street, Manchester road
Preston Place, Great Horton
Primrose Hill, Great Horton road
Primrose terrace, Wood street
Prince street, Manchester road
Prospect row, Silsbridge lane and Northwing
Prospect street, Silsbridge lane
Prospect terrace, Manor row
Providence Place, Clarence street, Manchester road
Providence Square, Bradford Moor
Providence street, Manchester road, Silsbridge lane and Westgate

Q

Quebec Terrace, Thornton road
Queen street, Bowling
Queen street, Manchester road and White Abbey

R

RANDALLWELL street, Great Horton road
Rawson's Arms Yard, Market street
Rawson's Buildings, Old Market place
Rawson Place, Darley street
Redgin, Bowling
Reform street, Westgate
Regent Place, Duke street
Regent street, Wood street
Richard street, Leeds road
Rich's Yard, Westgate
Roebuck Yard, Market street
Rooley lane, Bowling
Roundhill Place, Silsbridge lane

S

SALTPYE, Great Horton
Saltpye row, Black Abbey
Sams Mill, Great Horton
Sawrey Place, Little Horton lane
Scaife's Yard, Chapel lane
Scholemoor, Great Horton
School street, Cheapside
School street, Manchester road
Schuster's Buildings, Brook street
Shambles, New Market, Kirkgate
Sharp street, Manchester road
Shearbridge, Great Horton
Ship Alley, Well street
Shoulder of Mutton Yard, Kirkgate
Sidney Place, North Parade
Silsbridge lane, Westgate
Simes street, Westgate
Skinner lane, Manningham
Smiddles lane, Bowling
Smith street, Manchester road
Smithson's Place, Barkerend, High st
Smithville, Little Horton
Snap, Great Horton
Snow Hill, North Parade
Sodom, Little Horton
Solitary, Great Horton
Southfield Place, Green lane, Manningham
Southgate, Westgate
Southgate, Great Horton
Spink's Buildings, Black Abbey
Spinkwell Terrace, Bolton road
Springfield Place, Manningham lane
Spring Gardens, Manningham lane
Spring Lodge, Manningham lane
Spring row and place, Manningham la.
Spring street (High and Low), Manningham
Spring street, Wharf street, Bolton rd.
Squire lane, Manningham
St. George's street, Thornton road
St. James's Square, James street
St. James's street, Northwing
St. John's street, Prospect row
St. John's street, Northwing
St. Jude's Place, North Parade
St. Peter's row, Church steps
Sterling street, Manchester road
Sticker lane, Bowling
Stock's Green, Manningham
Stone street, Manor row
Stott Hill, Churchbank
Sugden's Yard, Bridge street
Summerseat Place, Gt. Horton road
Sunbridge, Bridge street
Swaine's Buildings, Tyrrel street
Swaine street, Hall Ings

T

Tankard's row, Silsbridge lane
Tanner Beck, Great Horron
Tanner Hill, Great Horton
Thiefscore Bridge, Manningham
Thomas street, Manchester road
Thompson's Buildings, Silsbridge la.
Thornton lane, Little Horton
Thornton's Buildings, Bridge street and Market street
Thornton road, Tyrrel street
Thornton street, Thornton road
Threadneedle street, Bridge street
Throstle nest, Legrams and Manningham
Toller lane, Manningham
Townhill, Wakefield road
Townend, Great Horton
Trafalgar street, Manor row
Trees, Manningham
Triangle street, Manchester road
Turner's Buildings, Bolton road
Turpin Houses, Middleton field
Tyrrel Court, Tyrrel street
Tyrrel square, Tyrrel street
Tyrrel street, Bridge street

U

Undercliffe, Otley road, High street
Undercliffe lane, Northwing

Undercliffe, road, High street
Unicorn Yard, Ivegate
Union Passage, Kirkgate
Union street, Bridge street
Uppercroft, Laister Dyke
Upper Globe, Manningham
Upper Green, Great Horton
Upper West street, Prospect row

V

Vicar lane, Churchbank
Victoria street, North Parade
Victoria street, Manchester road, Manningham and Silsbridge lane
Victoria place, Clarence street
Victoria terrace, Bolton road

W

Wakefield road, Bridge street
Wales street, Spring row
Walmsley's Yard, Thornton road
Wapping, Northwing
Warwick street, White Abbey
Waterloo place, Adelaide street
Waterside, Manningham
Water street, Northwing
Well street, Kirkgate
Well Court, Well street
Well lane, Vicar lane
Wellclose House, Great Horton
Wellington place, Little Horton lane
Wellington street, Stott Hill
Westbrook place, Great Horton road
Westbrook House, Great Horton road
Westbrook street, Great Horton road
Westgate, Ivegate
Westgrove street, Cropper lane
West Parade, Brick lane and Manningham lane
West street (Upper and Lower), Prospect row
Wharf street, Broad stones
Whetley fold, Lower Globe, Manningham
Whetley Hill & Lane, Manningham
Whetley street, Spring row, Manningham
White Abbey, top of Westgate
White Lion Yard, Kirkgate
Wild Boar street, Bolton road
William's Court, Manchester road
Wood street, White Abbey
Woodhouse Buildings, White Abbey

Y

York street, Wakefield road

ADDITIONS AND REMOVALS

RECEIVED SINCE THE PRECEDING PART OF THE DIRECTORY WAS PRINTED.

Armitage & Ibbetson, engravers and printers, Thornton's Buildings, Bridge street
Bayley John, agent for the Mentor Insurance Company; office Hustler's Buildings, Leeds road.—(*See advertisement.*)
Berry John, agent for the London Indisputable Life Policy Co. office, Leeds road.—(*See advertisement.*)
Drake William, veterinary surgeon, Angel Inn, Westgate.
Fawcett Ralph, printer, bookseller, binder, and stationer, 38 Westgate
Holgate Adamson, grocer, 24 Ivegate
Horsman Simon, grocer, 80 Westgate
Ingle & Smith, land and building agents, 32 Darley street
Lapish Hiram, linen draper, &c. 16 Westgate
Macleod William, M.D. 15 Albion Passage—Tuesdays only
Martin J. F. & Co. stuff merchants, Leeds road
Purchon James, auctioneer, 23 Piecehall Yard, Kirkgate
Raisbeck Edward, auctioneer, &c. Westbrook place.—(*See advertisement.*)
Sharp Richard Hey, architect, Albion Court, Kirkgate
Taylor Thomas, provision merchant, Leeds road
Wade Thomas, hair dresser, Tyrrel street

RATES AND FARES OF HACKNEY COACHES.

The following rates and fares shall be allowed and taken for hackney coaches plying for hire as aforesaid, from half-past seven o'clock in the morning to ten o'clock at night, and such fares shall be, for either time or distance, at the option of the driver, viz.—

If for Distance.	If on 4 wheels & constructed to cary 4 inside and 1 out.	If on 2 wheeels or if constructed to carry fewer than 4 inside & 1 out.
For every Carriage hired or taken any distance not exceeding one mile..................	1s. 0d.	0s. 8d.
Exceeding a mile and not exceeding a mile and a half............................	1s. 6d.	1s. 0d.
And for every succeeding half mile...........	0s. 6d.	0s. 4d.
If for Time, then for any time not exceeding a quarter of an hour......................	1s. 0d.	0s. 8d.
For every succeeding quarter or any part thereof	0s. 6d.	0s. 4d.

Every hackney coach retained or employed after the hour of ten at night, and before half-past seven in the morning, shall be allowed for every fare, or so much of any fare as may be performed between those hours, double the day fares, to be calculated in manner aforesaid.

That the fares above mentioned shall be deemed a compensation for any reasonable amount of luggage which the passenger may think fit to take.

RETURN FARES OF HACKNEY COACHES.

That where the fare for any hackney coach taking shilling fares shall amount to 2s. or upwards, or for any hackney coach taking eightpenny fares shall amount to 1s. 4d. or upwards, it shall be at the option of the hirer to detain such hackney coach to return in the same, on payment of half fare, provided it be not detained more than thirty minutes, for which detention no additional sum shall be demanded, and that when the fare for any hackney coach shall amount to less than the sum specified with respect to such hackney coach as aforesaid, it shall be at the option of the hirer to detain such hackney coach to return in the same, on payment of half fare, provided it be not so detained more than ten minutes, and for which detention no additional sum shall be demanded.

GENERAL POST OFFICE,

UNION PASSAGE, KIRKGATE.

Mr. William Coates—*Post Master.*

Receiving Houses.—*Bradford*—Mr. Squire Farrar, High street; Mr. Joshua Sharp, Goodmansend; Mr. David Medley, Manchester road; and Mr. William Savage, Westgate.

Horton—Mr. John Wood, Great Horton road.—*Bowling*—Mr. John Mitchell, Dudley Hill—*Manningham*—Mr. Henry Heppinstall, Lillycroft.—*New Leeds* not appointed.

DEPATURE OF THE MAILS.

For Shipley, Bingley, Keighley, Skipton, &c. The Box closes at half-past six, a. m. and the mail is despatched at a quarter past seven, a. m.

For LEEDS, York, Hull, Wakefield, Dewsbury, Sheffield, Huddersfield, Halifax, Rochdale, Manchester, Liverpool, Lancaster, Chester, Cumberland, Hereford, Monmouth, Salop, Stafford, Warwick, Westmoreland, West parts of Scotland, and Ireland. The Box closes at ten minutes before ten a. m. and the mail is despatched at half-past ten. a.m.

For LONDON and Foreign, Leeds and all the counties East, South and South West, but no part of Lancashire except Liverpool. The Box closes at ten minutes after five, p. m. and the Mail is despatched at ten minutes before six, p. m.

FOREIGN, and all parts of England, Ireland, Scotland, and Wales. The Box is closed at a quarter past seven, p. m. and the Mail is despatched at eight, p. m.

LATE LETTERS may be sent by the Mail about to be despached, till within five minutes of such, provided they are posted at the window, and that the *Late Fees as well as the Postage be paid*, by attaching the requisite Stamps. N. B.—This applies to all Late Letters, Foreign as well as English.

MESSENGERS are despatched *Daily*, Sundays excepted, at half-past eight morning, to Horton, Clayton, Thornton, West Bowling, Wibsey, Low Moor, Eccleshill, Idle, Wilsden, Cullingworth, East Bowling, Dudley Hill, Manningham, Heaton, Allerton, New Leeds, Bradford Moor and Undercliffe.

DELIVERIES.

The FIRST DELIVERY commences at seven in the morning in summer, and half-past seven in winter, and includes letters from London and Counties beyond London, (including Foreign) Leeds, Wakefield, Huddersfield, Hull, York, and the North Riding, Newcastle, Durham, Northumberland, East parts of Scotland, Edinburgh, &c.

The SECOND DELIVERY commences at half-past eight in the morning, and includes Foreign Letters, and Letters from all parts of England, Ireland, Scotland and Wales.

The THIRD DELIVERY commences at half-past one afternoon, and includes letters from Leeds, Hull, Wakefield, Dewsbury, Sheffield, Huddersfield, Halifax, Rochdale, Manchester, Liverpool, West parts of Scotland and Ireland.

The FOURTH DELIVERY (from private boxes only) commences at a quarter before seven evening, and includes letters from the neighbouring villages, and Bingley, Keighley, Skipton, Settle, Colne, Burnley, Blackburn, &c.

☞ On SUNDAYS the Office is closed from 10 a. m. to 5 p. m., after which hour it is open for the receipt of Paid Letters only.

YORKSHIRE BANKERS,

WITH THE HOUSES ON WHICH THEY DRAW IN LONDON.

BARNSLEY—Banking Company, S. Linley, manager, draw on Barnett and Co.; Wakefield and Barnsley Bank, J. Frudd, man. on Glyn & Co.

BEVERLEY—Yorkshire Banking Company, Joseph Lambert, manager, on Williams & Co-

BRADFORD—Harris & Co., on Barnett & Co.; Banking Company, S. Laycock, manager, on Jones, Loyd & Co.; Commercial Banking Company, J. Hill, man. on Glyn & Co.; Yorkshire Banking Company, W. Duckitt, man. on Williams & Co.

DEWSBURY—West Riding Union Banking Company, J. G. Berry, manager, on Masterman & Co.; Huddersfield Banking Company, Joshua Walker, man. on Smith, Payne & Co.

HALIFAX—Joint Stock Banking Co. John Caw, manager, on Jones, Loyd & Co.; Commercial Banking Co. F. Hardcastle, man. on Williams and Co.; Halifax and Huddersfield Union Banking Co. J. Bowman, man. on Glyn & Co.

HUDDERSFIELD—Yorkshire Banking Co. Jno. Barwick, man. on Williams & Co.;Halifax and Huddersfield Union Banking Co. J. T. Patchett man. on Glyn & Co.; Huddersfield Banking Co. David Marsden man. on Smith, Payne, & Co.; West-Riding Union Banking Co., James Heron man. on Masterman & Co.

HULL—Harrison, Watson & Co. on Price & Co.; Pease & Liddells (Old Bank), on Glyn & Co.; Thomas & Robert Raikes & Co. on Curries and Co.; Samuel Smith, Brothers & Co. on Smith, Payne & Co.; Bank of England, G. A. Shee, man. on Bank of England; Yorkshire Banking Co. E. W. Englishman., man on Williams & Co.; Hull Banking Co. George Cobbman. on Barclay & Co.

KEIGHLEY—Alcocks, Birkbecks & Co. on Barnard & Co.

KNARESBOROUGH—Terry & Harrisons, on Willis & Co. Yorkshire Banking Company, on Williams & Co.; Knaresborough and Claro Banking Co. John Hall man., on Barnett & Co.

LEEDS—Beckett & Co. on Glyn & Co.; William W. Brown & Co. on Brown & Co.; Bank of England, C. E. MCarthy, man. on Bank of England; Leeds Banking Co. Ed. Greenland, man. on Smith, Payne & Co.; Yorkshire Banking Co. J. W. Scott, man. on Williams & Co.

LEYBURN—Swaledale and Wensleydale Banking Co. J. Grime man. on Hankeys & Co.

OTLEY—Yorkshire Banking Co. Christopher Jackson, man. on Williams and Co.

PATELEY BRIDGE—Yorkshire Banking Co. on Williams & Co.

PONTEFRACT—Leatham, Tew & Co. on Denison & Co.; Yorkshire Banking Co. Richard Chambers man. on Williams & Co.

ROTHERHAM—Sheffield and Rotherham Banking Co. E. J. Heseltine, man. on Barclay & Co—Sheffield Banking Co. Charles Storey man. on Smith, Payne and Co.

SELBY—York City and County Bank, Robert Morrell man. on Barnett & Co.; Yorkshire Banking Co. Joseph Dobson man. on Williams & Co.

SHEFFIELD—Rimingtons and Youngs, on Masterman & Co.; Sheffield Banking Co. A. F. Hammond man. on Smith, Payne & Co.; Sheffield and Hallamshire Banking Co. W. Waterfall man. on Glyn & Co.; Sheffield & Rotherham Banking Co. W. Brown man. on Barclay & Co.; Sheffield Union Banking Co. E. Liddell man. on Prescott & Co.

SKIPTON—Alcocks, Birkbecks & Co. on Barnard & Co.; Yorkshire Banking Co. W. Gatenby man. on Williams & Co.

WAKEFIELD—Leatham, Tew & Co. Union Bank, on Barclay & Co.; Wakefield & Barnsley Banking Co. W. H. Dikes, man. on Glyn & Co.; West Riding Union Banking Co. on Masterman & Co.

YORK—Swan & Co. John Provis, man. on Glyn & Co.; Yorkshire Banking Co. M. Murray man. on Williams & Co.; York City and County Bank, Robert Barnes man. on Barnett & Co.; York Union Banking Company, B. T. Wilkinson man. on Glyn & Co.

IBBETSON'S BRADFORD
DIRECTORY ADVERTISER,

FOR 1849—50.

T. R. CHARLESWORTH

Begs most respectfully to intimate to the Solicitors, Merchants, Manufacturers, Tradesmen, and the Public of Bradford and its Vicinity, that he has commenced business as an

ACCOUNTANT & GENERAL AGENT,

NO. 49, DARLEY STREET,

OPPOSITE CHRIST CHURCH, BRADFORD.

From his knowledge of Accounts and of Business Transactions generally, T. R. C. hopes to give every satisfaction to his friends and the public, and pledges himself to use every exertion in order to promote the interests of those who may favour him with their commands.

Bankrupts' and Insolvents' Balance Sheets made out, Compositions effected, Tradesmen's Books audited and Accounts collected, on the most reasonable terms.

T. R. CHARLESWORTH begs respectfully to inform the members of the Medical Profession, that having engaged an active and highly respectable Man as a collector, he has great facilities for getting in small accounts, at considerably less expense than is generally incurred.

Security will be given if required.

References kindly permitted to E. A. Barret, Esq., Solicitor, Charles Street, Bradford; and Wm. Field, Esq., Surgeon, Bowling, near Bradford.

Agent for the Church of England Fire & Life Insurance Company.

49, *Darley Street, May 5th*, 1849.

HENRY W. BLACKBURN,

ACCOUNTANT,

2, DISPENSARY BUILDINGS, BRADFORD.

Auditor of Railway and other Public Company's Accounts: Trustees' & Receivers' Accounts in Chancery, or for any of the Courts of Equity or Bankruptcy, carefully made out.

Residuary Accounts for Executors, or for Arbitrators, in Settlement of Disputed Claims.—Tradesmen's Books posted or balanced.

THE COCOA-TREE TEA ESTABLISHMENT,

34, KIKGATE, BRADFORD,

CLARANCE & CO.,

TEA AND COFFEE MERCHANTS.

Purchasers of TEAS and COFFEES are respectfully informed, that the choicest selections are constantly on sale at this establishment, consisting of the finest Souchong, Gunpowder, Hyson, Young Hyson, Imperial, and the much-admired choice flavoured Assam, Orange Pekoes, &c.

COFFEES:

In addition to the following, CLARANCE & Co. have the best procurable from every country—

		s.	d.		s.	d.	
CEYLON,	Common Coffee,	0	9	to	0	11	per lb.
	Good quality	1	0	to	1	2	"
	Fine Plantation	1	4	to	1	6	"
JAVA,	Fine to Finest	1	1	to	1	6	"
JAMIACA	Good to fine	0	11	to	1	4	"
	Very fine to finest	1	6	to	1	8	"
COSTA RICA	A strong, good coffee	1	2	to	1	6	"
MOCHA,	Choice to finest old	1	5	to	1	8	"

TURKEY OR MOCHA COFFEE.

This beautiful Coffee may be had in Bottles containing 1lb. and 2lbs. each, ground and packed immediately after it is roasted, by which means it remains uninjured by the atmosphere, and for a lengthened period retains it full fragrant freshness.

Price, 1s. 8d. per Pound, Bottle included.

Raw and Refined Sugars at Wholesale Prices.

CLARANCE & CO.,

TEA & COFFEE MERCHANTS,

THE COCOA TREE TEA ESTABLISHMENT,

34, KIRKGATE, BRADFORD,

Opposite the Chapel.

In the event of Fire in the HALIFAX, BRADFORD and KEIGHLEY Districts application for the Company's Engines must be made to Mr. Isaac Swaine, 20 Horton street,...... HALIFAX.

To Mr. John Gill, Street Surveyor, Vicar lane, or to Mr. Joseph Farrar, the Company's Agent,........................ BRADFORD.

At the Gas Company's Office........................... KEIGHLEY.

AGENTS.

BRADFORD.....Mr. Joseph Farrar, No.8, Kirkgate, Corner of Market Street
Halifax......Mr. Thomas Barker, Office of the Company, Waterhouse Street,
Keighley......Mr. Thomas Waterworth, Solicitor.
Birstall......Mr. John Battye.
Huddersfield. .Mr. William Hornblower, Fox Street, Market Street.
Leeds........Mr. H. J. Morton, 13, Albion Street.
Kirkstall......Mr. Thomas Nellist, Kirkstall Mills.
Otley, Ilkley, &c. Mr. James Duncan, Westgate.
Bingley ......Mr. Edward Wood, Elm Tree.
Wakefield....Mr. Thomas Nightingale, Broker.
Rochdale..... Mr. James Turner, East Street, Townhead.
Cumberworth, &c...Mr. Charles Fitton.
Manchester...Mr. James Drew, 26 Brown Street.

BENJAMIN WALKER,

GLUE MANUFACTURER,

SHIPLEY.

Attends the Wellington Inn, High Street, on Thursdays.

EDWARD RAISBECK,

(LATE OF THORNHILL LEES IRON WORKS,)

Begs most respectfully to inform his friends and the public generally, that he has commenced business as a

COMMISSION AGENT, AUCTIONEER,

Arbitrator and Valuer,

In which branches any property entrusted to his care will be esteemed a favour, and have his most strict and prompt attention.

Westbrook Place, Bradford, Oct. 1849.

Printed in the United Kingdom by
Lightning Source UK Ltd., Milton Keynes
140371UK00001B/45/P

15